DEAR CREATURE

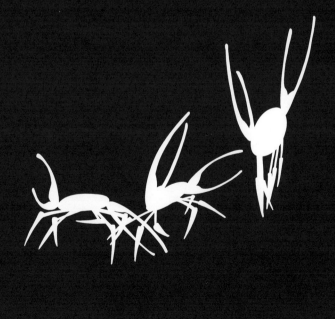

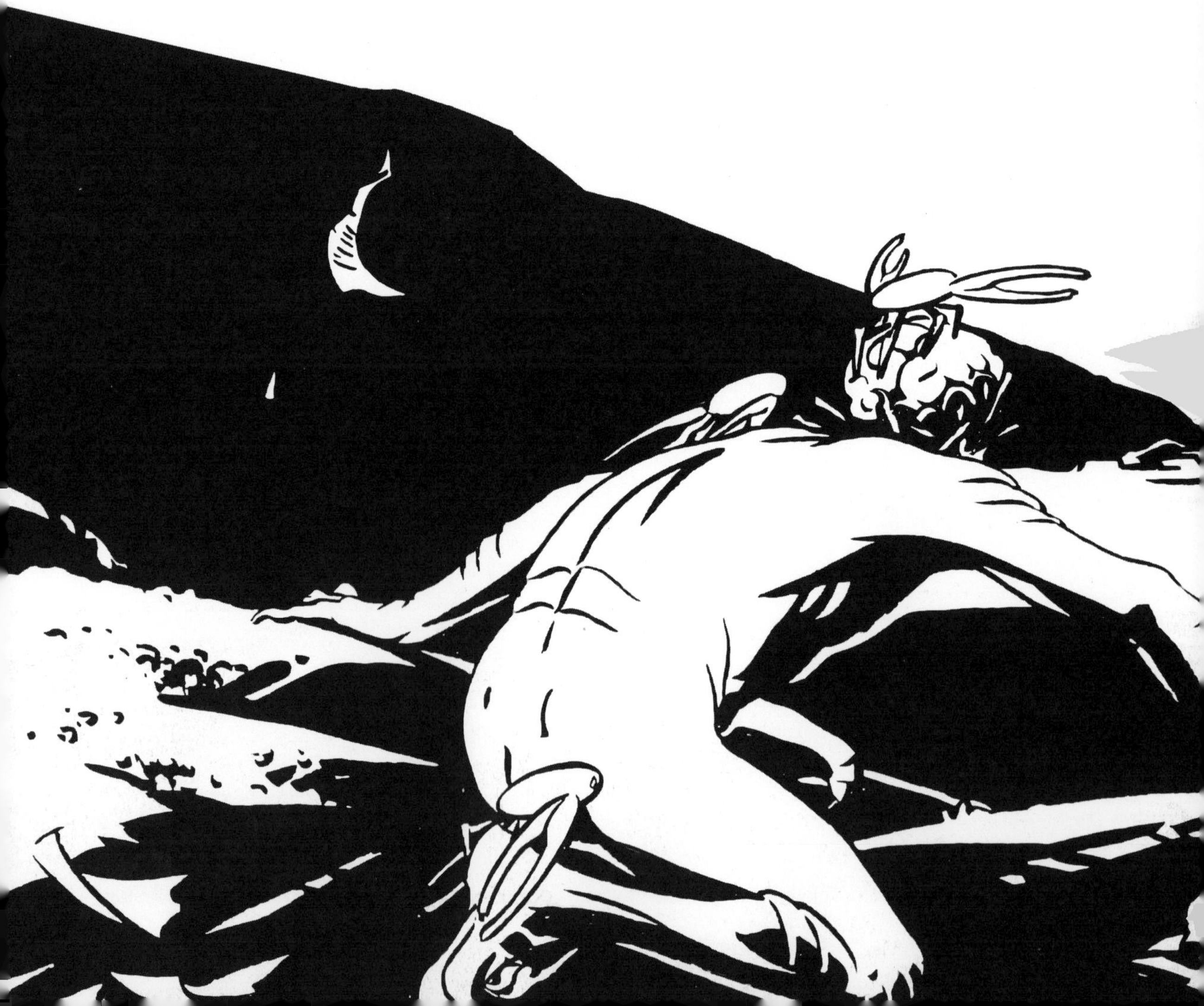

JONATHAN CASE
DEAR CREATURE

DARK HORSE BOOKS

President & Publisher
MIKE RICHARDSON

Dark Horse Edition Editor
SPENCER CUSHING

Dark Horse Edition Assistant Editor
KEVIN BURKHALTER

Designer
ETHAN KIMBERLING

Digital Art Technician
CHRISTINA McKENZIE

Neil Hankerson, Executive Vice President • Tom Weddle, Chief Financial Officer • Randy Stradley, Vice President of Publishing
Michael Martens, Vice President of Book Trade Sales • Matt Parkinson, Vice President of Marketing • David Scroggy, Vice
President of Product Development • Dale LaFountain, Vice President of Information Technology • Cara Niece, Vice President of
Production and Scheduling • Nick McWhorter, Vice President of Media Licensing • Ken Lizzi, General Counsel • Dave Marshall,
Editor in Chief • Davey Estrada, Editorial Director • Scott Allie, Executive Senior Editor • Chris Warner, Senior Books Editor
Cary Grazzini, Director of Specialty Projects • Lia Ribacchi, Art Director • Vanessa Todd, Director of Print Purchasing
Matt Dryer, Director of Digital Art and Prepress • Mark Bernardi, Director of Digital Publishing • Sarah Robertson, Director of
Product Sales • Michael Gombos, Director of International Publishing and Licensing

Published by Dark Horse Books
A division of Dark Horse Comics, Inc.
10956 SE Main Street
Milwaukie, OR 97222

First Dark Horse edition: September 2016
ISBN 978-1-50670-095-3

10 9 8 7 6 5 4 3 2 1
Printed in China

International Licensing: (503) 905-2377
Comic Shop Locator Service: (888) 266-4226

Library of Congress Cataloging-in-Publication Data

Names: Case, Jonathan, author, illustrator.
Title: Dear creature / by Jonathan Case.
Description: First Dark Horse edition. | Milwaukie, OR : Dark Horse Books,
  2016.
Identifiers: LCCN 2016021882 | ISBN 9781506700953 (hardback)
Subjects: LCSH: Sea monsters–Comic books, strips, etc. | Graphic novels. |
  BISAC: COMICS & GRAPHIC NOVELS / Literary.
Classification: LCC PN6727.C3875 D43 2016 | DDC 741.5/973–dc23
LC record available at https://lccn.loc.gov/2016021882

TABLE OF CONTENTS

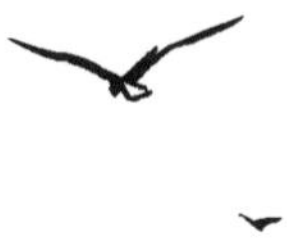

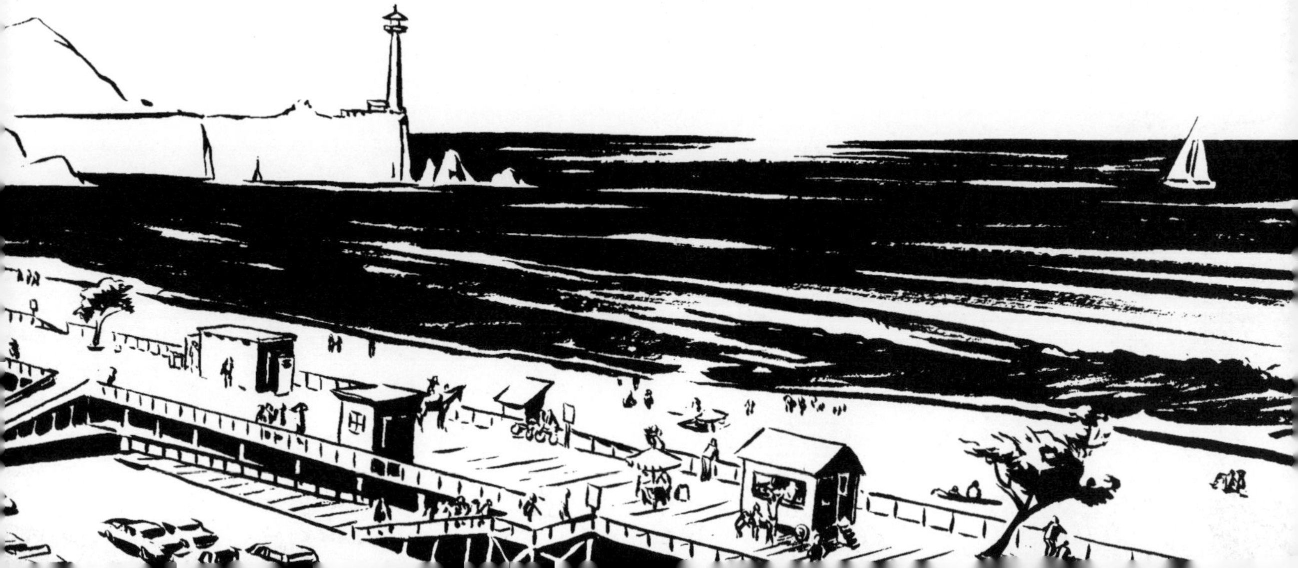

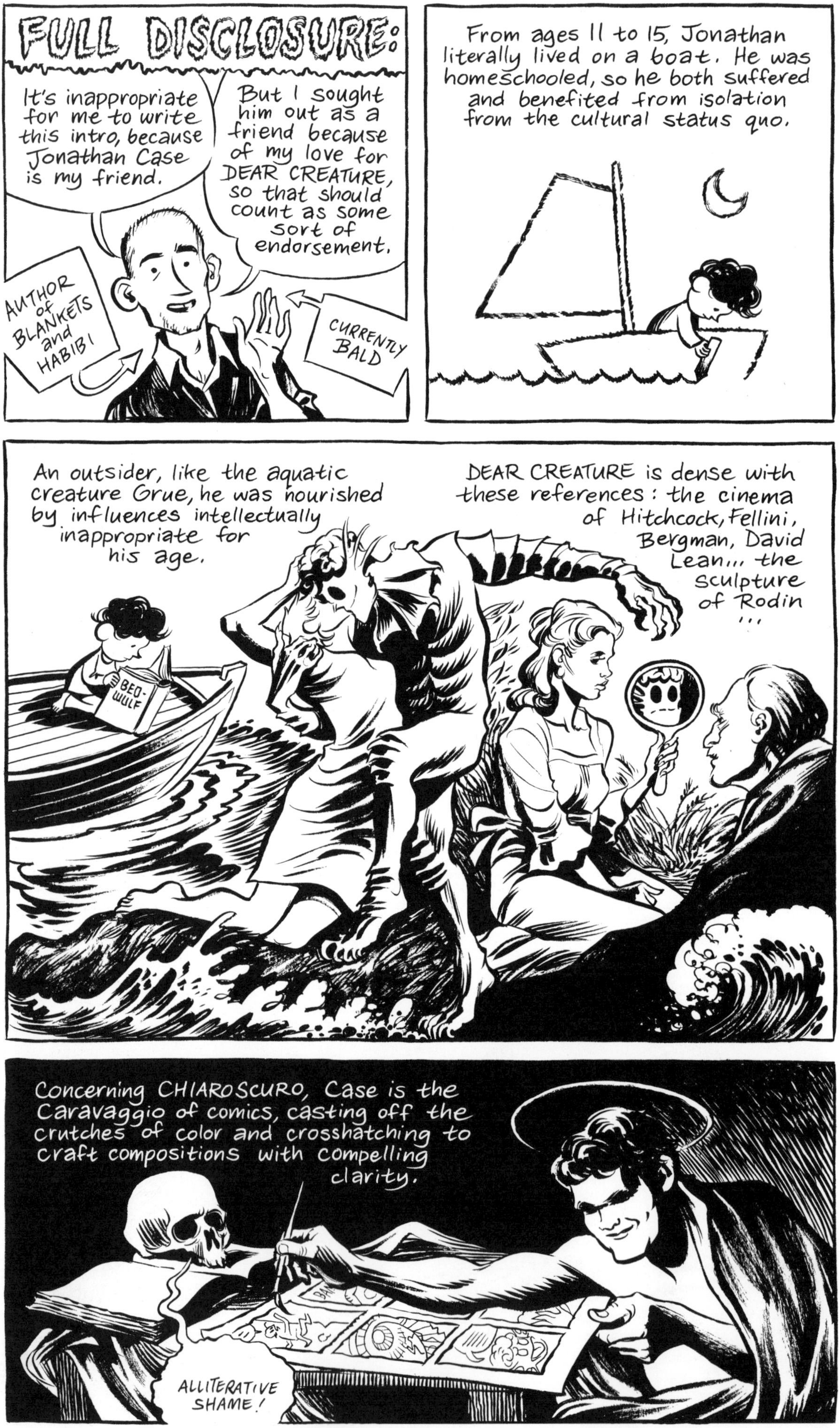
FULL DISCLOSURE:
It's inappropriate for me to write this intro, because Jonathan Case is my friend.
But I sought him out as a friend because of my love for DEAR CREATURE, so that should count as some sort of endorsement.
AUTHOR of BLANKETS and HABIBI
CURRENTLY BALD
From ages 11 to 15, Jonathan literally lived on a boat. He was homeschooled, so he both suffered and benefited from isolation from the cultural status quo.
An outsider, like the aquatic creature Grue, he was nourished by influences intellectually inappropriate for his age.
BEO-WULF
DEAR CREATURE is dense with these references: the cinema of Hitchcock, Fellini, Bergman, David Lean... the sculpture of Rodin ...
Concerning CHIAROSCURO, Case is the Caravaggio of comics, casting off the crutches of color and crosshatching to craft compositions with compelling clarity.
ALLITERATIVE SHAME!

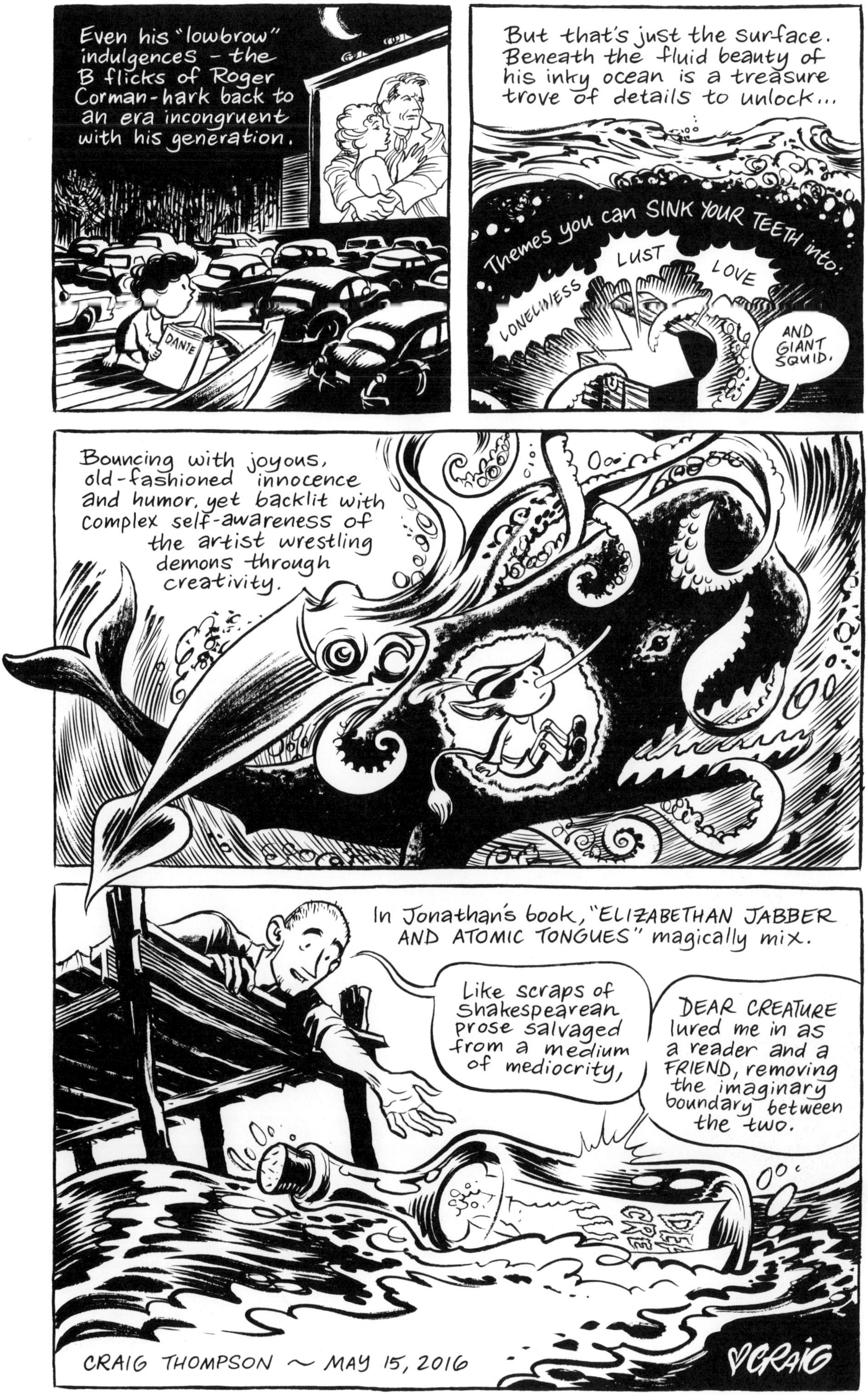
Even his "lowbrow" indulgences - the B flicks of Roger Corman-hark back to an era incongruent with his generation.
DANTE
But that's just the surface. Beneath the fluid beauty of his inky ocean is a treasure trove of details to unlock...
Themes you can SINK YOUR TEETH into:
LONELINESS
LUST
LOVE
AND GIANT SQUID.
Bouncing with joyous, old-fashioned innocence and humor, yet backlit with complex self-awareness of the artist wrestling demons through creativity.
In Jonathan's book, "ELIZABETHAN JABBER AND ATOMIC TONGUES" magically mix.
Like scraps of Shakespearean prose salvaged from a medium of mediocrity,
DEAR CREATURE lured me in as a reader and a FRIEND, removing the imaginary boundary between the two.
CRAIG THOMPSON ~ MAY 15, 2016
♥CRAIG

INTRODUCTION

to the 2011 edition by Steve Lieber, Eisner Award–winning
artist of *Whiteout* and *The Fix*

It's hard to imagine a more impressive comics debut than *Dear Creature* by Jonathan Case. He's come out of nowhere with one of the best original graphic novels anyone has seen in years, flooring everyone with his triple-threat abilities.

It's common for a new comic book creator to produce handsome drawings or have a fresh ear for dialogue. It's considerably less common for a cartoonist to arrive on the scene displaying fluency with the formal aspects of comic book storytelling. But that happens, too. All three? You just don't see debuts like that. Until now.

In his drawing, Jonathan deploys a palette of stark black and white. There's no cross-hatching to make soft grays, just perfectly chosen lines and shapes. His technique is simple, but the result is never sterile, cold, or distancing. Every panel is bursting with graphic energy: dynamic compositions, expressive gestures, and thoroughly imagined and varied people, monsters, props, and environments.

The writing in *Dear Creature* is equally accomplished. There's such joy and variety in the cast's voices. If you black out the pictures and only read the balloons, the characters are still vivid and distinct: Grue's Elizabethan iambic pentameter; the crab chorus's Runyonesque wise-guy chatter; Zola's passionate, operatic English as a second language; Officer Craw's cowboy straight talk; Giulietta's fearful hesitation.

But in comics, it's impossible to separate the pictures from the writing. This isn't illustrated prose, with pictures included to decorate the text. This is comics; the pictures ARE the text. Every scene in *Dear Creature* turns on purely visual storytelling choices.

Comics is also a rhythmic art, and this story gets much of its impact from the way abstract visual elements are juxtaposed. In these pages, Case displays an unerring instinct for leading the eye around the page. He knows when to build pictures out of drifting horizontals or bursting diagonals. He designs cool areas of unmarked white or black and juxtaposes them with warm tracts of precisely rendered texture. He arranges forms in space to create calm or chaos, as appropriate. This is one of the most difficult things about making comics.

But all this would be empty technique if it wasn't in service of a great story. *Dear Creature* is a glorious mash-up of wildly disparate influences: Fellini, *Frankenstein*, Frankie and Annette, Shakespeare, Roy Orbison, and God only knows what else. There's humor, horror, adventure, compassion, lunatic spectacle, and a couple of unlikely romances. It's a big, risky story and it shouldn't work at all. But it does, unified by its compelling atmosphere, appealing characters, utterly sincere love story, and the considerable taste and talent of its creator.

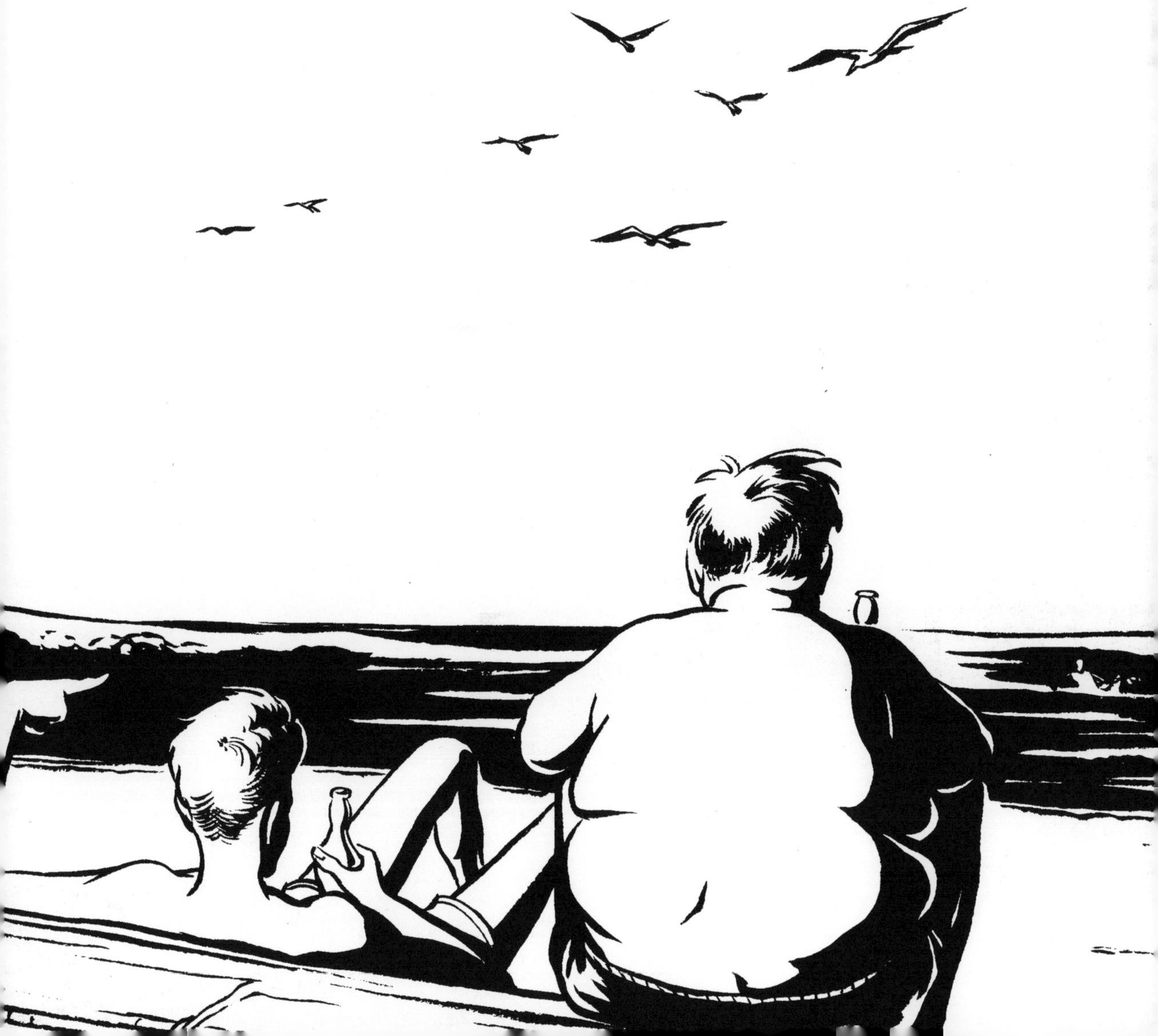

ANTIPHOLUS OF SYRACUSE:

Sweet mistress—what your name is else, I know not,
Nor by what wonder you do hit of mine—
Less in your knowledge and your grace you show not
Than our earth's wonder, more than earth divine.
Teach me, dear creature, how to think and speak;
Lay open to my earthy-gross conceit,
Smother'd in errors, feeble, shallow, weak,
The folded meaning of your words' deceit.

—*William Shakespeare*, The Comedy of Errors, *Act 3, Scene 2*

CHAPTER ONE

ONLY THE LONELY

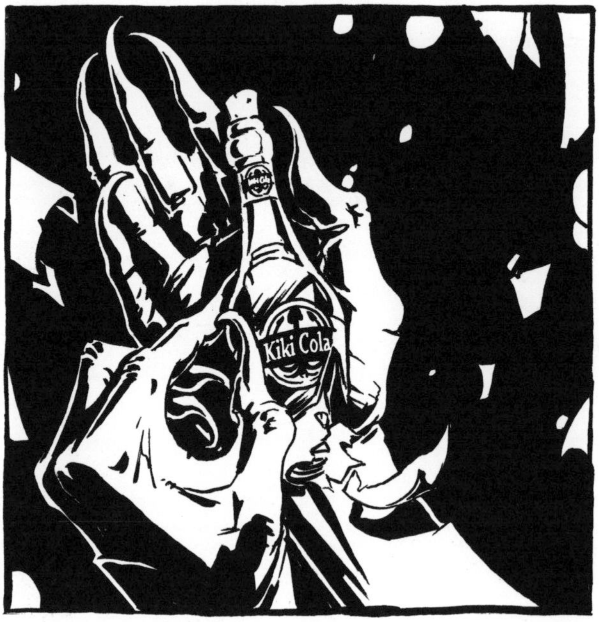
Kiki Cola

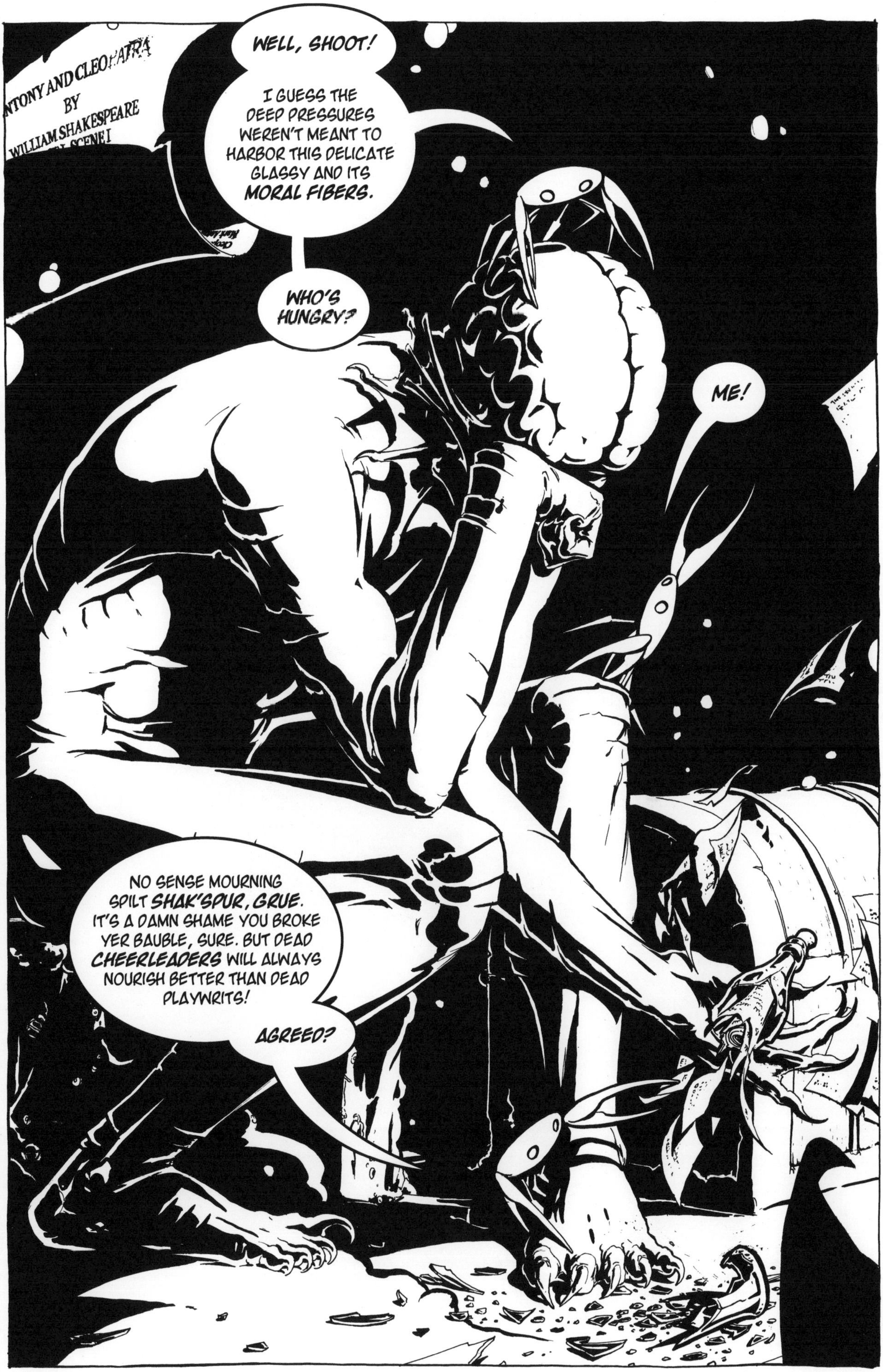
NTONY AND CLEO ATRA
BY
WILLIAM SHAKESPEARE
WELL, SHOOT!
I GUESS THE DEEP PRESSURES WEREN'T MEANT TO HARBOR THIS DELICATE GLASSY AND ITS MORAL FIBERS.
WHO'S HUNGRY?
ME!
NO SENSE MOURNING SPILT SHAK'SPUR, GRUE. IT'S A DAMN SHAME YOU BROKE YER BAUBLE, SURE. BUT DEAD CHEERLEADERS WILL ALWAYS NOURISH BETTER THAN DEAD PLAYWRITS!
AGREED?

OKAY...

LEMME ASK YOU THIS:

GRANTED, I'M A *CRAB* WITH HUMBLE CONCERNS.

I SIMPLY CAN'T KNOW WHAT A SEA MUTANT COULD WANT FOR MORE THAN THIS LOVELY INTERIOR BELOW THE BRINE, NO NATURAL *PREDATORS—*

AND A CHEST FULL OF DELICIOUS *HUMAN REMAINS!*

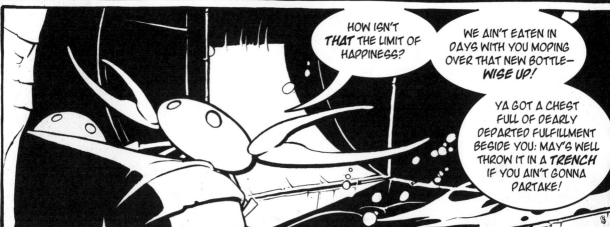

HOW ISN'T *THAT* THE LIMIT OF HAPPINESS?

WE AIN'T EATEN IN DAYS WITH YOU MOPING OVER THAT NEW BOTTLE— *WISE UP!*

YA GOT A CHEST FULL OF DEARLY DEPARTED FULFILLMENT BESIDE YOU: MAY'S WELL THROW IT IN A *TRENCH* IF YOU AIN'T GONNA PARTAKE!

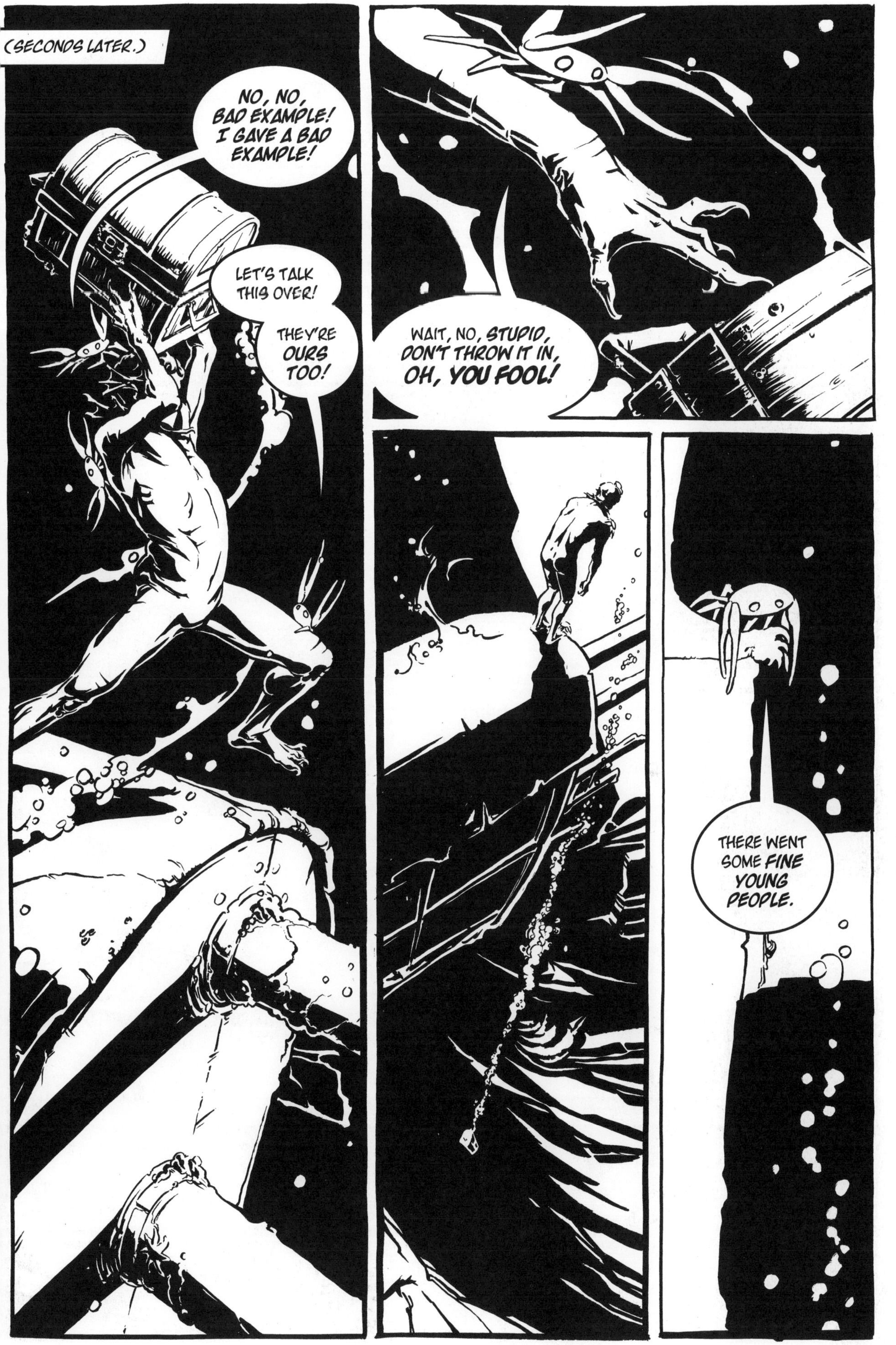
(SECONDS LATER.)
NO, NO, BAD EXAMPLE! I GAVE A BAD EXAMPLE!
LET'S TALK THIS OVER!
THEY'RE OURS TOO!
WAIT, NO, STUPID, DON'T THROW IT IN, OH, YOU FOOL!
THERE WENT SOME FINE YOUNG PEOPLE.

5. NO NIGHT SWIMM
BY ORDINANCE OF SANTA LUCIA COUNTY
CLASS OF 62
JOE! YOU MAKE ME FEEL THINGS I'VE NEVER FELT!
RIGHT-
I GOT A TINGLE...
ALL THE WAY DOWN TO MY TOES!

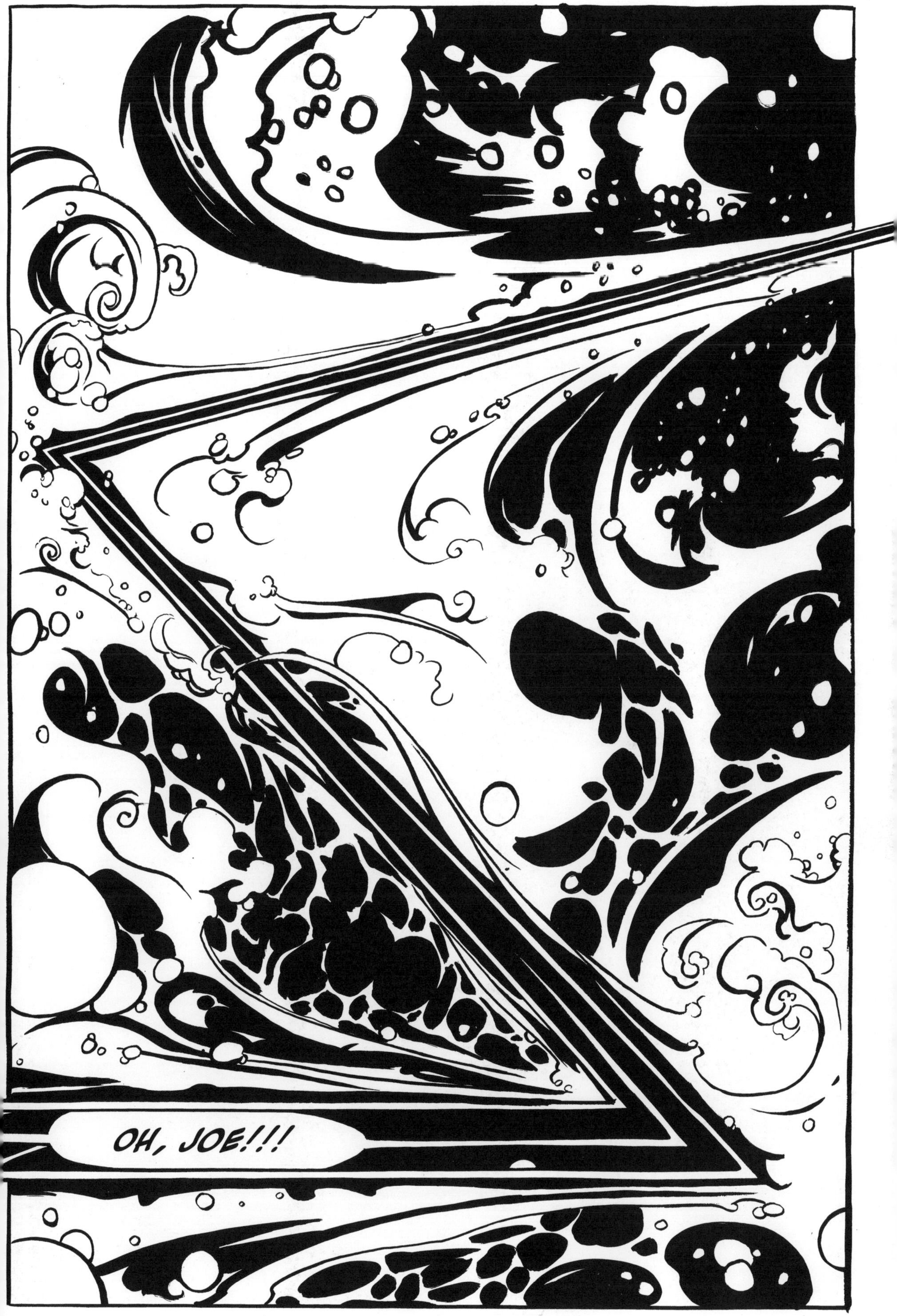
OH, JOE!!!

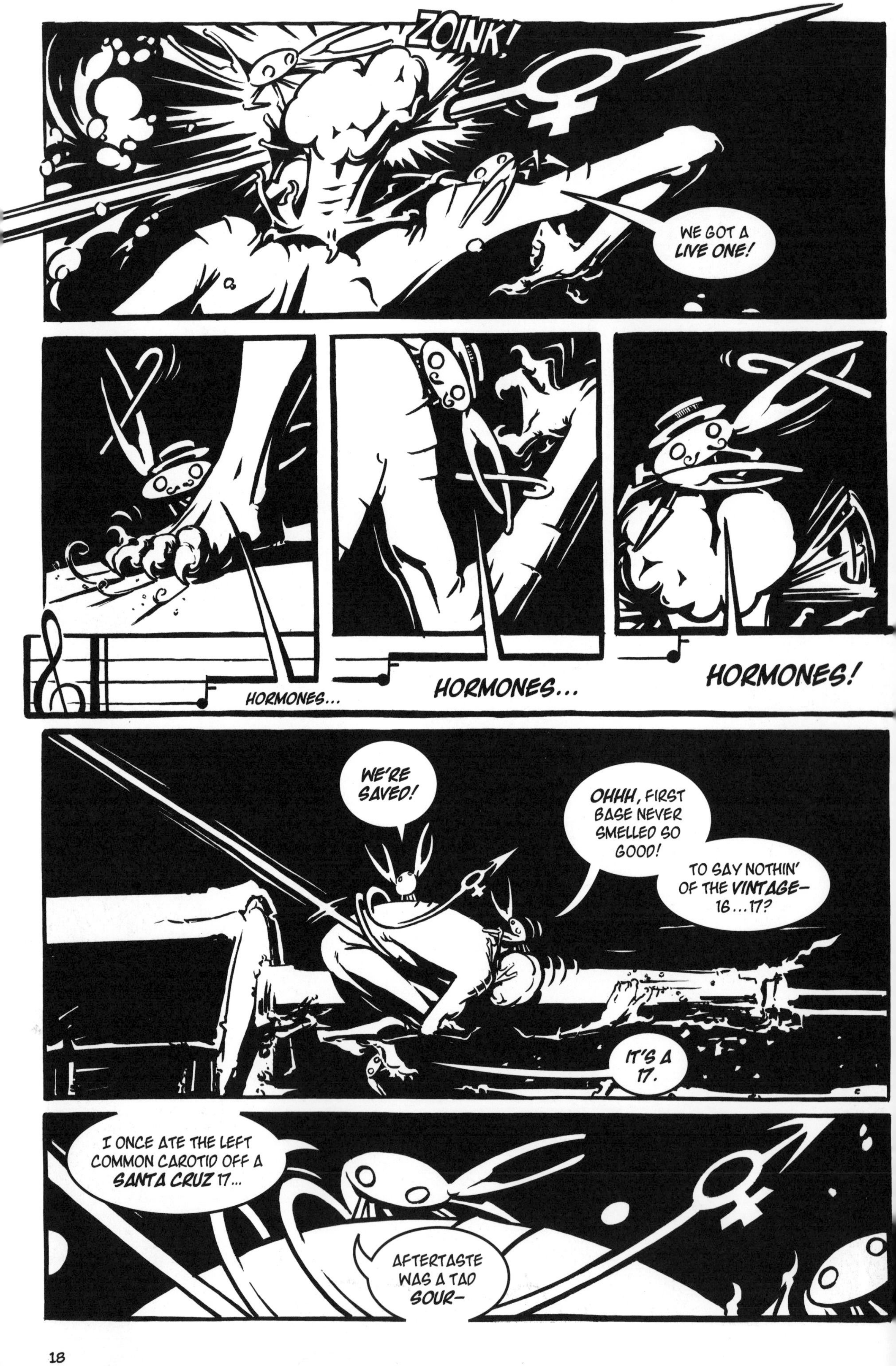
ZOINK!
WE GOT A LIVE ONE!
HORMONES...
HORMONES...
HORMONES!
WE'RE SAVED!
OHHH, FIRST BASE NEVER SMELLED SO GOOD!
TO SAY NOTHIN' OF THE VINTAGE— 16...17?
IT'S A 17.
I ONCE ATE THE LEFT COMMON CAROTID OFF A SANTA CRUZ 17...
AFTERTASTE WAS A TAD SOUR—

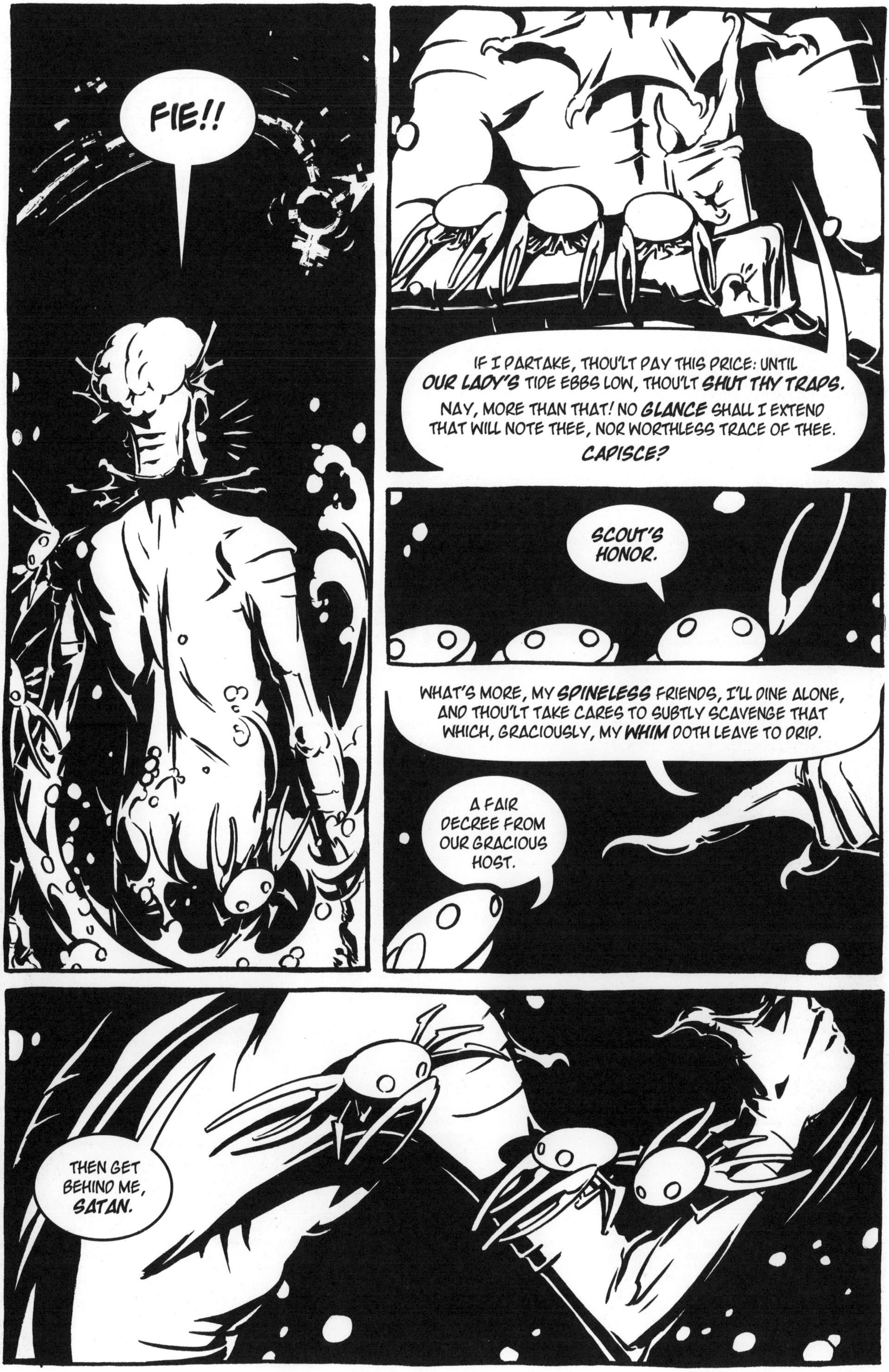
FIE!!
IF I PARTAKE, THOU'LT PAY THIS PRICE: UNTIL OUR LADY'S TIDE EBBS LOW, THOU'LT SHUT THY TRAPS.
NAY, MORE THAN THAT! NO GLANCE SHALL I EXTEND THAT WILL NOTE THEE, NOR WORTHLESS TRACE OF THEE. CAPISCE?
SCOUT'S HONOR.
WHAT'S MORE, MY SPINELESS FRIENDS, I'LL DINE ALONE, AND THOU'LT TAKE CARES TO SUBTLY SCAVENGE THAT WHICH, GRACIOUSLY, MY WHIM DOTH LEAVE TO DRIP.
A FAIR DECREE FROM OUR GRACIOUS HOST.
THEN GET BEHIND ME, SATAN.

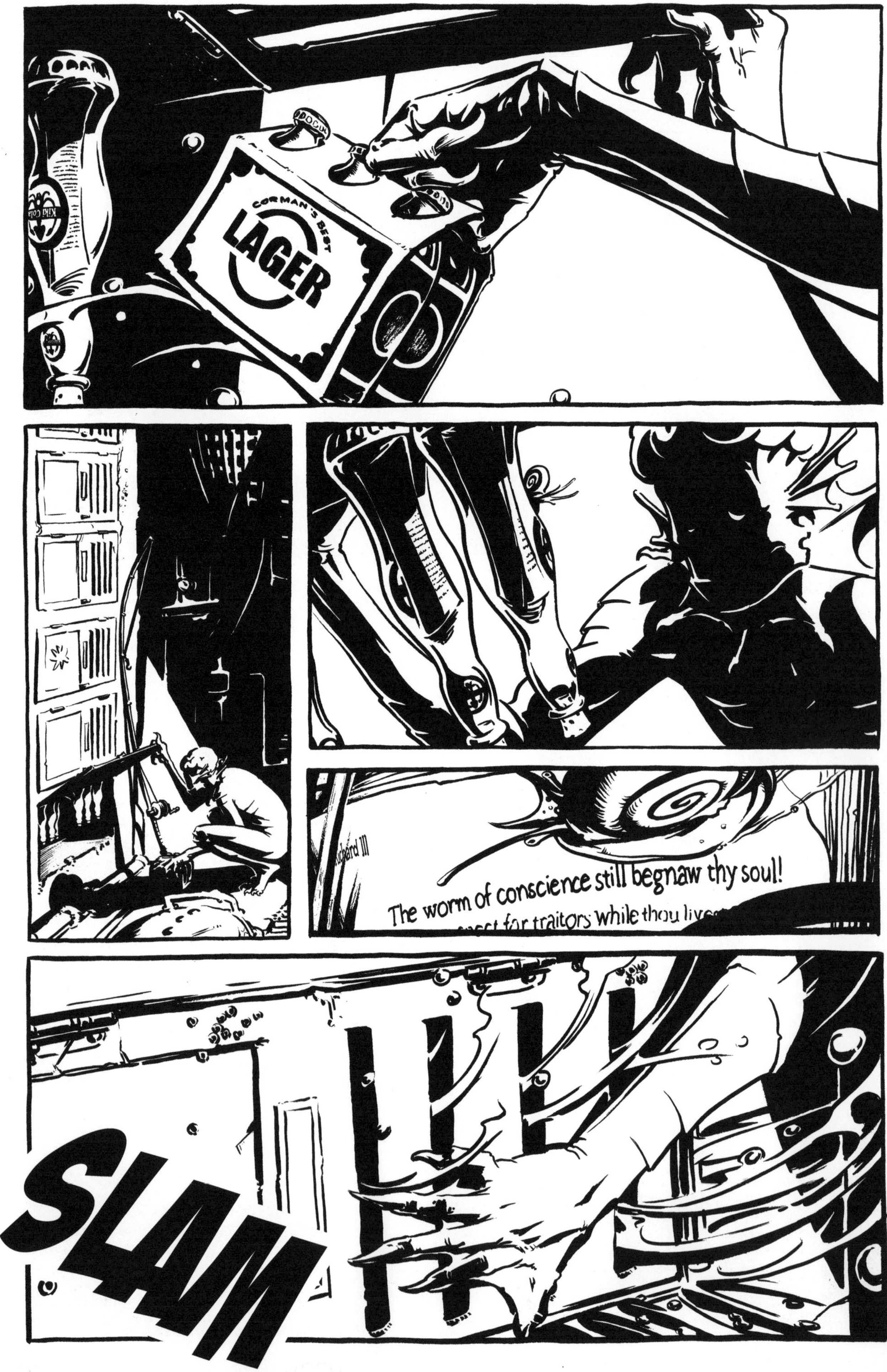
CORMAN'S BEST
LAGER
Richard III
The worm of conscience still begnaw thy soul!
SLAM

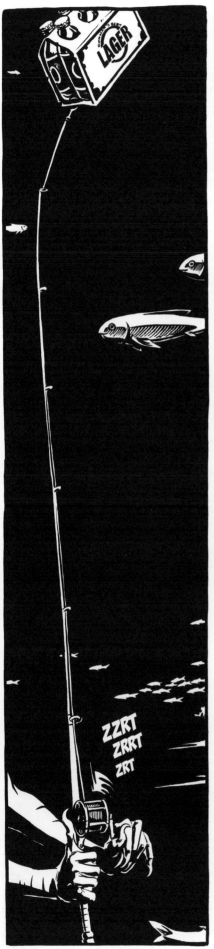

YOU'RE SO GOOD!
OH, JOE!...TELL ME
YOU LOVE ME!

ZZRT
ZRRT
ZRT

TELL ME, JOE!
THERE'S NOTHING
I WANT MORE!

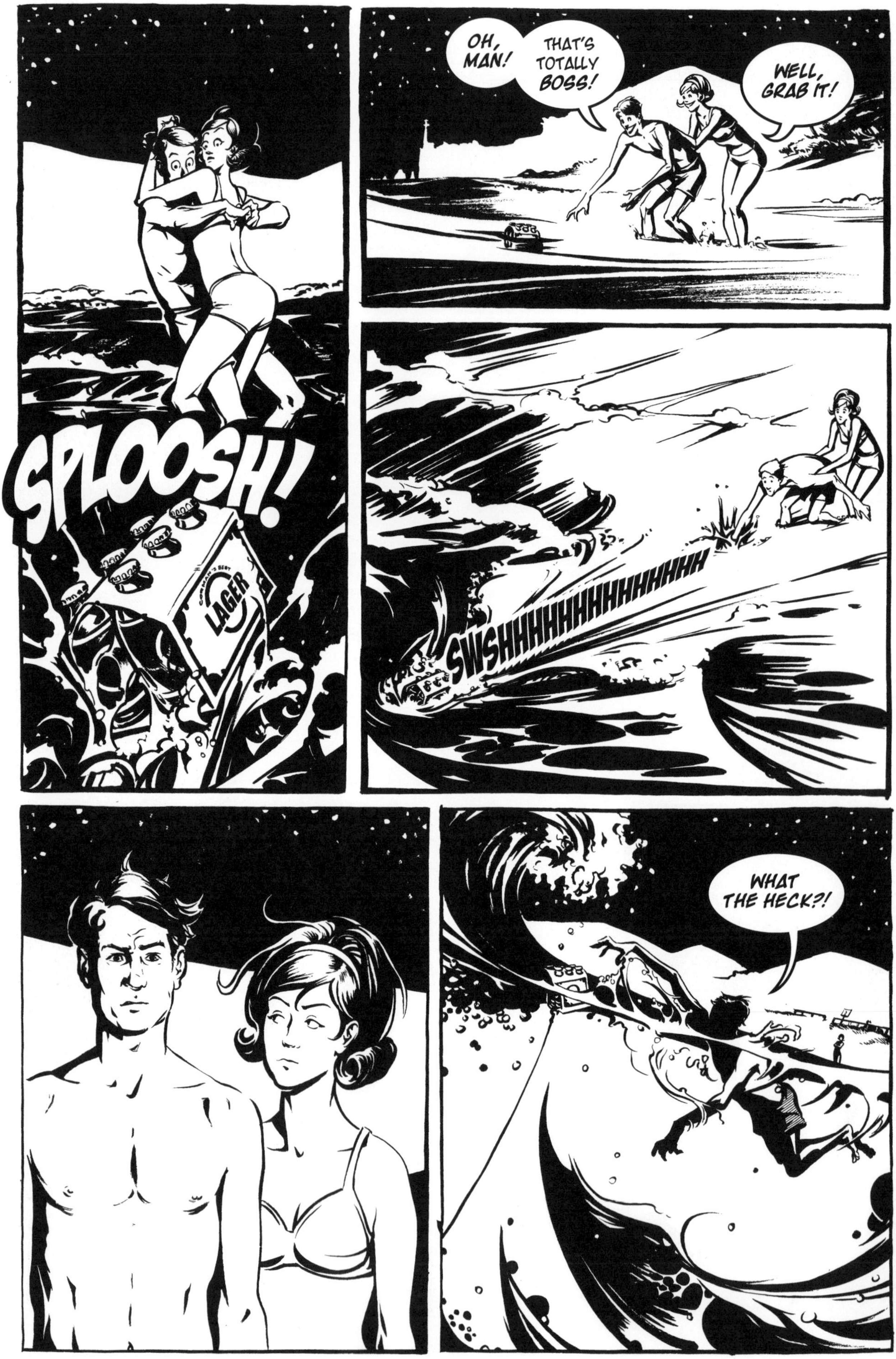
SPLOOSH!
LAGER
OH, MAN!
THAT'S TOTALLY BOSS!
WELL, GRAB IT!
SWSHHHHHHHHHHHHHHHH
WHAT THE HECK?!

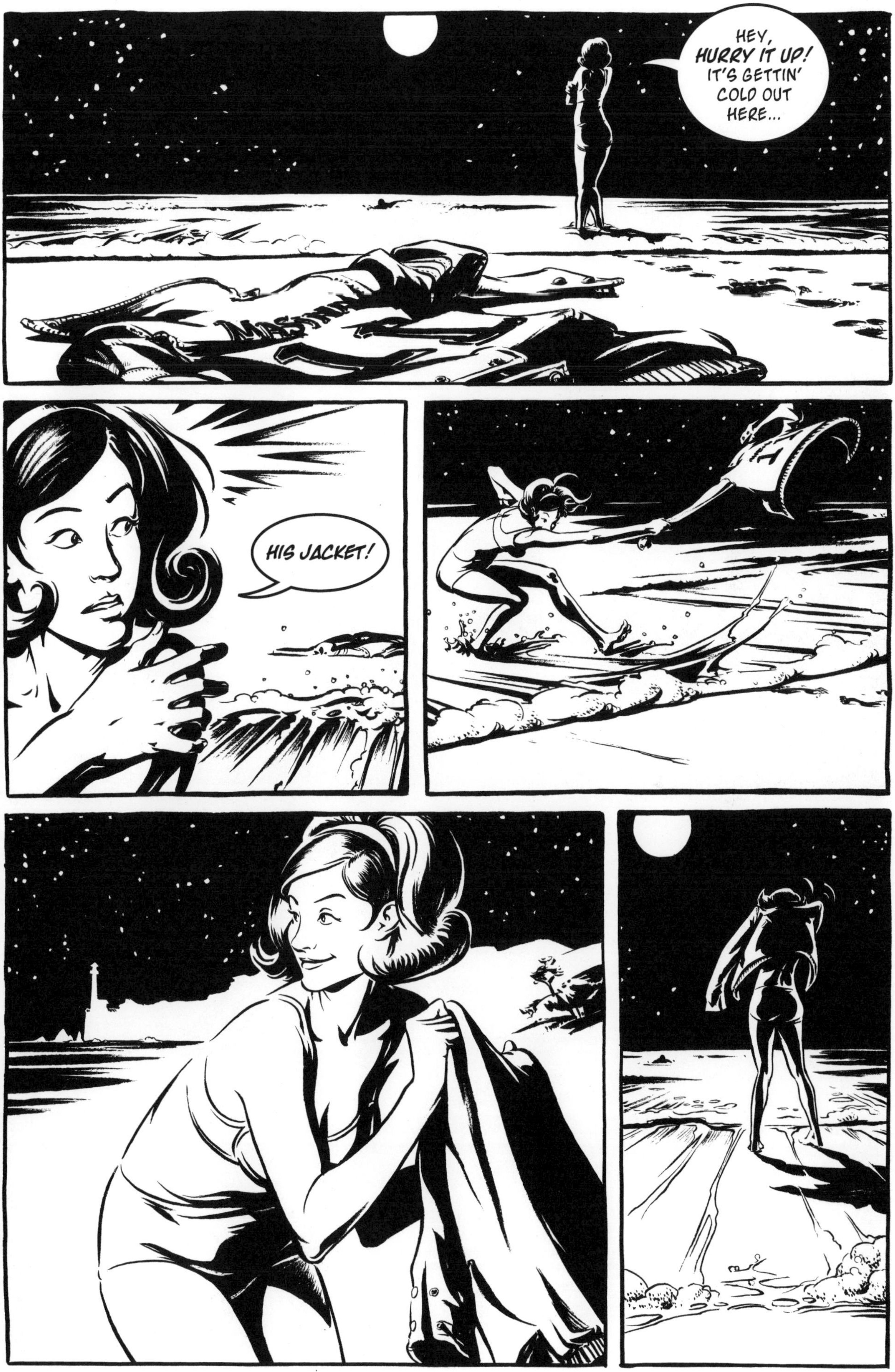
HEY, HURRY IT UP! IT'S GETTIN' COLD OUT HERE...
HIS JACKET!

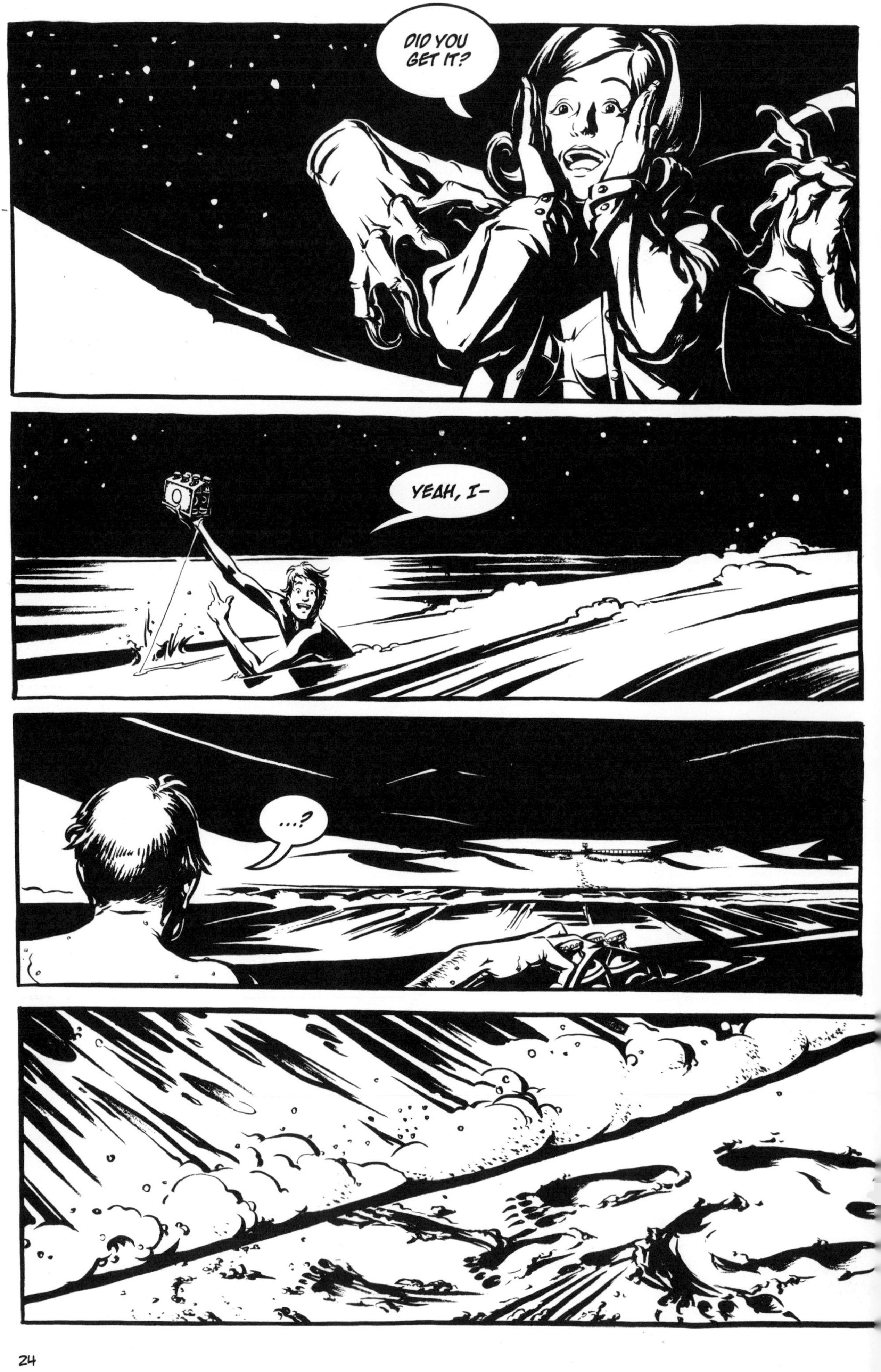
DID YOU GET IT?
YEAH, I-
...?

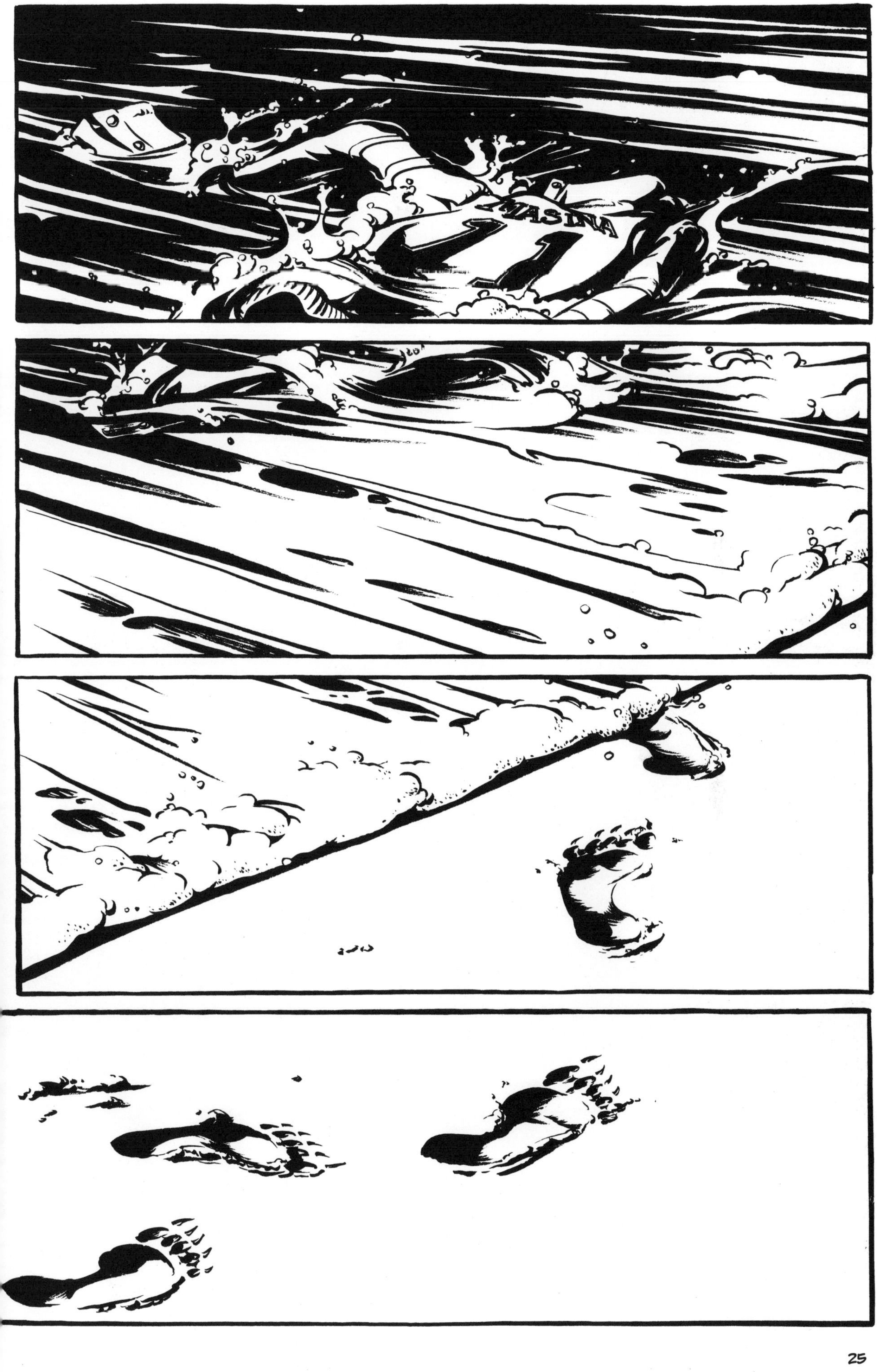
MASINA
11

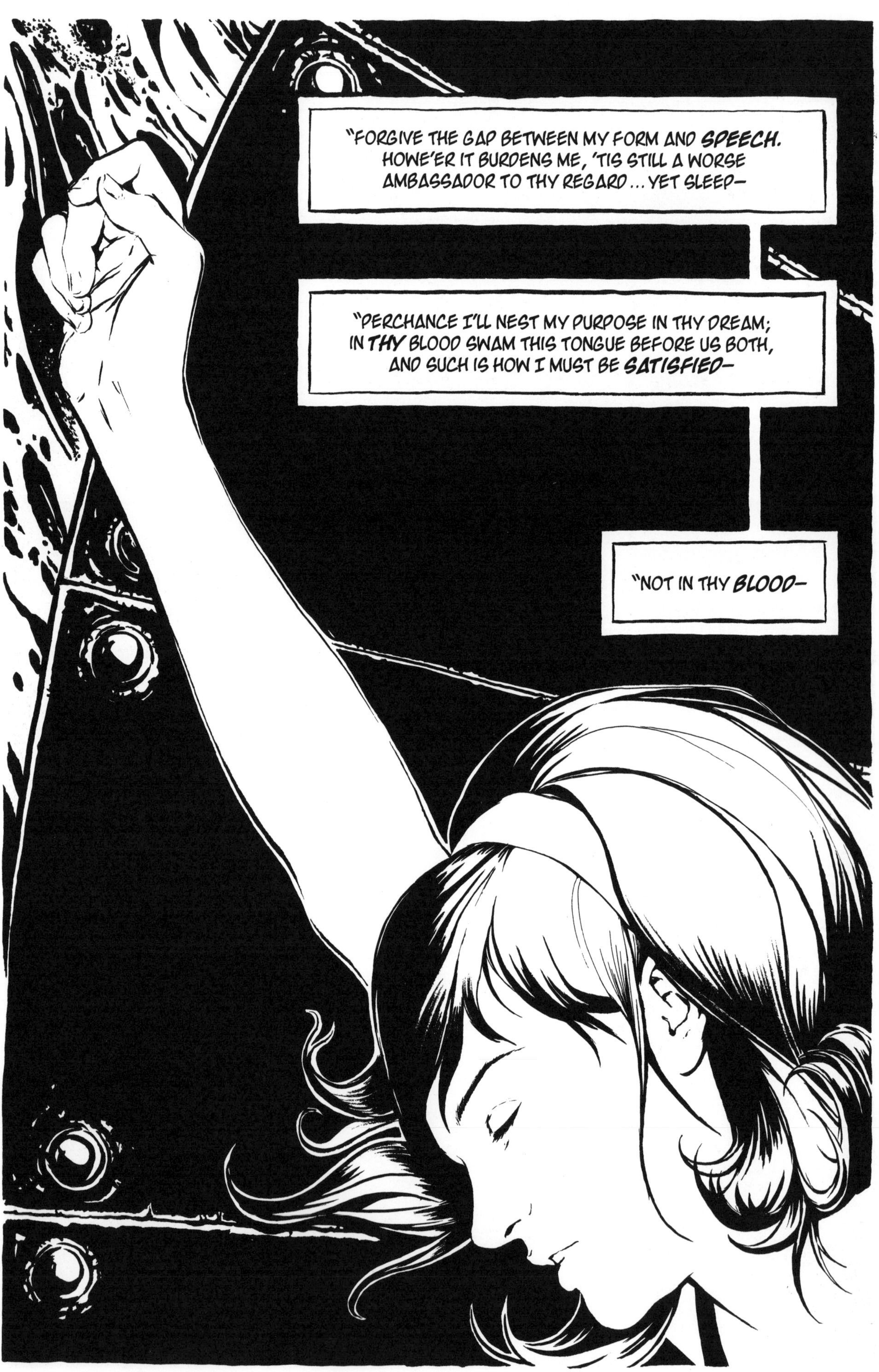
"FORGIVE THE GAP BETWEEN MY FORM AND SPEECH. HOWE'ER IT BURDENS ME, 'TIS STILL A WORSE AMBASSADOR TO THY REGARD ... YET SLEEP–
"PERCHANCE I'LL NEST MY PURPOSE IN THY DREAM; IN THY BLOOD SWAM THIS TONGUE BEFORE US BOTH, AND SUCH IS HOW I MUST BE SATISFIED–
"NOT IN THY BLOOD–

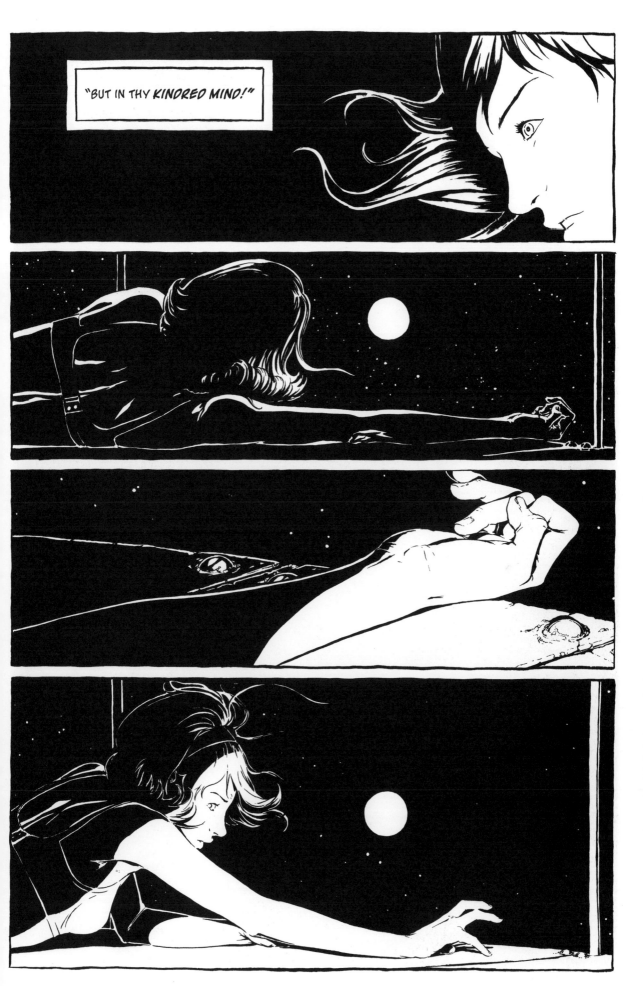

"BUT IN THY *KINDRED MIND!*"

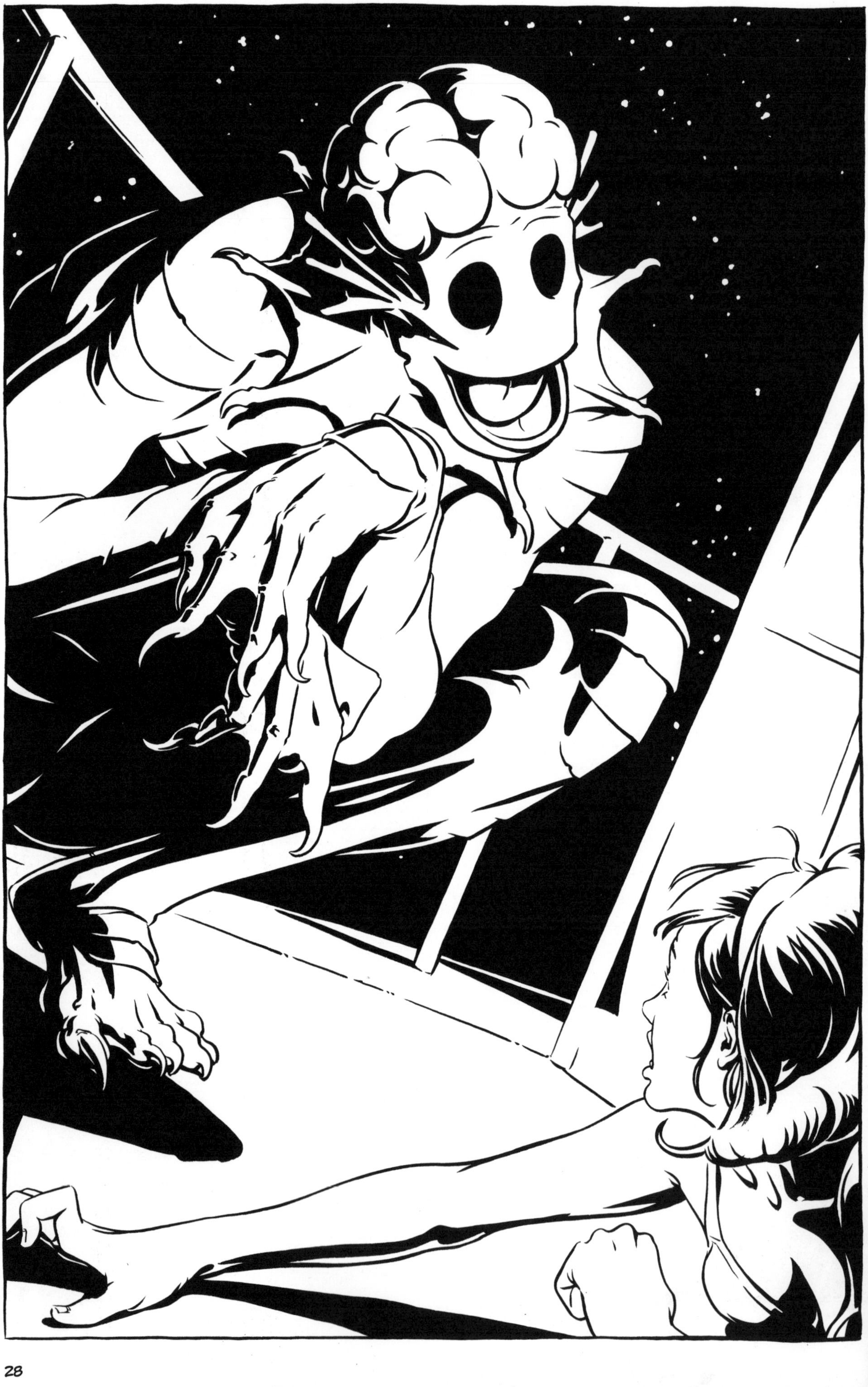

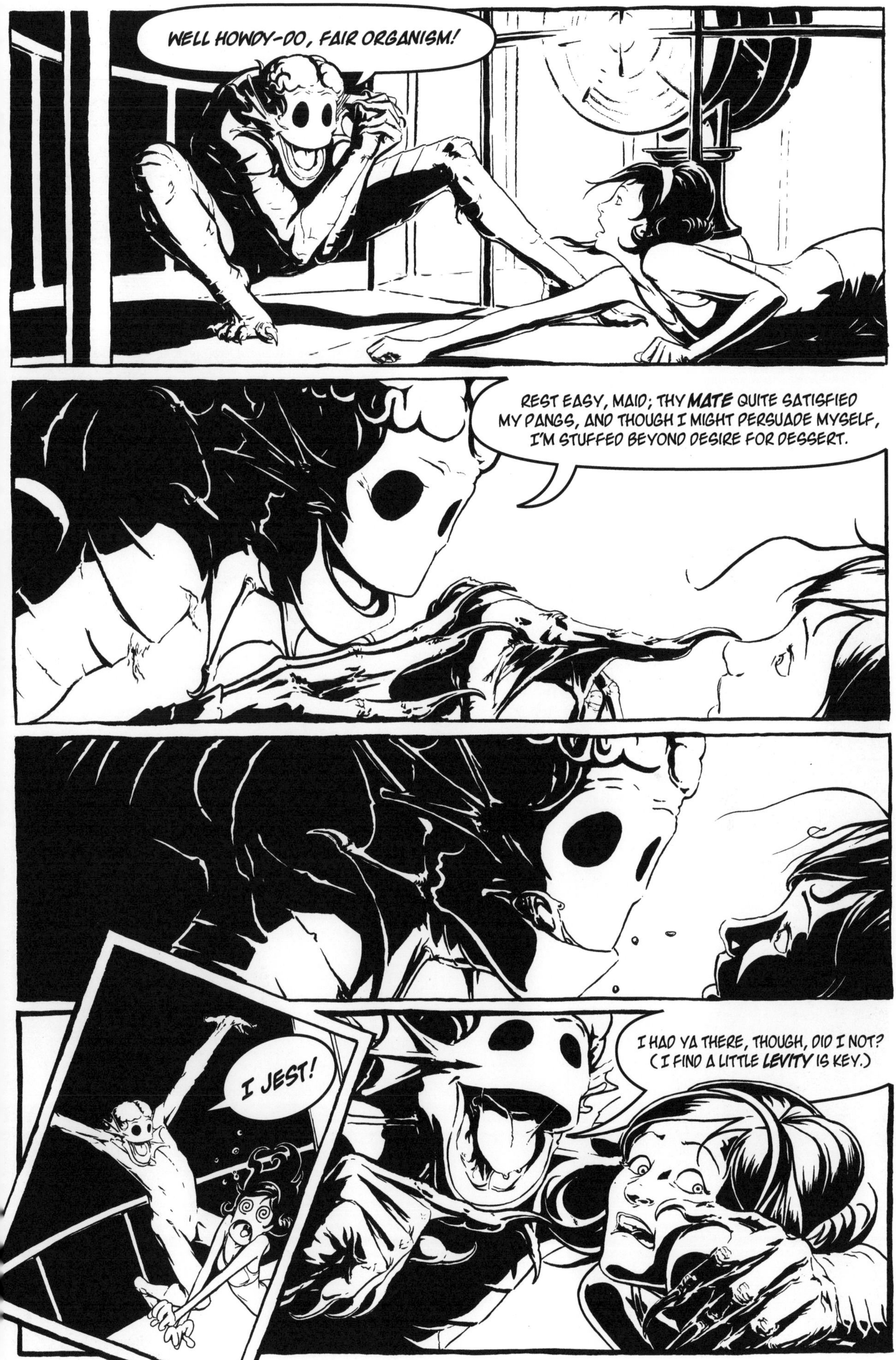
WELL HOWDY-DO, FAIR ORGANISM!
REST EASY, MAID; THY MATE QUITE SATISFIED MY PANGS, AND THOUGH I MIGHT PERSUADE MYSELF, I'M STUFFED BEYOND DESIRE FOR DESSERT.
I JEST!
I HAD YA THERE, THOUGH, DID I NOT? (I FIND A LITTLE LEVITY IS KEY.)

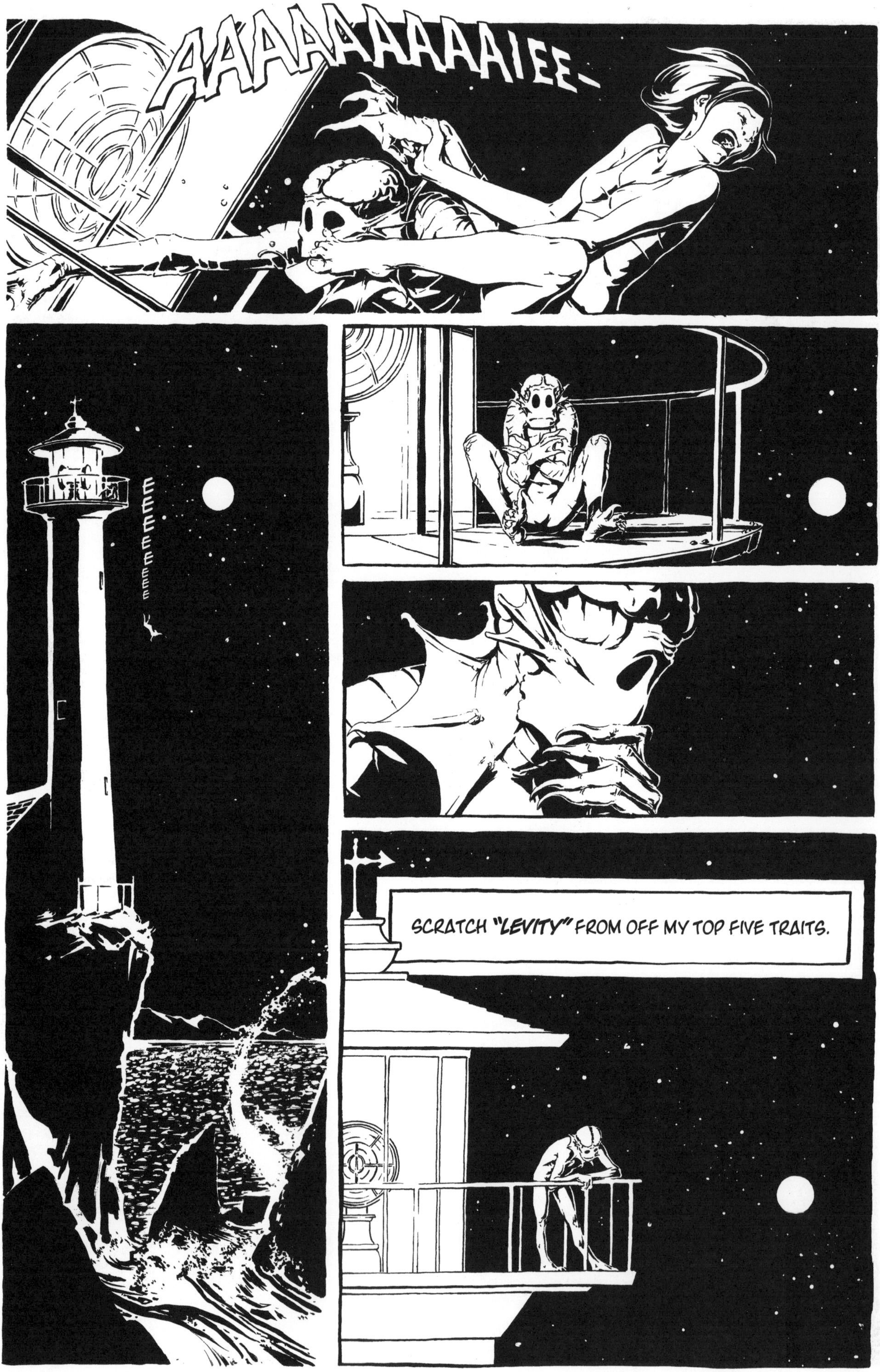
AAAAAAAAAIEE-
EEEEEEEE
SCRATCH "LEVITY" FROM OFF MY TOP FIVE TRAITS.

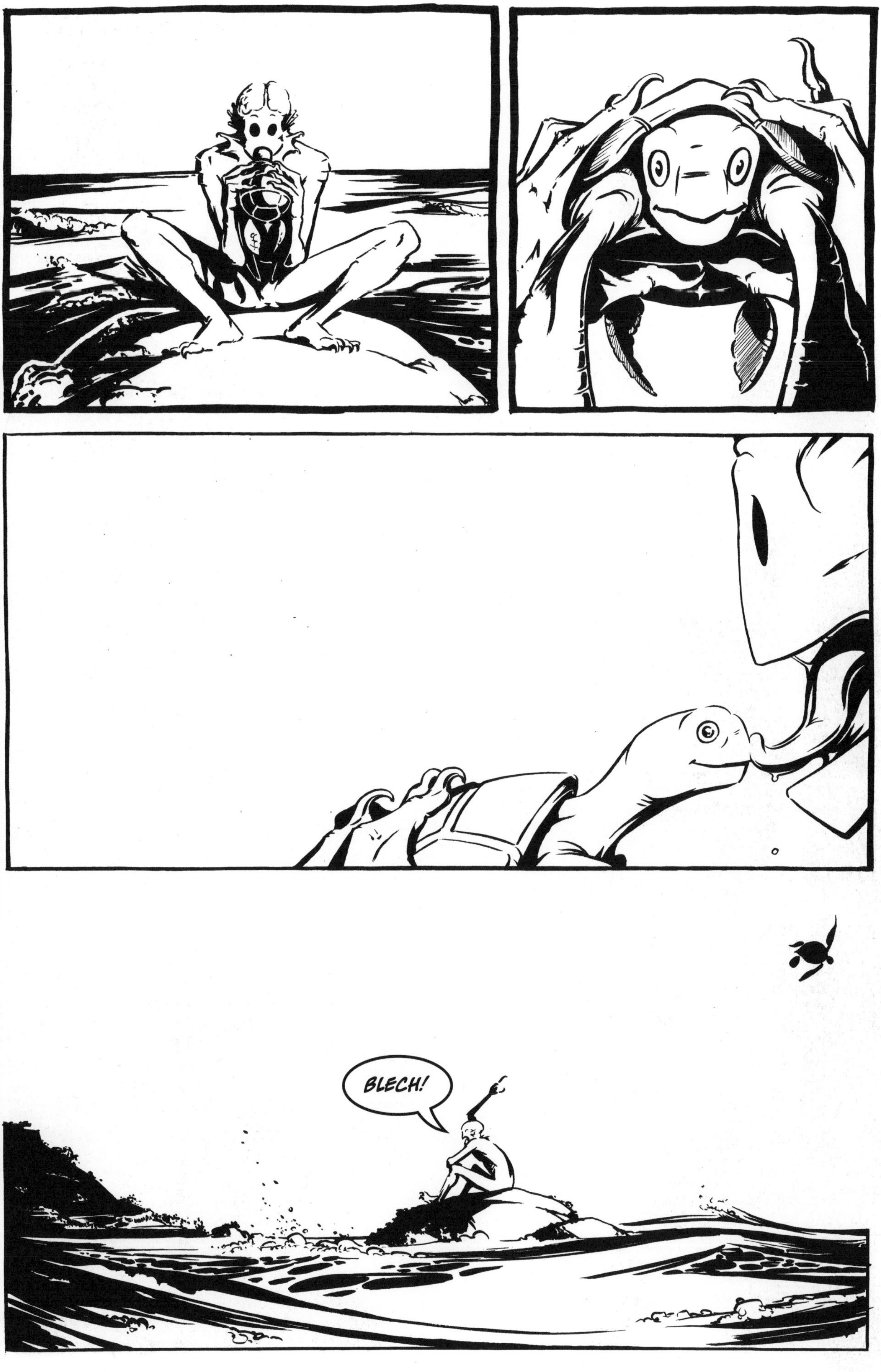
BLECH!

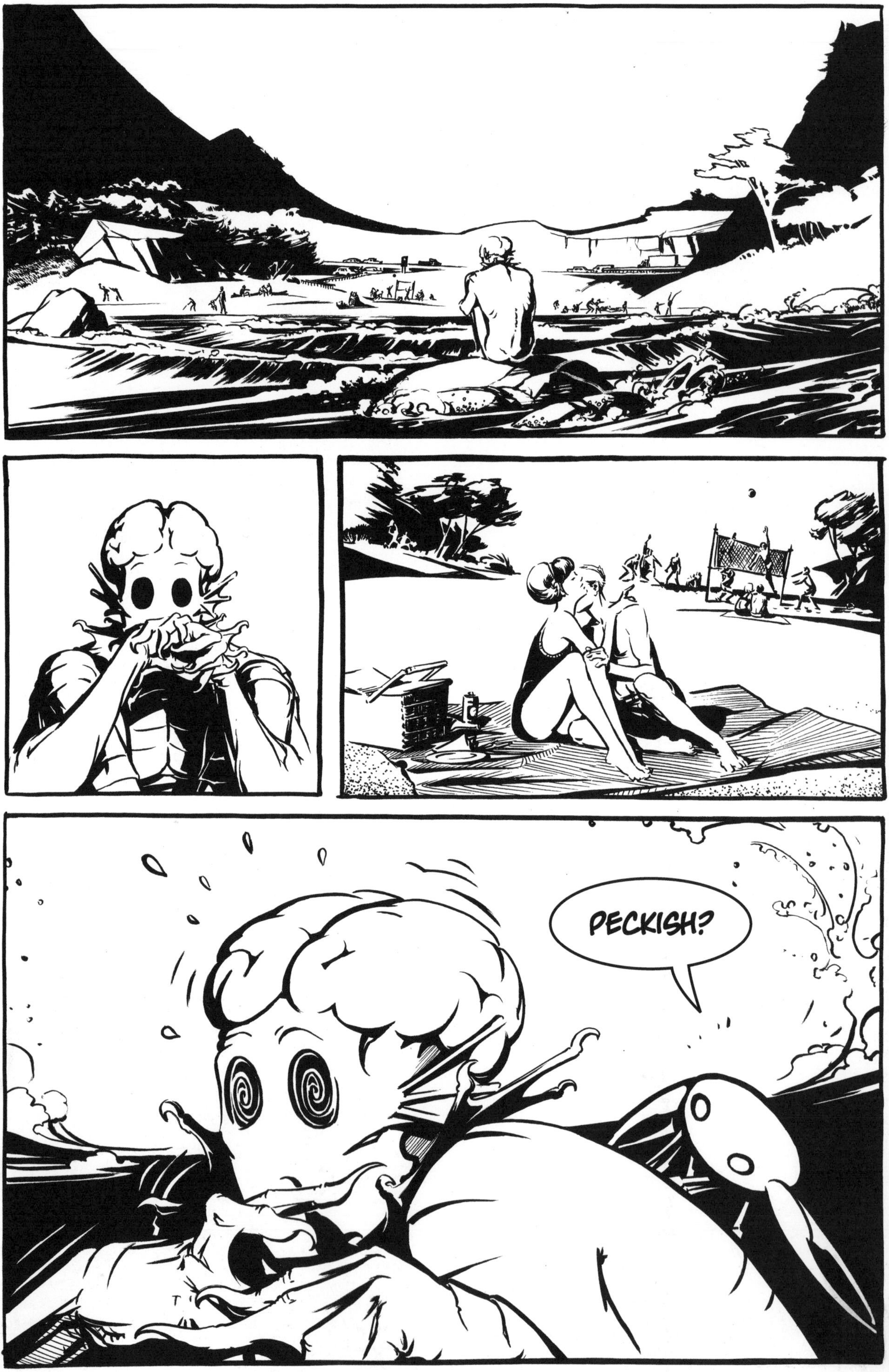
PECKISH?

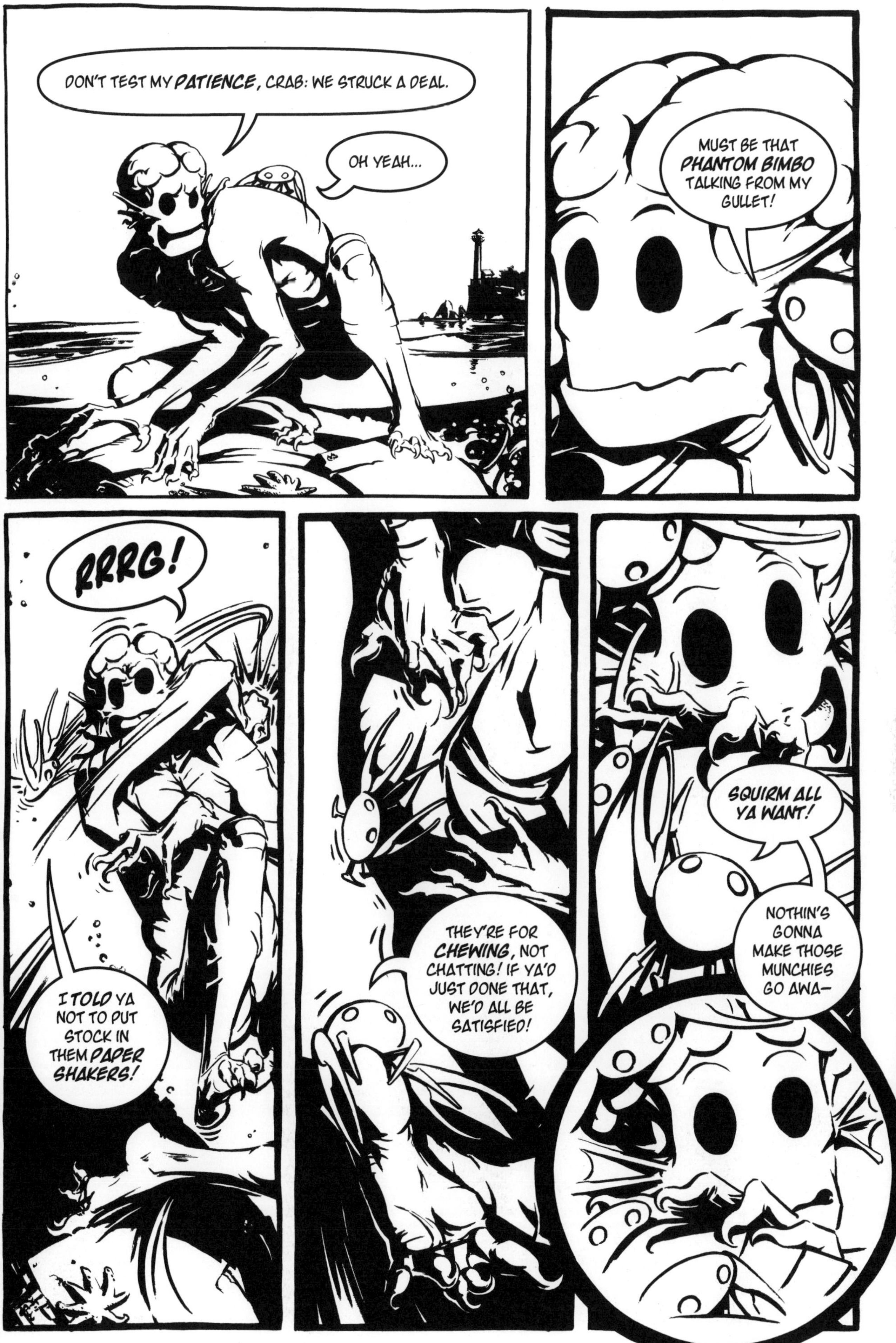

DON'T TEST MY PATIENCE, CRAB: WE STRUCK A DEAL.
OH YEAH...
MUST BE THAT PHANTOM BIMBO TALKING FROM MY GULLET!
RRRG!
I TOLD YA NOT TO PUT STOCK IN THEM PAPER SHAKERS!
THEY'RE FOR CHEWING, NOT CHATTING! IF YA'D JUST DONE THAT, WE'D ALL BE SATISFIED!
SQUIRM ALL YA WANT!
NOTHIN'S GONNA MAKE THOSE MUNCHIES GO AWA—

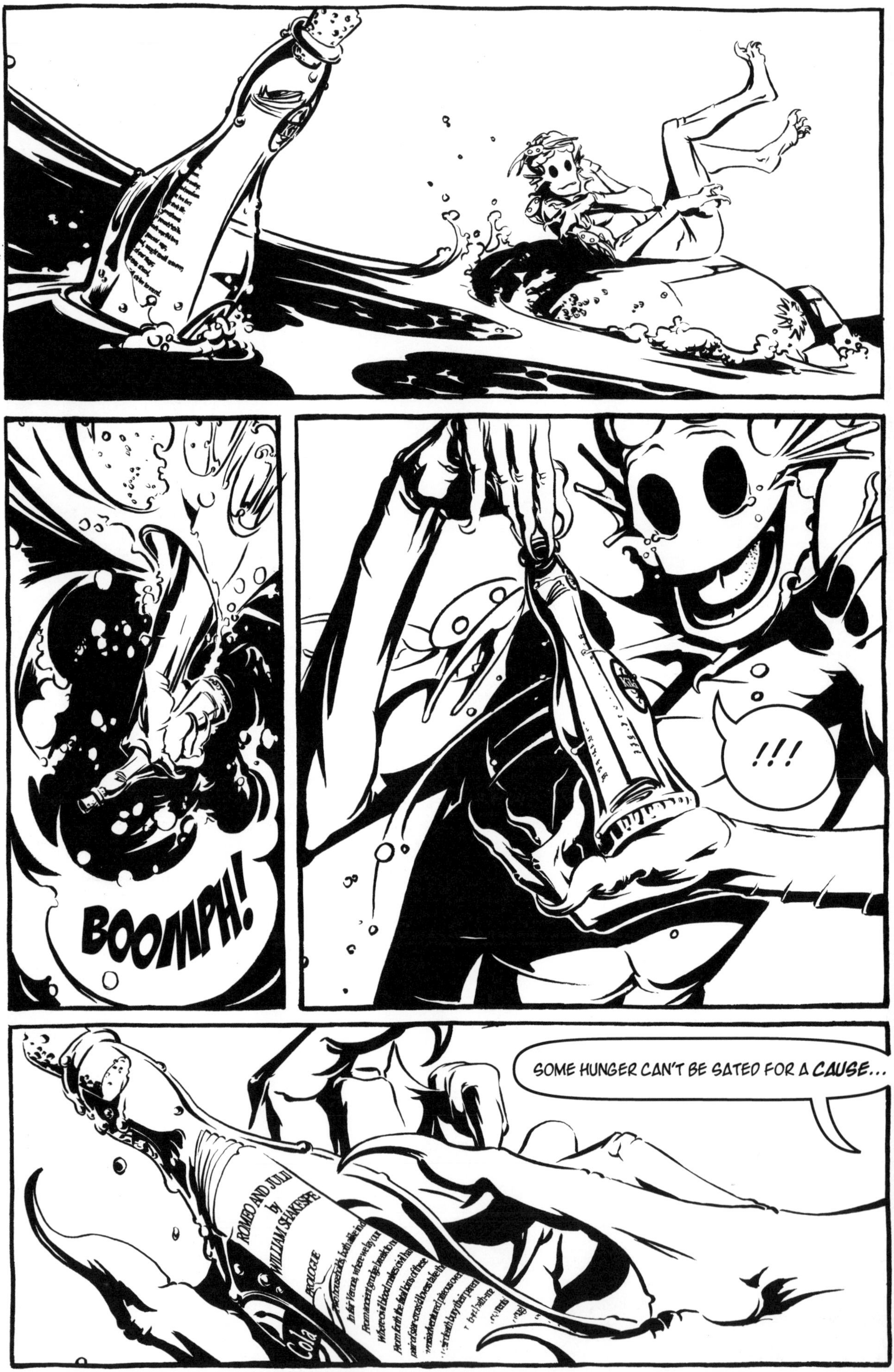
BOOMPH!
!!!
SOME HUNGER CAN'T BE SATED FOR A CAUSE...

IT AIN'T NATURAL TO MAKE NICE WITH YER FOOD, *GRUE*. AND YOU SEEN IT YERSELF—THESE BOTTLES DON'T EVEN HELP WITH *THAT*.

YER JUST GONNA LOSE IT AGAIN.

?

I SEE NOW MY *CONCILIATION'S* PLOT!

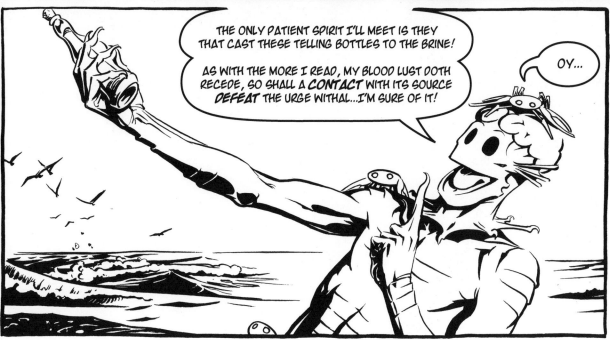

THE ONLY PATIENT SPIRIT I'LL MEET IS THEY THAT CAST THESE TELLING BOTTLES TO THE BRINE!

AS WITH THE MORE I READ, MY BLOOD LUST DOTH RECEDE, SO SHALL A *CONTACT* WITH ITS SOURCE *DEFEAT* THE URGE WITHAL...I'M SURE OF IT!

OY...

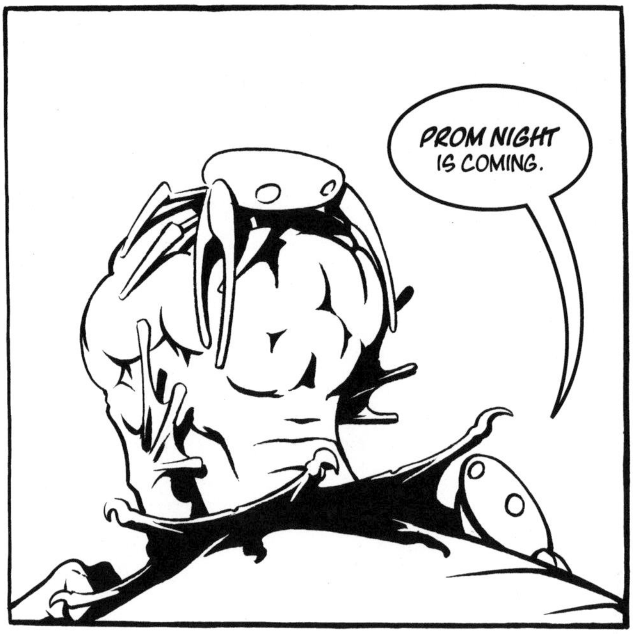
PROM NIGHT IS COMING.

CHAPTER TWO

RIDE AWAY

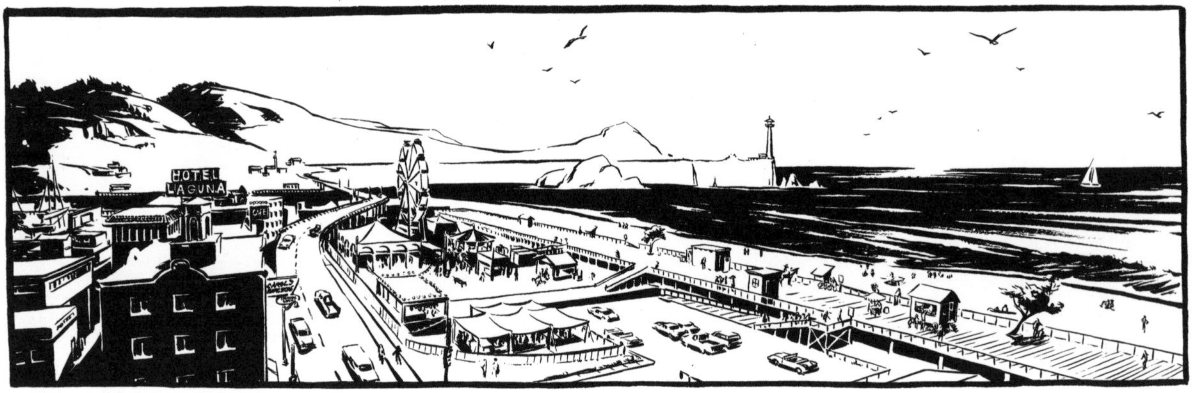
HOTEL
LAGUNA

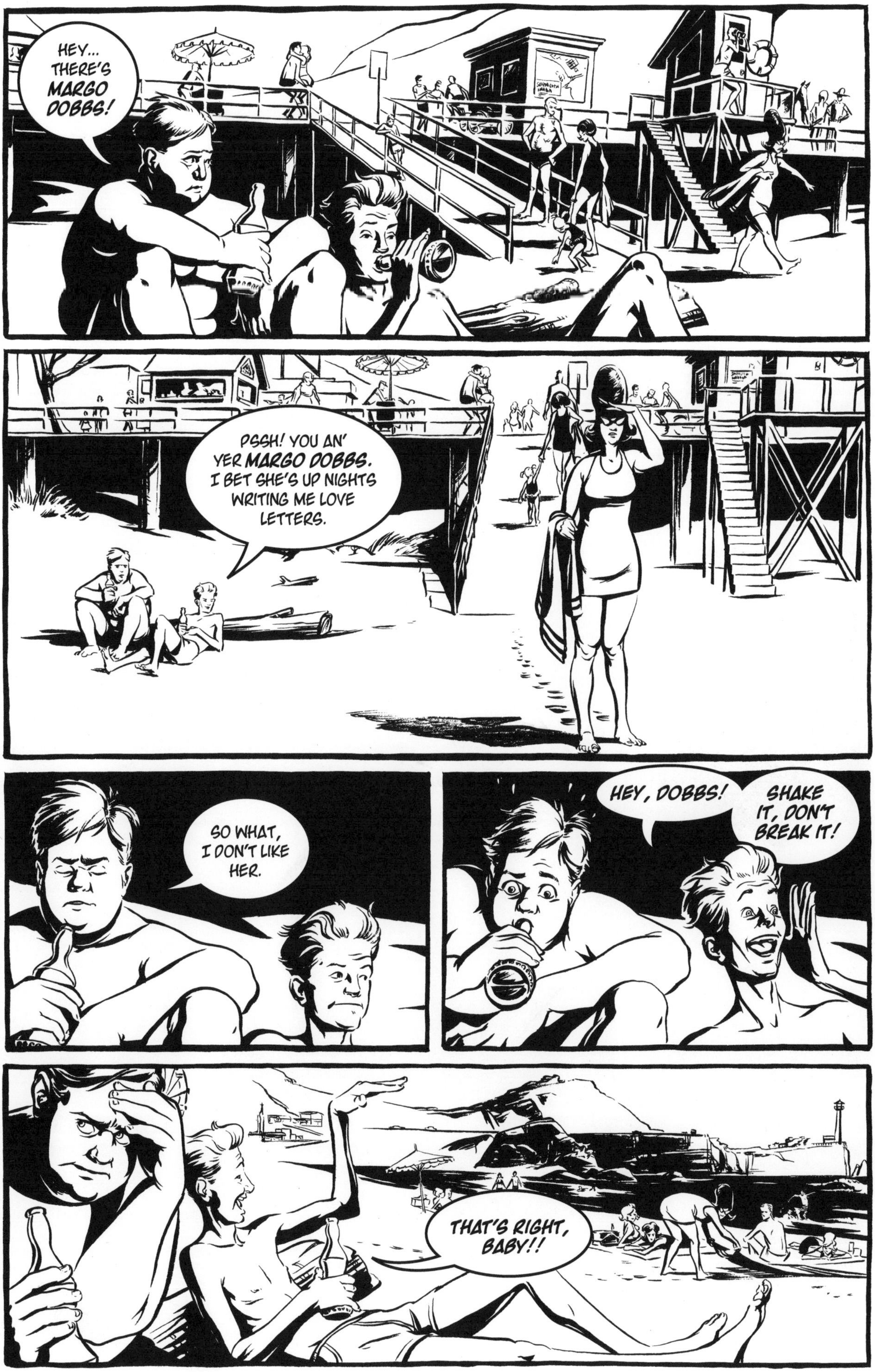
HEY... THERE'S MARGO DOBBS!
PSSH! YOU AN' YER MARGO DOBBS. I BET SHE'S UP NIGHTS WRITING ME LOVE LETTERS.
SO WHAT, I DON'T LIKE HER.
HEY, DOBBS!
SHAKE IT, DON'T BREAK IT!
THAT'S RIGHT, BABY!!

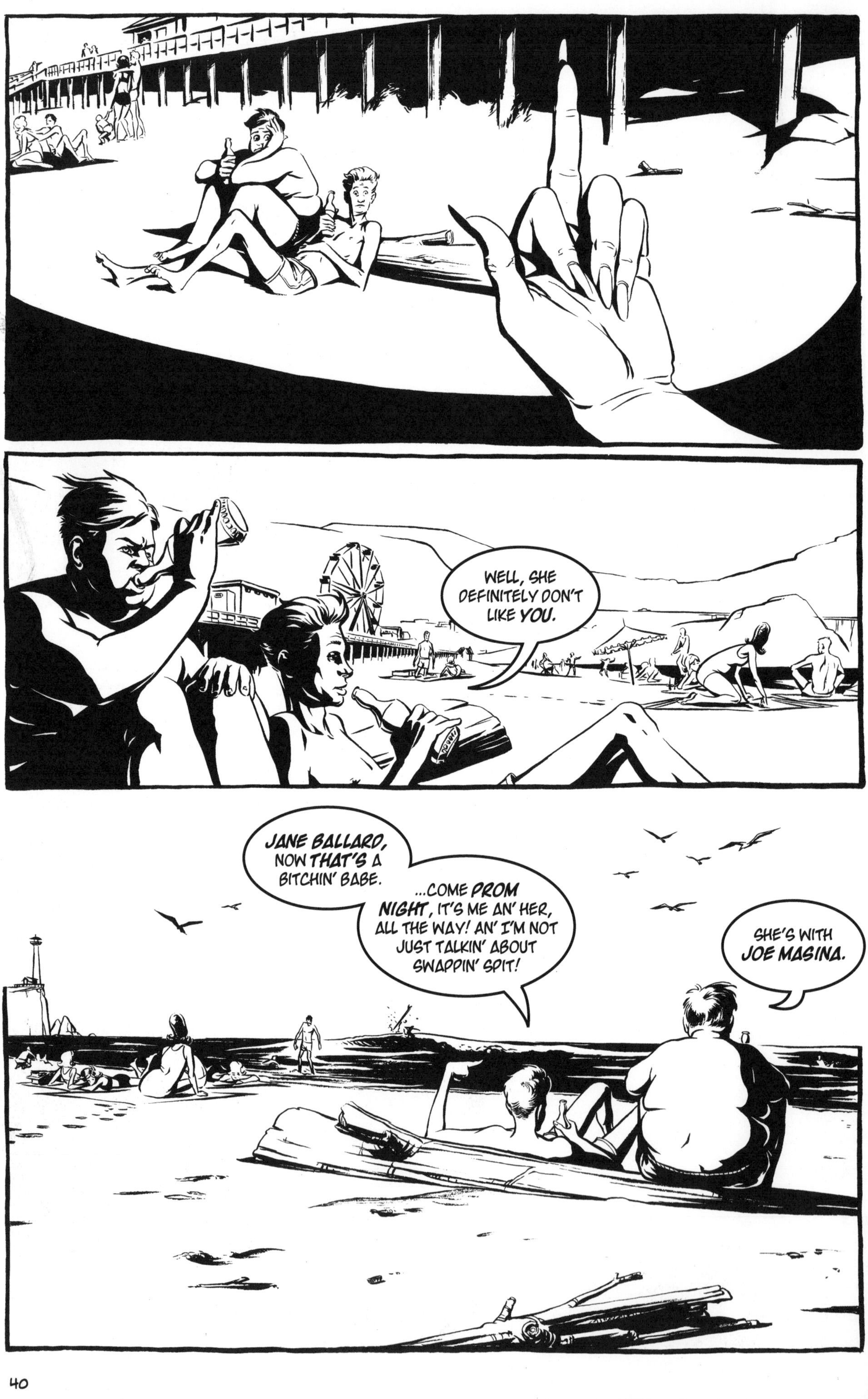
WELL, SHE DEFINITELY DON'T LIKE YOU.
JANE BALLARD, NOW THAT'S A BITCHIN' BABE.
...COME PROM NIGHT, IT'S ME AN' HER, ALL THE WAY! AN' I'M NOT JUST TALKIN' ABOUT SWAPPIN' SPIT!
SHE'S WITH JOE MASINA.

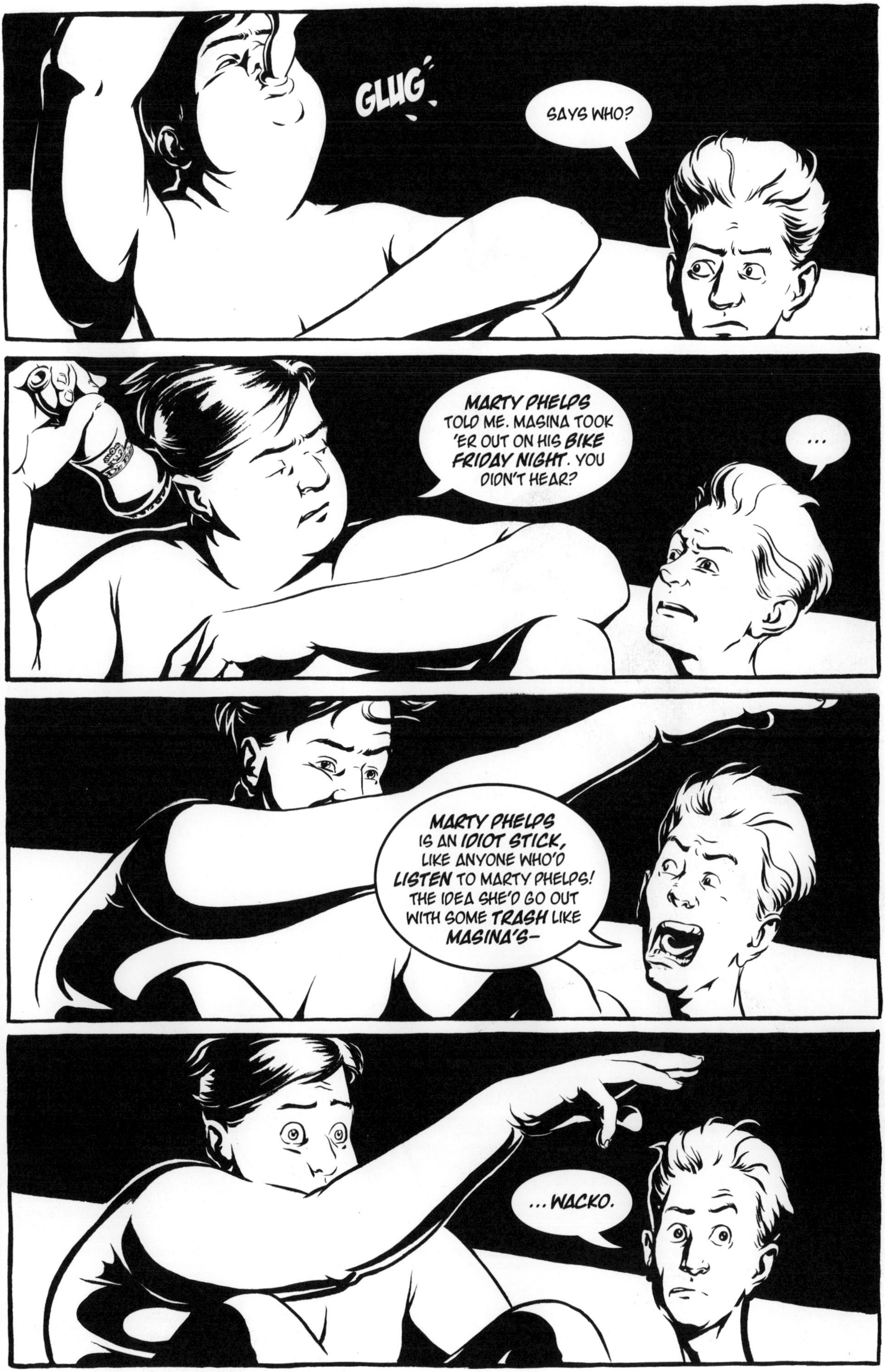
GLUG
SAYS WHO?
MARTY PHELPS TOLD ME. MASINA TOOK 'ER OUT ON HIS BIKE FRIDAY NIGHT. YOU DIDN'T HEAR?
...
MARTY PHELPS IS AN IDIOT STICK, LIKE ANYONE WHO'D LISTEN TO MARTY PHELPS! THE IDEA SHE'D GO OUT WITH SOME TRASH LIKE MASINA'S–
...WACKO.

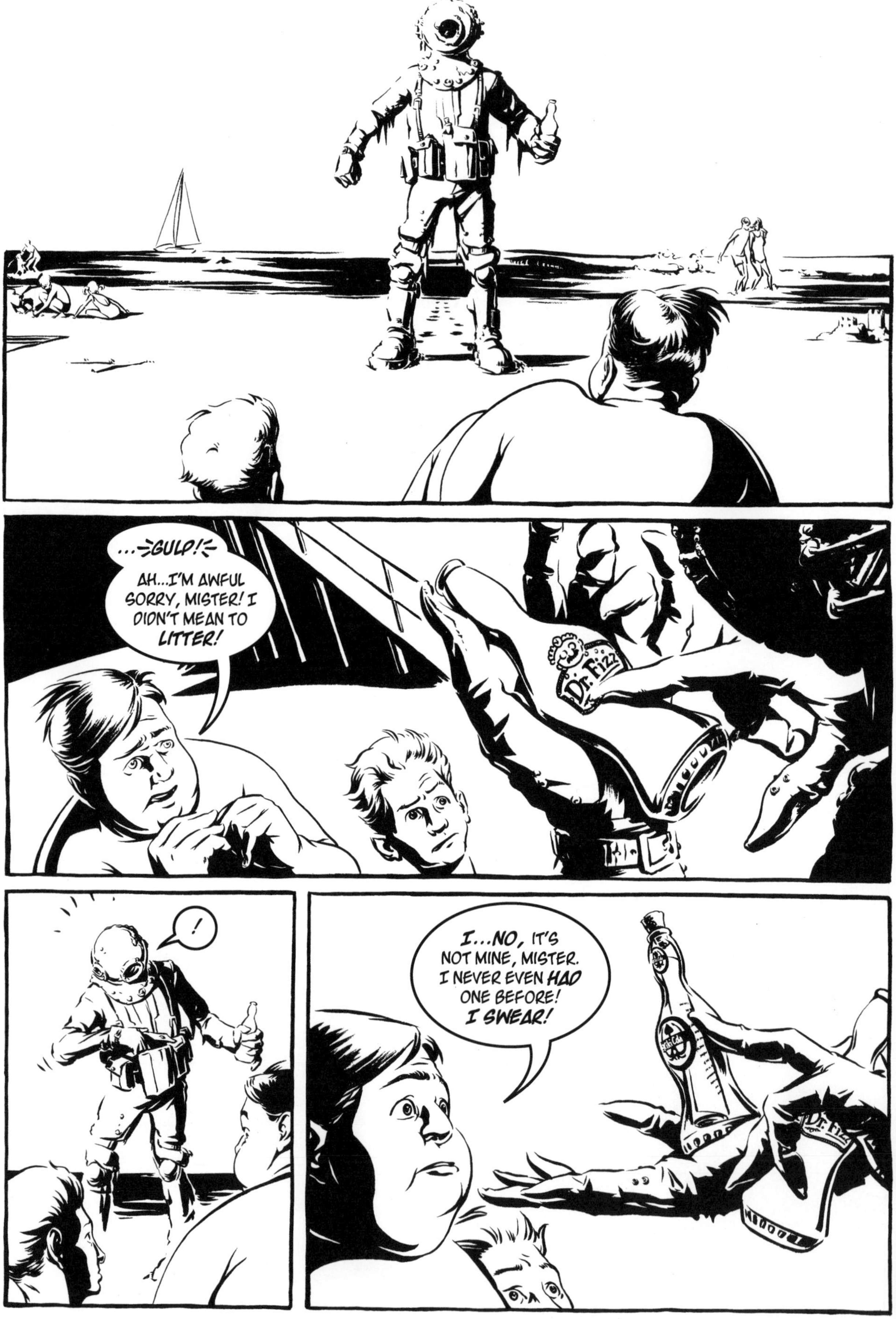
...GULP!
AH...I'M AWFUL SORRY, MISTER! I DIDN'T MEAN TO LITTER!
Dr. Fizz
!
I...NO, IT'S NOT MINE, MISTER. I NEVER EVEN HAD ONE BEFORE! I SWEAR!

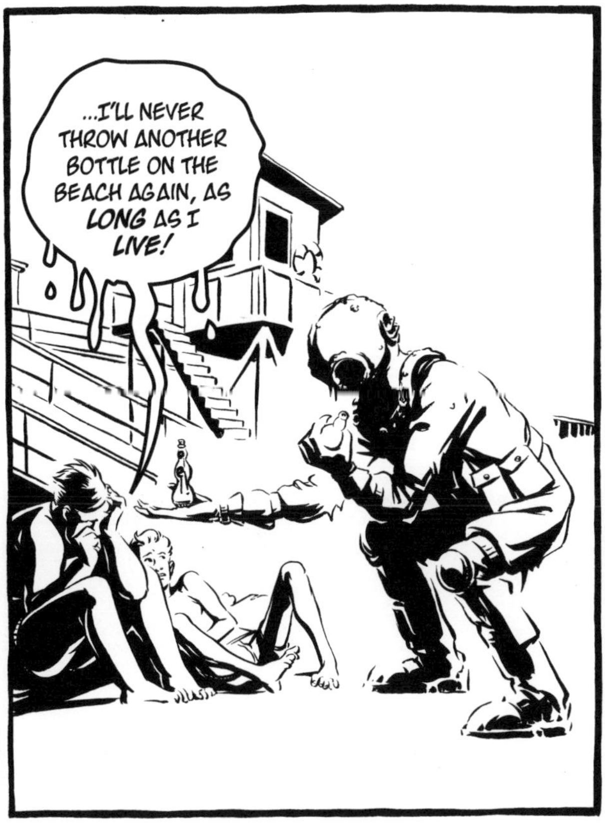
...I'LL NEVER THROW ANOTHER BOTTLE ON THE BEACH AGAIN, AS LONG AS I LIVE!

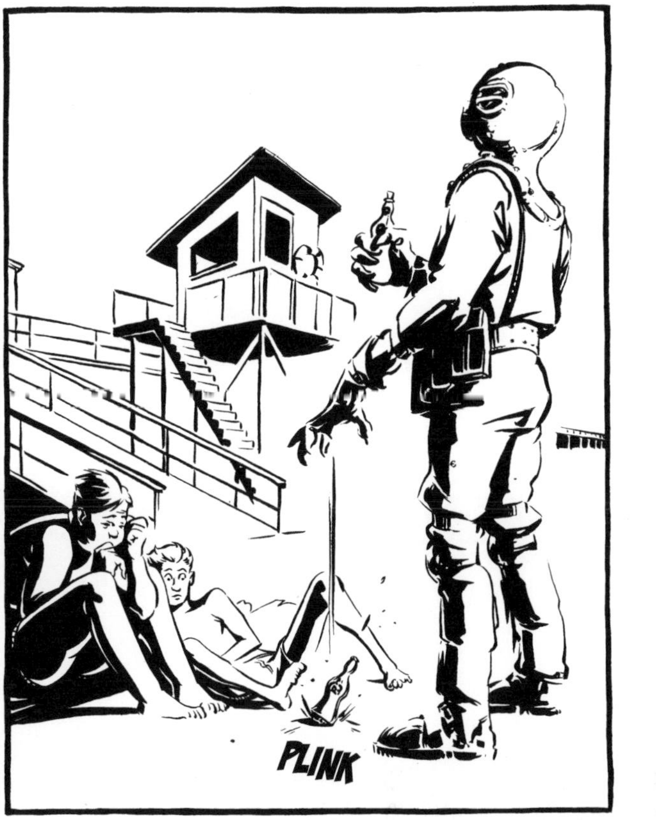
PLINK

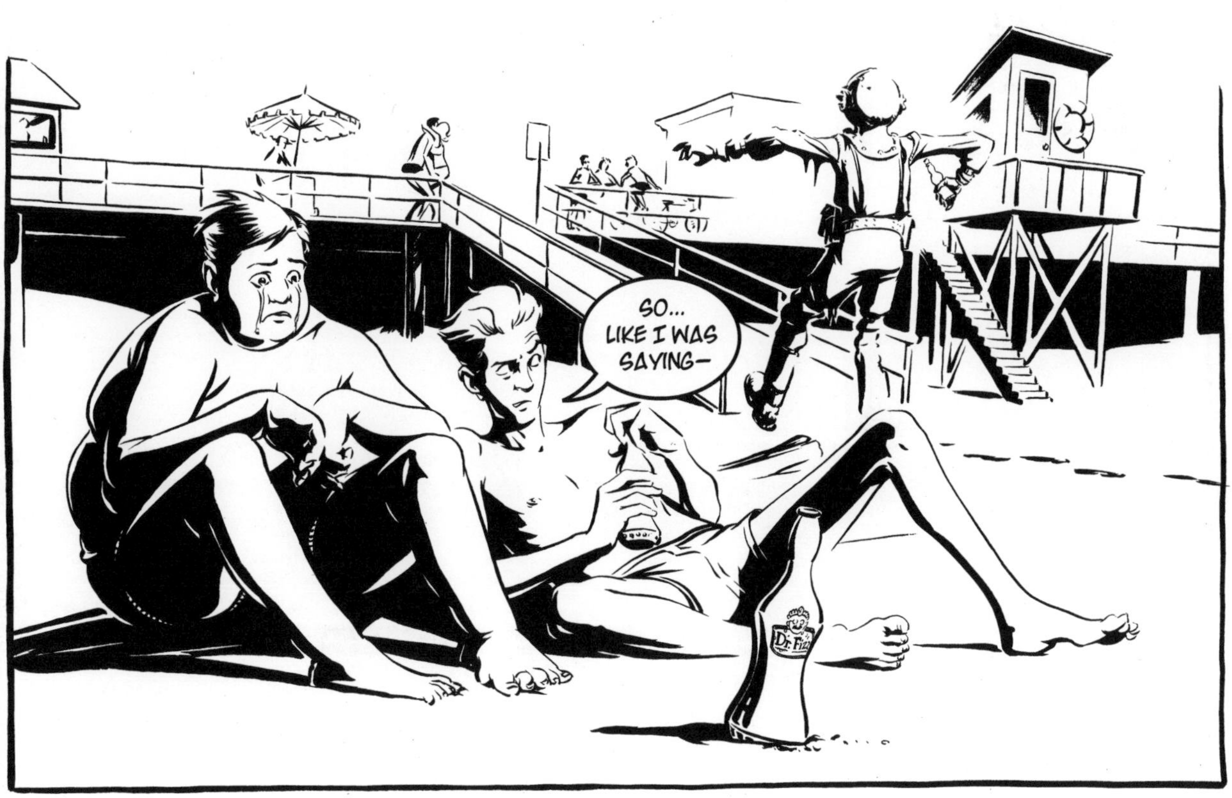
SO... LIKE I WAS SAYING–
Dr. Fizz

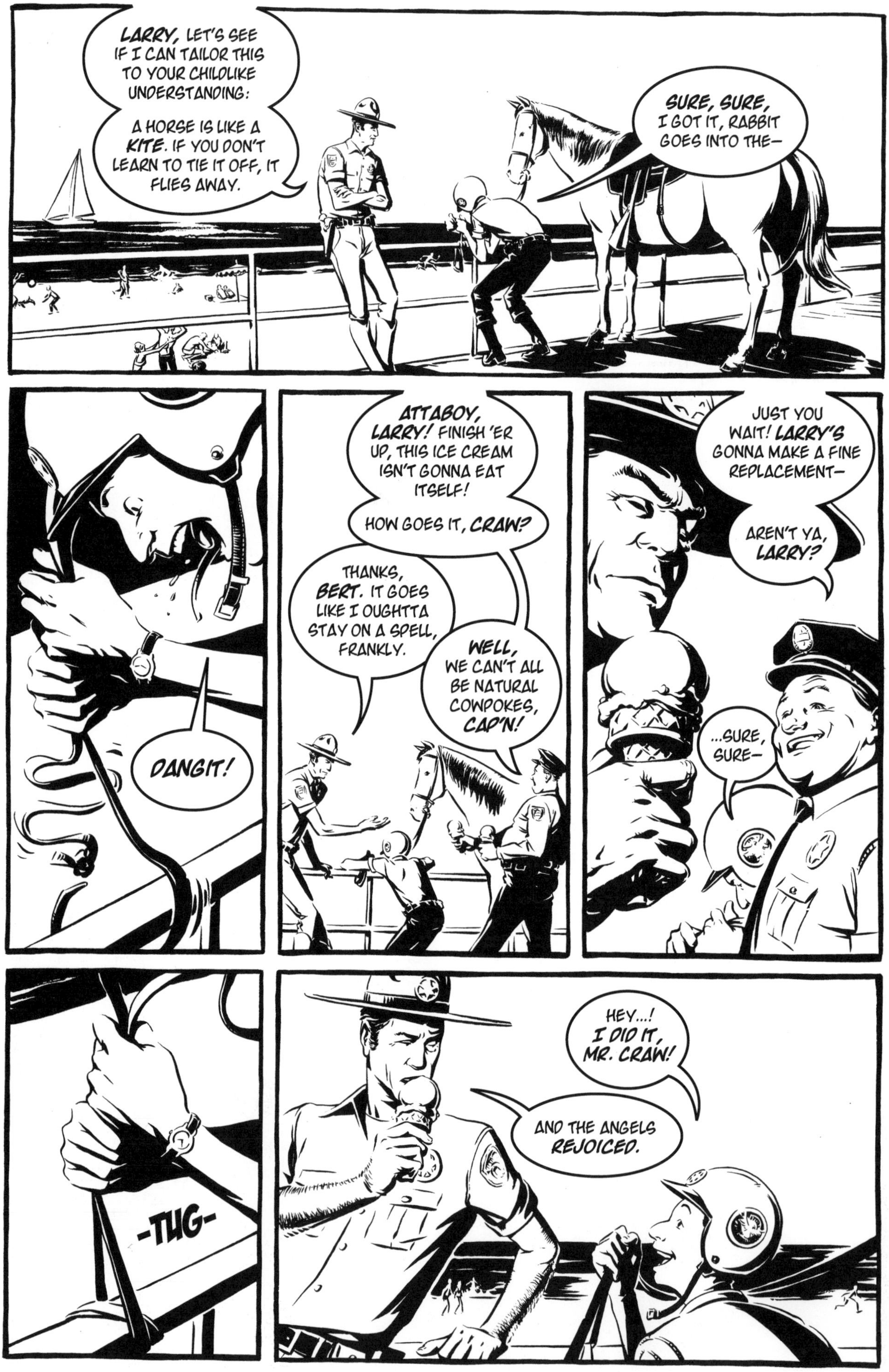
LARRY, LET'S SEE IF I CAN TAILOR THIS TO YOUR CHILDLIKE UNDERSTANDING:
A HORSE IS LIKE A KITE. IF YOU DON'T LEARN TO TIE IT OFF, IT FLIES AWAY.
SURE, SURE, I GOT IT, RABBIT GOES INTO THE—
DANGIT!
ATTABOY, LARRY! FINISH 'ER UP, THIS ICE CREAM ISN'T GONNA EAT ITSELF!
HOW GOES IT, CRAW?
THANKS, BERT. IT GOES LIKE I OUGHTTA STAY ON A SPELL, FRANKLY.
WELL, WE CAN'T ALL BE NATURAL COWPOKES, CAP'N!
JUST YOU WAIT! LARRY'S GONNA MAKE A FINE REPLACEMENT—
AREN'T YA, LARRY?
...SURE, SURE—
-TUG-
HEY...! I DID IT, MR. CRAW!
AND THE ANGELS REJOICED.

TAKE FIVE ON ME, SON. I GOTTA YAK AT THE *CAP'N.*

THANK YOU, SIR!

!

WE FOUND THE *MASINA* KID'S JACKET DOWN BY THE WATER. WORD AROUND IS, HE WAS OUT WITH HER.

YOU THINK THAT BOY'S *SMART ENOUGH* TO CARRY THIS OFF?

THERE'S TOO MANY INCIDENTS OVER THE YEAR.

WE'RE MISSING SOMETHING.

CRAW, LISTEN...

I KNOW YOU GOT SOME YEARS OF EXPERIENCE ON YA. BUT THE KIDS TODAY ARE A NEW KIND OF TROUBLE. NO VALUES, NO ASPIRATIONS...

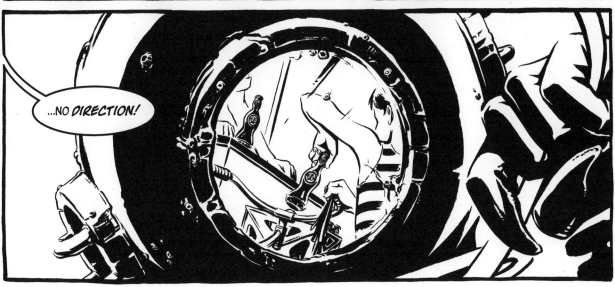

...NO *DIRECTION!*

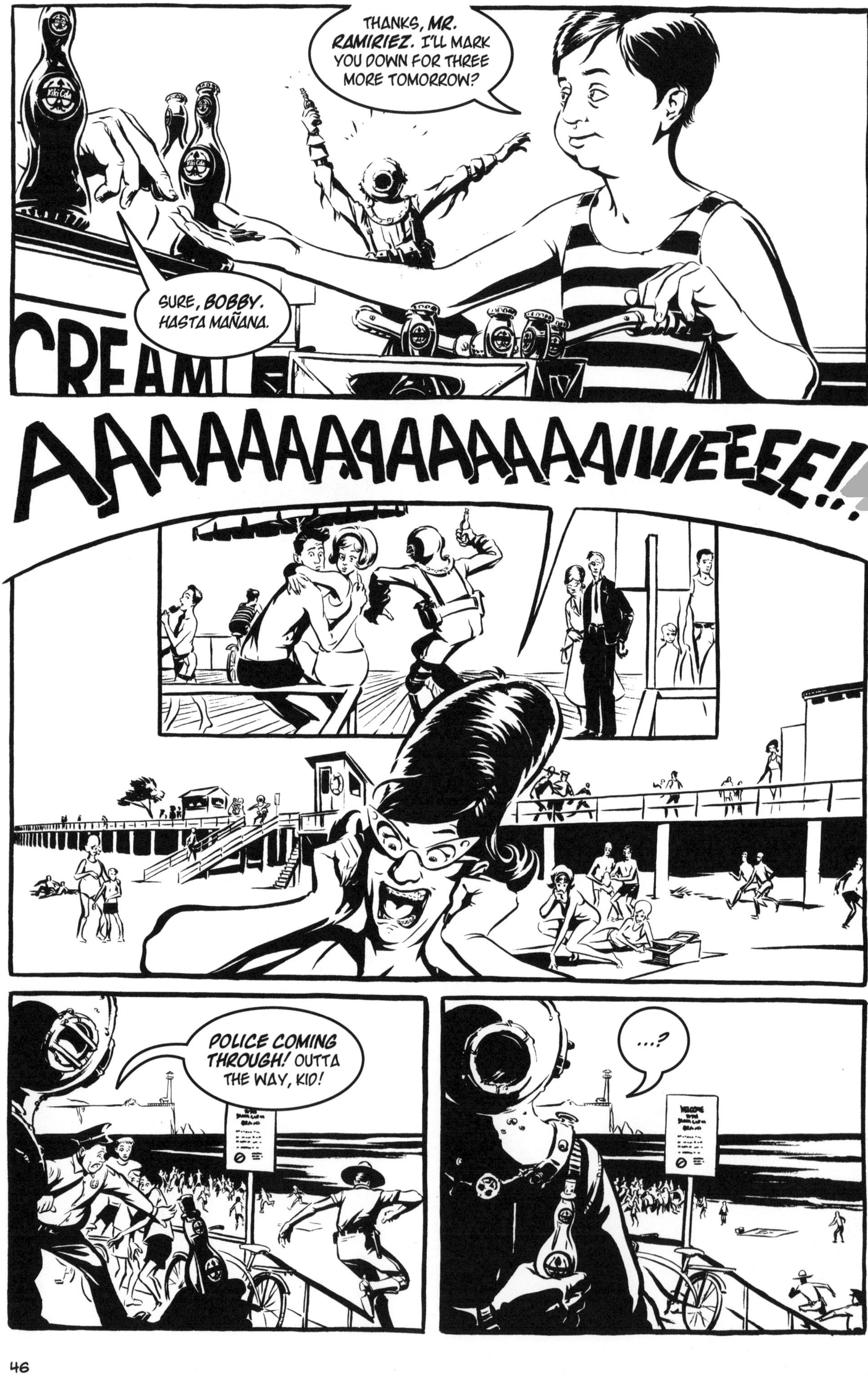
THANKS, MR. RAMIRIEZ. I'LL MARK YOU DOWN FOR THREE MORE TOMORROW?
SURE, BOBBY. HASTA MAÑANA.
CREAM
AAAAAAAAAAAAAAIIIIEEEEE!!
POLICE COMING THROUGH! OUTTA THE WAY, KID!
...?

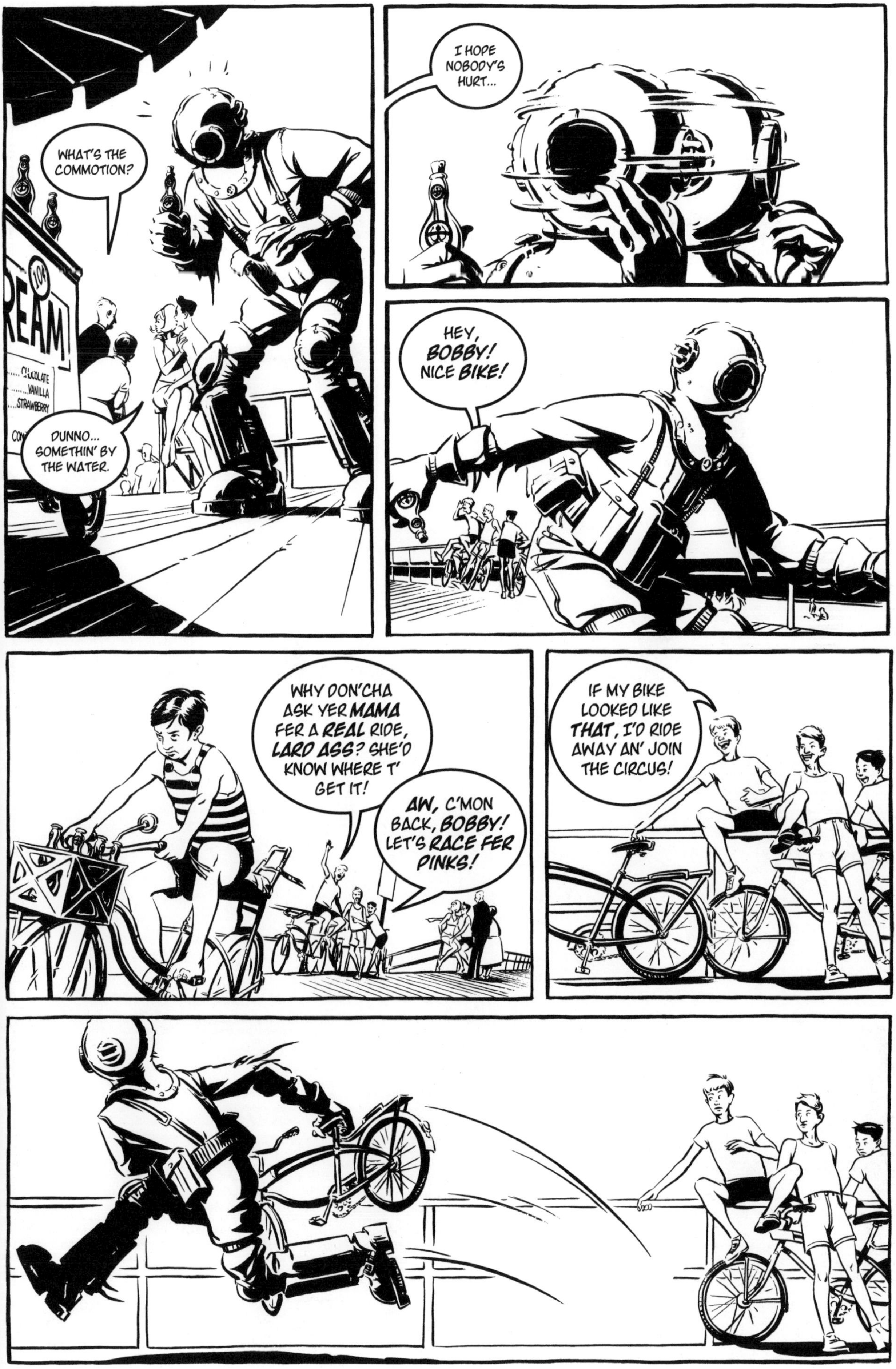
WHAT'S THE COMMOTION?
DUNNO... SOMETHIN' BY THE WATER.
REAM
CHOCOLATE
VANILLA
STRAWBERRY
I HOPE NOBODY'S HURT...
HEY, BOBBY! NICE BIKE!
WHY DON'CHA ASK YER MAMA FER A REAL RIDE, LARD ASS? SHE'D KNOW WHERE T' GET IT!
AW, C'MON BACK, BOBBY! LET'S RACE FER PINKS!
IF MY BIKE LOOKED LIKE THAT, I'D RIDE AWAY AN' JOIN THE CIRCUS!

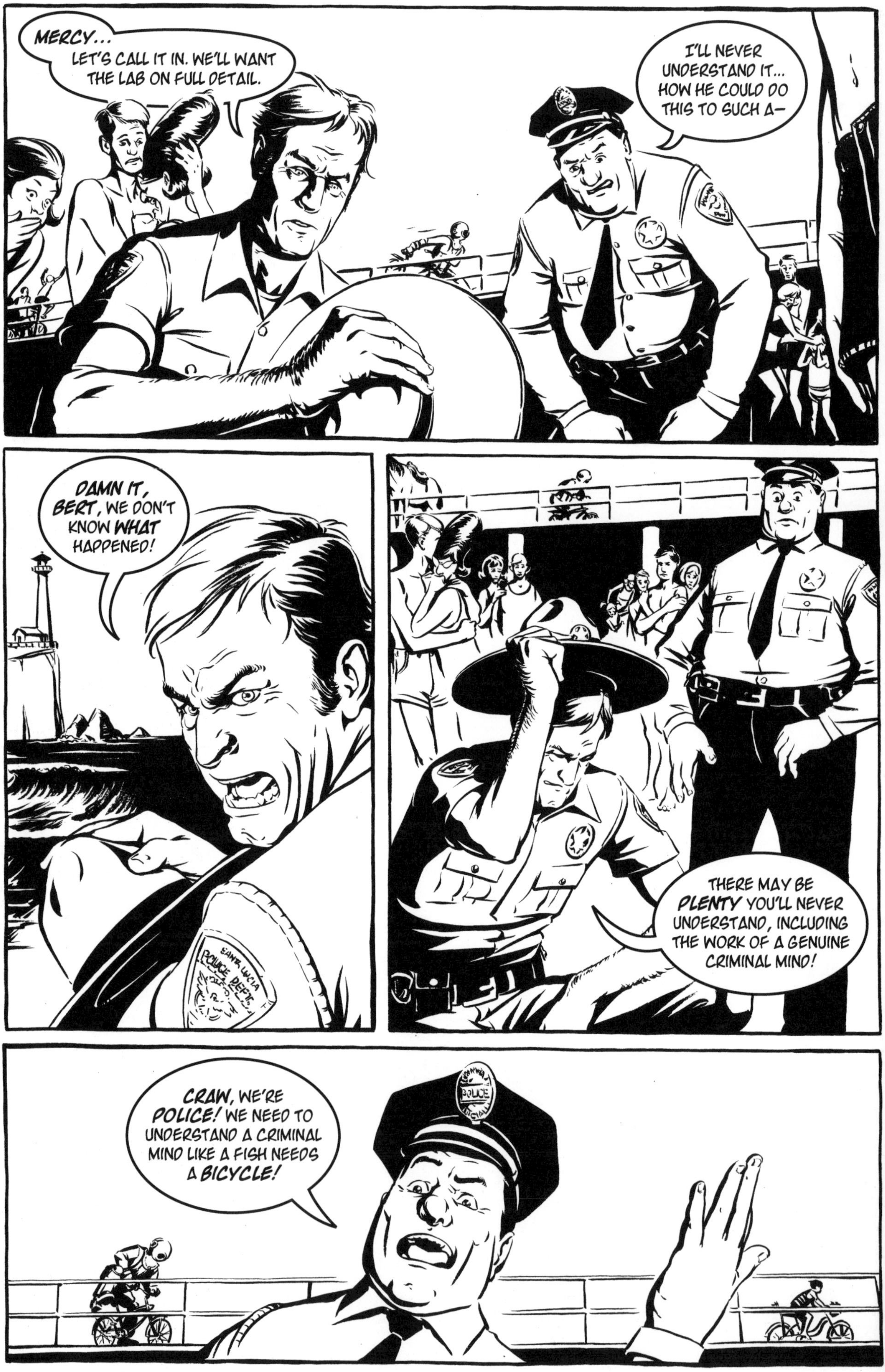
MERCY... LET'S CALL IT IN. WE'LL WANT THE LAB ON FULL DETAIL.
I'LL NEVER UNDERSTAND IT... HOW HE COULD DO THIS TO SUCH A—
DAMN IT, BERT, WE DON'T KNOW WHAT HAPPENED!
THERE MAY BE PLENTY YOU'LL NEVER UNDERSTAND, INCLUDING THE WORK OF A GENUINE CRIMINAL MIND!
CRAW, WE'RE POLICE! WE NEED TO UNDERSTAND A CRIMINAL MIND LIKE A FISH NEEDS A BICYCLE!

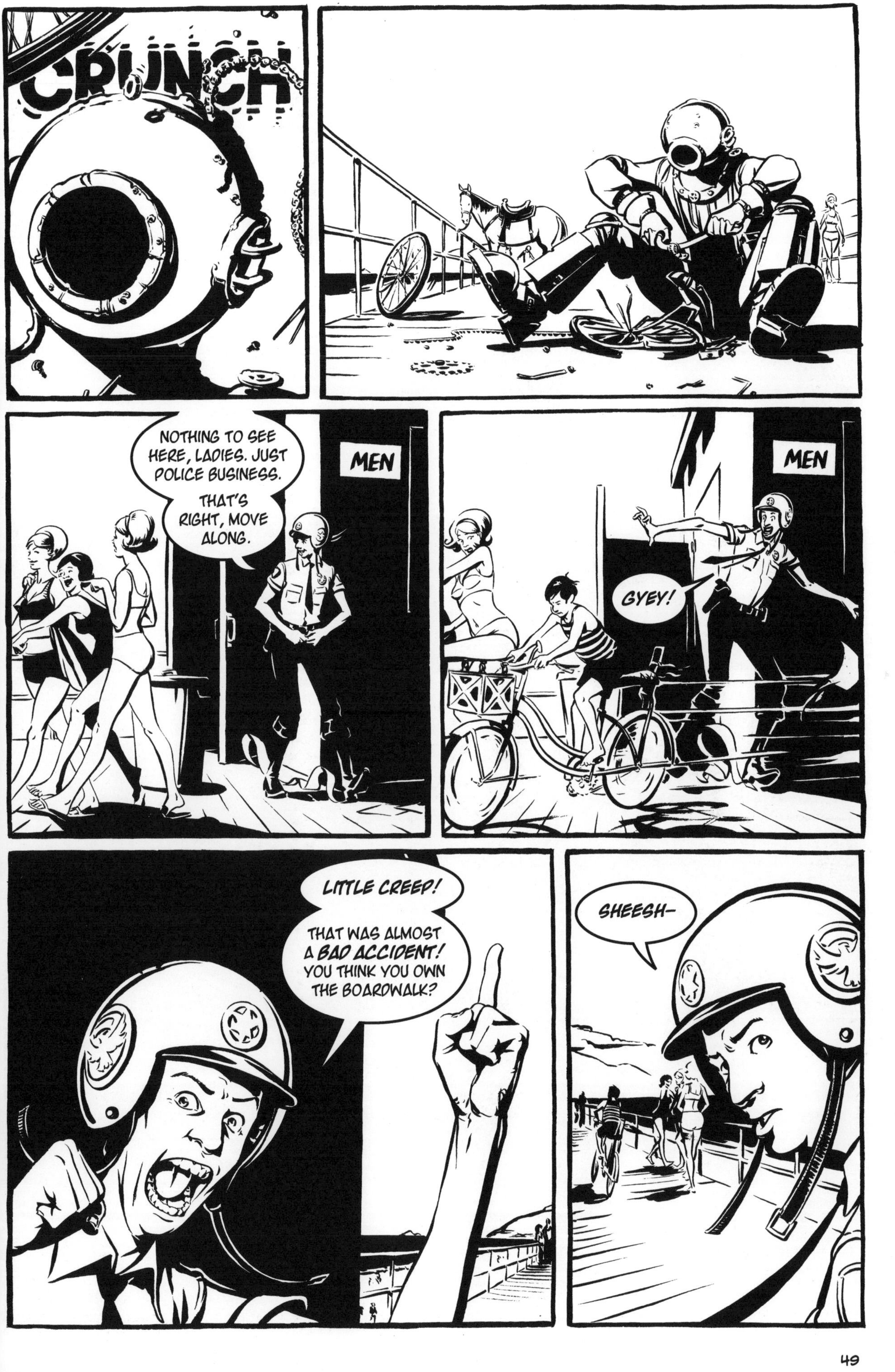
CRUNCH
NOTHING TO SEE HERE, LADIES. JUST POLICE BUSINESS.
THAT'S RIGHT, MOVE ALONG.
MEN
MEN
GYEY!
LITTLE CREEP!
THAT WAS ALMOST A BAD ACCIDENT! YOU THINK YOU OWN THE BOARDWALK?
SHEESH-

CLOPPA-CLOP

CLOPPA-
CLOP

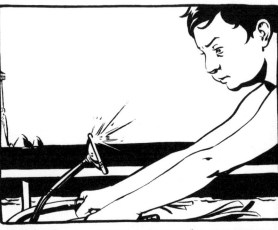

AH!

SKREECH!

SANTA LUCIA
FAIRGROUNDS
ENTRANCE
A WHOLE
WORLD OF FUN!

CLOPPA-CLOP

NEEEIGH!

WATER-FRONT

SMASH!

COTTON CANDY

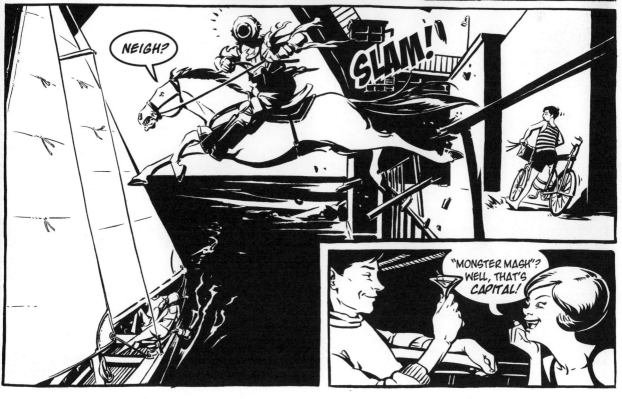

NEIGH?

SLAM!

"MONSTER MASH"? WELL, THAT'S CAPITAL!

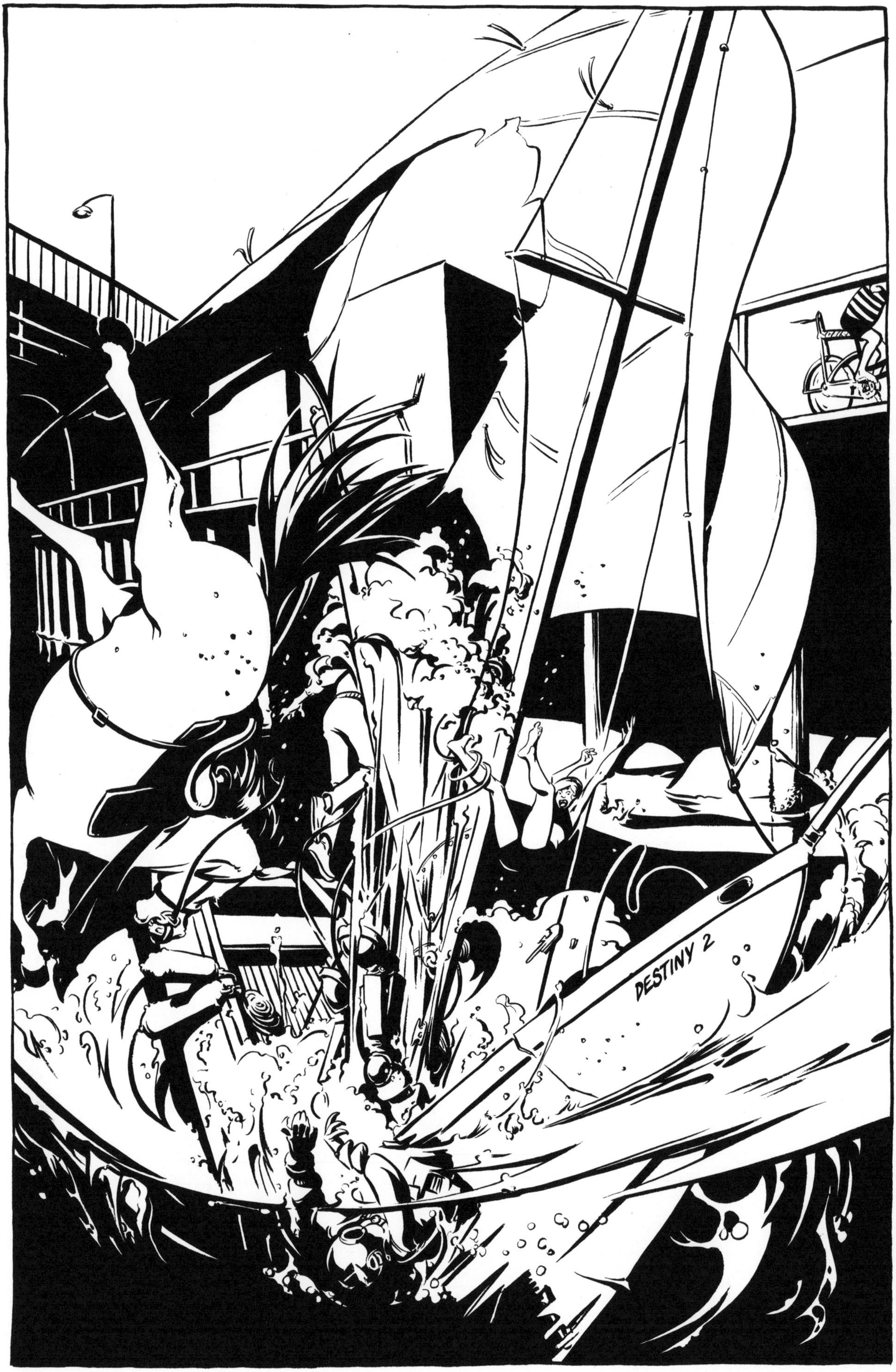
DESTINY 2

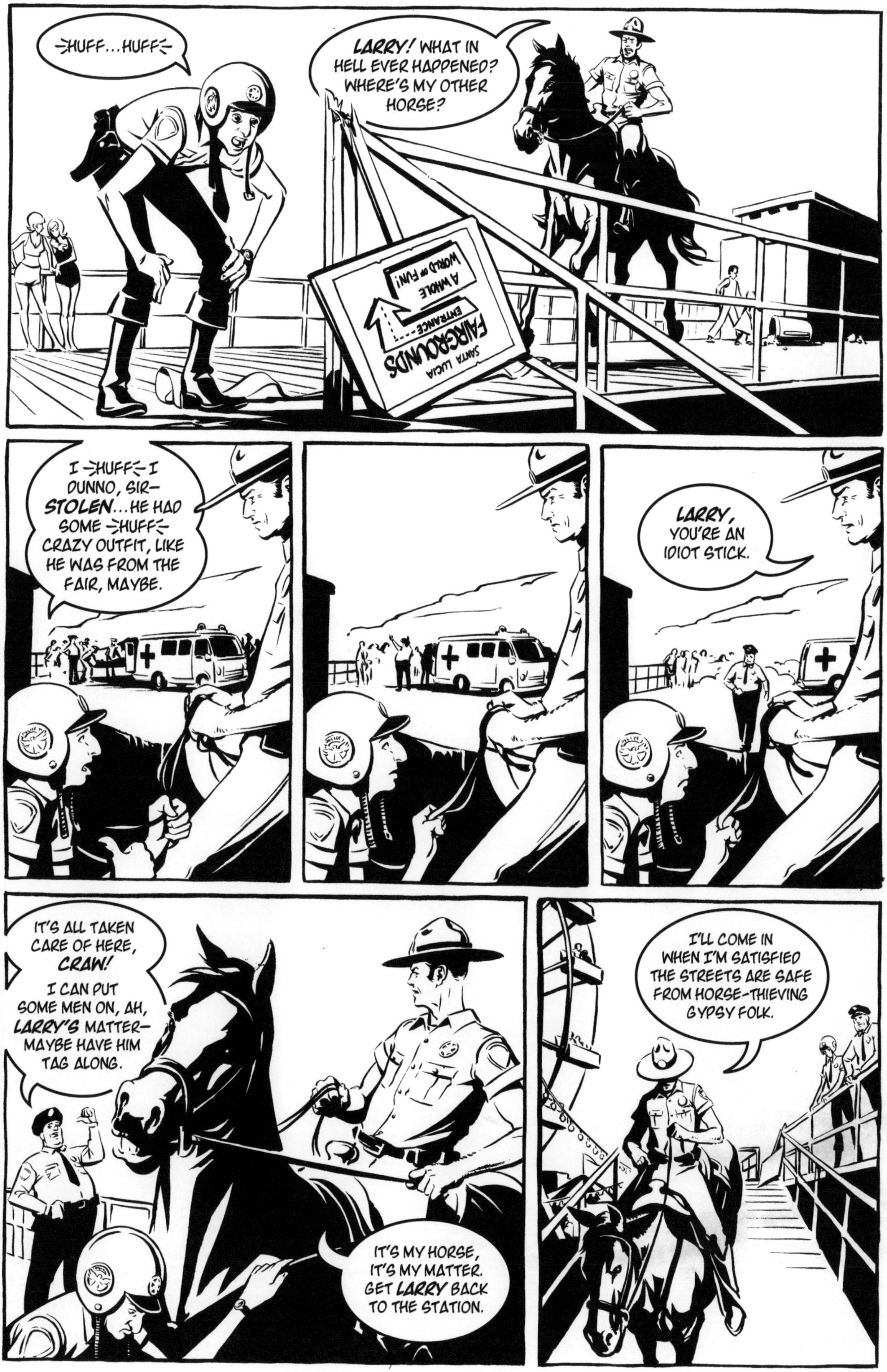

≡HUFF...HUFF≡
LARRY! WHAT IN HELL EVER HAPPENED? WHERE'S MY OTHER HORSE?
SANTA LUCIA FAIRGROUNDS ENTRANCE A WHOLE WORLD OF FUN!
I ≡HUFF≡ I DUNNO, SIR– STOLEN...HE HAD SOME ≡HUFF≡ CRAZY OUTFIT, LIKE HE WAS FROM THE FAIR, MAYBE.
LARRY, YOU'RE AN IDIOT STICK.
IT'S ALL TAKEN CARE OF HERE, CRAW!
I CAN PUT SOME MEN ON, AH, LARRY'S MATTER– MAYBE HAVE HIM TAG ALONG.
IT'S MY HORSE, IT'S MY MATTER. GET LARRY BACK TO THE STATION.
I'LL COME IN WHEN I'M SATISFIED THE STREETS ARE SAFE FROM HORSE-THIEVING GYPSY FOLK.

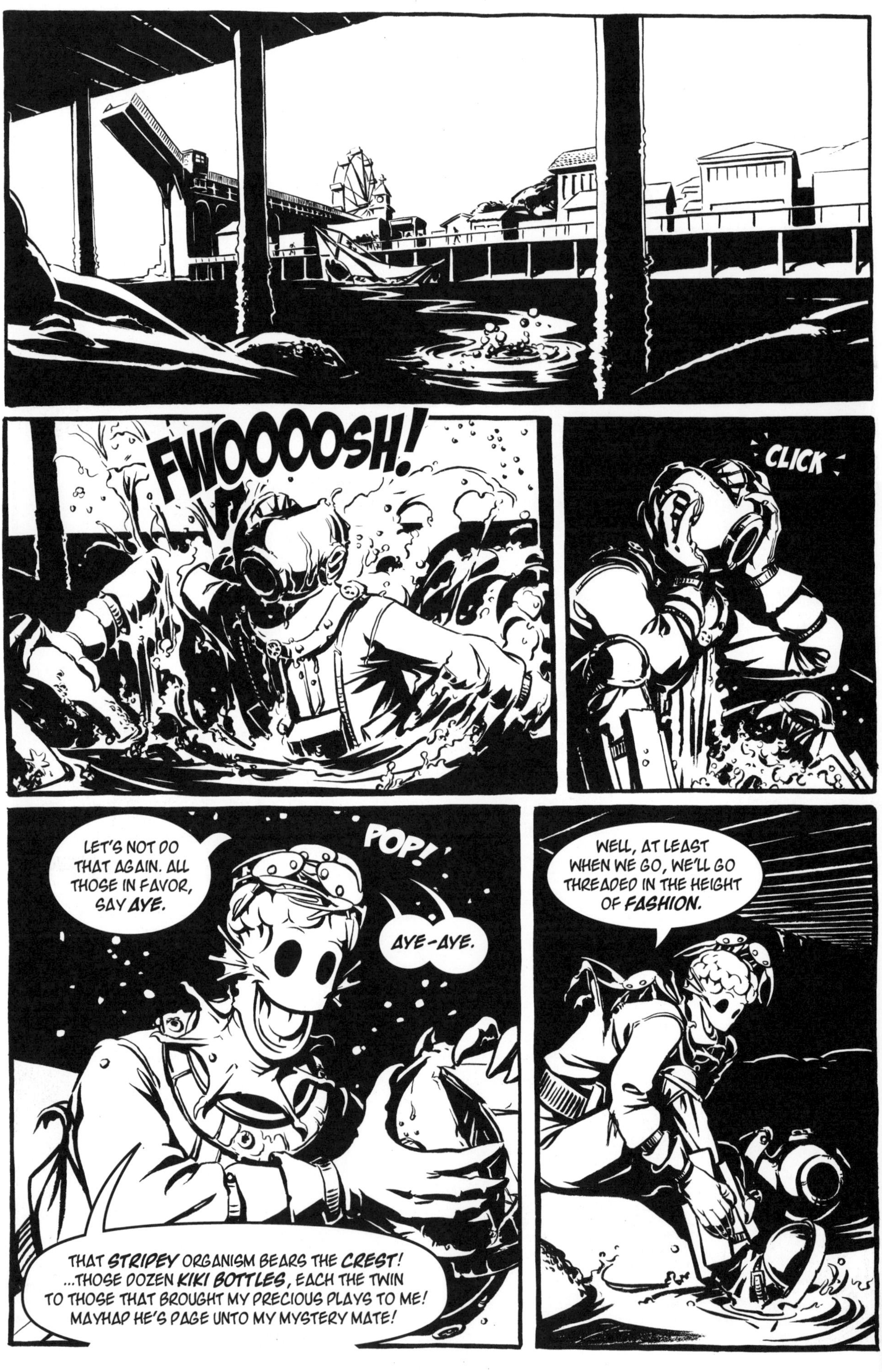
FWOOOOSH!
CLICK
LET'S NOT DO THAT AGAIN. ALL THOSE IN FAVOR, SAY AYE.
POP!
AYE-AYE.
THAT STRIPEY ORGANISM BEARS THE CREST! ...THOSE DOZEN KIKI BOTTLES, EACH THE TWIN TO THOSE THAT BROUGHT MY PRECIOUS PLAYS TO ME! MAYHAP HE'S PAGE UNTO MY MYSTERY MATE!
WELL, AT LEAST WHEN WE GO, WE'LL GO THREADED IN THE HEIGHT OF FASHION.

NOT SO, INVERTEBRATE! THIS SUIT HATH SERVED, BUT NOW'S A WELL-LOVED *LIABILITY*... WE NEEDS MUST FIND ANOTHER WAY TO HIDE!

I DON'T LIKE THE WHOLE BUSINESS—

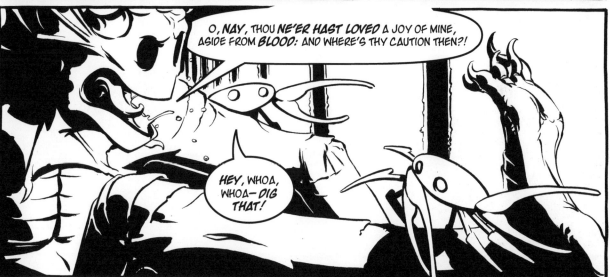

O, *NAY*, THOU *NE'ER HAST LOVED* A JOY OF MINE, ASIDE FROM *BLOOD*: AND WHERE'S THY CAUTION THEN?!

HEY, WHOA, WHOA—*DIG THAT!*

SANTA LUCIA **DRY DOCK**

THE *STRIPEY!* GOD BE PRAISED! I MIGHT HAVE MISSED THE CATCH FOR RAMBLING SO: NO MORE OF THAT!

WHAT *WOULD* I DO WITHOUT THEE, GENTLE CRAB?

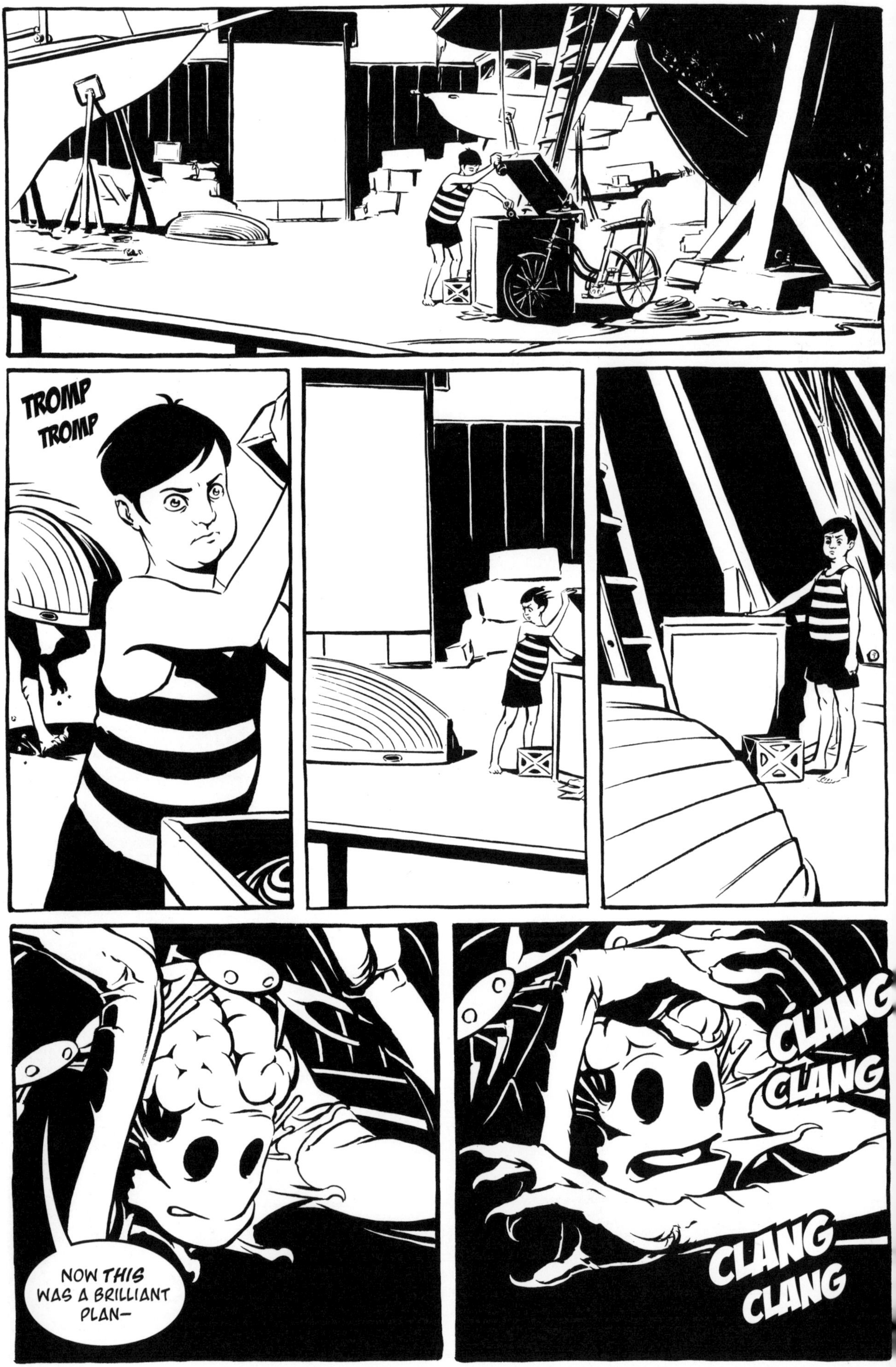
TROMP
TROMP
NOW THIS WAS A BRILLIANT PLAN–
CLANG
CLANG
CLANG
CLANG

CLANG
CLANG

LOOK WHERE THE *STRIPEY* CLIMBS! A MIGHTY SHIP!

CLANG

I DARE NOT GUESS WHAT *WONDERS* LIE WITHIN!

CLA-

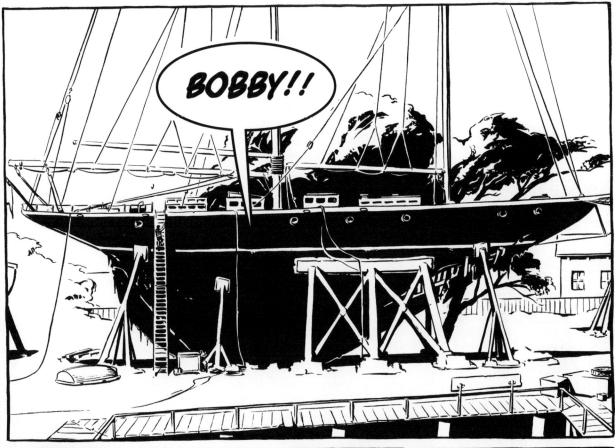

BOBBY!!

STOMP...
STOMP...
STOMP...
STOMP

UNHOLY ZEUS!

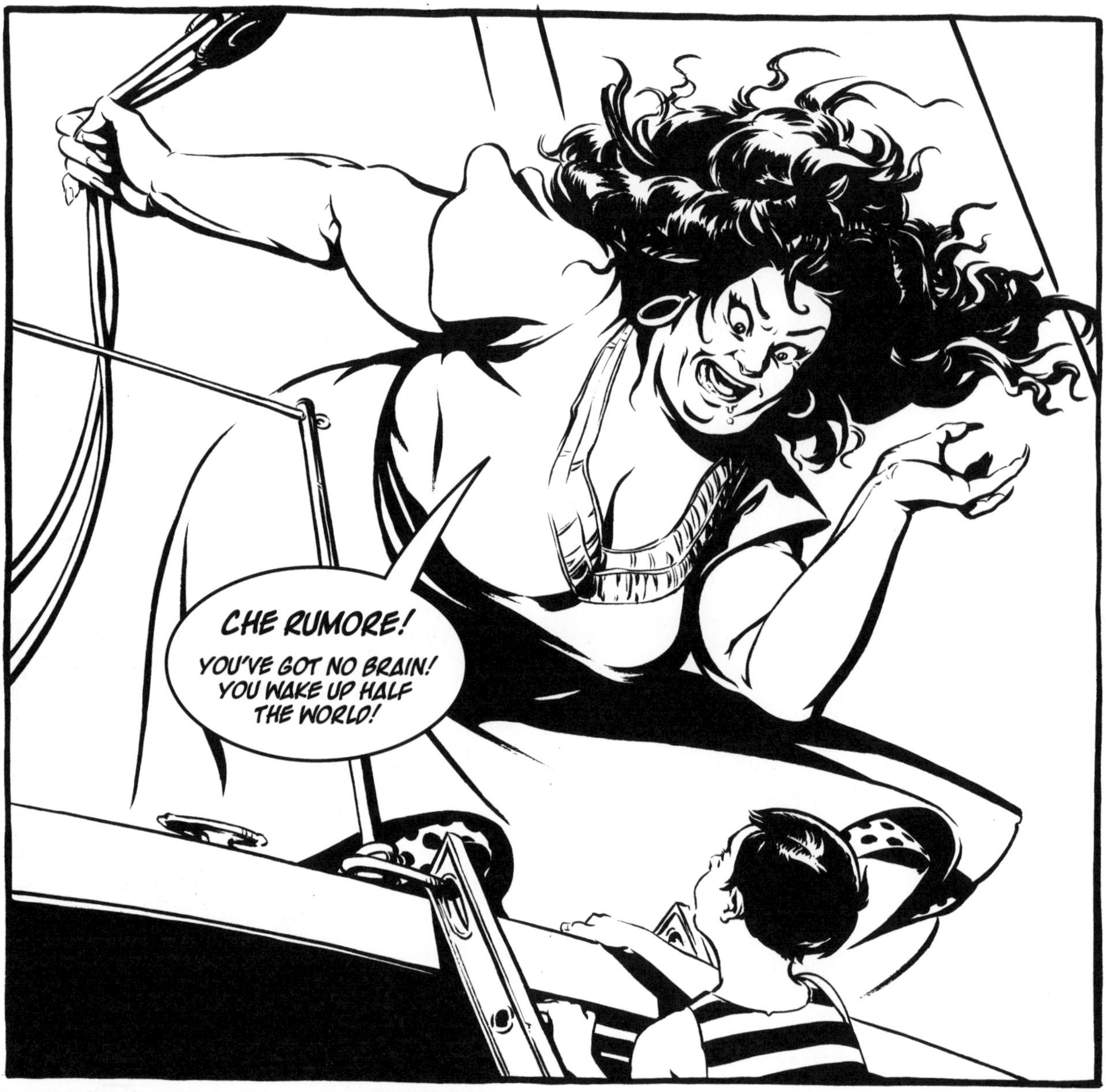
CHE RUMORE!
YOU'VE GOT NO BRAIN! YOU WAKE UP HALF THE WORLD!

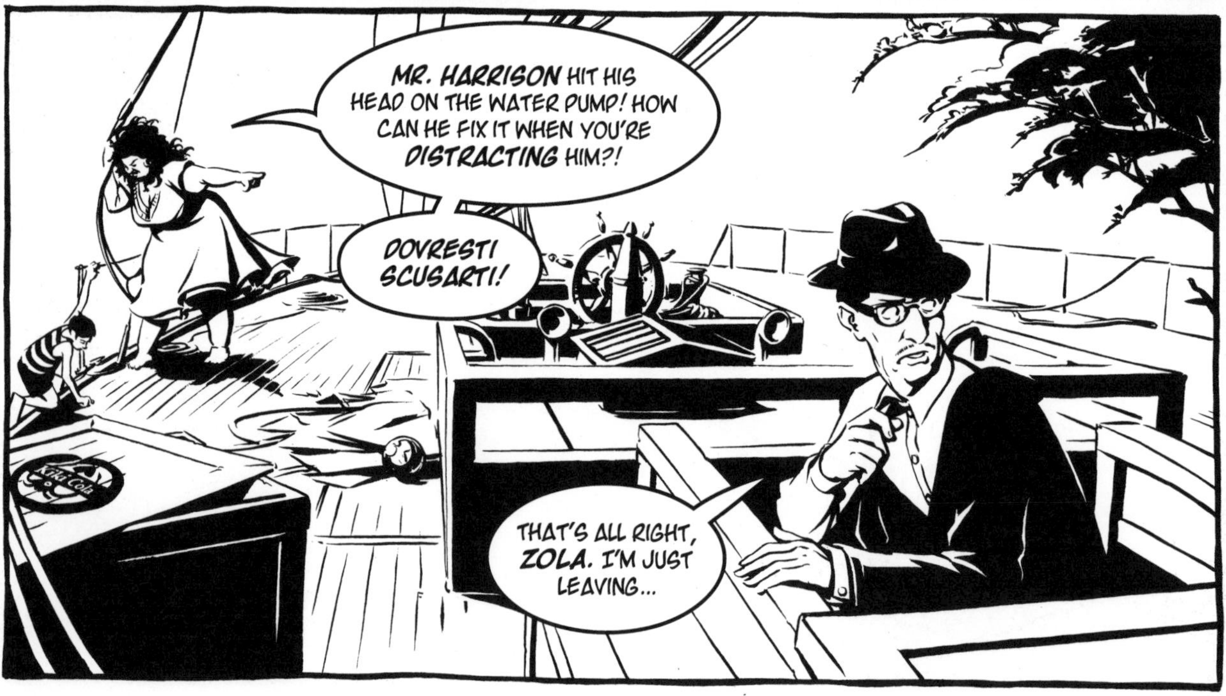
MR. HARRISON HIT HIS HEAD ON THE WATER PUMP! HOW CAN HE FIX IT WHEN YOU'RE DISTRACTING HIM?!
DOVRESTI SCUSARTI!
THAT'S ALL RIGHT, ZOLA. I'M JUST LEAVING...

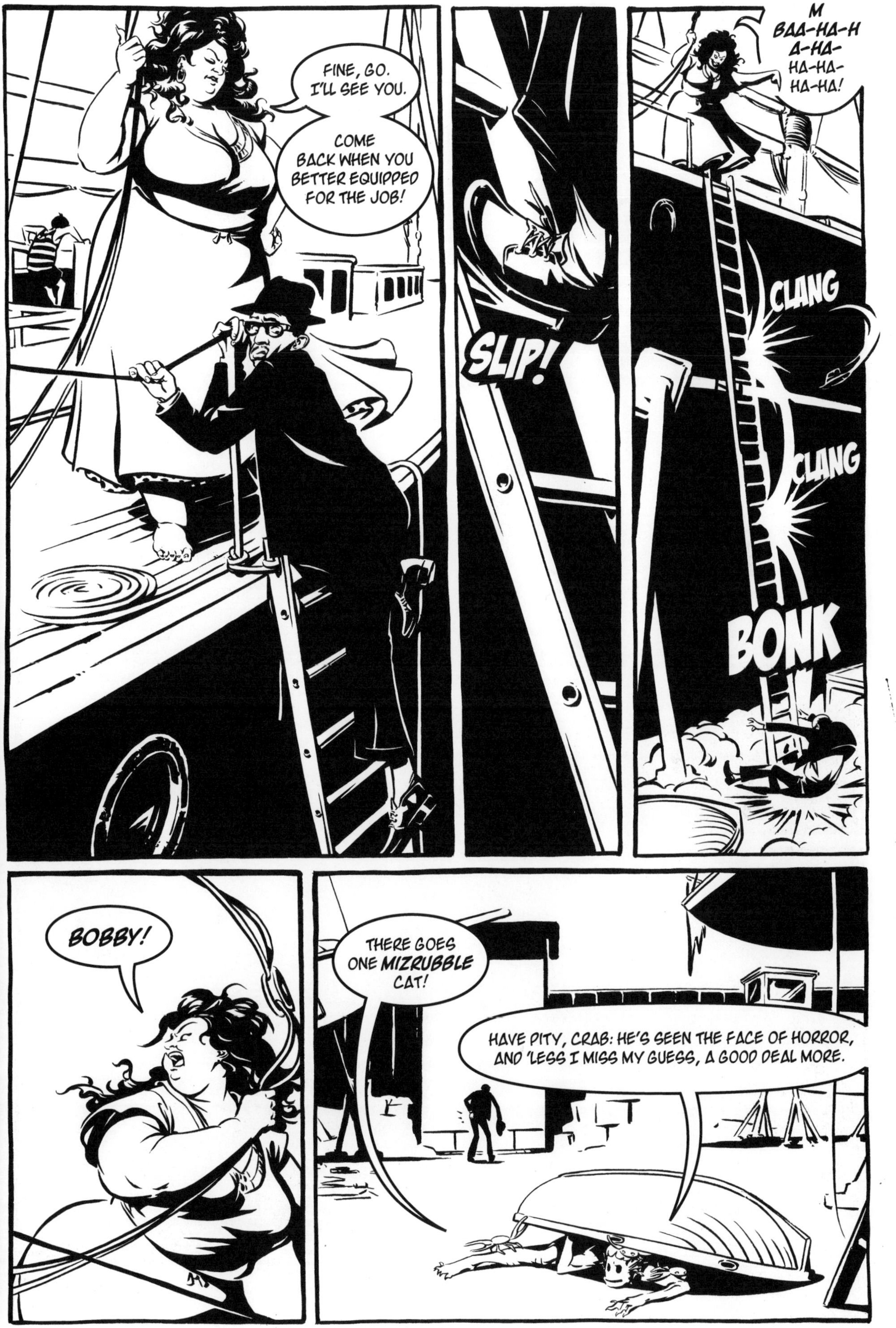
FINE, GO. I'LL SEE YOU.
COME BACK WHEN YOU BETTER EQUIPPED FOR THE JOB!
SLIP!
M BAA-HA-H A-HA-HA-HA-HA-HA!
CLANG
CLANG
BONK
BOBBY!
THERE GOES ONE MIZRUBBLE CAT!
HAVE PITY, CRAB: HE'S SEEN THE FACE OF HORROR, AND 'LESS I MISS MY GUESS, A GOOD DEAL MORE.

STOMP

STOMP

YOU KNOW WHAT YOUR *FATHER* WILL DO WHEN HE COMES BACK? WHEN HE SEES I HAVEN'T HAD THE BOAT REPAIRED LIKE HE WANTED?

HE'LL LEAVE AGAIN, AND WE'LL BE STUCK HERE FOR GOOD. YOU NEED TO STAY OUT WHEN SOMEONE'S HERE TO HELP. UNDERSTAND?

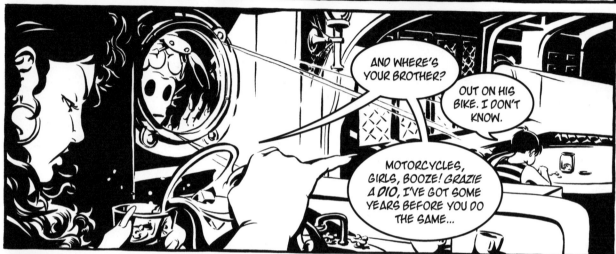

AND WHERE'S YOUR BROTHER?

OUT ON HIS BIKE. I DON'T KNOW.

MOTORCYCLES, GIRLS, BOOZE! GRAZIE *A DIO*, I'VE GOT SOME YEARS BEFORE YOU DO THE SAME...

HAVE YOU FED *GIULIETTA*?

NO...

YOU FINISH YOUR ROUTE, YOU FEED AUNT *GIULIETTA*! SHOW ME YOU CAN DO SOMETHING WORTHWHILE!

NO COMPRENDE, BIRDIE?

YOU AIN'T ALONE.

BE SILENT, CRABS! THE *STRIPEY* RISES! LOOK...

THE *BOTTLE*!

Kiki Cola

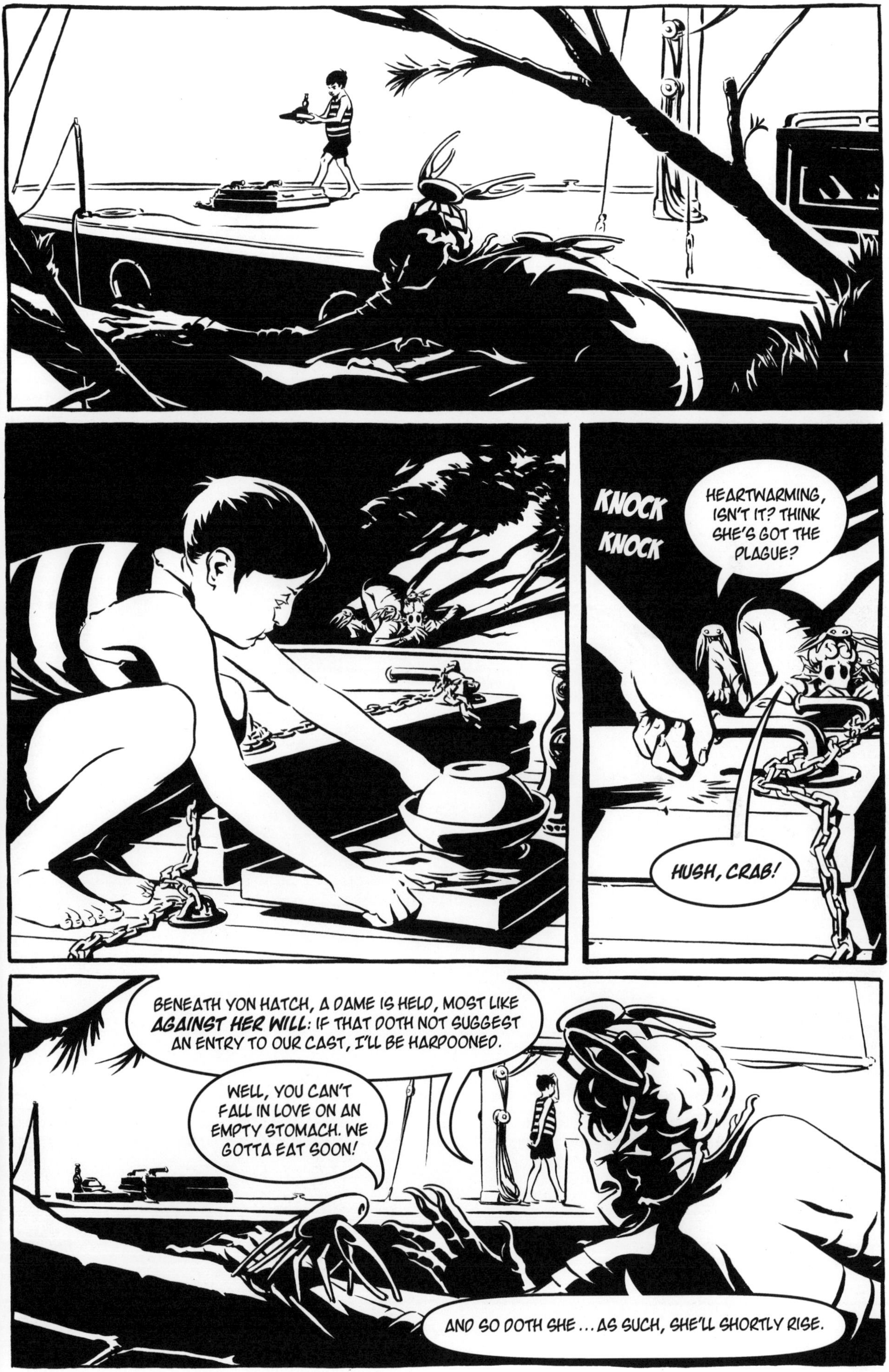
KNOCK
KNOCK
HEARTWARMING, ISN'T IT? THINK SHE'S GOT THE PLAGUE?
HUSH, CRAB!
BENEATH YON HATCH, A DAME IS HELD, MOST LIKE AGAINST HER WILL: IF THAT DOTH NOT SUGGEST AN ENTRY TO OUR CAST, I'LL BE HARPOONED.
WELL, YOU CAN'T FALL IN LOVE ON AN EMPTY STOMACH. WE GOTTA EAT SOON!
AND SO DOTH SHE . . . AS SUCH, SHE'LL SHORTLY RISE.

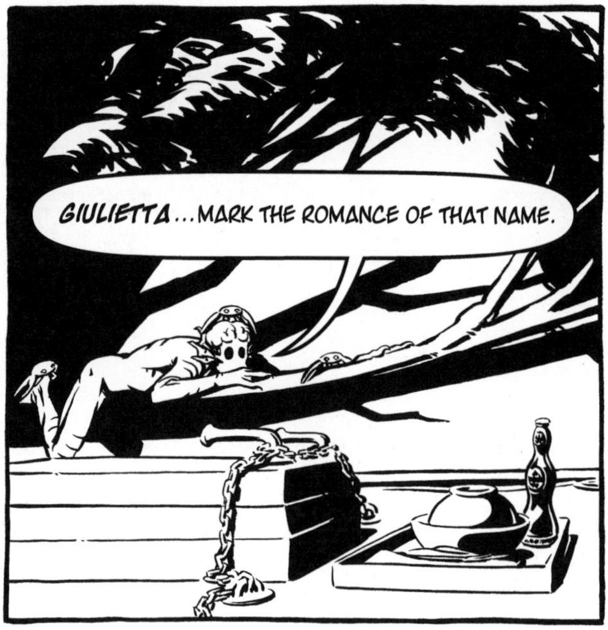
GIULIETTA... MARK THE ROMANCE OF THAT NAME.

CHAPTER THREE

IN DREAMS

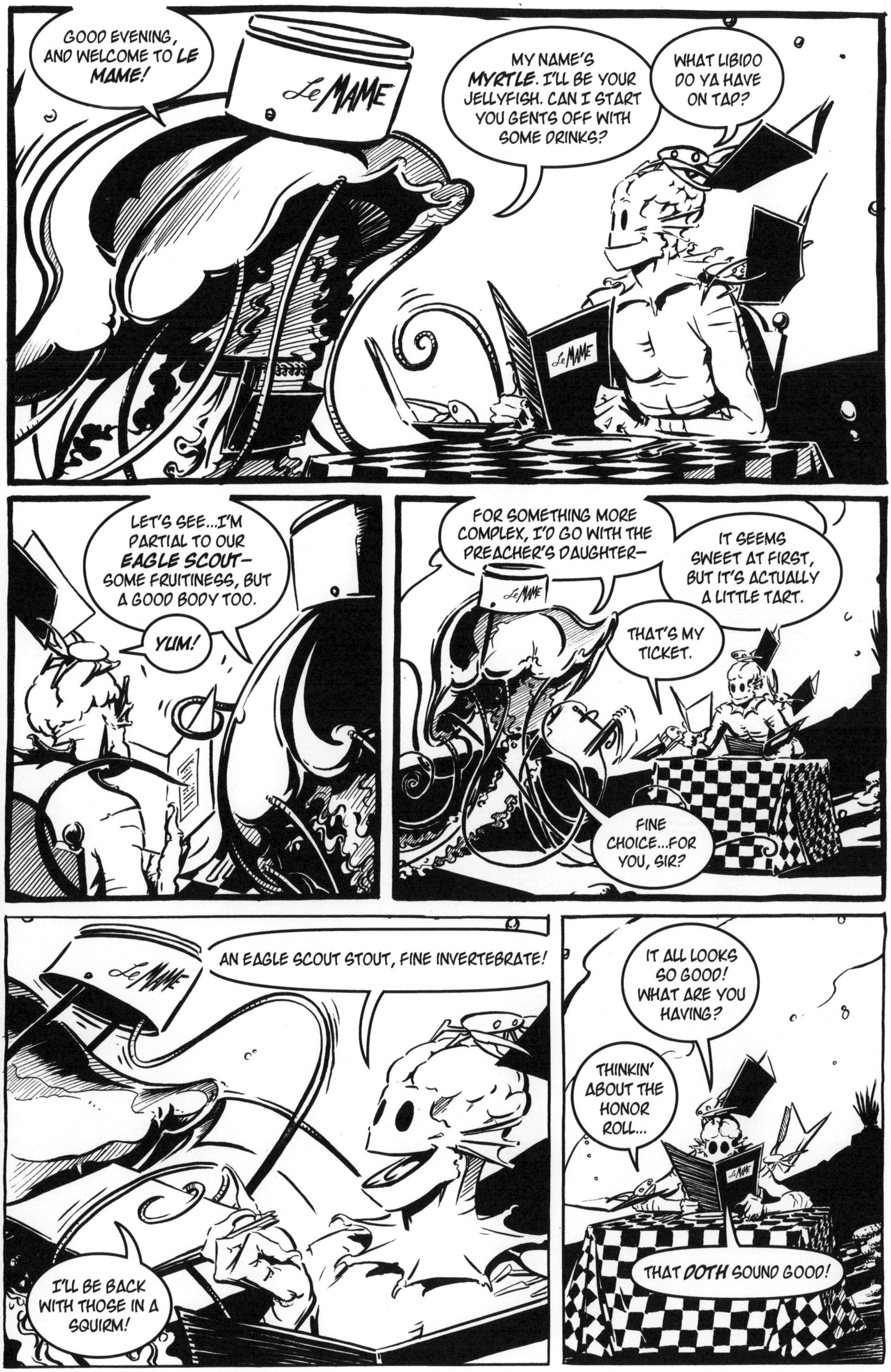
GOOD EVENING, AND WELCOME TO LE MAME!
Le MAME
MY NAME'S MYRTLE. I'LL BE YOUR JELLYFISH. CAN I START YOU GENTS OFF WITH SOME DRINKS?
WHAT LIBIDO DO YA HAVE ON TAP?
Le MAME
LET'S SEE...I'M PARTIAL TO OUR EAGLE SCOUT—SOME FRUITINESS, BUT A GOOD BODY TOO.
YUM!
FOR SOMETHING MORE COMPLEX, I'D GO WITH THE PREACHER'S DAUGHTER—
IT SEEMS SWEET AT FIRST, BUT IT'S ACTUALLY A LITTLE TART.
Le MAME
THAT'S MY TICKET.
FINE CHOICE...FOR YOU, SIR?
Le MAME
AN EAGLE SCOUT STOUT, FINE INVERTEBRATE!
I'LL BE BACK WITH THOSE IN A SQUIRM!
IT ALL LOOKS SO GOOD! WHAT ARE YOU HAVING?
THINKIN' ABOUT THE HONOR ROLL...
THAT DOTH SOUND GOOD!

HERE WE ARE! AND JUST TO LET YOU KNOW, OUR SPECIAL TONIGHT IS A PROM NIGHT COMBINATION PLATE: *STOOD UP* AND *STAG* IN A SPIKED-PUNCH SAUCE. THIS IS ALSO *HAPPY HOUR*, SO SPECIAL ED IS HALF PRICE 'TIL SIX.

DO THEY COME IN THE HELMETS?

NO SIR, WE SHELL THEM.

YOU GENTS NEED ANY MORE TIME?

LET'S *BOOGIE!*

DOES THE *HONOR ROLL* COME WITH A SPREAD OF SOME SORT?

CHEERLEADER. THAT OKAY?

PERFECT. ONE OF THOSE, PLEASE.

I'LL HAVE THE CHESS CLUB, OPENED FACES.

VERY GOOD... AND FOR THE SEA MUTANT?

PRAY, HOW'S THE BEACH BUNNY SERVED?

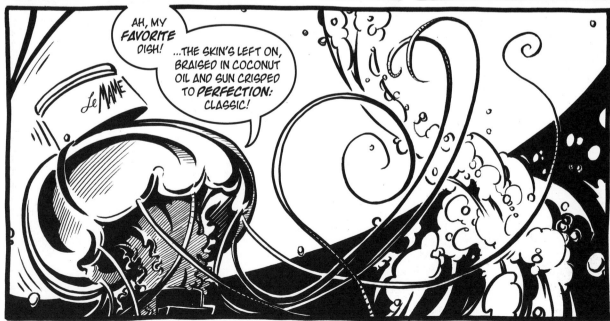

AH, MY *FAVORITE* DISH!

...THE SKIN'S LEFT ON, BRAISED IN COCONUT OIL AND SUN CRISPED TO *PERFECTION:* CLASSIC!

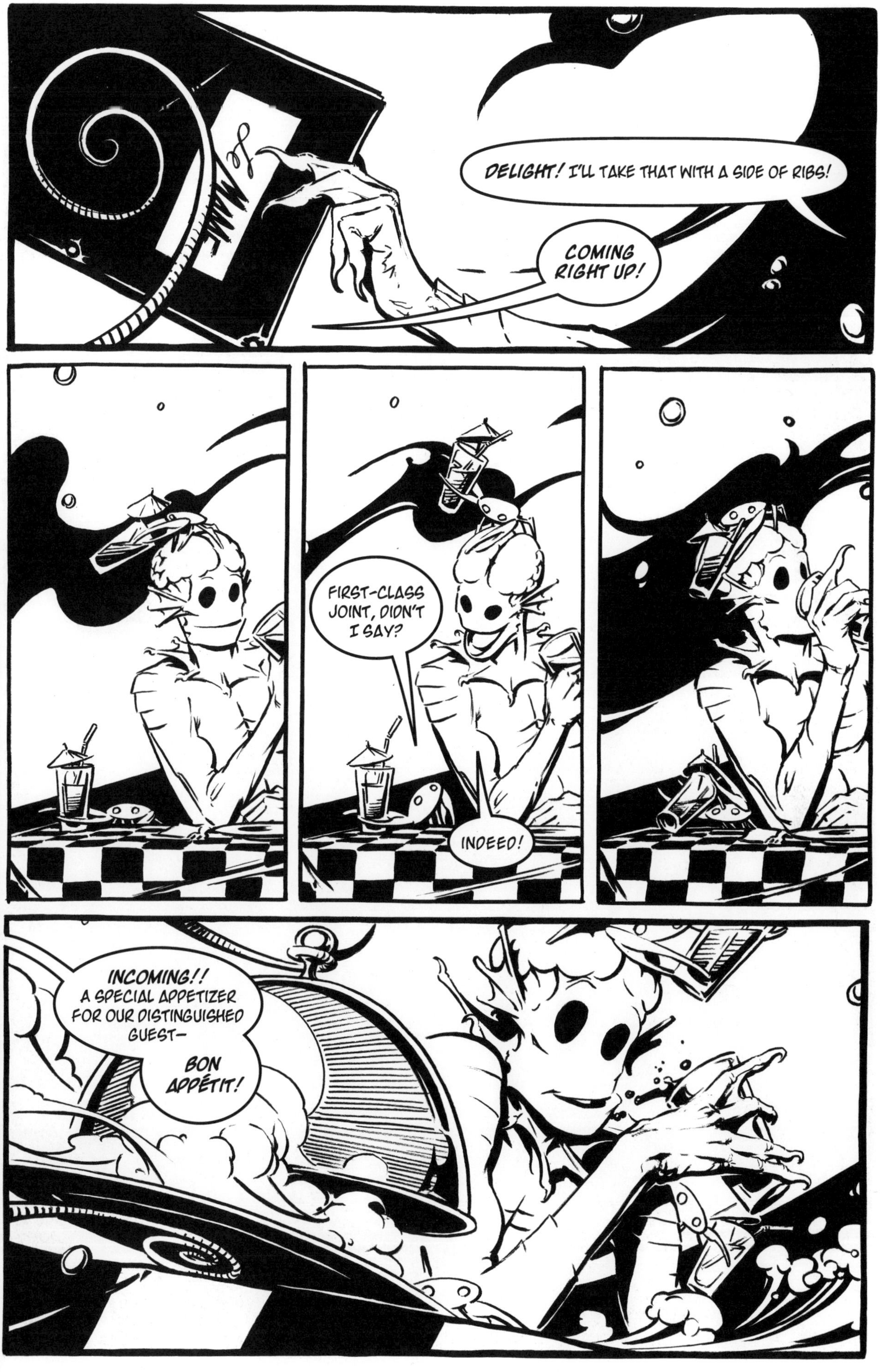
DELIGHT! I'LL TAKE THAT WITH A SIDE OF RIBS!
COMING RIGHT UP!
FIRST-CLASS JOINT, DIDN'T I SAY?
INDEED!
INCOMING!! A SPECIAL APPETIZER FOR OUR DISTINGUISHED GUEST—
BON APPÉTIT!

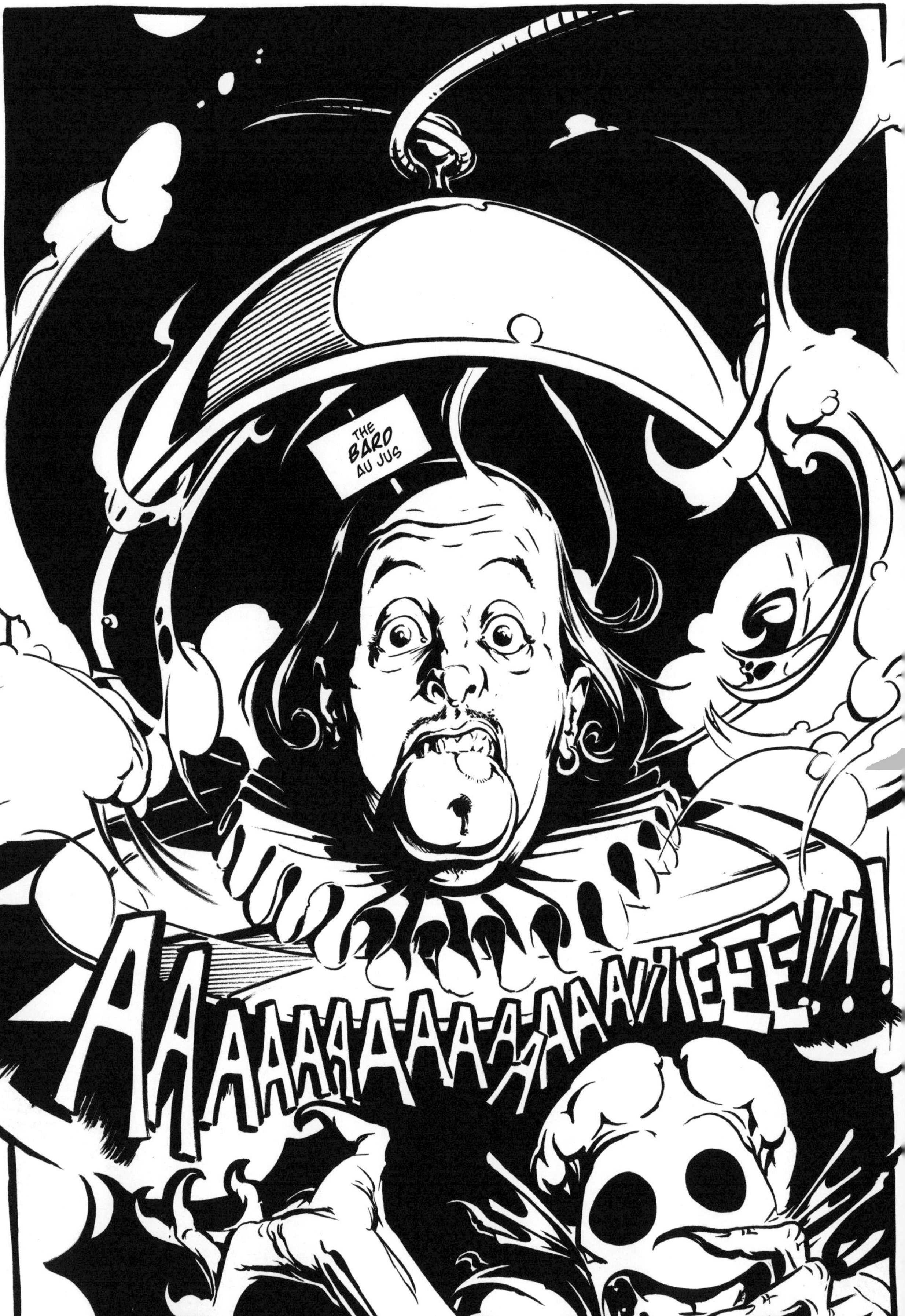
THE BARD AU JUS
AAAAAAAAAAAAAAAAAIIEEE!!!

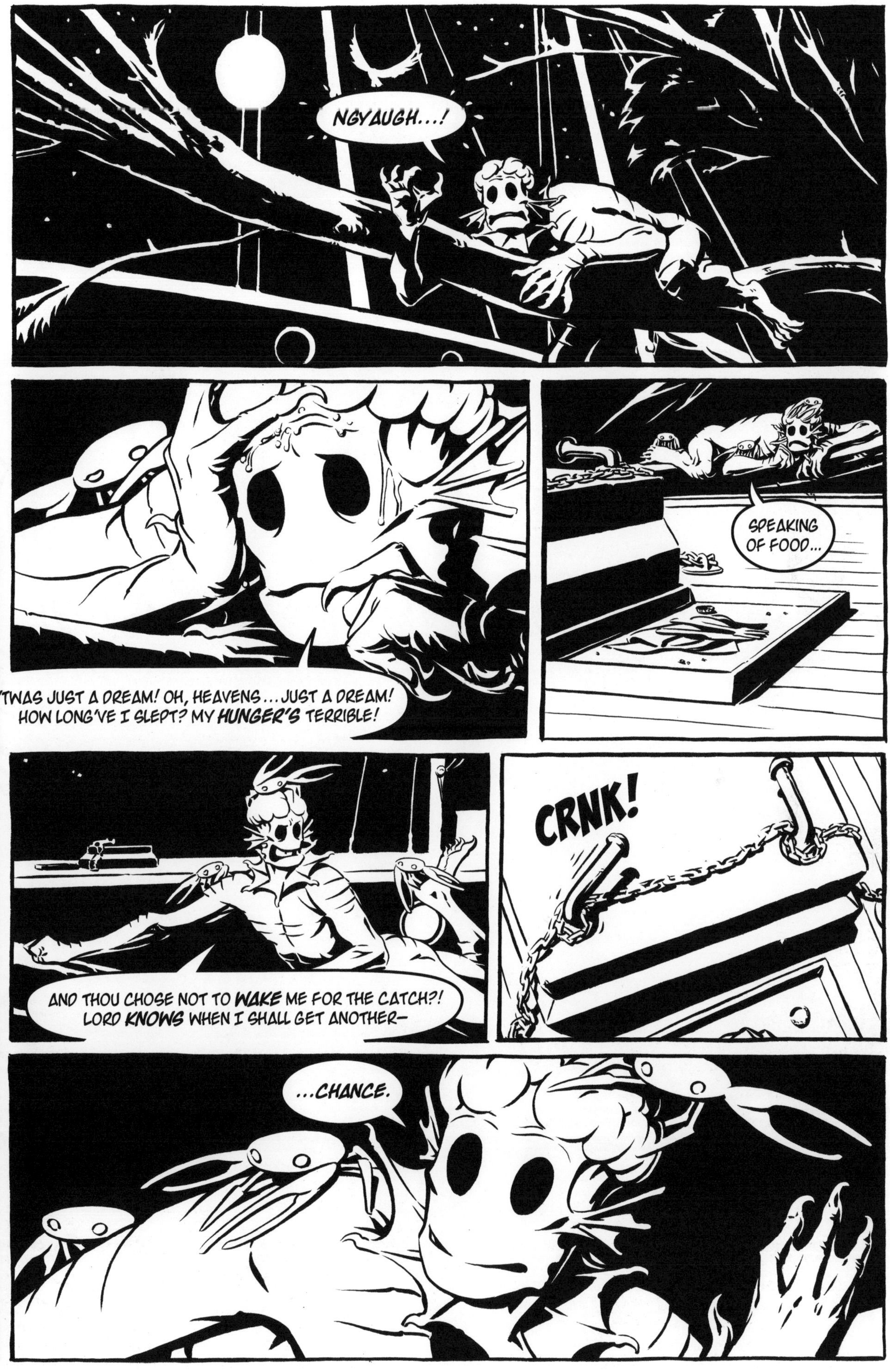
NGYAUGH...!
'TWAS JUST A DREAM! OH, HEAVENS... JUST A DREAM! HOW LONG'VE I SLEPT? MY HUNGER'S TERRIBLE!
SPEAKING OF FOOD...
AND THOU CHOSE NOT TO WAKE ME FOR THE CATCH?! LORD KNOWS WHEN I SHALL GET ANOTHER—
CRNK!
...CHANCE.

SPLINK!

CLOMP!

IT'S TRULY *SHE!* I'LL MAKE A LOVE OF WORDS UNTO HER *PORTHOLE—*

EW!

FIRST, THE PLAY RETRIEVE!

SO FRUITFUL EVERY TURN HATH BEEN WITHIN MY QUEST, AND ALL I'VE DONE IS TAKE A STEP IN FAITH! *HURRAH* UNTO THE HIGHER PATH!

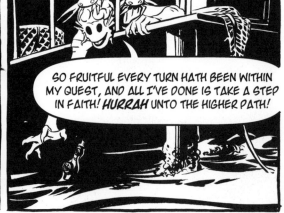

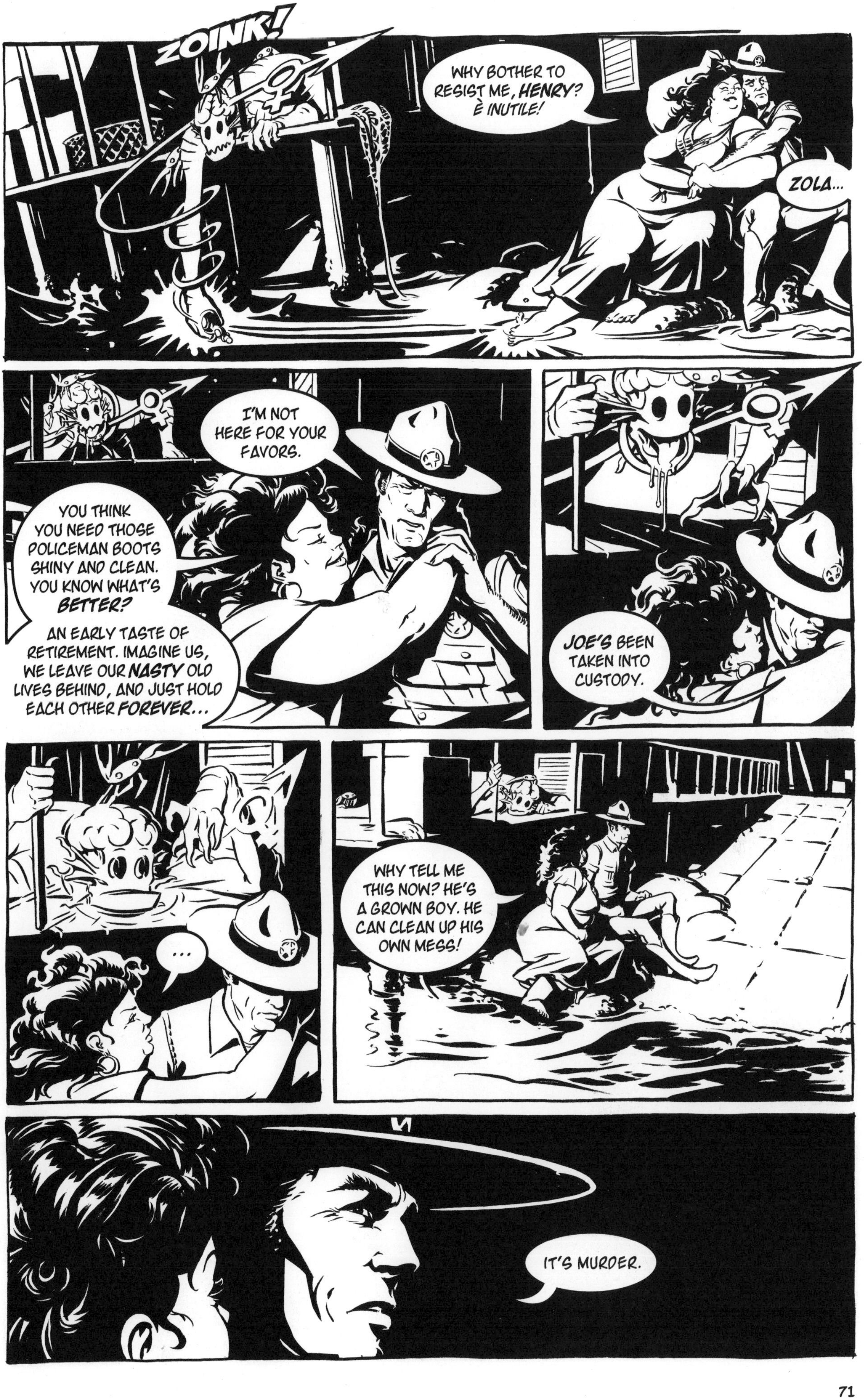
ZOINK!
WHY BOTHER TO RESIST ME, HENRY? È INUTILE!
ZOLA...
I'M NOT HERE FOR YOUR FAVORS.
YOU THINK YOU NEED THOSE POLICEMAN BOOTS SHINY AND CLEAN. YOU KNOW WHAT'S BETTER?
AN EARLY TASTE OF RETIREMENT. IMAGINE US, WE LEAVE OUR NASTY OLD LIVES BEHIND, AND JUST HOLD EACH OTHER FOREVER...
JOE'S BEEN TAKEN INTO CUSTODY.
...
WHY TELL ME THIS NOW? HE'S A GROWN BOY. HE CAN CLEAN UP HIS OWN MESS!
IT'S MURDER.

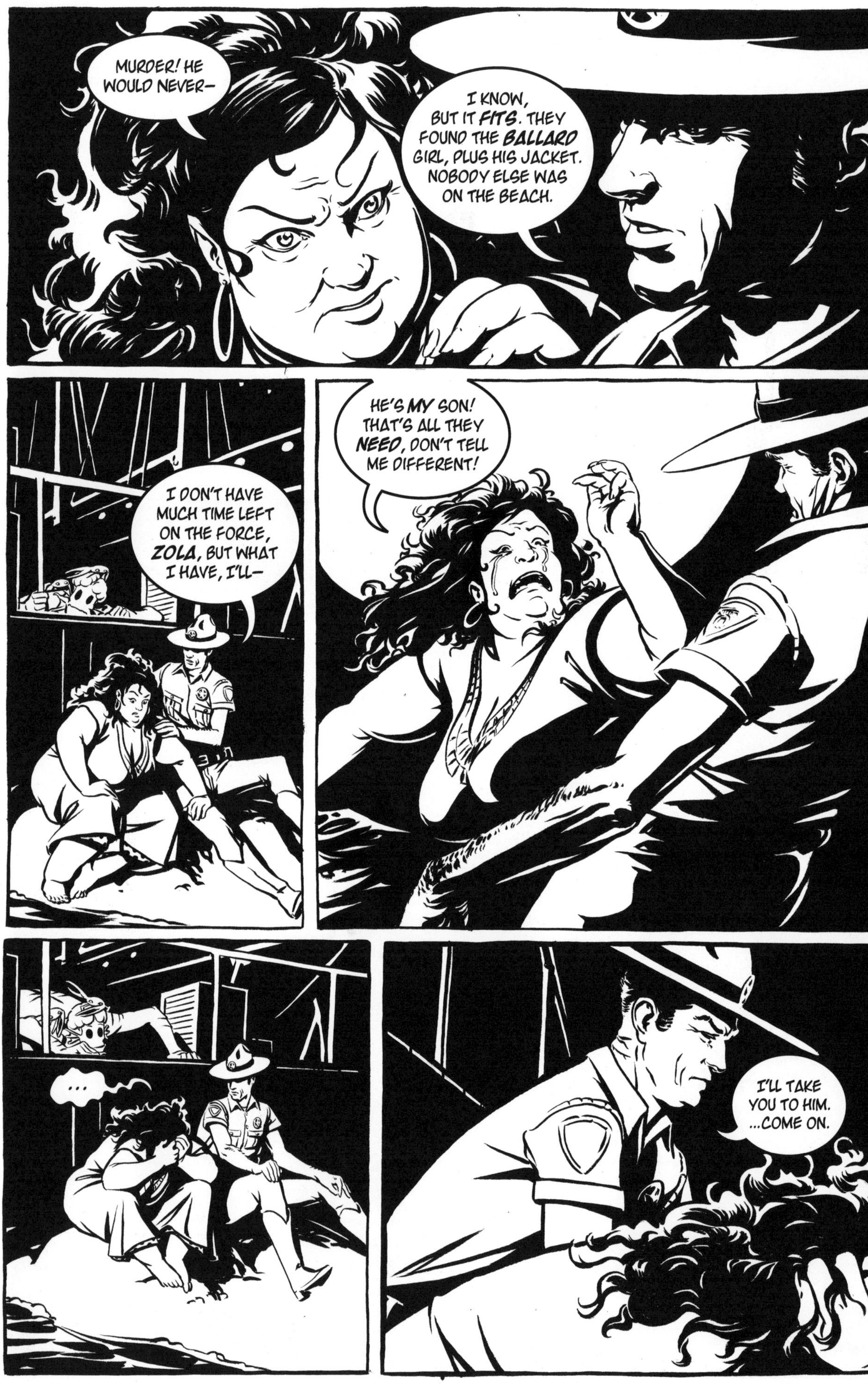
MURDER! HE WOULD NEVER—
I KNOW, BUT IT FITS. THEY FOUND THE BALLARD GIRL, PLUS HIS JACKET. NOBODY ELSE WAS ON THE BEACH.
I DON'T HAVE MUCH TIME LEFT ON THE FORCE, ZOLA, BUT WHAT I HAVE, I'LL—
HE'S MY SON! THAT'S ALL THEY NEED, DON'T TELL ME DIFFERENT!
...
I'LL TAKE YOU TO HIM. ...COME ON.

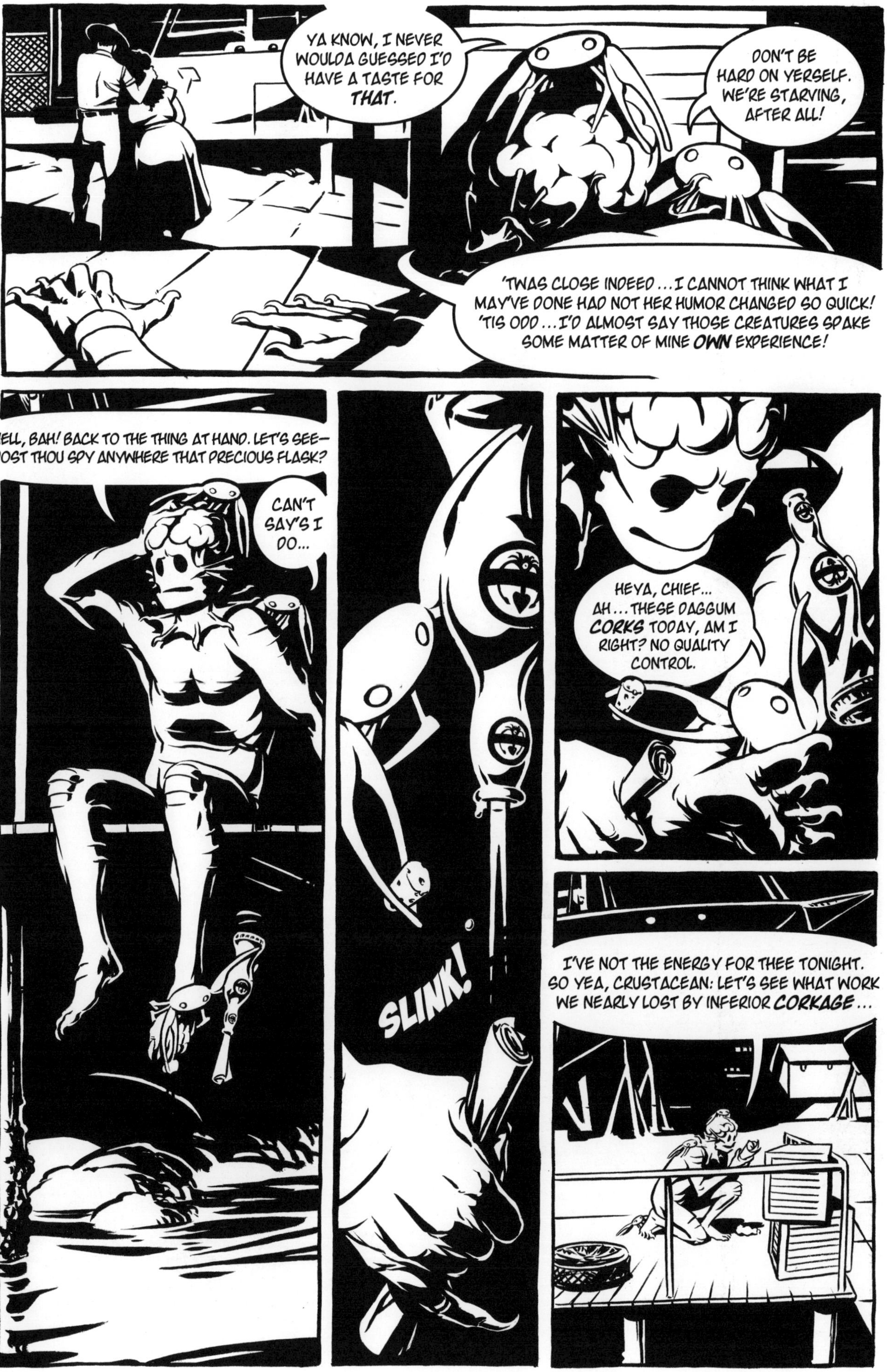
YA KNOW, I NEVER WOULDA GUESSED I'D HAVE A TASTE FOR **THAT**.
DON'T BE HARD ON YERSELF. WE'RE STARVING, AFTER ALL!
'TWAS CLOSE INDEED... I CANNOT THINK WHAT I MAY'VE DONE HAD NOT HER HUMOR CHANGED SO QUICK! 'TIS ODD... I'D ALMOST SAY THOSE CREATURES SPAKE SOME MATTER OF MINE **OWN** EXPERIENCE!
WELL, BAH! BACK TO THE THING AT HAND. LET'S SEE-- DOST THOU SPY ANYWHERE THAT PRECIOUS FLASK?
CAN'T SAY'S I DO...
SLINK!
HEYA, CHIEF... AH... THESE DAGGUM **CORKS** TODAY, AM I RIGHT? NO QUALITY CONTROL.
I'VE NOT THE ENERGY FOR THEE TONIGHT. SO YEA, CRUSTACEAN: LET'S SEE WHAT WORK WE NEARLY LOST BY INFERIOR **CORKAGE**...

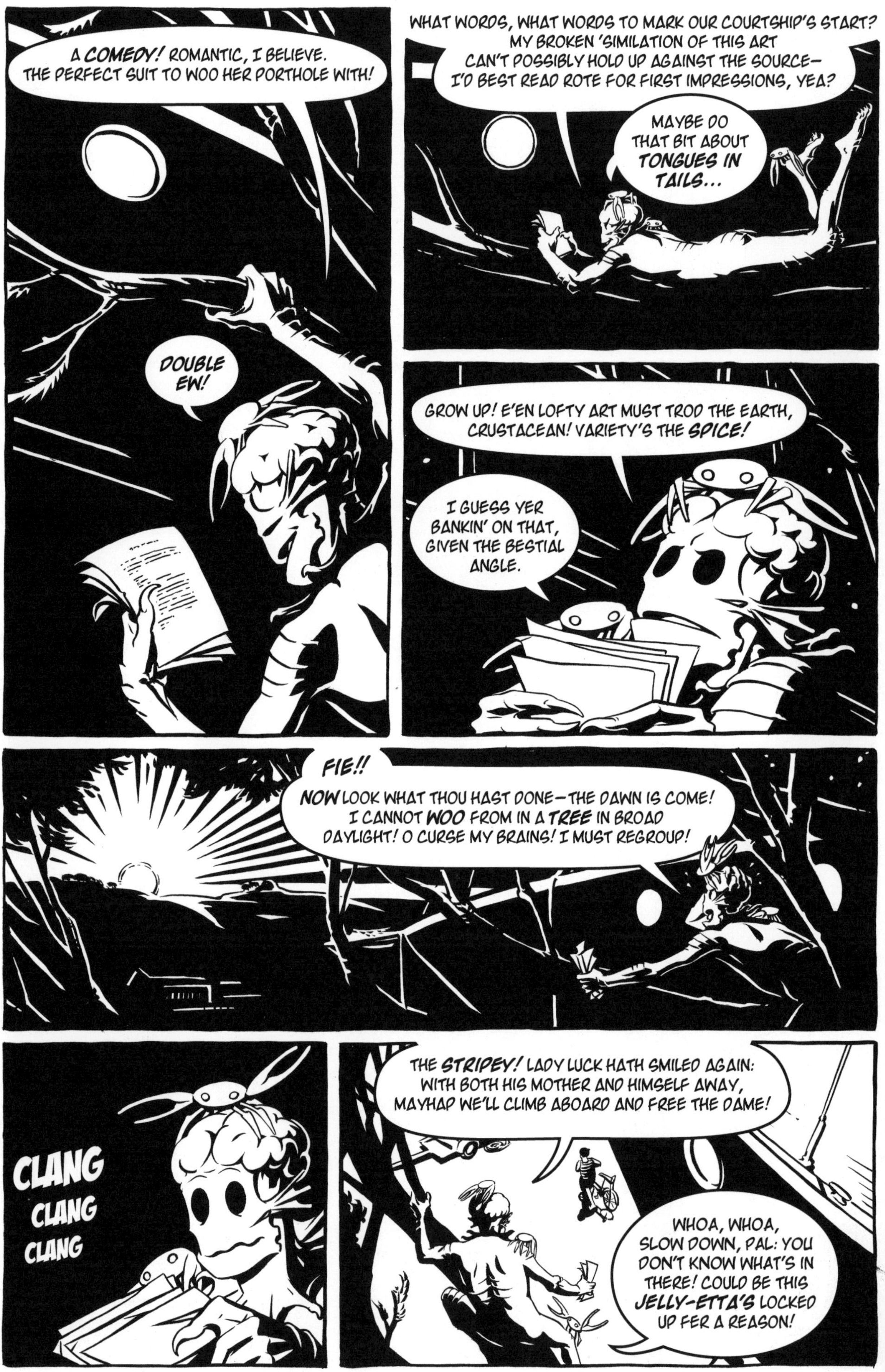
A COMEDY! ROMANTIC, I BELIEVE. THE PERFECT SUIT TO WOO HER PORTHOLE WITH!
DOUBLE EW!
WHAT WORDS, WHAT WORDS TO MARK OUR COURTSHIP'S START? MY BROKEN 'SIMILATION OF THIS ART CAN'T POSSIBLY HOLD UP AGAINST THE SOURCE— I'D BEST READ ROTE FOR FIRST IMPRESSIONS, YEA?
MAYBE DO THAT BIT ABOUT TONGUES IN TAILS...
GROW UP! E'EN LOFTY ART MUST TROD THE EARTH, CRUSTACEAN! VARIETY'S THE SPICE!
I GUESS YER BANKIN' ON THAT, GIVEN THE BESTIAL ANGLE.
FIE!!
NOW LOOK WHAT THOU HAST DONE—THE DAWN IS COME! I CANNOT WOO FROM IN A TREE IN BROAD DAYLIGHT! O CURSE MY BRAINS! I MUST REGROUP!
CLANG
CLANG
CLANG
THE STRIPEY! LADY LUCK HATH SMILED AGAIN: WITH BOTH HIS MOTHER AND HIMSELF AWAY, MAYHAP WE'LL CLIMB ABOARD AND FREE THE DAME!
WHOA, WHOA, SLOW DOWN, PAL: YOU DON'T KNOW WHAT'S IN THERE! COULD BE THIS JELLY-ETTA'S LOCKED UP FER A REASON!

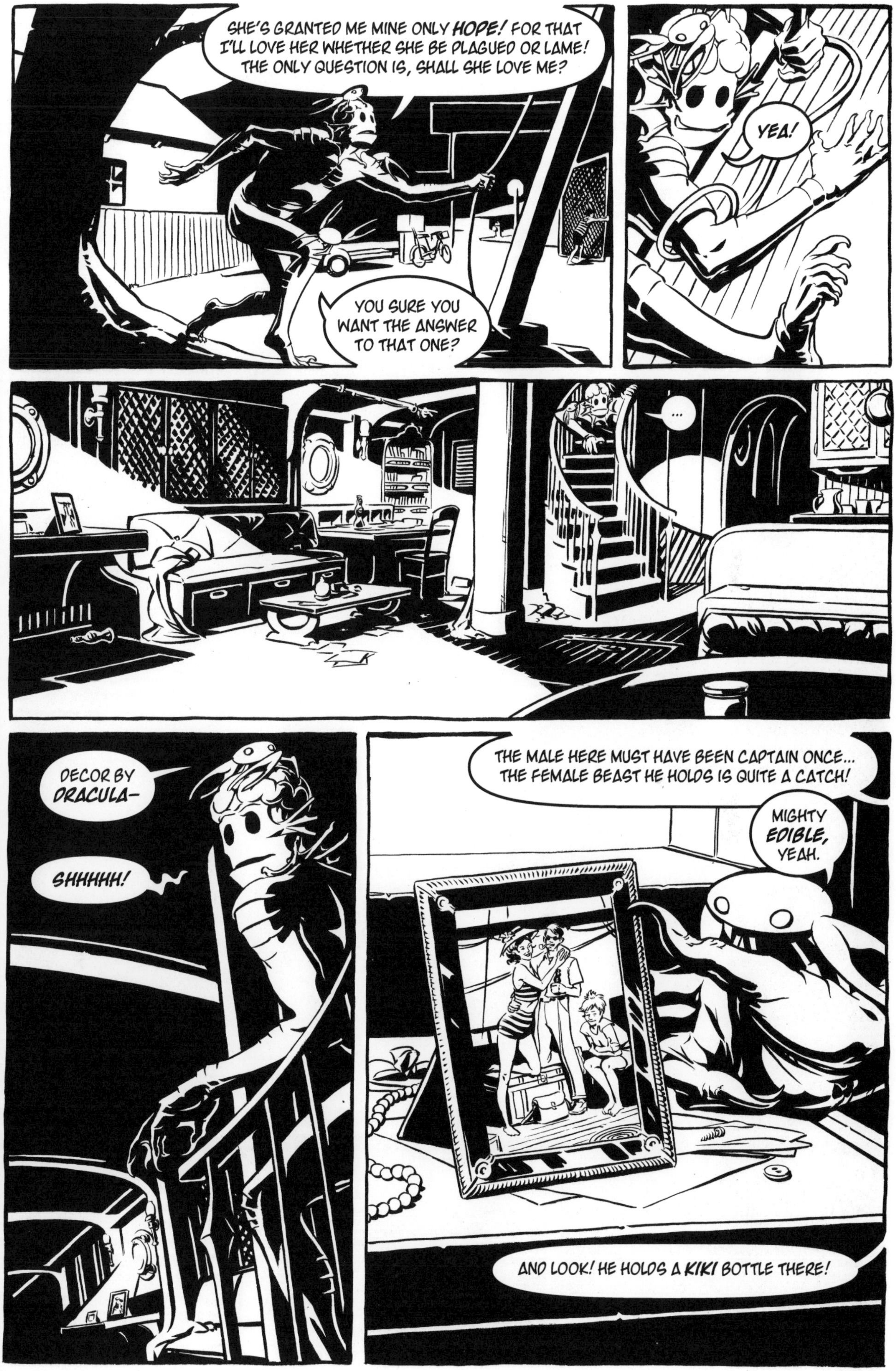
SHE'S GRANTED ME MINE ONLY HOPE! FOR THAT I'LL LOVE HER WHETHER SHE BE PLAGUED OR LAME! THE ONLY QUESTION IS, SHALL SHE LOVE ME?
YOU SURE YOU WANT THE ANSWER TO THAT ONE?
YEA!
...
DECOR BY DRACULA-
SHHHHH!
THE MALE HERE MUST HAVE BEEN CAPTAIN ONCE... THE FEMALE BEAST HE HOLDS IS QUITE A CATCH!
MIGHTY EDIBLE, YEAH.
AND LOOK! HE HOLDS A KIKI BOTTLE THERE!

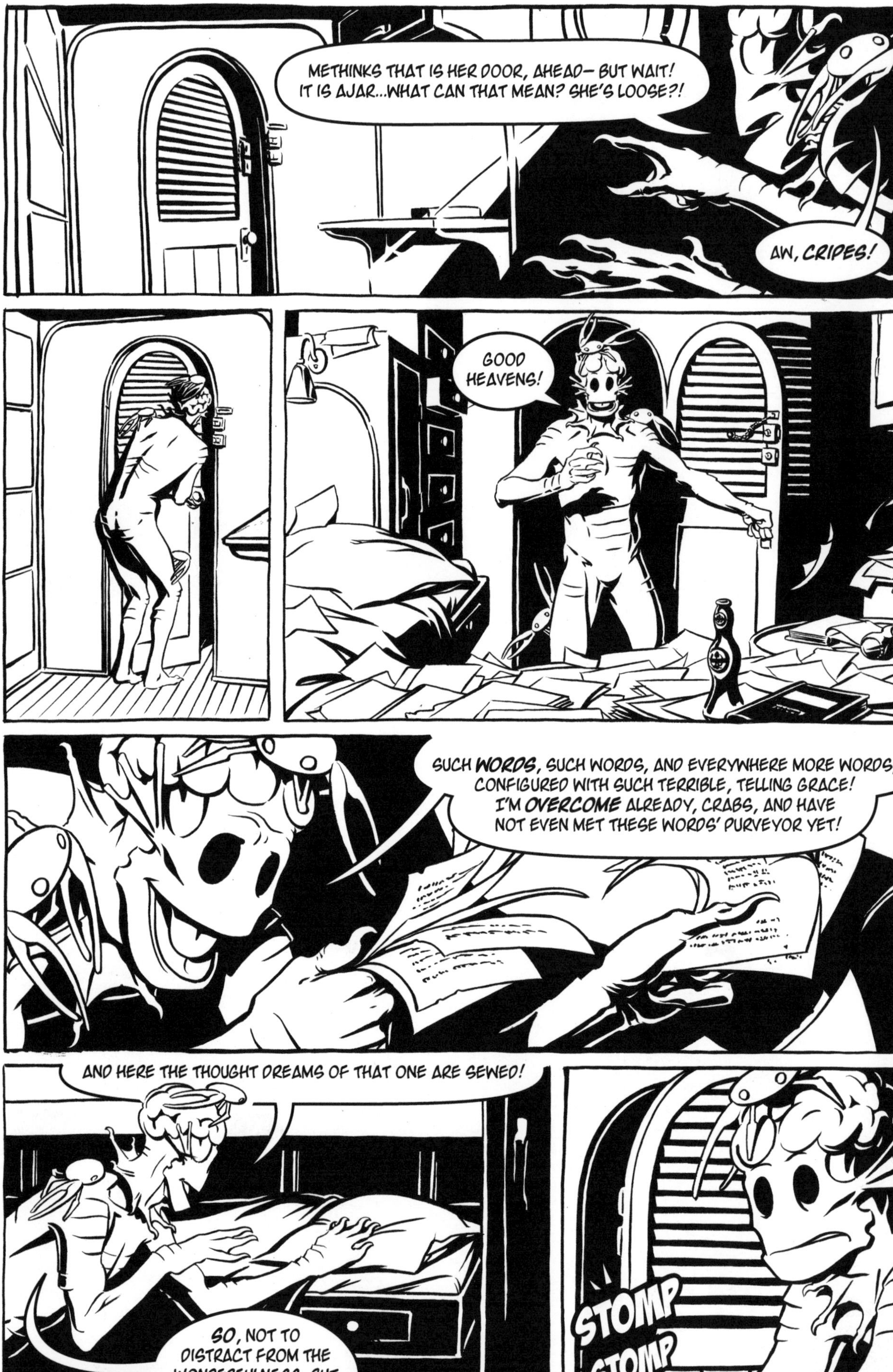
METHINKS THAT IS HER DOOR, AHEAD— BUT WAIT! IT IS AJAR...WHAT CAN THAT MEAN? SHE'S LOOSE?!
AW, CRIPES!
GOOD HEAVENS!
SUCH WORDS, SUCH WORDS, AND EVERYWHERE MORE WORDS, CONFIGURED WITH SUCH TERRIBLE, TELLING GRACE! I'M OVERCOME ALREADY, CRABS, AND HAVE NOT EVEN MET THESE WORDS' PURVEYOR YET!
AND HERE THE THOUGHT DREAMS OF THAT ONE ARE SEWED!
SO, NOT TO DISTRACT FROM THE WONDERFULNESS, BUT WHERE IS THIS GAL—?
STOMP
STOMP

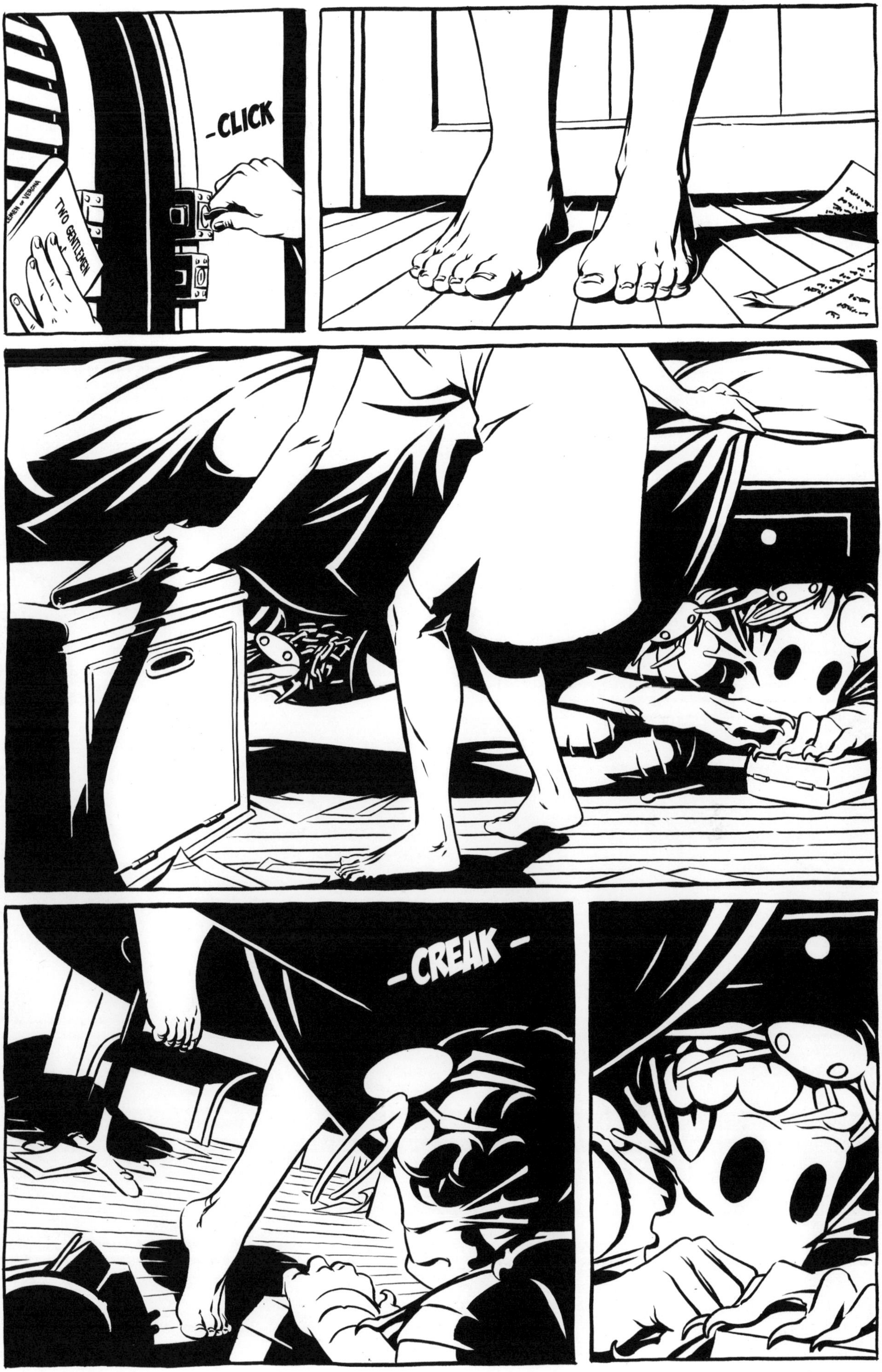
-CLICK
TWO GENTLEMEN
-CREAK-

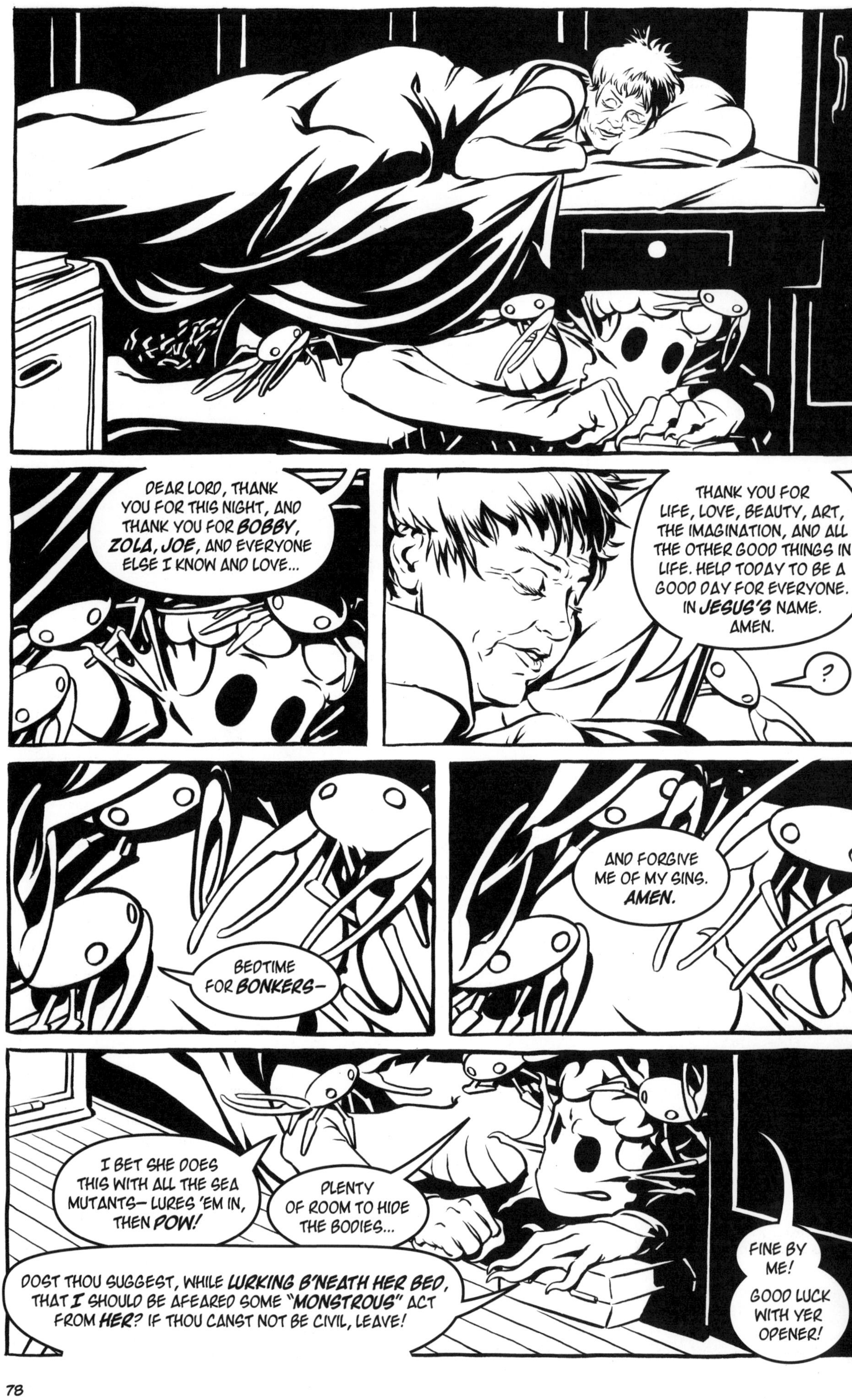
DEAR LORD, THANK YOU FOR THIS NIGHT, AND THANK YOU FOR BOBBY, ZOLA, JOE, AND EVERYONE ELSE I KNOW AND LOVE...
THANK YOU FOR LIFE, LOVE, BEAUTY, ART, THE IMAGINATION, AND ALL THE OTHER GOOD THINGS IN LIFE. HELP TODAY TO BE A GOOD DAY FOR EVERYONE. IN JESUS'S NAME. AMEN.
?
BEDTIME FOR BONKERS–
AND FORGIVE ME OF MY SINS. AMEN.
I BET SHE DOES THIS WITH ALL THE SEA MUTANTS– LURES 'EM IN, THEN POW!
PLENTY OF ROOM TO HIDE THE BODIES...
DOST THOU SUGGEST, WHILE LURKING B'NEATH HER BED, THAT I SHOULD BE AFEARED SOME "MONSTROUS" ACT FROM HER? IF THOU CANST NOT BE CIVIL, LEAVE!
FINE BY ME!
GOOD LUCK WITH YER OPENER!

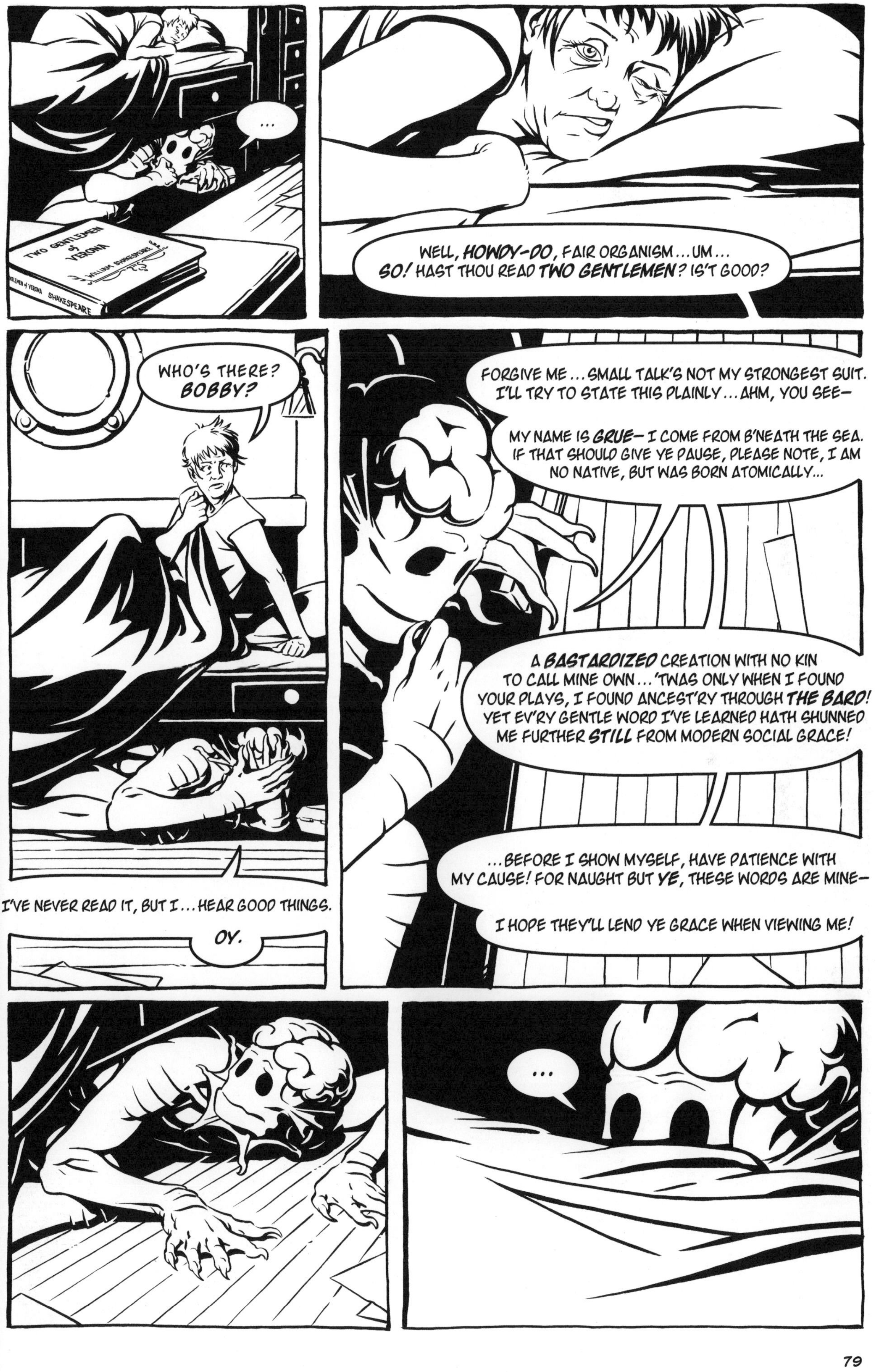
...
TWO GENTLEMEN of VERONA
WILLIAM SHAKESPEARE
SHAKESPEARE
WELL, HOWDY-DO, FAIR ORGANISM... UM... SO! HAST THOU READ TWO GENTLEMEN? IS'T GOOD?
WHO'S THERE? BOBBY?
I'VE NEVER READ IT, BUT I... HEAR GOOD THINGS.
OY.
FORGIVE ME... SMALL TALK'S NOT MY STRONGEST SUIT. I'LL TRY TO STATE THIS PLAINLY... AHM, YOU SEE–
MY NAME IS GRUE– I COME FROM B'NEATH THE SEA. IF THAT SHOULD GIVE YE PAUSE, PLEASE NOTE, I AM NO NATIVE, BUT WAS BORN ATOMICALLY...
A BASTARDIZED CREATION WITH NO KIN TO CALL MINE OWN... 'TWAS ONLY WHEN I FOUND YOUR PLAYS, I FOUND ANCEST'RY THROUGH THE BARD! YET EV'RY GENTLE WORD I'VE LEARNED HATH SHUNNED ME FURTHER STILL FROM MODERN SOCIAL GRACE!
...BEFORE I SHOW MYSELF, HAVE PATIENCE WITH MY CAUSE! FOR NAUGHT BUT YE, THESE WORDS ARE MINE–
I HOPE THEY'LL LEND YE GRACE WHEN VIEWING ME!
...

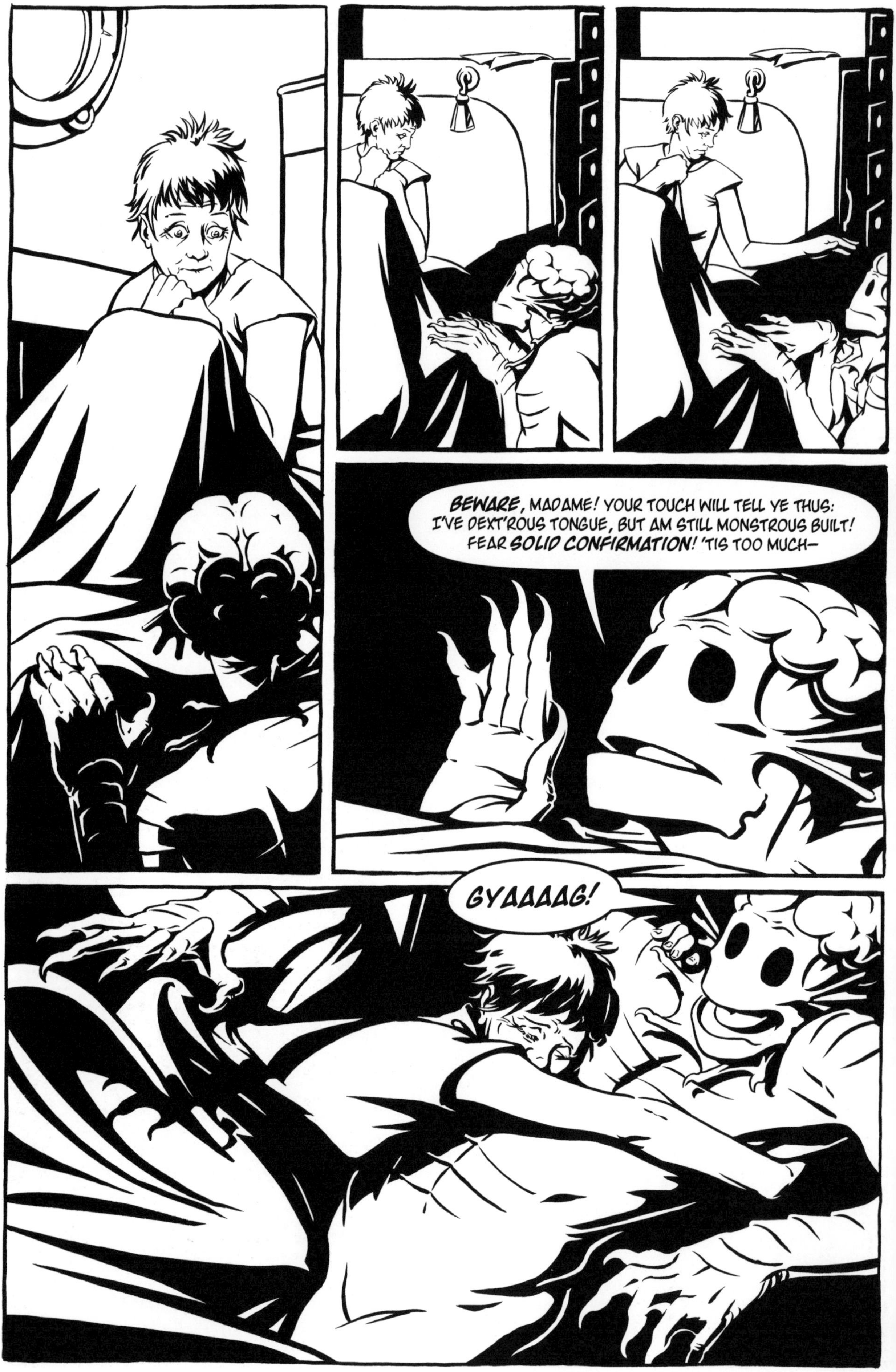
BEWARE, MADAME! YOUR TOUCH WILL TELL YE THUS: I'VE DEXT'ROUS TONGUE, BUT AM STILL MONSTROUS BUILT! FEAR SOLID CONFIRMATION! 'TIS TOO MUCH—
GYAAAAG!

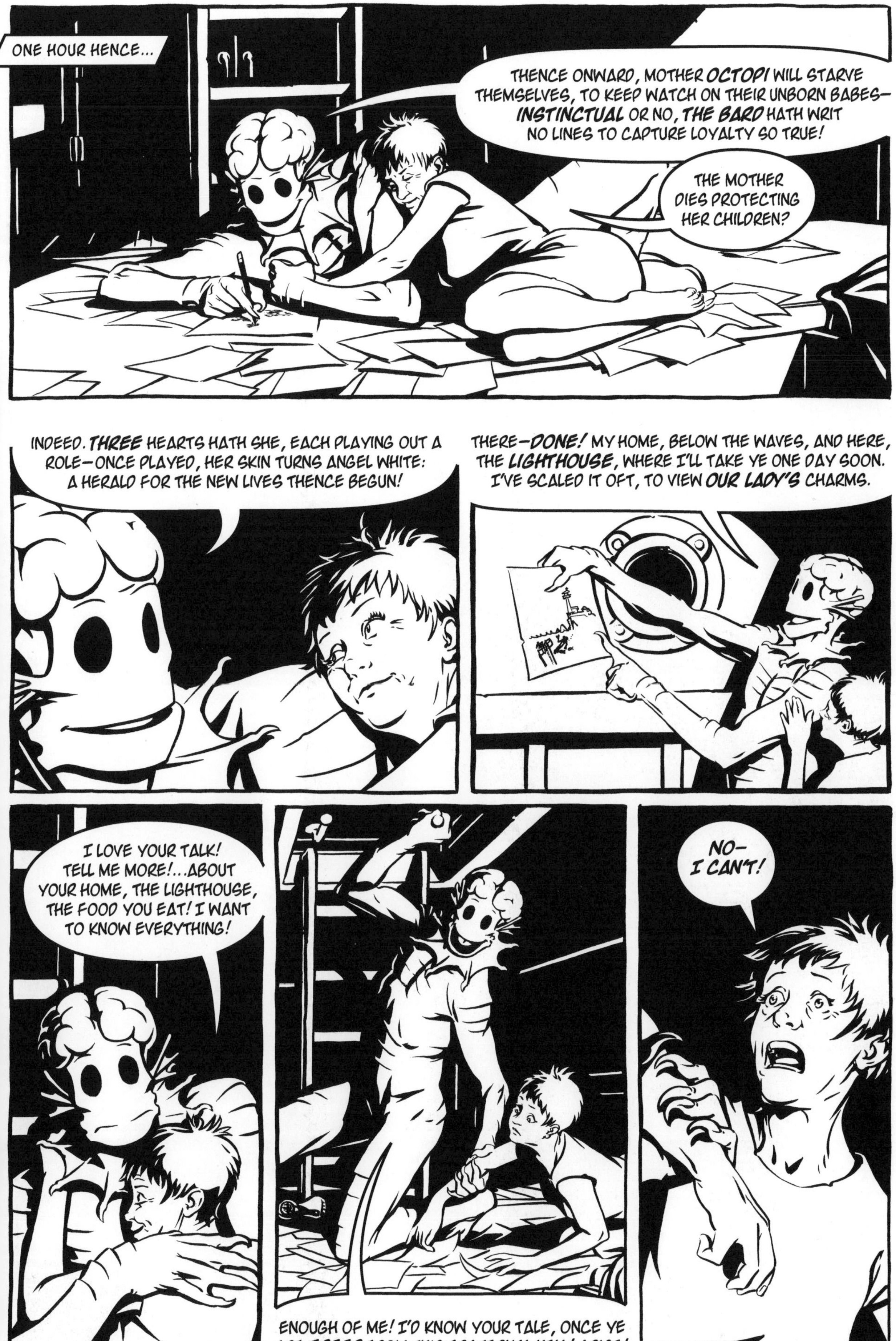

ONE HOUR HENCE...
THENCE ONWARD, MOTHER OCTOPI WILL STARVE THEMSELVES, TO KEEP WATCH ON THEIR UNBORN BABES—INSTINCTUAL OR NO, THE BARD HATH WRIT NO LINES TO CAPTURE LOYALTY SO TRUE!
THE MOTHER DIES PROTECTING HER CHILDREN?
INDEED. THREE HEARTS HATH SHE, EACH PLAYING OUT A ROLE—ONCE PLAYED, HER SKIN TURNS ANGEL WHITE: A HERALD FOR THE NEW LIVES THENCE BEGUN!
THERE—DONE! MY HOME, BELOW THE WAVES, AND HERE, THE LIGHTHOUSE, WHERE I'LL TAKE YE ONE DAY SOON. I'VE SCALED IT OFT, TO VIEW OUR LADY'S CHARMS.
I LOVE YOUR TALK! TELL ME MORE!...ABOUT YOUR HOME, THE LIGHTHOUSE, THE FOOD YOU EAT! I WANT TO KNOW EVERYTHING!
ENOUGH OF ME! I'D KNOW YOUR TALE, ONCE YE ARE FREED FROM THIS FRATERNAL HELL! ARISE!
NO—I CAN'T!

YOU'RE CAPTIVE: AS YOUR CHAMPION, I'M OBLIGED!

IT'S NOT SAFE!

NOT SAFE?! 'TIS NOTHING OF THE SORT! OUT THERE, THERE'S *ONLY* ORGANISMS LIKE TO YE, SO FAR'S THE EYE CAN SEE! YE NEED NOT HIDE YOURSELF, AS I REQUIRE! YOUR POD IS GREAT!

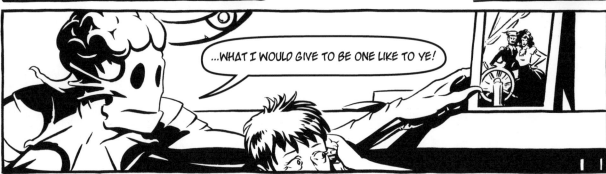

...WHAT I WOULD GIVE TO BE ONE LIKE TO YE!

WHO ARE THESE ORGANISMS? FRIENDS OF YOURS?

NO, THAT'S *ZOLA* AND *BOBBY*.

I'D NE'ER HAVE GUESSED! HOW MUCH YE CREATURES CHANGE! BUT WAIT—IS *BOBBY* NOT YOUR SISTER'S SPAWN?

BOBBY WAS CAPTAIN OF THE SHIP, AND *ZOLA* LOVED HIM... HE LEFT A LONG TIME AGO, AND US WITH THE SHIP. *ZOLA* NAMED BOBBY AFTER HIM, BUT BOBBY'S NOT HIS.

IT WAS A LONG TIME AGO.

SHE STILL TALKS LIKE HE'S COMING BACK FOR HER. I WISH HE WOULD.

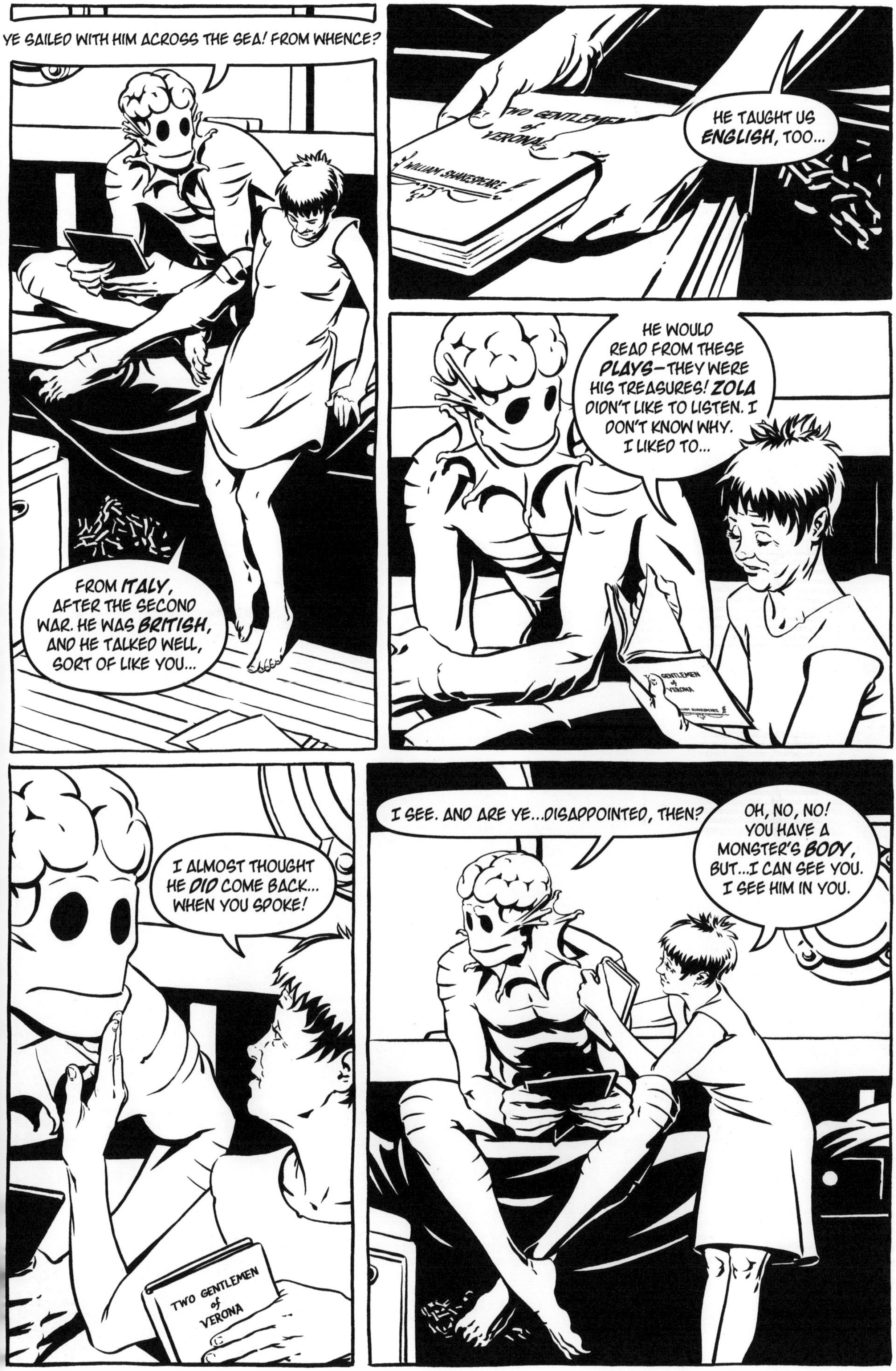
YE SAILED WITH HIM ACROSS THE SEA! FROM WHENCE?
FROM ITALY, AFTER THE SECOND WAR. HE WAS BRITISH, AND HE TALKED WELL, SORT OF LIKE YOU...
TWO GENTLEMEN of VERONA
WILLIAM SHAKESPEARE
HE TAUGHT US ENGLISH, TOO...
HE WOULD READ FROM THESE PLAYS—THEY WERE HIS TREASURES! ZOLA DIDN'T LIKE TO LISTEN. I DON'T KNOW WHY. I LIKED TO...
GENTLEMEN of VERONA
I ALMOST THOUGHT HE DID COME BACK... WHEN YOU SPOKE!
TWO GENTLEMEN of VERONA
I SEE. AND ARE YE...DISAPPOINTED, THEN?
OH, NO, NO! YOU HAVE A MONSTER'S BODY, BUT...I CAN SEE YOU. I SEE HIM IN YOU.

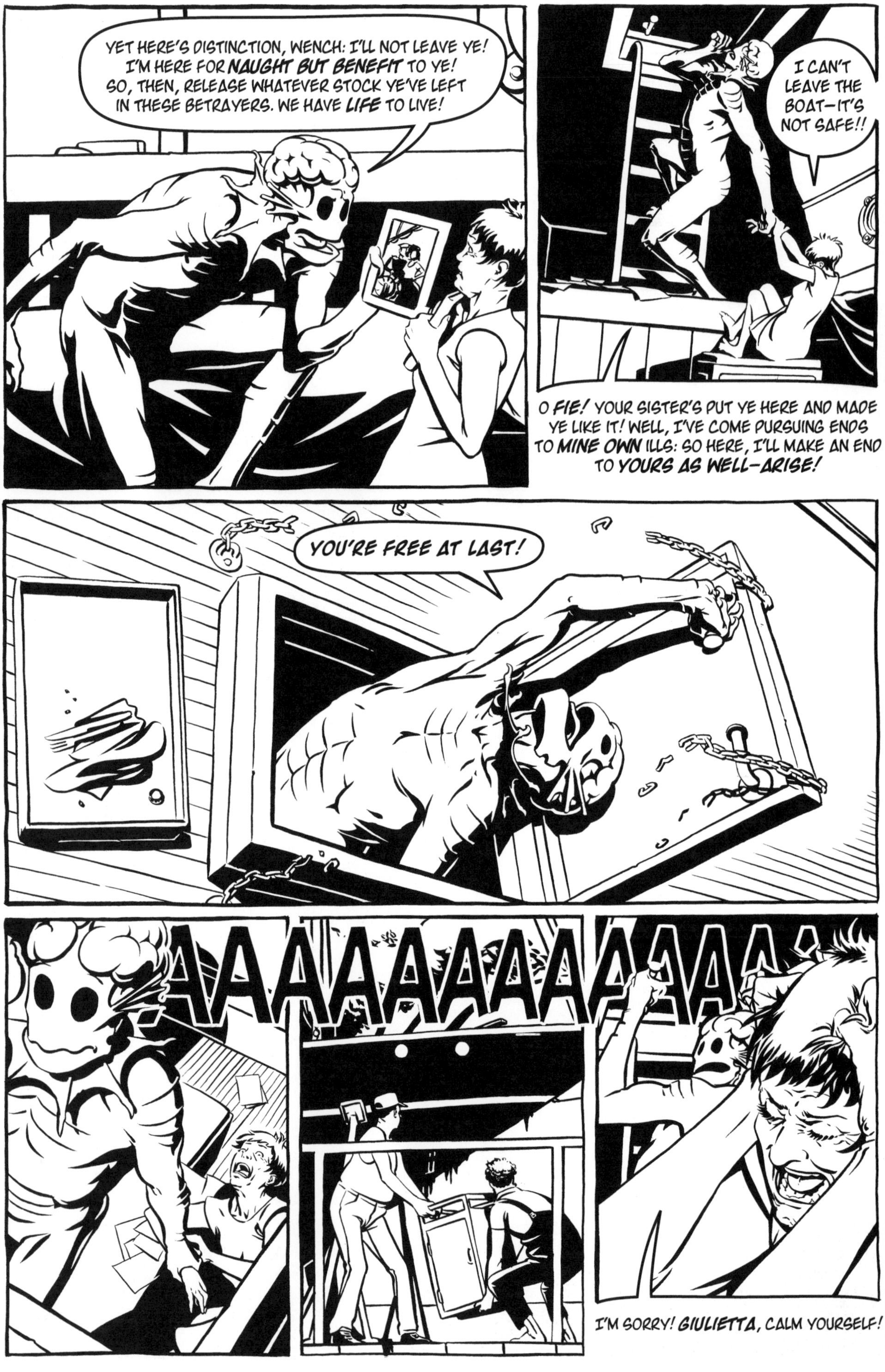
YET HERE'S DISTINCTION, WENCH: I'LL NOT LEAVE YE! I'M HERE FOR NAUGHT BUT BENEFIT TO YE! SO, THEN, RELEASE WHATEVER STOCK YE'VE LEFT IN THESE BETRAYERS. WE HAVE LIFE TO LIVE!
I CAN'T LEAVE THE BOAT—IT'S NOT SAFE!!
O FIE! YOUR SISTER'S PUT YE HERE AND MADE YE LIKE IT! WELL, I'VE COME PURSUING ENDS TO MINE OWN ILLS: SO HERE, I'LL MAKE AN END TO YOURS AS WELL—ARISE!
YOU'RE FREE AT LAST!
AAAAAAAAAAAAAA!
I'M SORRY! GIULIETTA, CALM YOURSELF!

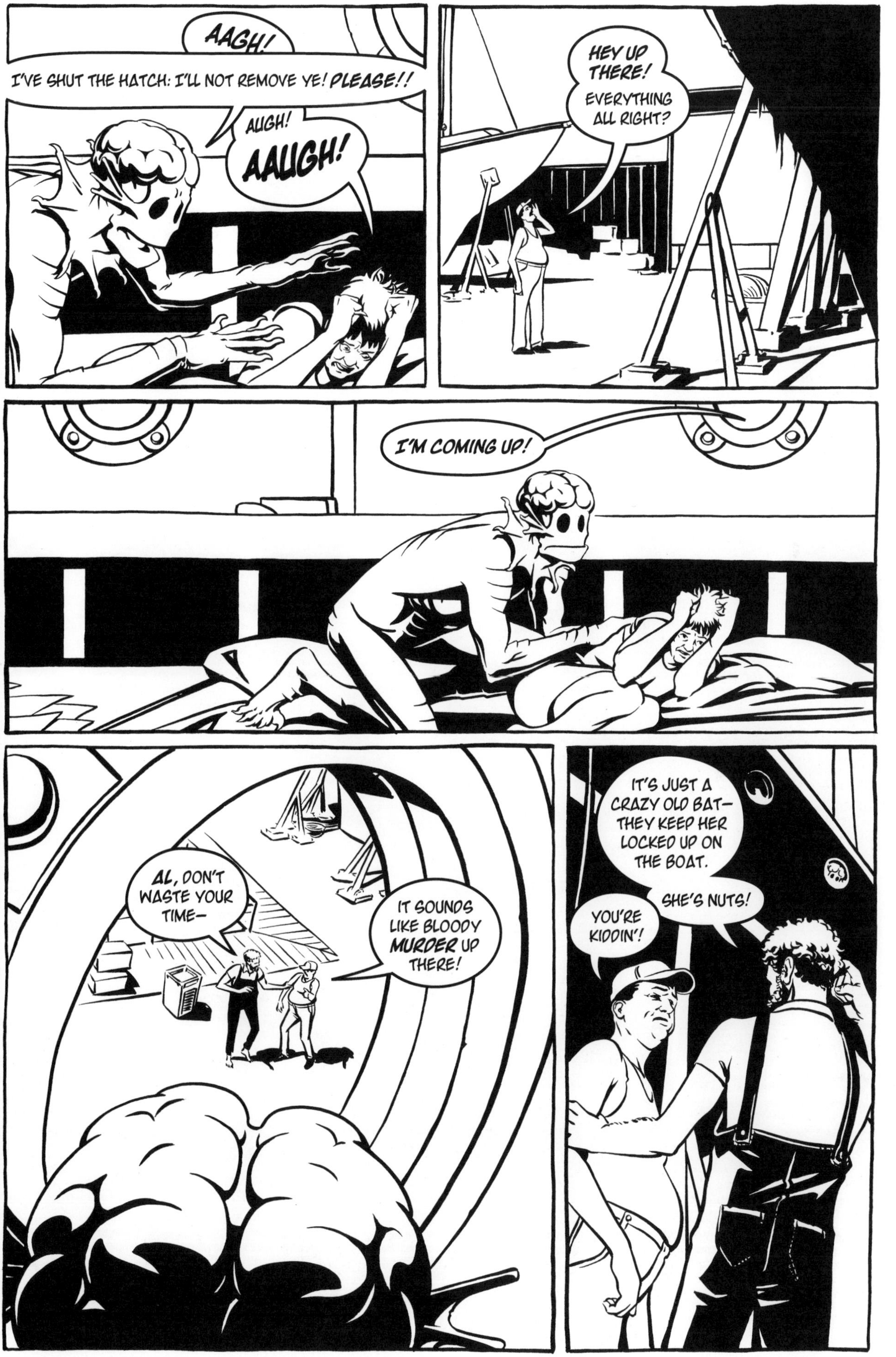
AAGH!
I'VE SHUT THE HATCH: I'LL NOT REMOVE YE! PLEASE!!
AUGH!
AAUGH!
HEY UP THERE!
EVERYTHING ALL RIGHT?
I'M COMING UP!
AL, DON'T WASTE YOUR TIME—
IT SOUNDS LIKE BLOODY MURDER UP THERE!
IT'S JUST A CRAZY OLD BAT— THEY KEEP HER LOCKED UP ON THE BOAT.
SHE'S NUTS!
YOU'RE KIDDIN'!

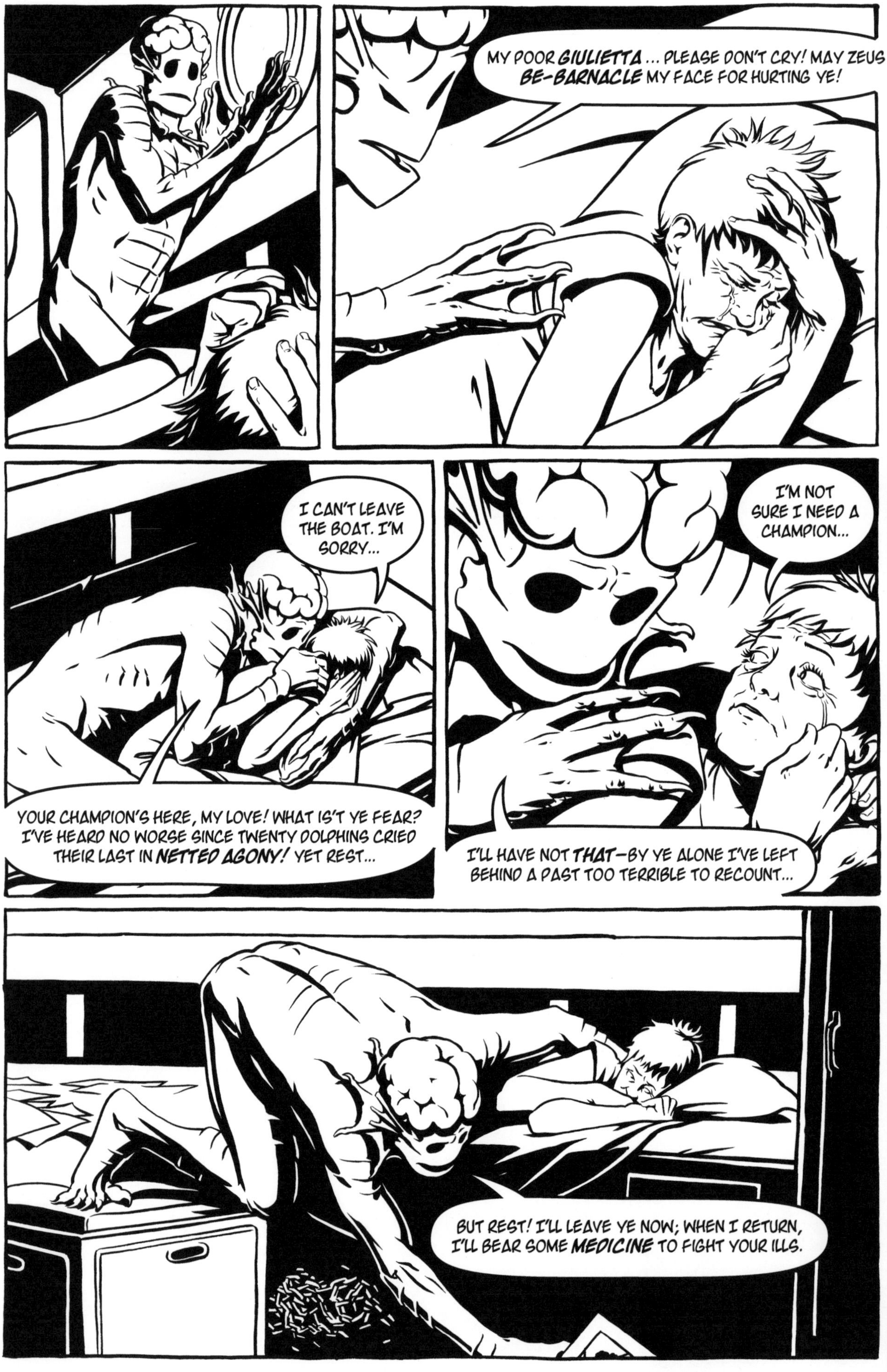
MY POOR GIULIETTA ... PLEASE DON'T CRY! MAY ZEUS BE-BARNACLE MY FACE FOR HURTING YE!
I CAN'T LEAVE THE BOAT. I'M SORRY...
YOUR CHAMPION'S HERE, MY LOVE! WHAT IS'T YE FEAR? I'VE HEARD NO WORSE SINCE TWENTY DOLPHINS CRIED THEIR LAST IN NETTED AGONY! YET REST...
I'M NOT SURE I NEED A CHAMPION...
I'LL HAVE NOT THAT—BY YE ALONE I'VE LEFT BEHIND A PAST TOO TERRIBLE TO RECOUNT...
BUT REST! I'LL LEAVE YE NOW; WHEN I RETURN, I'LL BEAR SOME MEDICINE TO FIGHT YOUR ILLS.

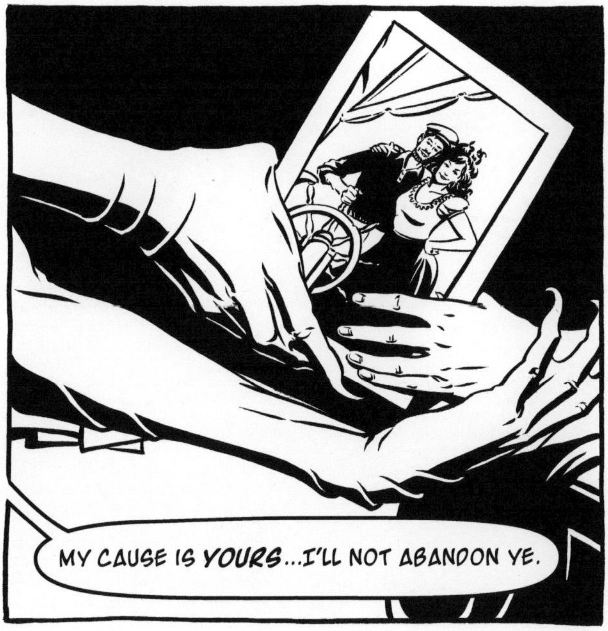
MY CAUSE IS YOURS...I'LL NOT ABANDON YE.

CHAPTER FOUR
CRYING

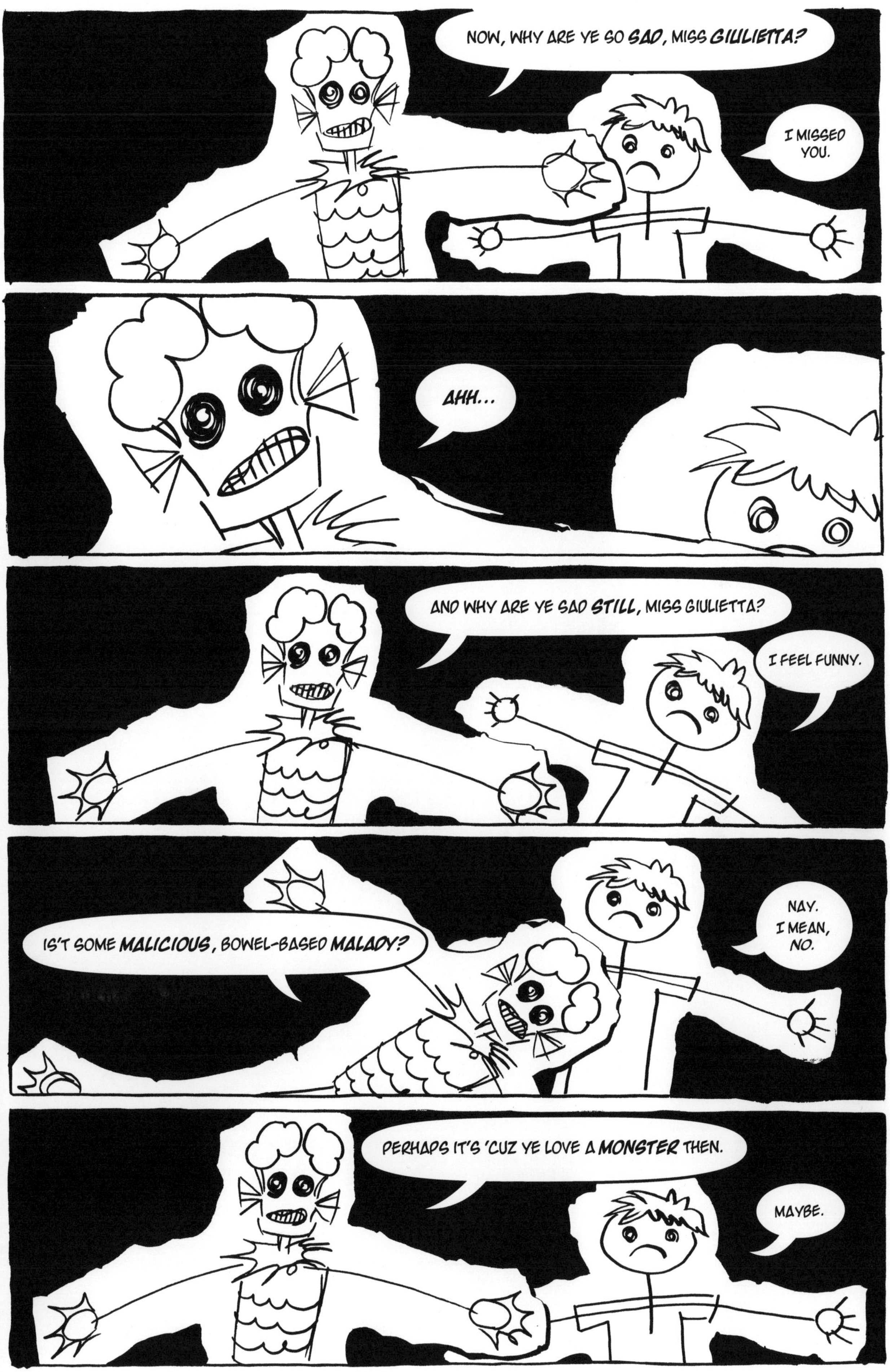
NOW, WHY ARE YE SO SAD, MISS GIULIETTA?
I MISSED YOU.
AHH...
AND WHY ARE YE SAD STILL, MISS GIULIETTA?
I FEEL FUNNY.
IS'T SOME MALICIOUS, BOWEL-BASED MALADY?
NAY. I MEAN, NO.
PERHAPS IT'S 'CUZ YE LOVE A MONSTER THEN.
MAYBE.

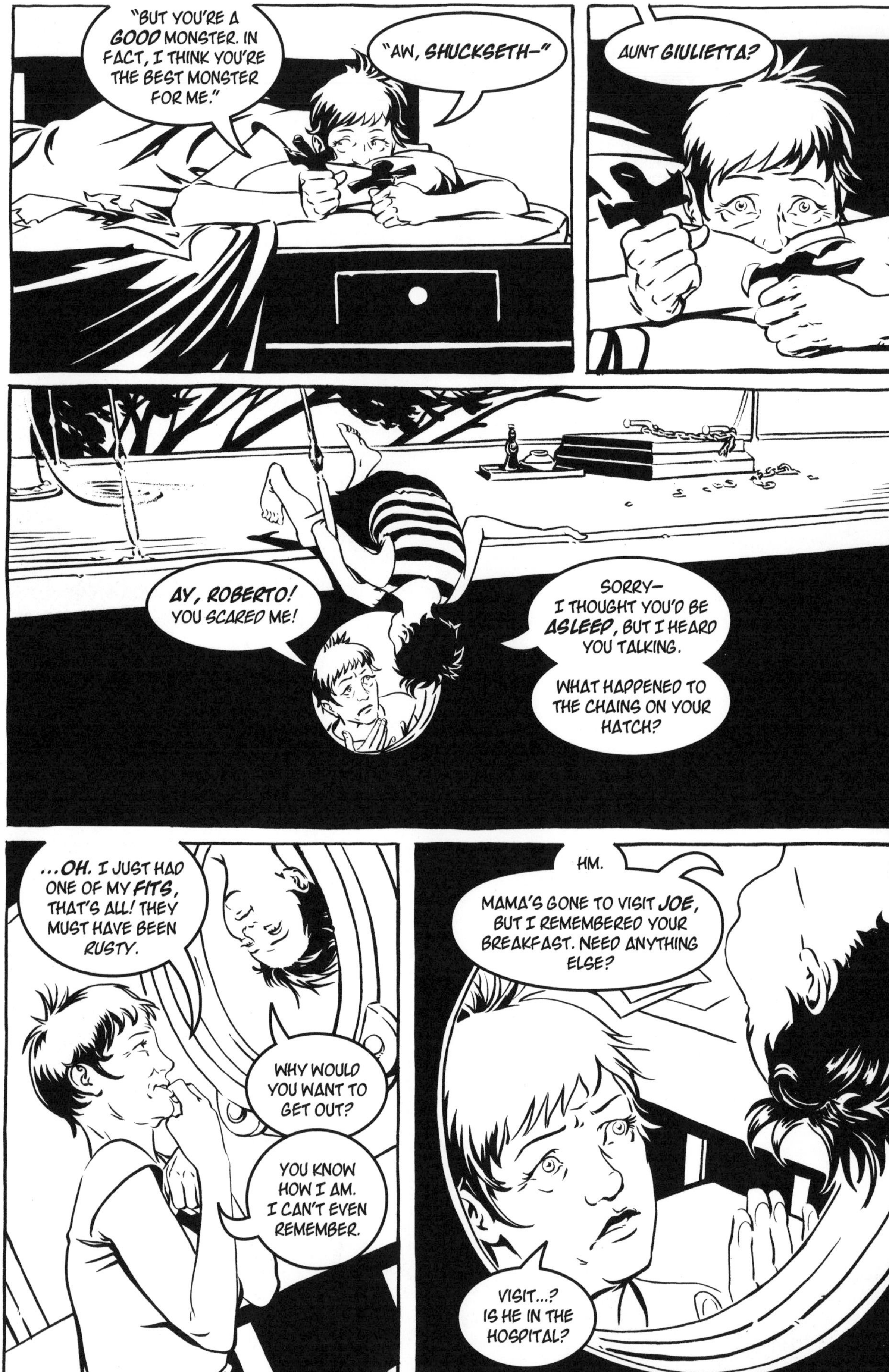
"BUT YOU'RE A GOOD MONSTER. IN FACT, I THINK YOU'RE THE BEST MONSTER FOR ME."
"AW, SHUCKSETH–"
AUNT GIULIETTA?
AY, ROBERTO! YOU SCARED ME!
SORRY– I THOUGHT YOU'D BE ASLEEP, BUT I HEARD YOU TALKING.
WHAT HAPPENED TO THE CHAINS ON YOUR HATCH?
...OH. I JUST HAD ONE OF MY FITS, THAT'S ALL! THEY MUST HAVE BEEN RUSTY.
WHY WOULD YOU WANT TO GET OUT?
YOU KNOW HOW I AM. I CAN'T EVEN REMEMBER.
HM.
MAMA'S GONE TO VISIT JOE, BUT I REMEMBERED YOUR BREAKFAST. NEED ANYTHING ELSE?
VISIT...? IS HE IN THE HOSPITAL?

The Daily

SOUTHWESTERN

August 6th, 1962

LIGHTHOUSE KILLER CAPTURED!

Police link high school running back with rash of summertime disappearances. Trial Tuesday.

By JOHN CULLICOTT
(Asst Managing Editor)

In an unparalleled act of deductive reasoning, local police have linked Joe Masina, a senior at Santa Lucia High, with the murder of his school-mate, Jane Ballard. The first part of the Ballard girl's body was found washed up in front of the fairgrounds on Sunday afternoon. After a thorough search, police found the rest of the body lodged between the rocks below the Punchbowl Lighthouse. Montgomery Harrison, the lighthouse keeper, is being held for questioning at the downtown station.

It is also likely, based on police statements, that Masina is responsible for the disappearances of up to thir-

DEAR LORD...

"LIGHTHOUSE KILLER"...?

THEY SAY HE PUSHED HER OFF THE LIGHTHOUSE LAST *FRIDAY*...MAYBE OTHERS TOO.

CAPTAIN CRAW SAYS THEY'RE WRONG.

HE SAYS *MR. HARRISON*, THE LIGHTHOUSE KEEPER, ALWAYS LOCKS IT FROM BELOW SO NO ONE CAN GET TO THE *TOP* WHEN HE'S NOT *THERE*.

HARRISON— WHERE HAVE I HEARD HIS NAME BEFORE?

HE'S...A *FRIEND* OF MAMA'S.

OF COURSE!!! HE WAS *HERE* THAT NIGHT. I SAW HIM! IF I CAN EXPLAIN—OH, *BOBBY*! WE COULD HELP *JOE* CLEAR HIS NAME!

The Daily SOUTHWEST

LIGHTHOUSE KILLER CAPTURED!

YES! DON'T WORRY, BOBBY, WE'RE GOING TO HELP JOE, AND—

AUNT GIULIETTA?

HM?

...

HOW CAN YOU HELP IF YOU CAN'T LEAVE YOUR CABIN?

93

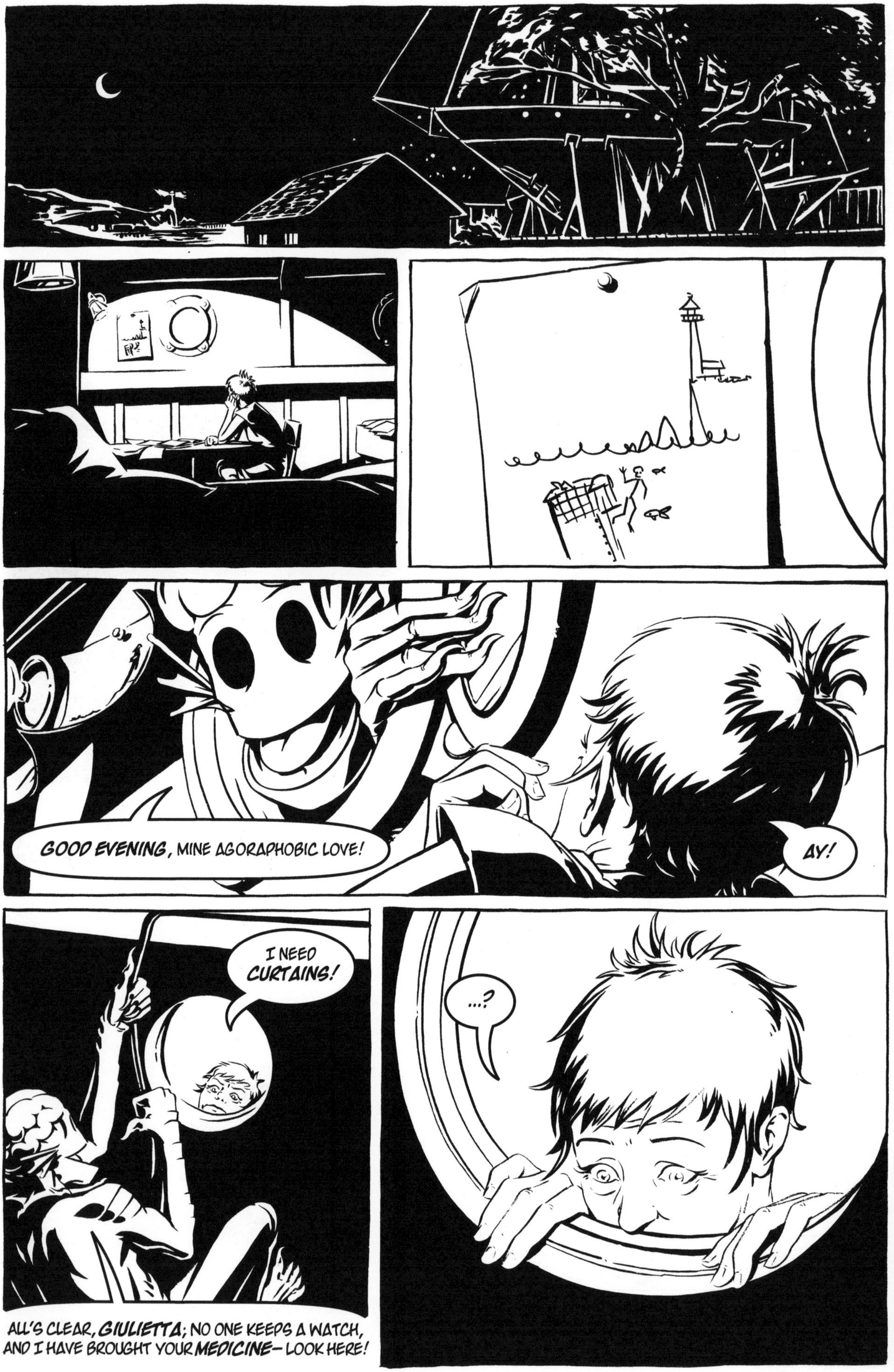
GOOD EVENING, MINE AGORAPHOBIC LOVE!
AY!
I NEED CURTAINS!
ALL'S CLEAR, GIULIETTA; NO ONE KEEPS A WATCH, AND I HAVE BROUGHT YOUR MEDICINE— LOOK HERE!
...?

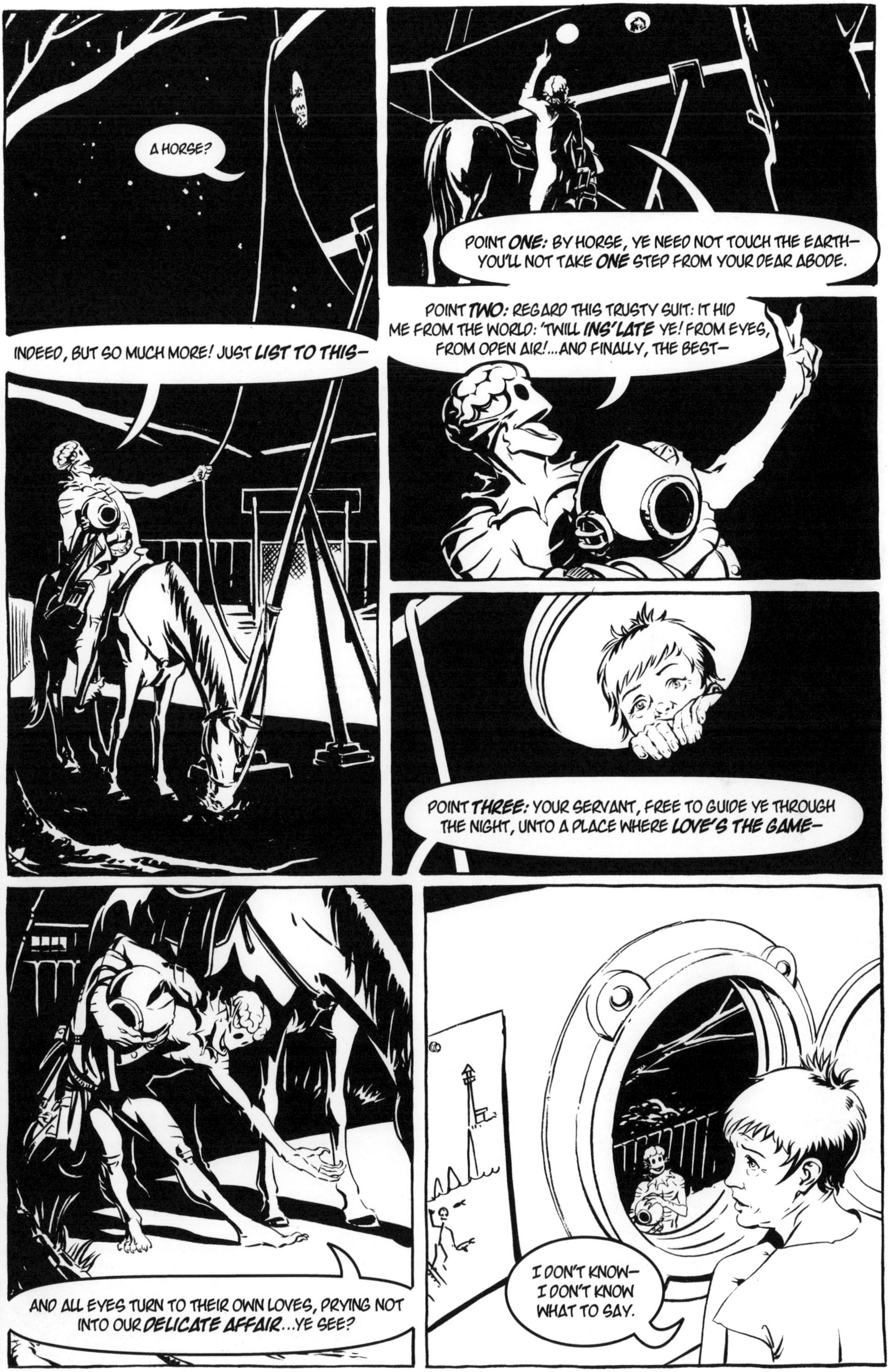
A HORSE?
POINT ONE: BY HORSE, YE NEED NOT TOUCH THE EARTH— YOU'LL NOT TAKE ONE STEP FROM YOUR DEAR ABODE.
INDEED, BUT SO MUCH MORE! JUST LIST TO THIS—
POINT TWO: REGARD THIS TRUSTY SUIT: IT HID ME FROM THE WORLD: 'TWILL INS'LATE YE! FROM EYES, FROM OPEN AIR!...AND FINALLY, THE BEST—
POINT THREE: YOUR SERVANT, FREE TO GUIDE YE THROUGH THE NIGHT, UNTO A PLACE WHERE LOVE'S THE GAME—
AND ALL EYES TURN TO THEIR OWN LOVES, PRYING NOT INTO OUR DELICATE AFFAIR...YE SEE?
I DON'T KNOW— I DON'T KNOW WHAT TO SAY.

NO NEED TO SAY A THING! SOME *BREVITY* IS BEST, SINCE WE'VE A *SCHEDULE* FOR TO KEEP!

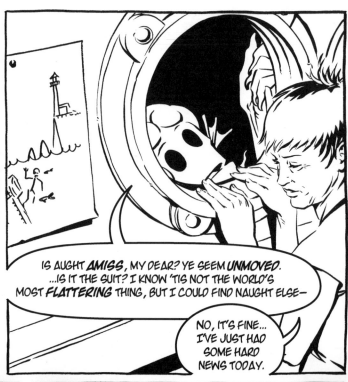

IS AUGHT *AMISS*, MY DEAR? YE SEEM *UNMOVED*. ...IS IT THE SUIT? I KNOW 'TIS NOT THE WORLD'S MOST *FLATTERING* THING, BUT I COULD FIND NAUGHT ELSE—

NO, IT'S FINE... I'VE JUST HAD SOME HARD NEWS TODAY.

DO TELL! IF I CAN BE OF ANY HELP—

IT'S *ZOLA'S* SON, *JOE.* HE WAS OUT ON THE BEACH WITH A *GIRL* A FEW NIGHTS AGO...

SHE *DISAPPEARED*, BUT THEY... THEY JUST FOUND HER *BODY*, AND—

THEY'RE TRYING HIM FOR *MURDER!* NOT ONLY FOR THIS GIRL, BUT MANY OTHER YOUNG PEOPLE WHO'VE DISAPPEARED...

I *KNOW* HE COULDN'T HAVE DONE IT, BUT I FEEL SOMETHING *TERRIBLE* I CAN'T PLACE... BEFORE YOU LEFT ME, YOU TALKED ABOUT *LEAVING SOMETHING BEHIND*...

AND I'VE BEEN WONDERING...

DO YOU KNOW ANYTHING ABOUT THIS?

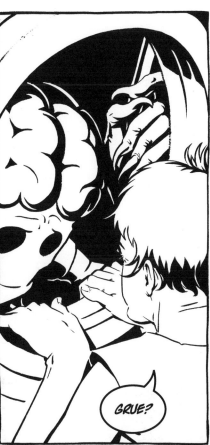

GRUE?

NAY! *NAY*— I'VE KEPT AN EYE UPON THE BEACH; THE LIGHTHOUSE TOO, AND NEVER SAW A *THING*. YOUR NEPHEW'S BLAMELESS AS AN ANGELFISH!

THANK YOU! JUST HEARING YOU SAY IT, I KNOW IT'S TRUE!

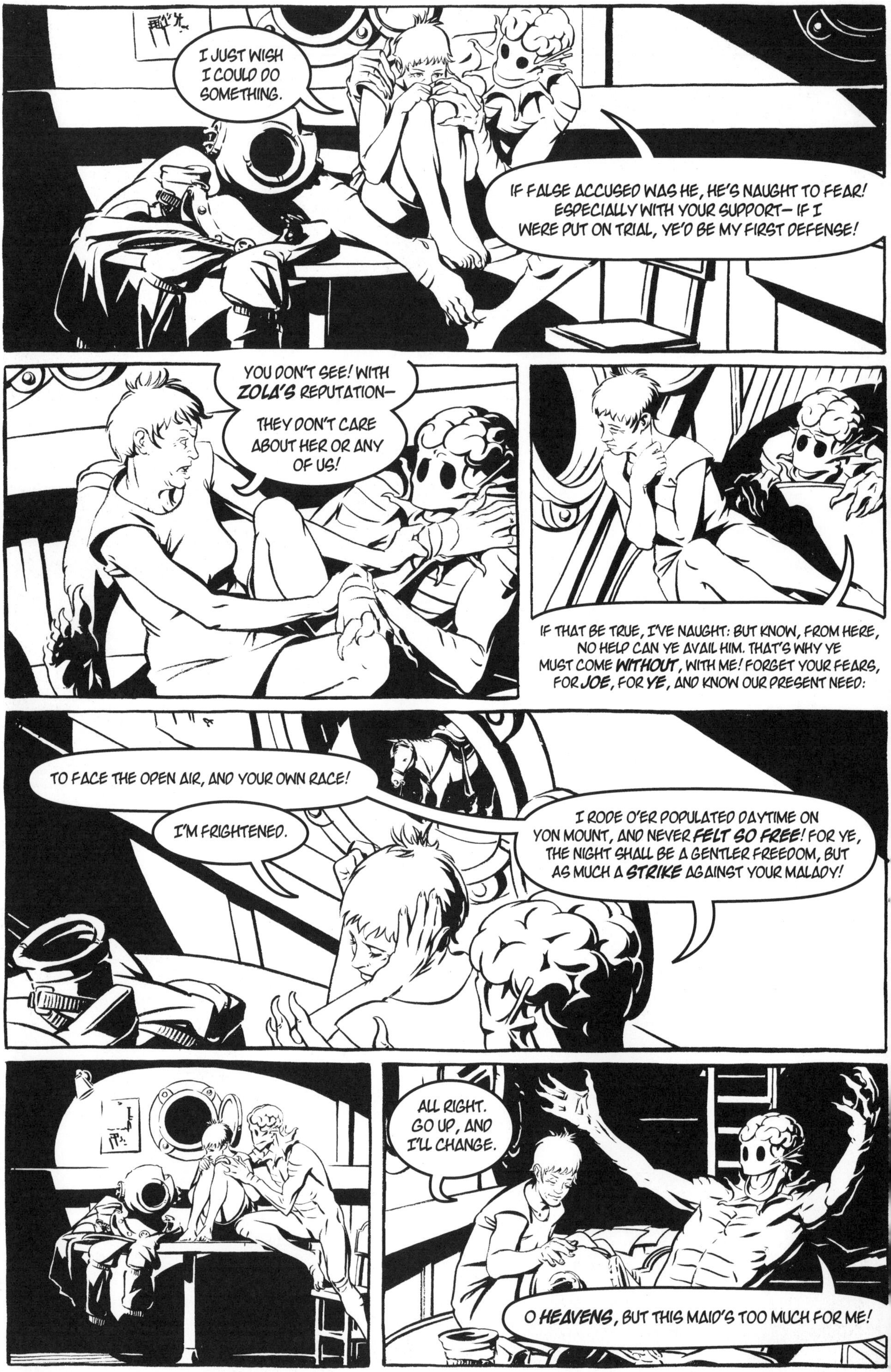
I JUST WISH I COULD DO SOMETHING.
IF FALSE ACCUSED WAS HE, HE'S NAUGHT TO FEAR! ESPECIALLY WITH YOUR SUPPORT— IF I WERE PUT ON TRIAL, YE'D BE MY FIRST DEFENSE!
YOU DON'T SEE! WITH ZOLA'S REPUTATION—
THEY DON'T CARE ABOUT HER OR ANY OF US!
IF THAT BE TRUE, I'VE NAUGHT: BUT KNOW, FROM HERE, NO HELP CAN YE AVAIL HIM. THAT'S WHY YE MUST COME WITHOUT, WITH ME! FORGET YOUR FEARS, FOR JOE, FOR YE, AND KNOW OUR PRESENT NEED:
TO FACE THE OPEN AIR, AND YOUR OWN RACE!
I'M FRIGHTENED.
I RODE O'ER POPULATED DAYTIME ON YON MOUNT, AND NEVER FELT SO FREE! FOR YE, THE NIGHT SHALL BE A GENTLER FREEDOM, BUT AS MUCH A STRIKE AGAINST YOUR MALADY!
ALL RIGHT. GO UP, AND I'LL CHANGE.
O HEAVENS, BUT THIS MAID'S TOO MUCH FOR ME!

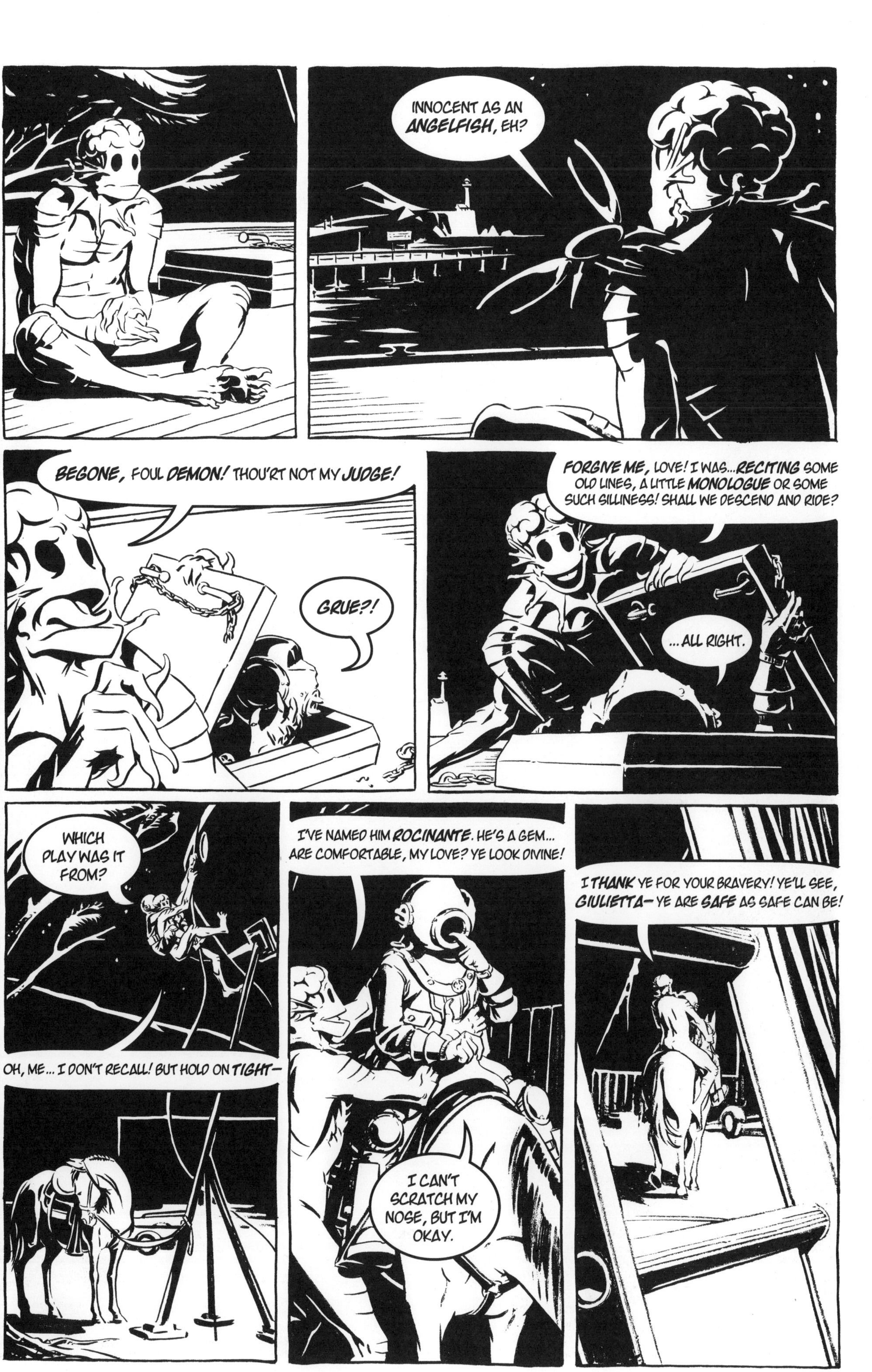
INNOCENT AS AN ANGELFISH, EH?
BEGONE, FOUL DEMON! THOU'RT NOT MY JUDGE!
GRUE?!
FORGIVE ME, LOVE! I WAS...RECITING SOME OLD LINES, A LITTLE MONOLOGUE OR SOME SUCH SILLINESS! SHALL WE DESCEND AND RIDE?
...ALL RIGHT.
WHICH PLAY WAS IT FROM?
OH, ME... I DON'T RECALL! BUT HOLD ON TIGHT—
I'VE NAMED HIM ROCINANTE. HE'S A GEM... ARE COMFORTABLE, MY LOVE? YE LOOK DIVINE!
I CAN'T SCRATCH MY NOSE, BUT I'M OKAY.
I THANK YE FOR YOUR BRAVERY! YE'LL SEE, GIULIETTA— YE ARE SAFE AS SAFE CAN BE!

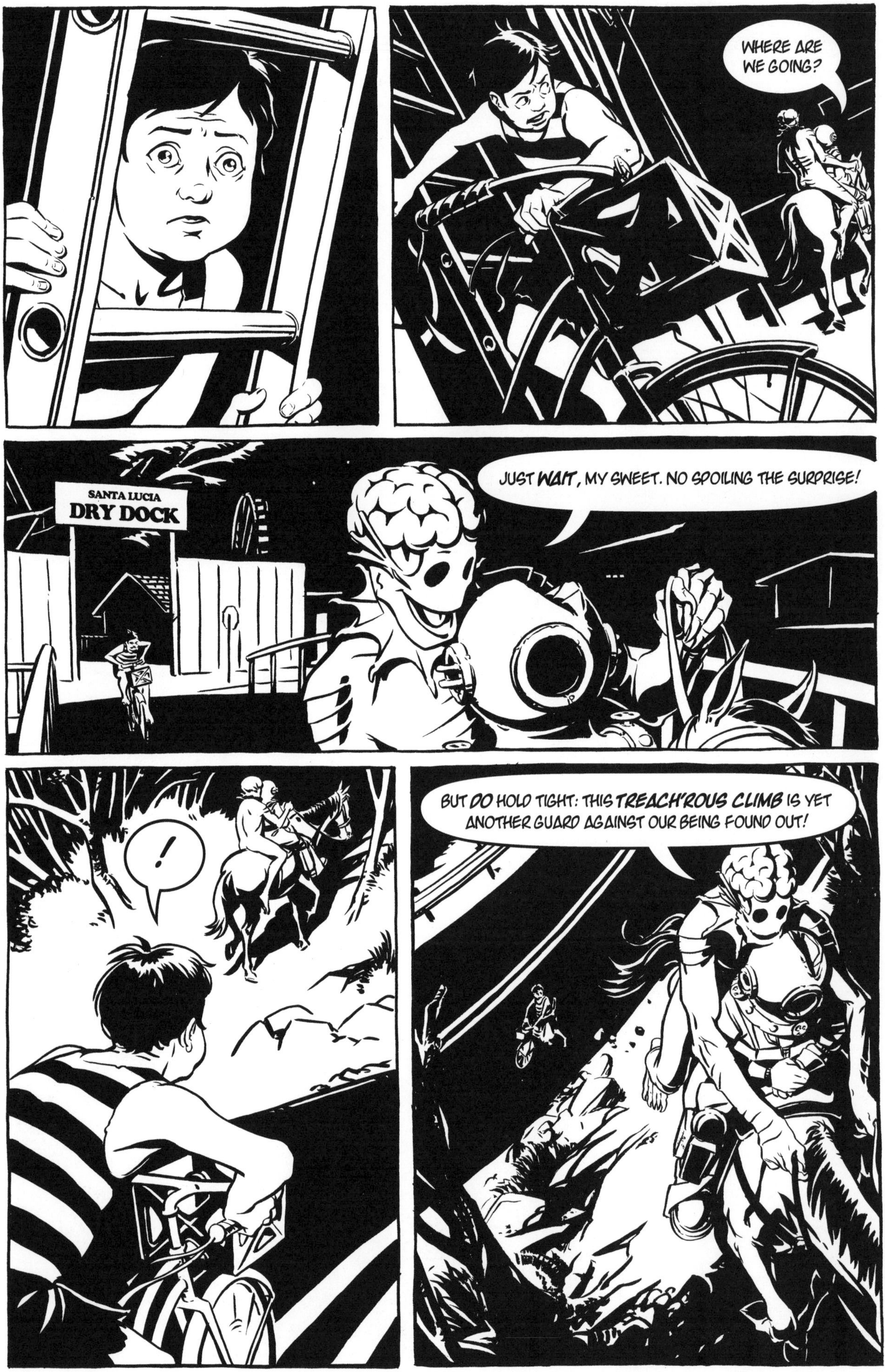
WHERE ARE WE GOING?
SANTA LUCIA DRY DOCK
JUST WAIT, MY SWEET. NO SPOILING THE SURPRISE!
!
BUT DO HOLD TIGHT: THIS TREACH'ROUS CLIMB IS YET ANOTHER GUARD AGAINST OUR BEING FOUND OUT!

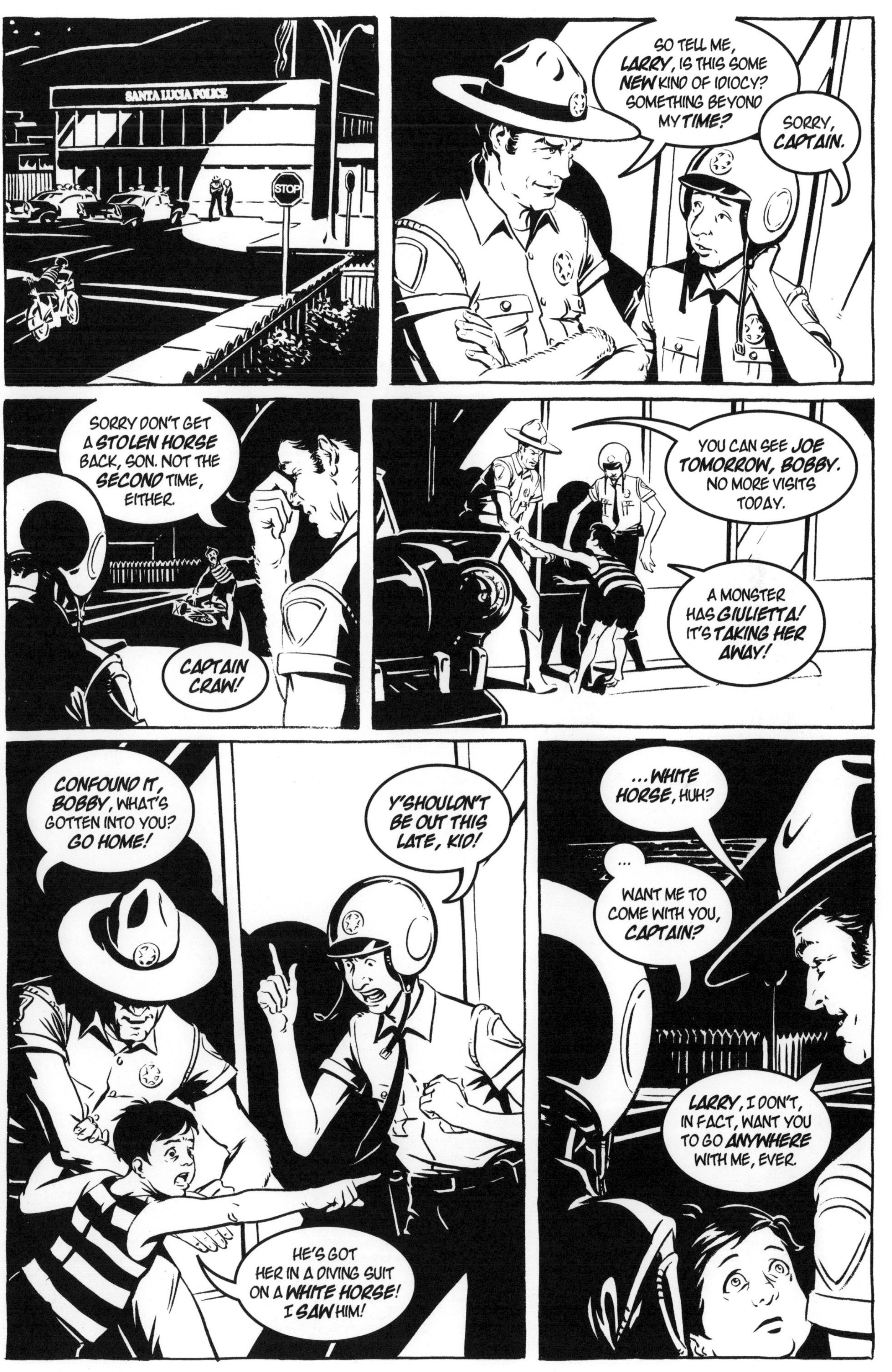
SANTA LUCIA POLICE
STOP
SO TELL ME, LARRY, IS THIS SOME NEW KIND OF IDIOCY? SOMETHING BEYOND MY TIME?
SORRY, CAPTAIN.
SORRY DON'T GET A STOLEN HORSE BACK, SON. NOT THE SECOND TIME, EITHER.
CAPTAIN CRAW!
YOU CAN SEE JOE TOMORROW, BOBBY. NO MORE VISITS TODAY.
A MONSTER HAS GIULIETTA! IT'S TAKING HER AWAY!
CONFOUND IT, BOBBY, WHAT'S GOTTEN INTO YOU? GO HOME!
Y'SHOULDN'T BE OUT THIS LATE, KID!
HE'S GOT HER IN A DIVING SUIT ON A WHITE HORSE! I SAW HIM!
...WHITE HORSE, HUH?
...
WANT ME TO COME WITH YOU, CAPTAIN?
LARRY, I DON'T, IN FACT, WANT YOU TO GO ANYWHERE WITH ME, EVER.

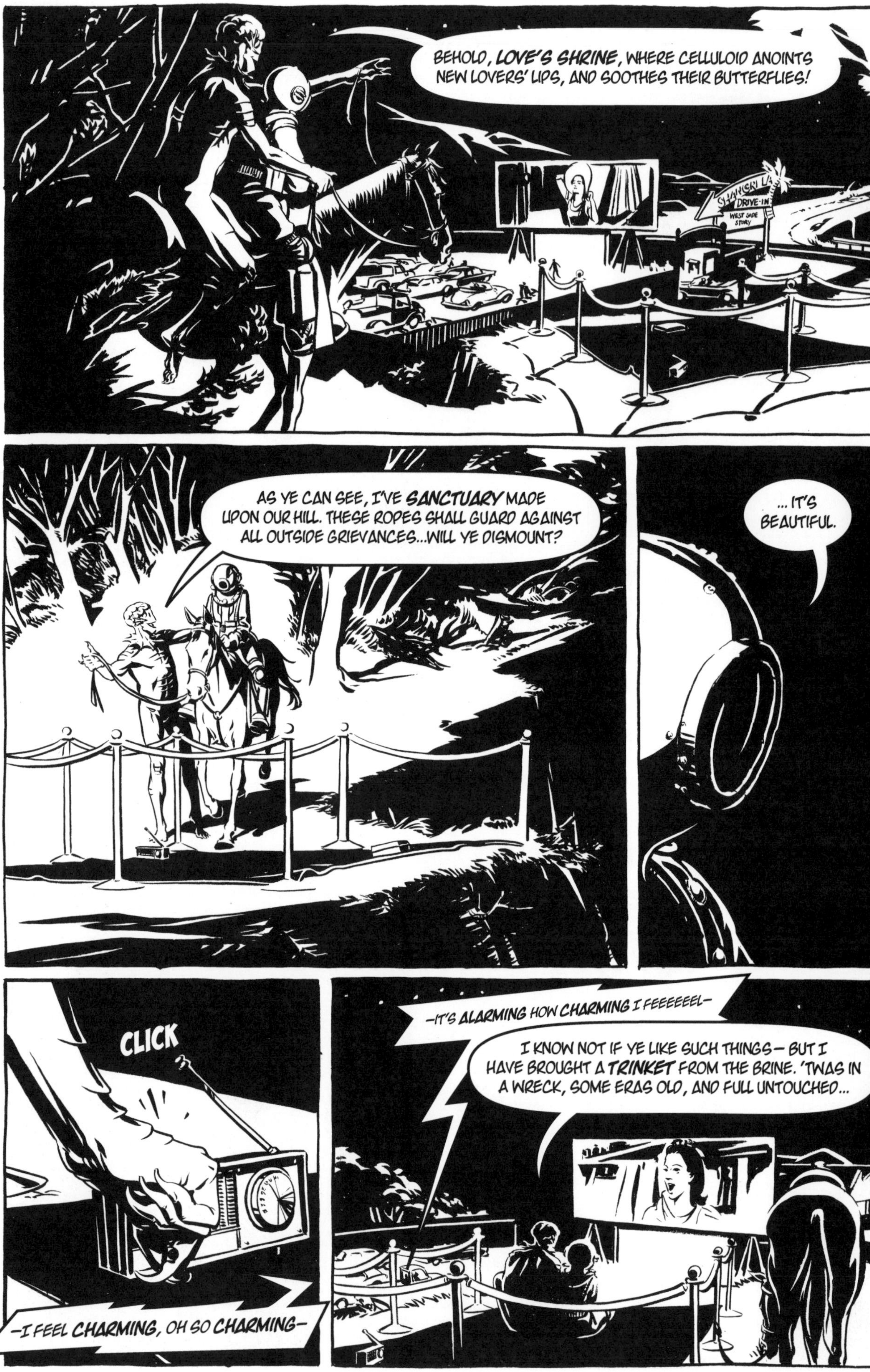

BEHOLD, LOVE'S SHRINE, WHERE CELLULOID ANOINTS NEW LOVERS' LIPS, AND SOOTHES THEIR BUTTERFLIES!
SHANGRI LA DRIVE-IN
WEST SIDE STORY
AS YE CAN SEE, I'VE SANCTUARY MADE UPON OUR HILL. THESE ROPES SHALL GUARD AGAINST ALL OUTSIDE GRIEVANCES...WILL YE DISMOUNT?
...IT'S BEAUTIFUL.
CLICK
—I FEEL CHARMING, OH SO CHARMING—
—IT'S ALARMING HOW CHARMING I FEEEEEEL—
I KNOW NOT IF YE LIKE SUCH THINGS— BUT I HAVE BROUGHT A TRINKET FROM THE BRINE. 'TWAS IN A WRECK, SOME ERAS OLD, AND FULL UNTOUCHED...

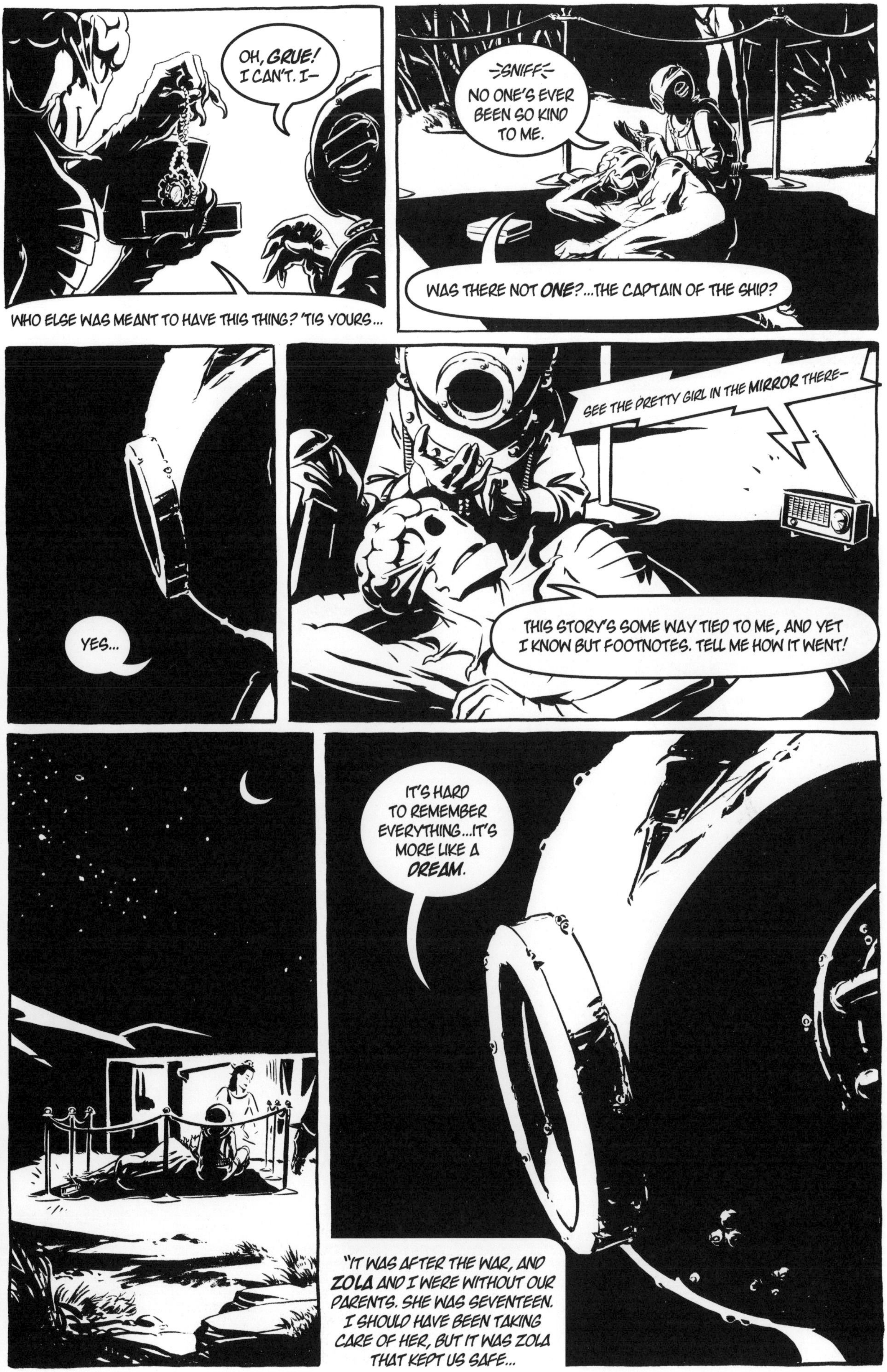
OH, GRUE! I CAN'T. I–
WHO ELSE WAS MEANT TO HAVE THIS THING? 'TIS YOURS...
SNIFF
NO ONE'S EVER BEEN SO KIND TO ME.
WAS THERE NOT ONE?...THE CAPTAIN OF THE SHIP?
YES...
SEE THE PRETTY GIRL IN THE MIRROR THERE–
THIS STORY'S SOME WAY TIED TO ME, AND YET I KNOW BUT FOOTNOTES. TELL ME HOW IT WENT!
IT'S HARD TO REMEMBER EVERYTHING...IT'S MORE LIKE A DREAM.
"IT WAS AFTER THE WAR, AND ZOLA AND I WERE WITHOUT OUR PARENTS. SHE WAS SEVENTEEN. I SHOULD HAVE BEEN TAKING CARE OF HER, BUT IT WAS ZOLA THAT KEPT US SAFE...

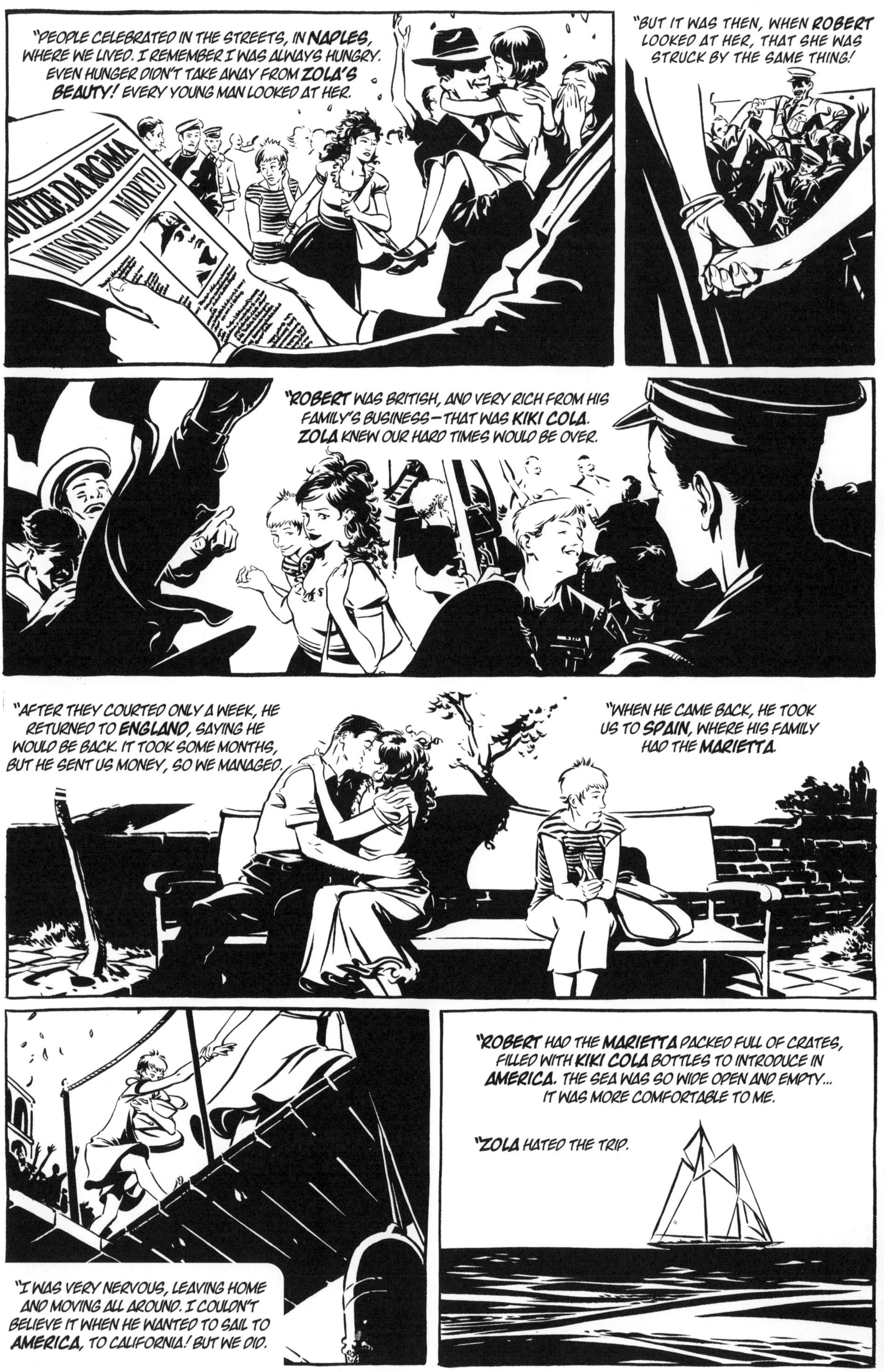
"PEOPLE CELEBRATED IN THE STREETS, IN NAPLES, WHERE WE LIVED. I REMEMBER I WAS ALWAYS HUNGRY. EVEN HUNGER DIDN'T TAKE AWAY FROM ZOLA'S BEAUTY! EVERY YOUNG MAN LOOKED AT HER.
NOTIZIE DA ROMA
MUSSOLINI MORTO
"BUT IT WAS THEN, WHEN ROBERT LOOKED AT HER, THAT SHE WAS STRUCK BY THE SAME THING!
"ROBERT WAS BRITISH, AND VERY RICH FROM HIS FAMILY'S BUSINESS—THAT WAS KIKI COLA. ZOLA KNEW OUR HARD TIMES WOULD BE OVER.
"AFTER THEY COURTED ONLY A WEEK, HE RETURNED TO ENGLAND, SAYING HE WOULD BE BACK. IT TOOK SOME MONTHS, BUT HE SENT US MONEY, SO WE MANAGED.
"WHEN HE CAME BACK, HE TOOK US TO SPAIN, WHERE HIS FAMILY HAD THE MARIETTA.
"I WAS VERY NERVOUS, LEAVING HOME AND MOVING ALL AROUND. I COULDN'T BELIEVE IT WHEN HE WANTED TO SAIL TO AMERICA, TO CALIFORNIA! BUT WE DID.
"ROBERT HAD THE MARIETTA PACKED FULL OF CRATES, FILLED WITH KIKI COLA BOTTLES TO INTRODUCE IN AMERICA. THE SEA WAS SO WIDE OPEN AND EMPTY... IT WAS MORE COMFORTABLE TO ME.
"ZOLA HATED THE TRIP.

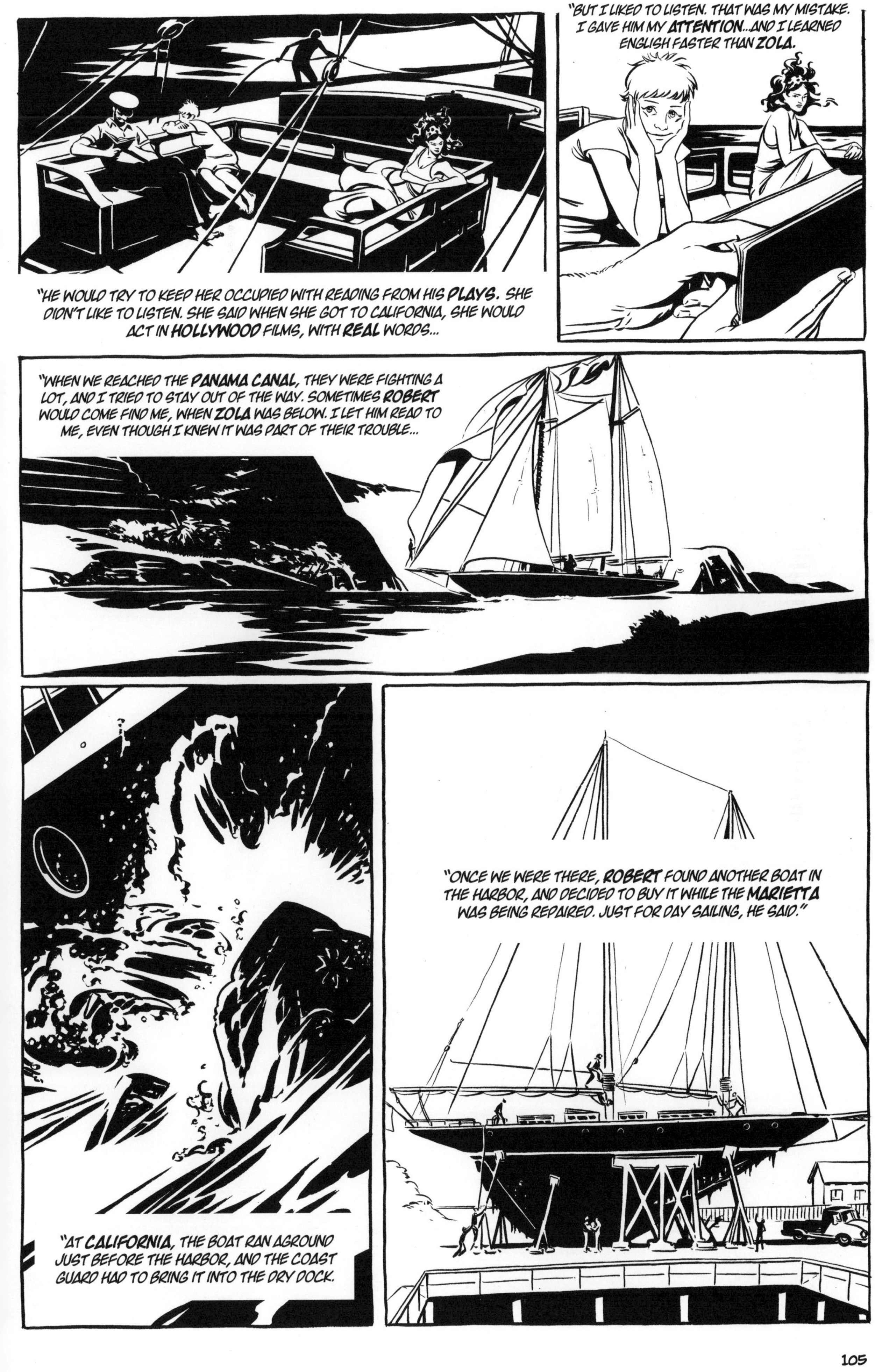
"HE WOULD TRY TO KEEP HER OCCUPIED WITH READING FROM HIS PLAYS. SHE DIDN'T LIKE TO LISTEN. SHE SAID WHEN SHE GOT TO CALIFORNIA, SHE WOULD ACT IN HOLLYWOOD FILMS, WITH REAL WORDS...
"BUT I LIKED TO LISTEN. THAT WAS MY MISTAKE. I GAVE HIM MY ATTENTION...AND I LEARNED ENGLISH FASTER THAN ZOLA.
"WHEN WE REACHED THE PANAMA CANAL, THEY WERE FIGHTING A LOT, AND I TRIED TO STAY OUT OF THE WAY. SOMETIMES ROBERT WOULD COME FIND ME, WHEN ZOLA WAS BELOW. I LET HIM READ TO ME, EVEN THOUGH I KNEW IT WAS PART OF THEIR TROUBLE...
"AT CALIFORNIA, THE BOAT RAN AGROUND JUST BEFORE THE HARBOR, AND THE COAST GUARD HAD TO BRING IT INTO THE DRY DOCK.
"ONCE WE WERE THERE, ROBERT FOUND ANOTHER BOAT IN THE HARBOR, AND DECIDED TO BUY IT WHILE THE MARIETTA WAS BEING REPAIRED. JUST FOR DAY SAILING, HE SAID."

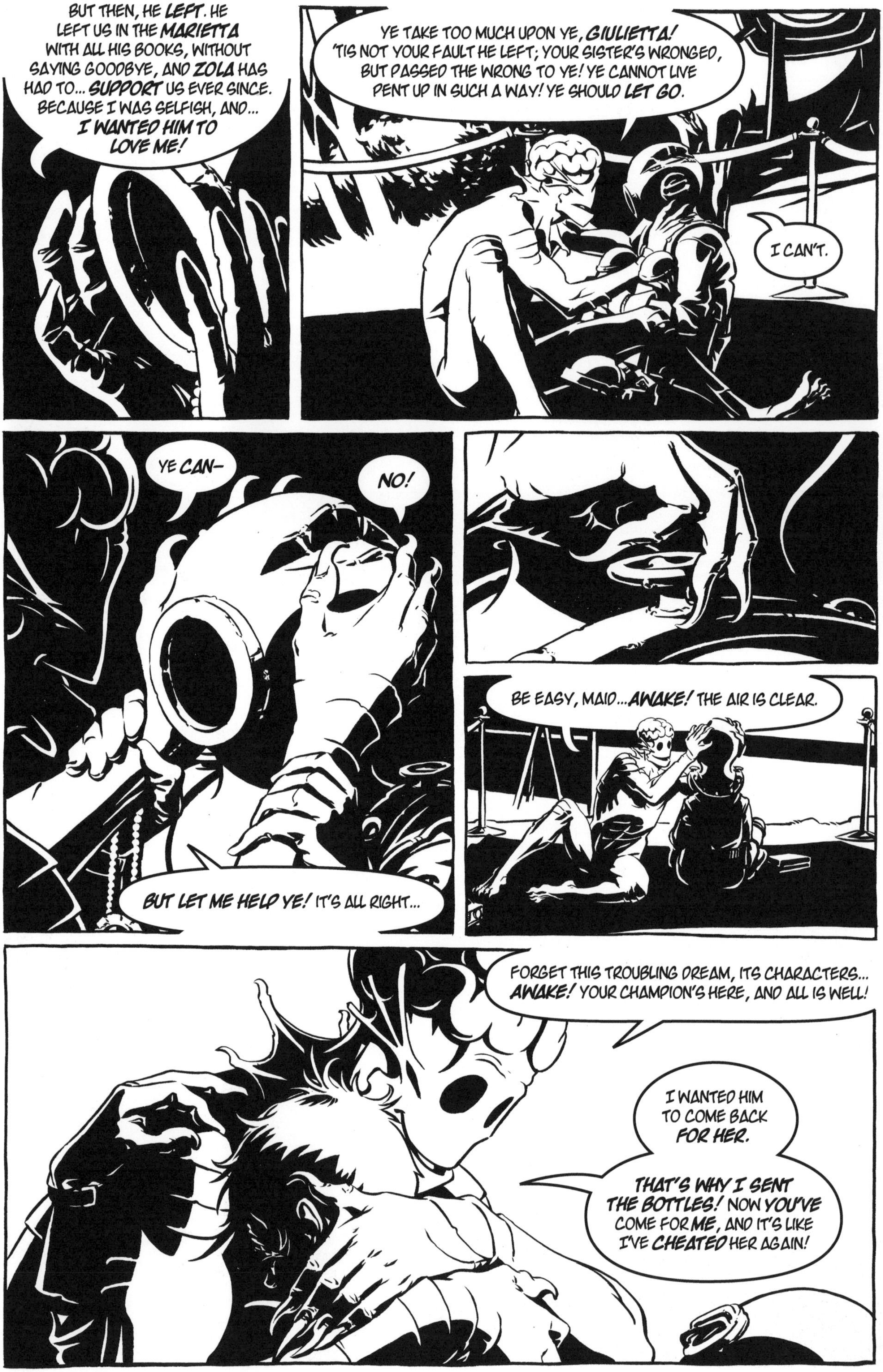
BUT THEN, HE LEFT. HE LEFT US IN THE MARIETTA WITH ALL HIS BOOKS, WITHOUT SAYING GOODBYE, AND ZOLA HAS HAD TO... SUPPORT US EVER SINCE. BECAUSE I WAS SELFISH, AND... I WANTED HIM TO LOVE ME!
YE TAKE TOO MUCH UPON YE, GIULIETTA! 'TIS NOT YOUR FAULT HE LEFT; YOUR SISTER'S WRONGED, BUT PASSED THE WRONG TO YE! YE CANNOT LIVE PENT UP IN SUCH A WAY! YE SHOULD LET GO.
I CAN'T.
YE CAN-
NO!
BUT LET ME HELP YE! IT'S ALL RIGHT...
BE EASY, MAID...AWAKE! THE AIR IS CLEAR.
FORGET THIS TROUBLING DREAM, ITS CHARACTERS... AWAKE! YOUR CHAMPION'S HERE, AND ALL IS WELL!
I WANTED HIM TO COME BACK FOR HER.
THAT'S WHY I SENT THE BOTTLES! NOW YOU'VE COME FOR ME, AND IT'S LIKE I'VE CHEATED HER AGAIN!

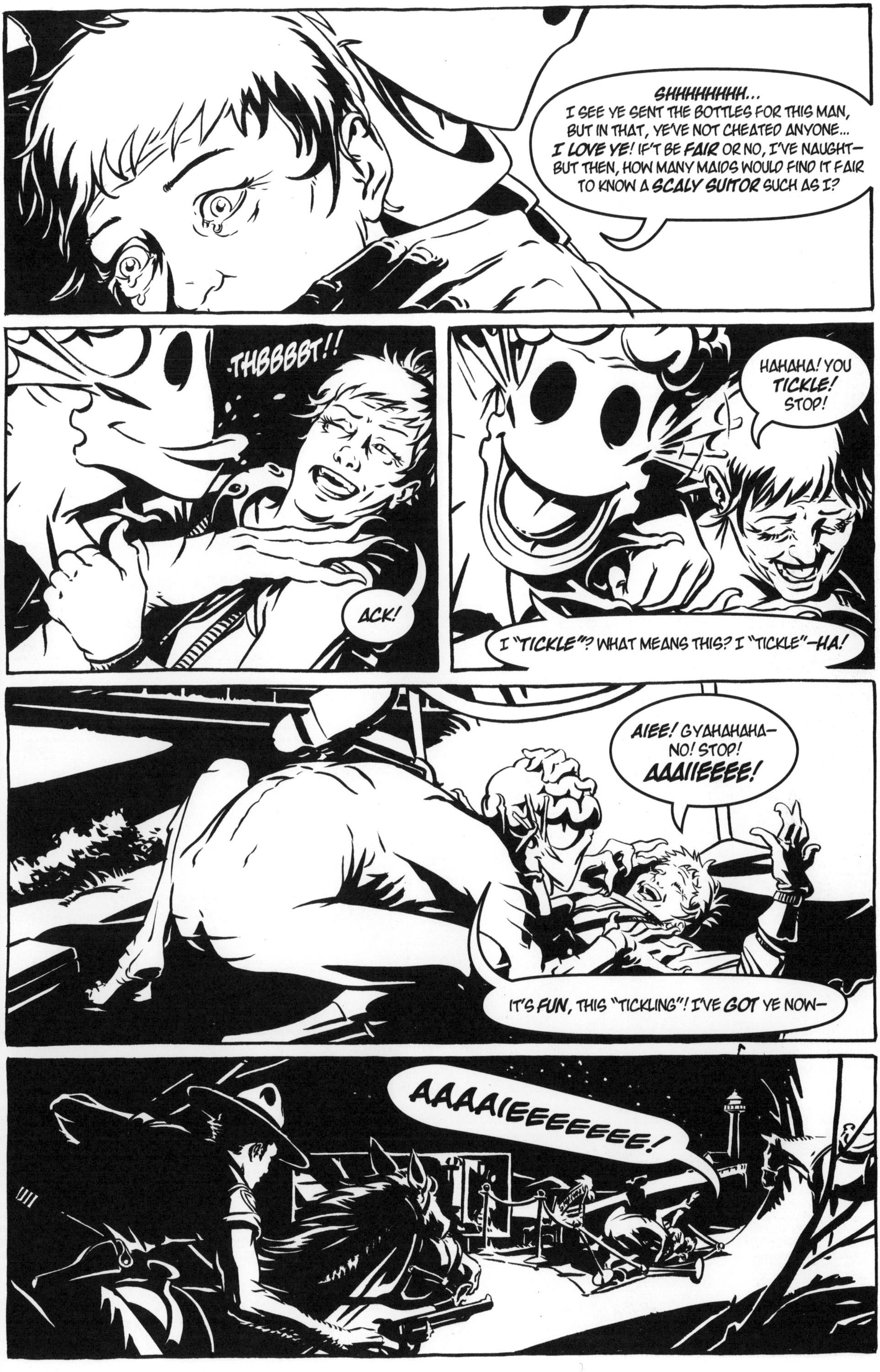
SHHHHHHHH...
I SEE YE SENT THE BOTTLES FOR THIS MAN, BUT IN THAT, YE'VE NOT CHEATED ANYONE... I LOVE YE! IF'T BE FAIR OR NO, I'VE NAUGHT— BUT THEN, HOW MANY MAIDS WOULD FIND IT FAIR TO KNOW A SCALY SUITOR SUCH AS I?
THBBBBT!!
ACK!
HAHAHA! YOU TICKLE! STOP!
I "TICKLE"? WHAT MEANS THIS? I "TICKLE"—HA!
AIEE! GYAHAHAHA— NO! STOP! AAAIIEEEE!
IT'S FUN, THIS "TICKLING"! I'VE GOT YE NOW—
AAAAIEEEEEEEE!

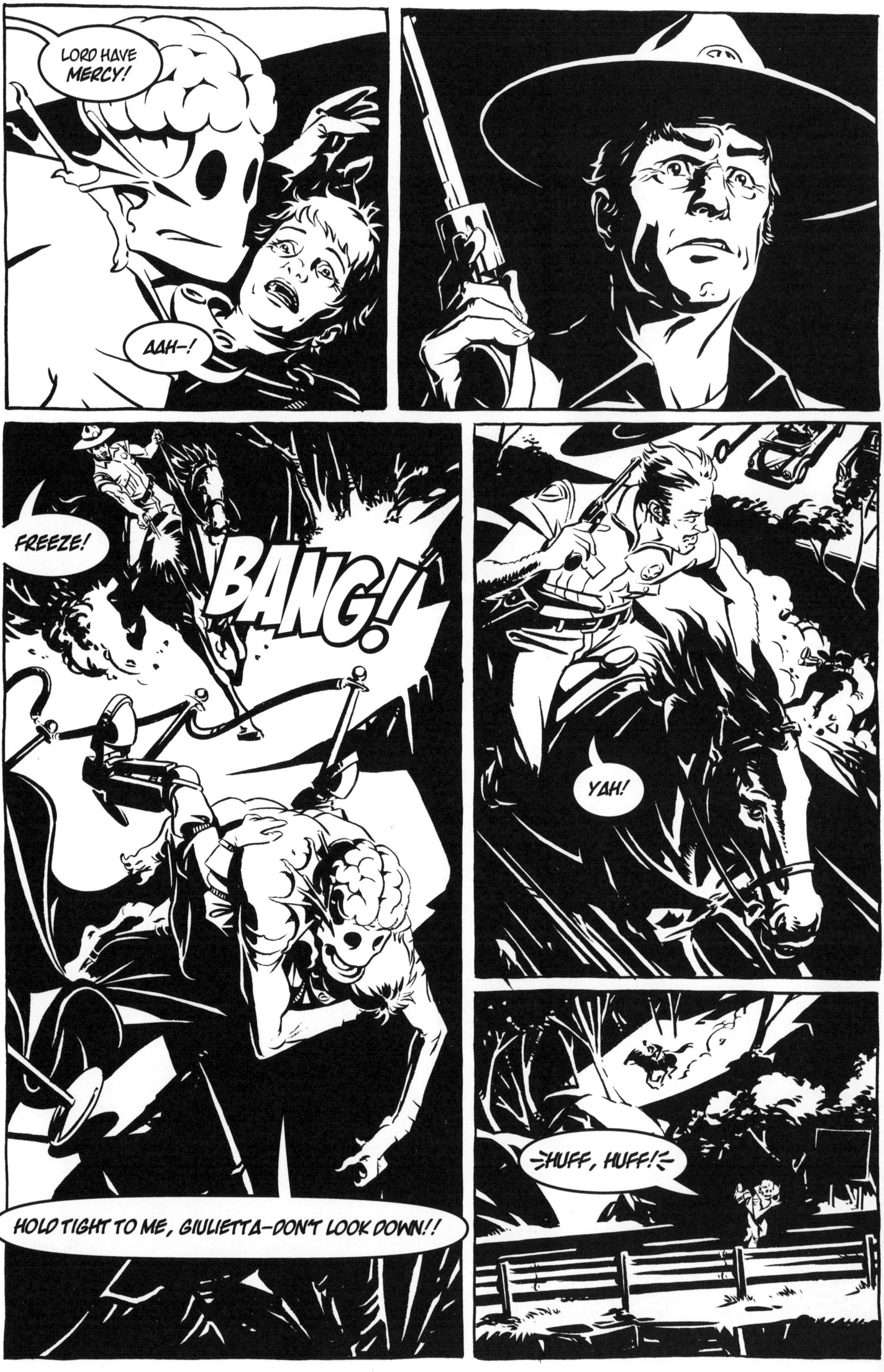
LORD HAVE MERCY!
AAH-!
FREEZE!
BANG!
HOLD TIGHT TO ME, GIULIETTA-DON'T LOOK DOWN!!
YAH!
HUFF, HUFF!

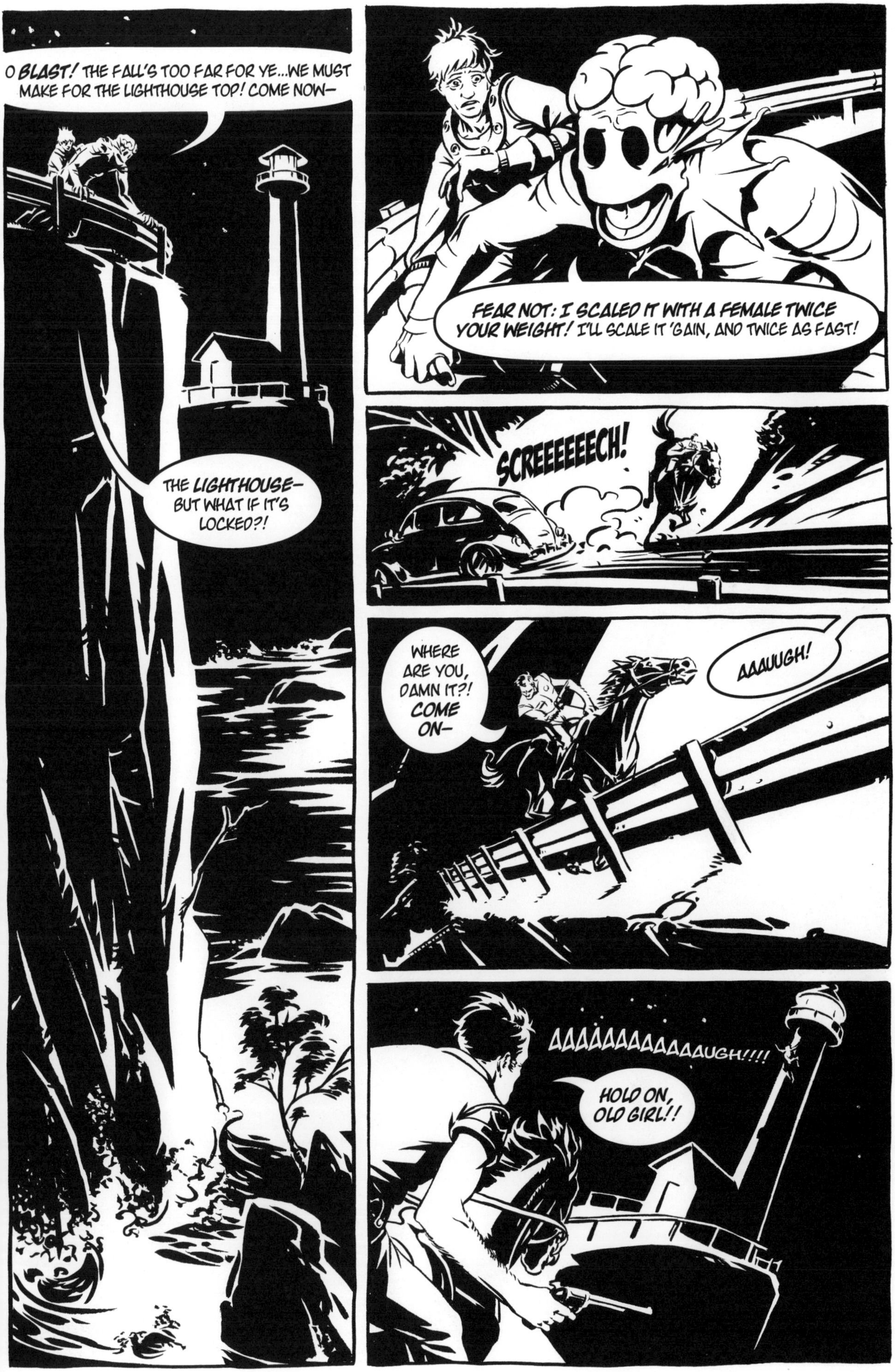
O BLAST! THE FALL'S TOO FAR FOR YE...WE MUST MAKE FOR THE LIGHTHOUSE TOP! COME NOW—
THE LIGHTHOUSE— BUT WHAT IF IT'S LOCKED?!
FEAR NOT: I SCALED IT WITH A FEMALE TWICE YOUR WEIGHT! I'LL SCALE IT 'GAIN, AND TWICE AS FAST!
SCREEEEEEECH!
WHERE ARE YOU, DAMN IT?! COME ON—
AAAUUGH!
AAAAAAAAAAAAAUGH!!!!
HOLD ON, OLD GIRL!!

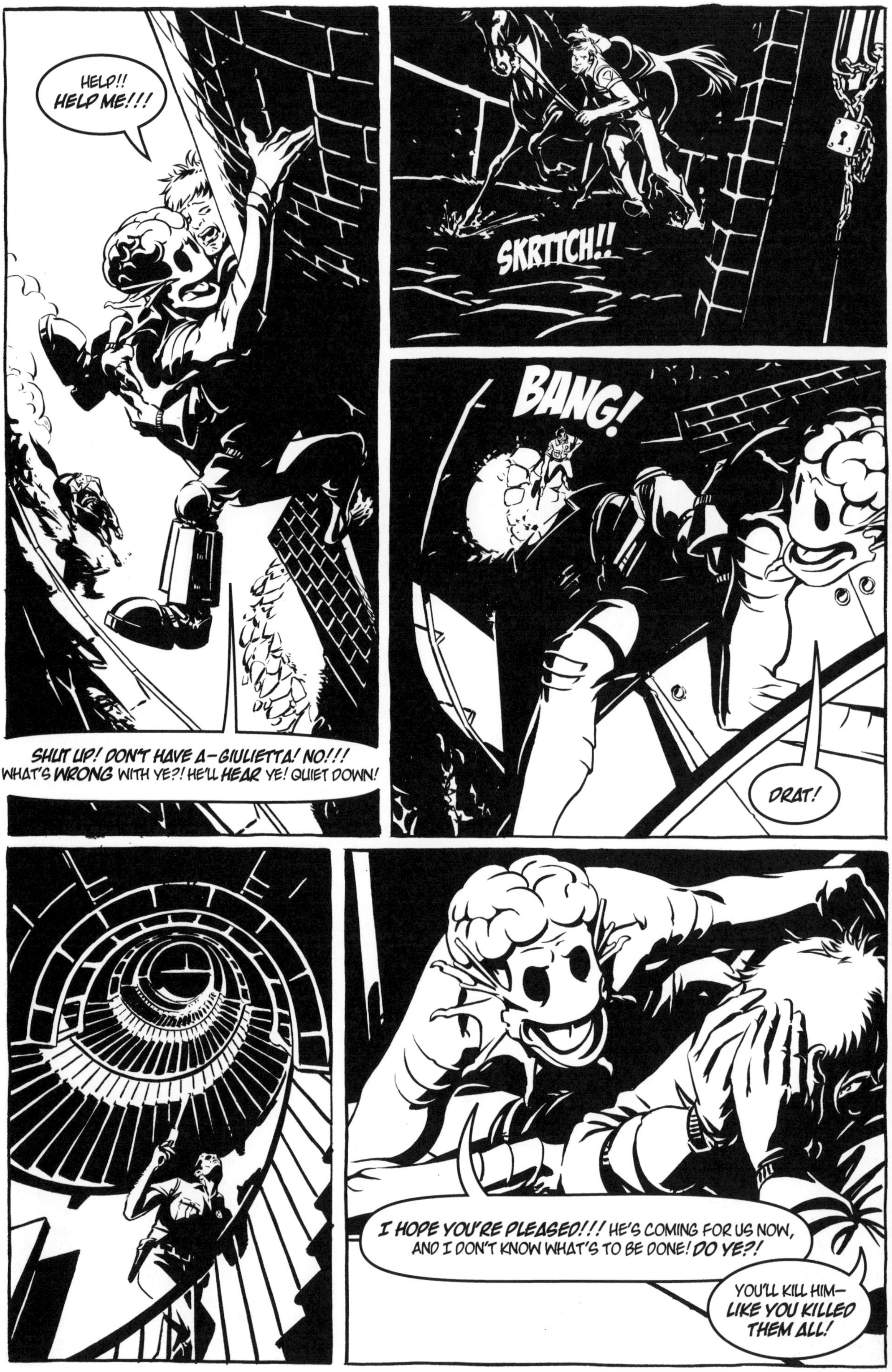
HELP!! HELP ME!!!
SKRTTCH!!
SHUT UP! DON'T HAVE A–GIULIETTA! NO!!! WHAT'S WRONG WITH YE?! HE'LL HEAR YE! QUIET DOWN!
BANG!
DRAT!
I HOPE YOU'RE PLEASED!!! HE'S COMING FOR US NOW, AND I DON'T KNOW WHAT'S TO BE DONE! DO YE?!
YOU'LL KILL HIM— LIKE YOU KILLED THEM ALL!

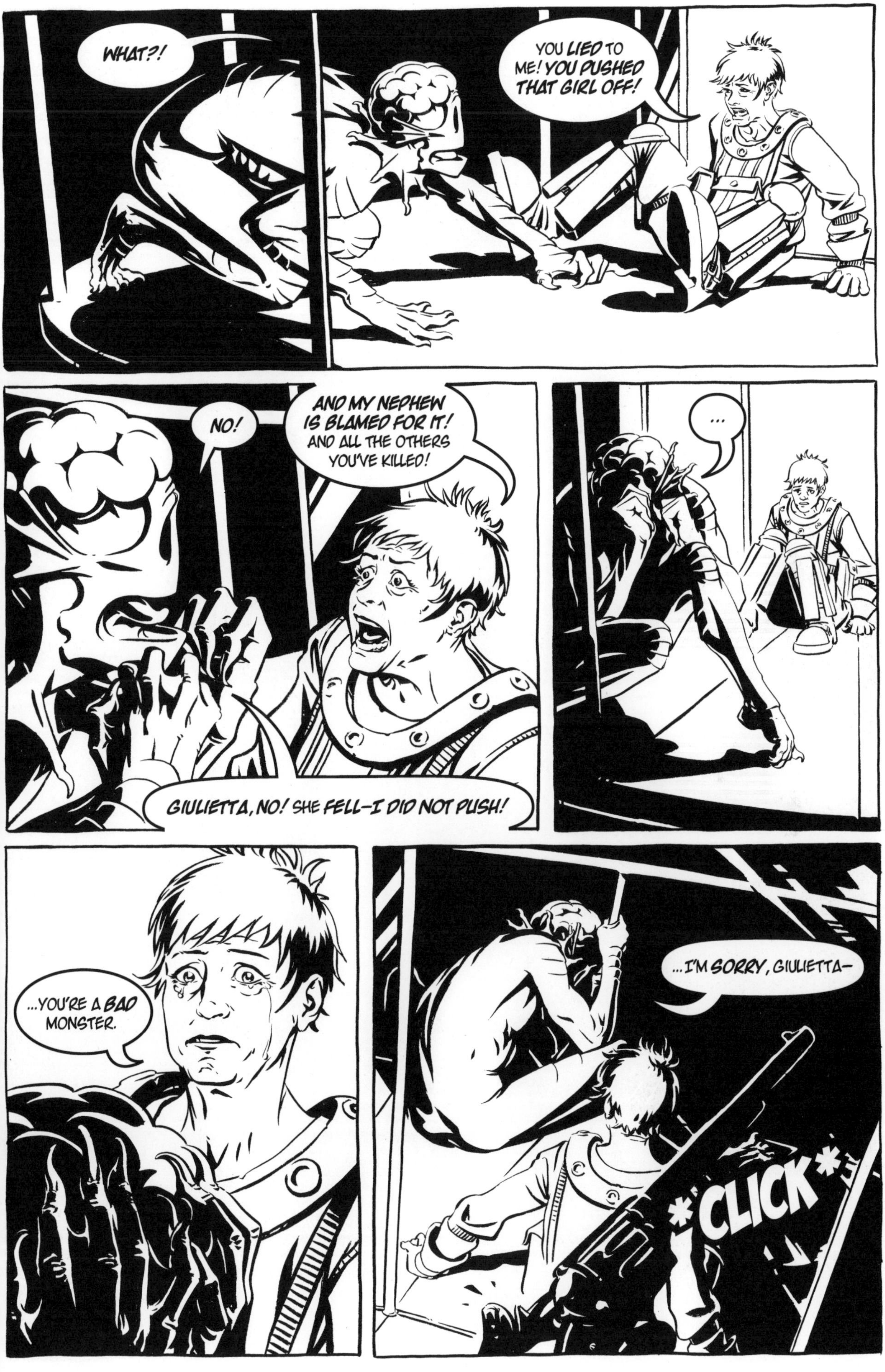
WHAT?!
YOU LIED TO ME! YOU PUSHED THAT GIRL OFF!
NO!
AND MY NEPHEW IS BLAMED FOR IT! AND ALL THE OTHERS YOU'VE KILLED!
GIULIETTA, NO! SHE FELL—I DID NOT PUSH!
...
...YOU'RE A BAD MONSTER.
...I'M SORRY, GIULIETTA—
CLICK

I'M SORRY–

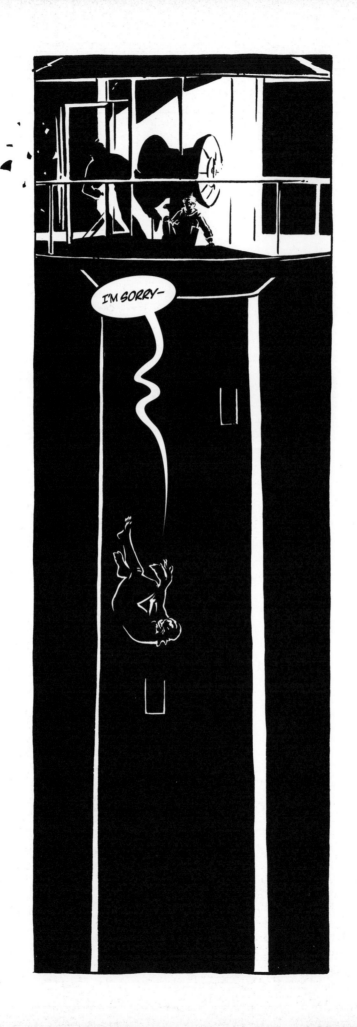

CHAPTER FIVE

IT'S OVER

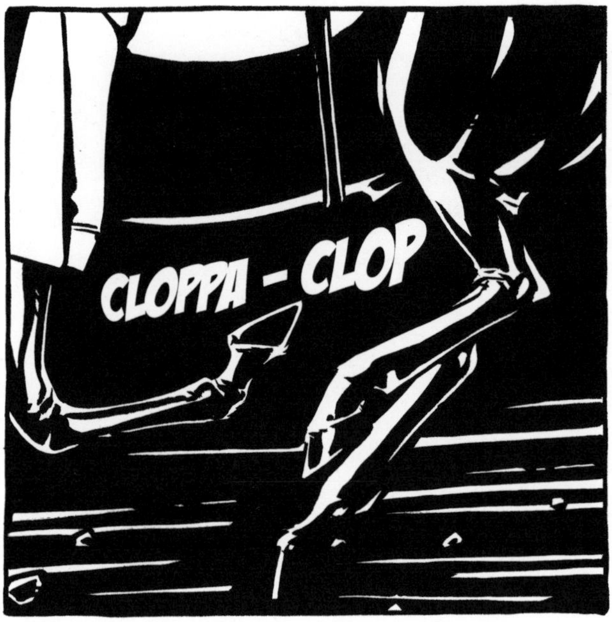
CLOPPA - CLOP

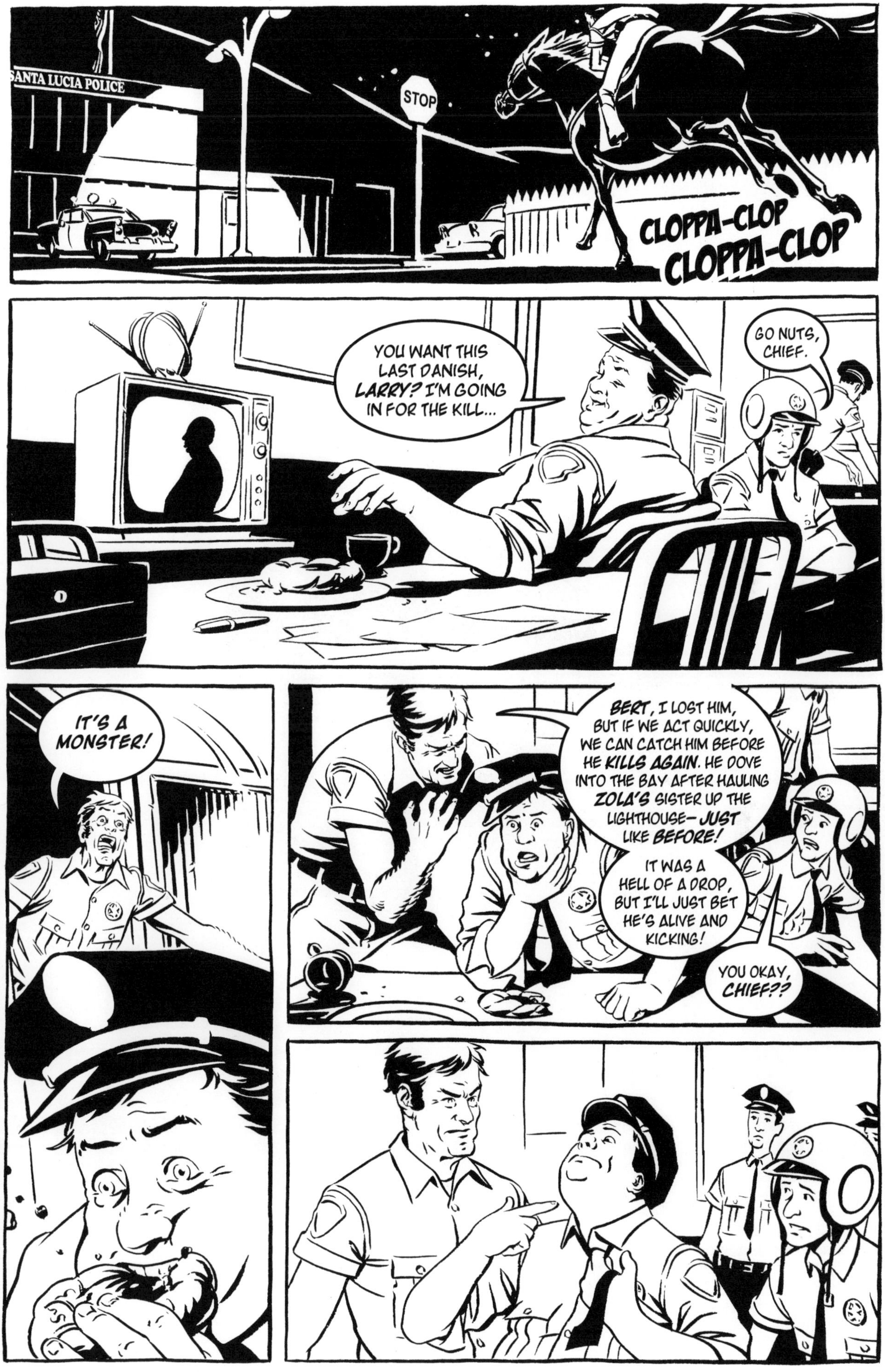
SANTA LUCIA POLICE
STOP
CLOPPA-CLOP
CLOPPA-CLOP
YOU WANT THIS LAST DANISH, LARRY? I'M GOING IN FOR THE KILL...
GO NUTS, CHIEF.
IT'S A MONSTER!
BERT, I LOST HIM, BUT IF WE ACT QUICKLY, WE CAN CATCH HIM BEFORE HE KILLS AGAIN. HE DOVE INTO THE BAY AFTER HAULING ZOLA'S SISTER UP THE LIGHTHOUSE– JUST LIKE BEFORE!
IT WAS A HELL OF A DROP, BUT I'LL JUST BET HE'S ALIVE AND KICKING!
YOU OKAY, CHIEF??

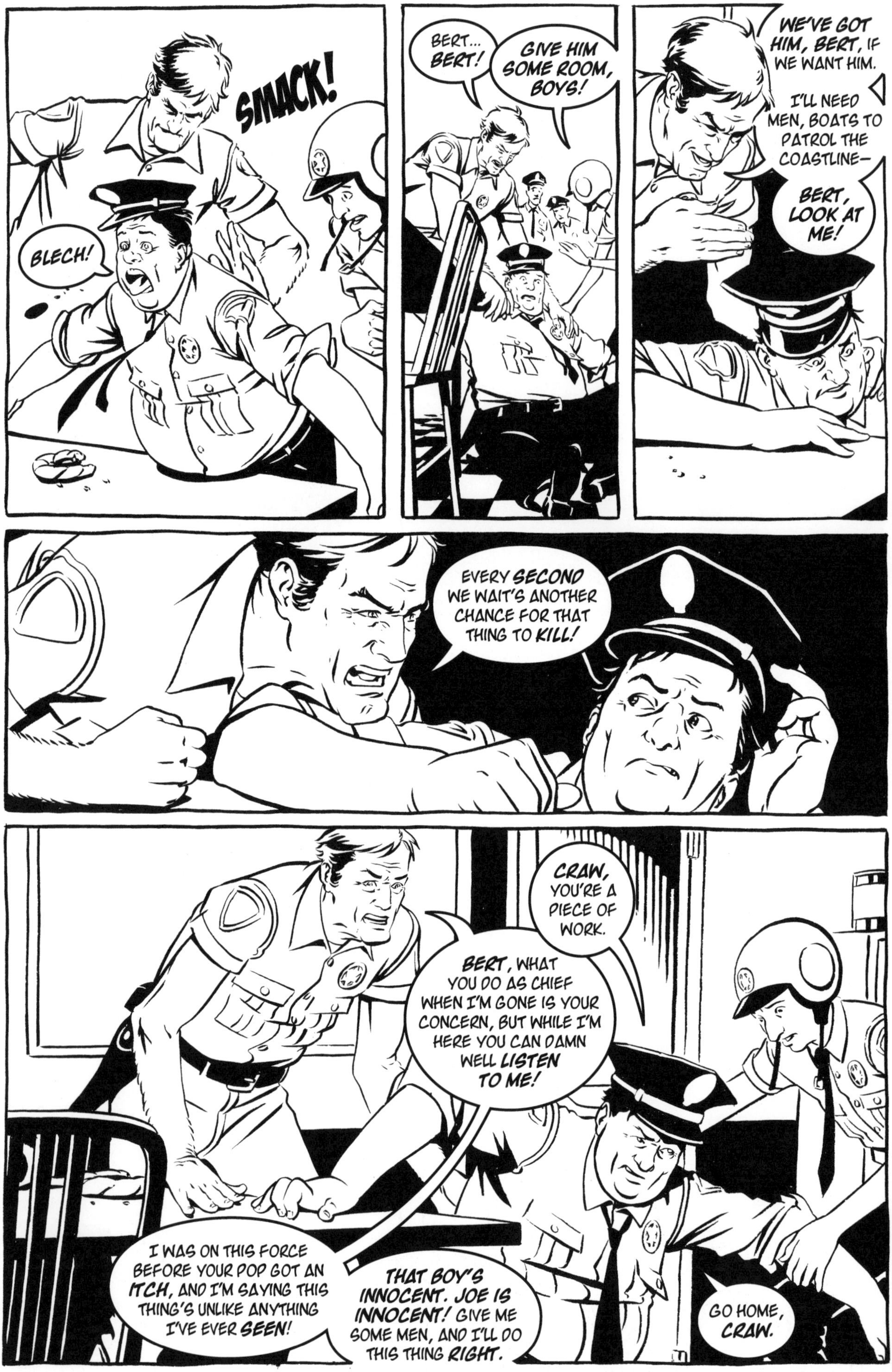
SMACK!
BLECH!
BERT... BERT!
GIVE HIM SOME ROOM, BOYS!
WE'VE GOT HIM, BERT, IF WE WANT HIM.
I'LL NEED MEN, BOATS TO PATROL THE COASTLINE—
BERT, LOOK AT ME!
EVERY SECOND WE WAIT'S ANOTHER CHANCE FOR THAT THING TO KILL!
CRAW, YOU'RE A PIECE OF WORK.
BERT, WHAT YOU DO AS CHIEF WHEN I'M GONE IS YOUR CONCERN, BUT WHILE I'M HERE YOU CAN DAMN WELL LISTEN TO ME!
I WAS ON THIS FORCE BEFORE YOUR POP GOT AN ITCH, AND I'M SAYING THIS THING'S UNLIKE ANYTHING I'VE EVER SEEN!
THAT BOY'S INNOCENT. JOE IS INNOCENT! GIVE ME SOME MEN, AND I'LL DO THIS THING RIGHT.
GO HOME, CRAW.

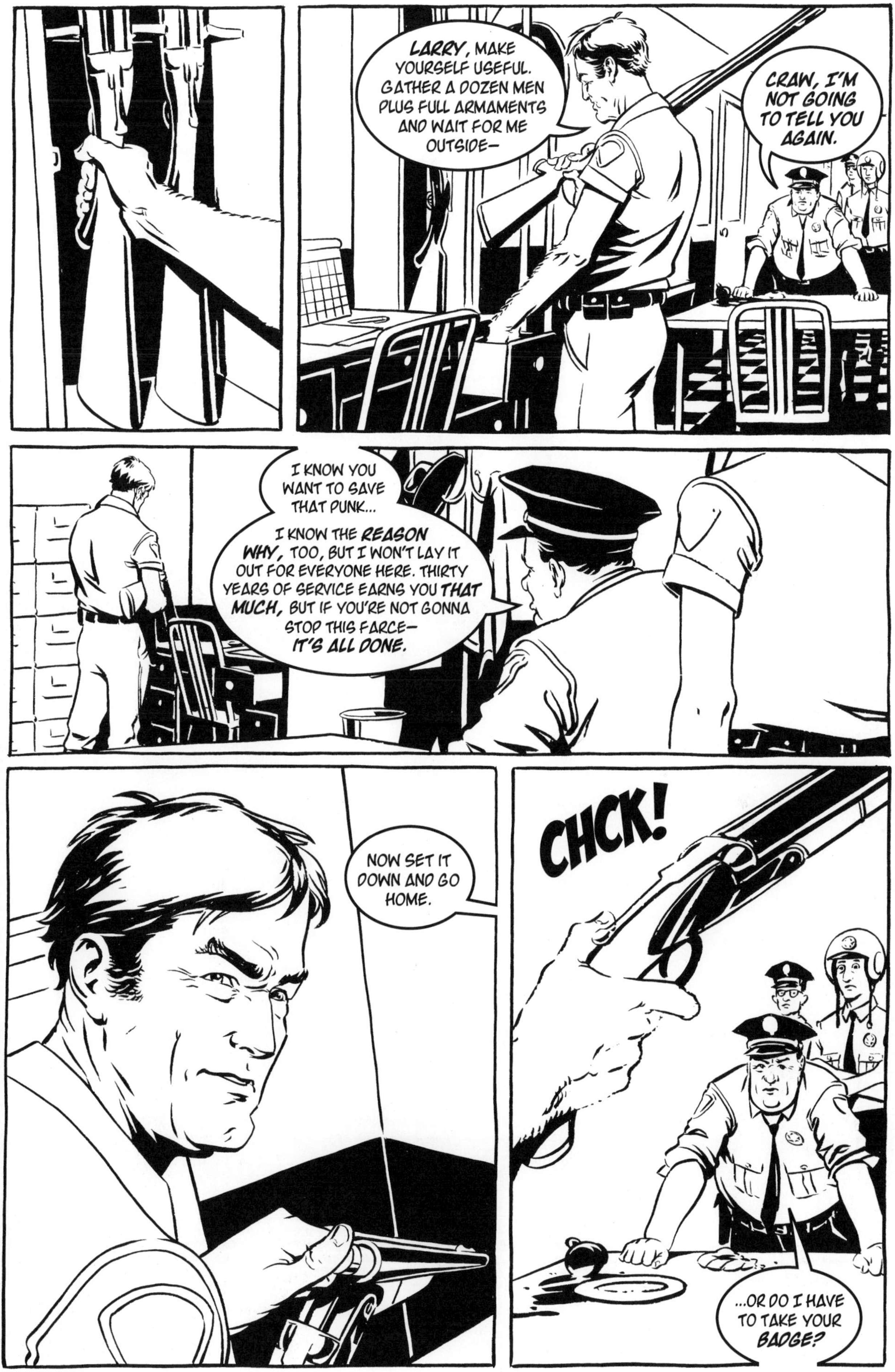
LARRY, MAKE YOURSELF USEFUL. GATHER A DOZEN MEN PLUS FULL ARMAMENTS AND WAIT FOR ME OUTSIDE—
CRAW, I'M NOT GOING TO TELL YOU AGAIN.
I KNOW YOU WANT TO SAVE THAT PUNK...
I KNOW THE REASON WHY, TOO, BUT I WON'T LAY IT OUT FOR EVERYONE HERE. THIRTY YEARS OF SERVICE EARNS YOU THAT MUCH, BUT IF YOU'RE NOT GONNA STOP THIS FARCE— IT'S ALL DONE.
NOW SET IT DOWN AND GO HOME.
CHCK!
...OR DO I HAVE TO TAKE YOUR BADGE?

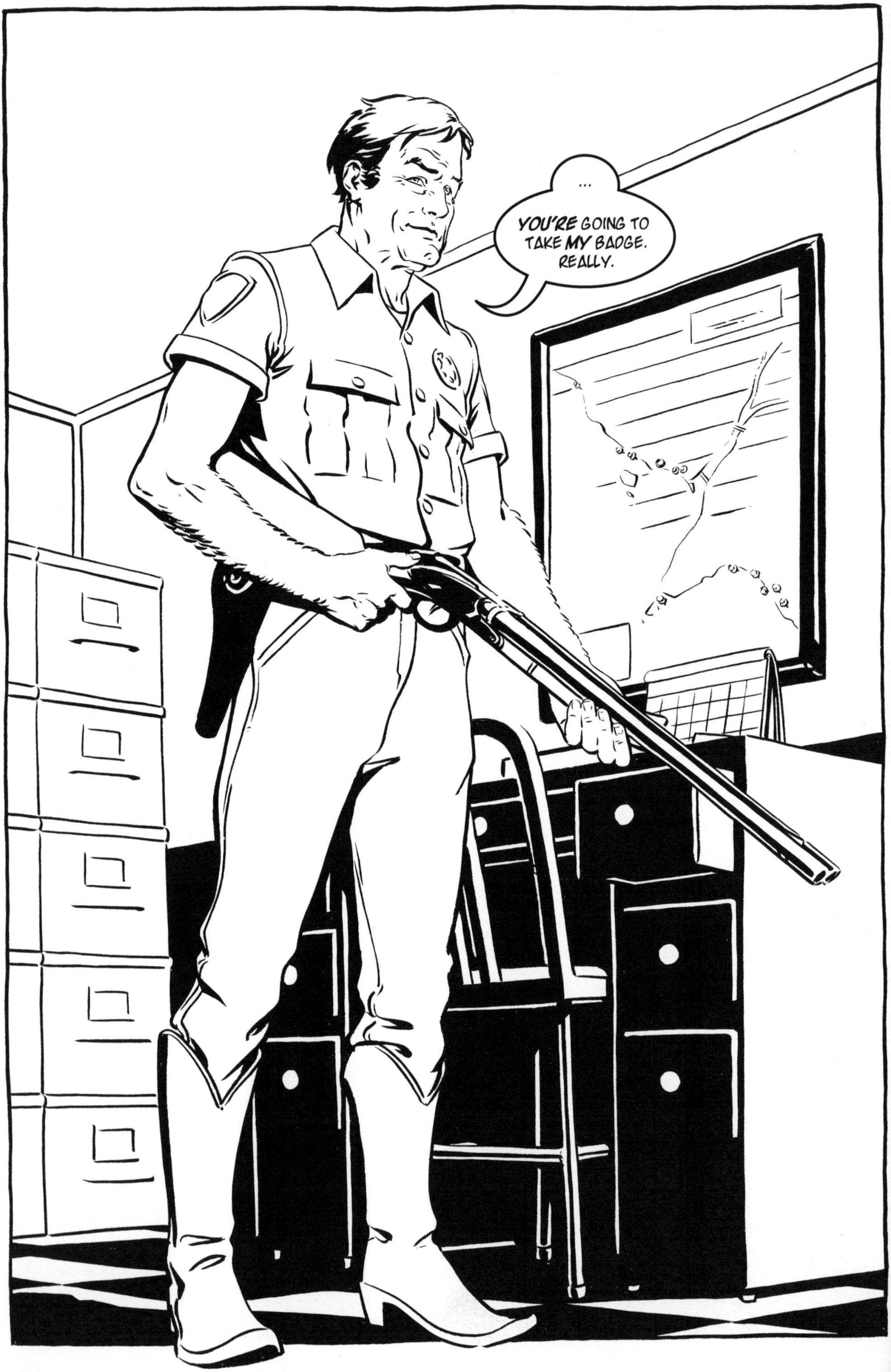
...
YOU'RE GOING TO TAKE MY BADGE. REALLY.

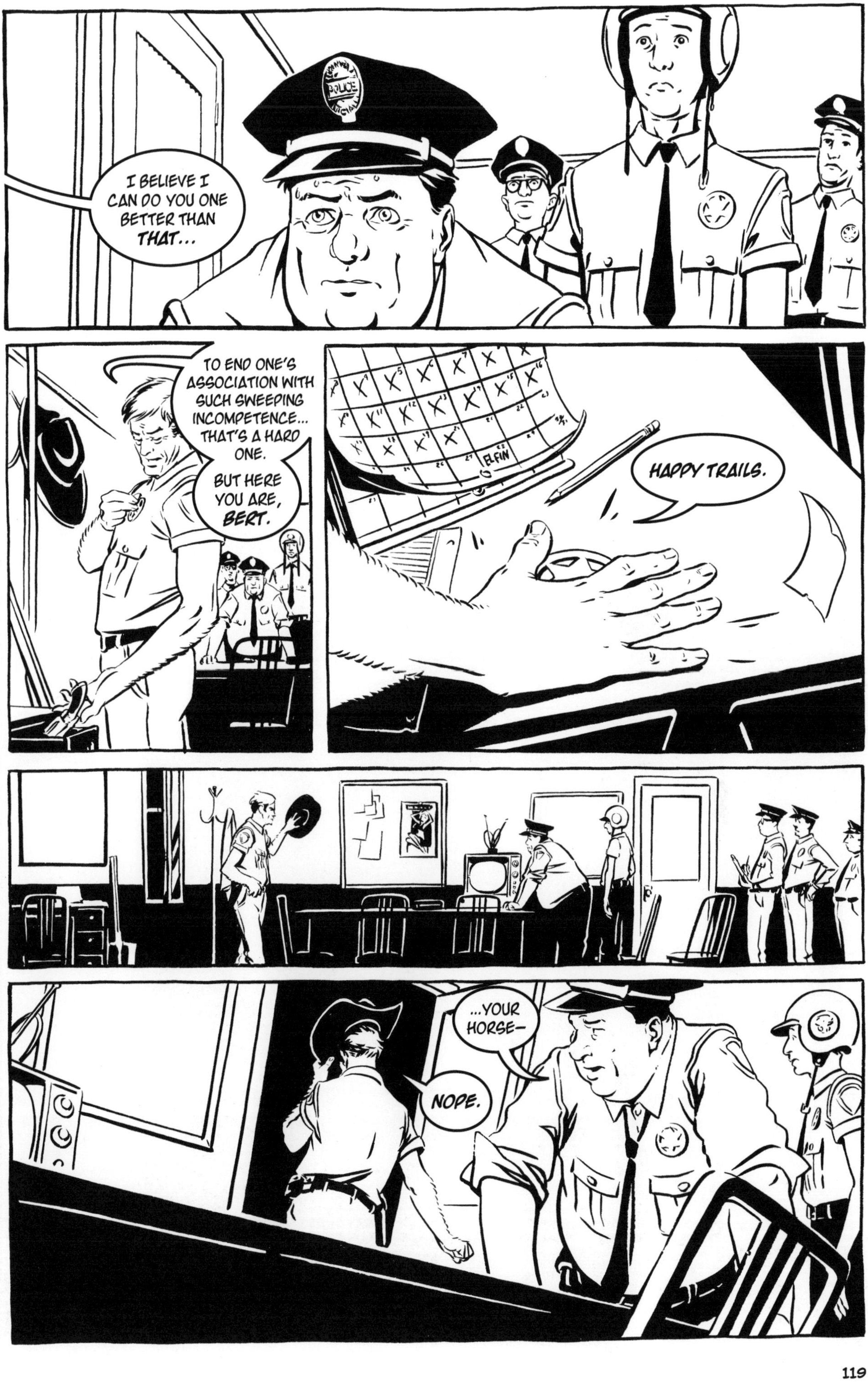
I BELIEVE I CAN DO YOU ONE BETTER THAN THAT...
TO END ONE'S ASSOCIATION WITH SUCH SWEEPING INCOMPETENCE... THAT'S A HARD ONE.
BUT HERE YOU ARE, BERT.
EL FIN
HAPPY TRAILS.
...YOUR HORSE-
NOPE.

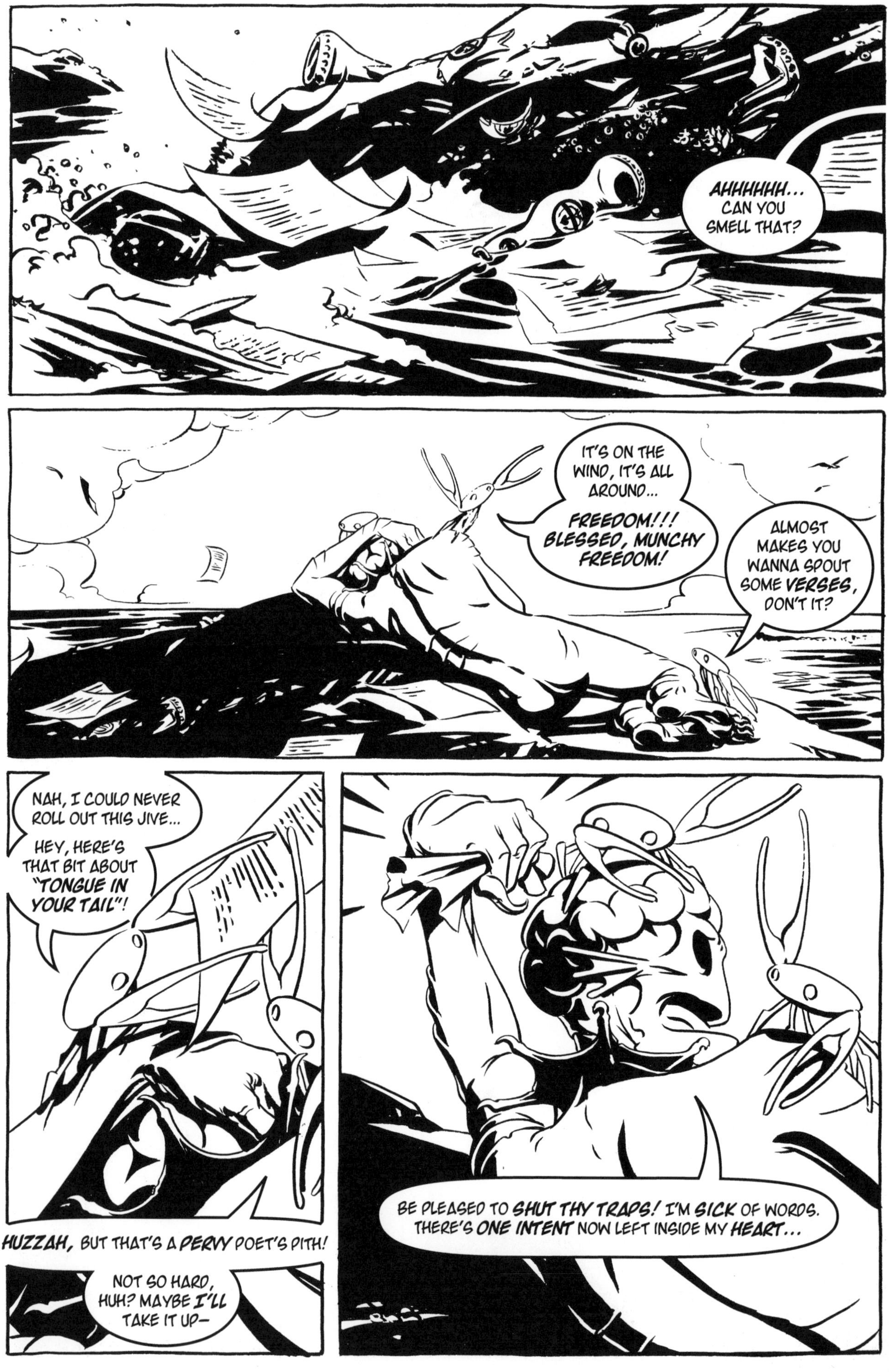

AHHHHHH... CAN YOU SMELL THAT?
IT'S ON THE WIND, IT'S ALL AROUND... FREEDOM!!! BLESSED, MUNCHY FREEDOM!
ALMOST MAKES YOU WANNA SPOUT SOME VERSES, DON'T IT?
NAH, I COULD NEVER ROLL OUT THIS JIVE...
HEY, HERE'S THAT BIT ABOUT "TONGUE IN YOUR TAIL"!
HUZZAH, BUT THAT'S A PERVY POET'S PITH!
NOT SO HARD, HUH? MAYBE I'LL TAKE IT UP—
BE PLEASED TO SHUT THY TRAPS! I'M SICK OF WORDS. THERE'S ONE INTENT NOW LEFT INSIDE MY HEART...

AND THAT'S TO *FEED* AS NE'ER WAS *FED BEFORE,* UPON THE LEWD: *CONSISTENT* IN THEIR *LUST, REQUITED* IN THEIR BAWDY LOVE AS NO DESIRE, PURE OR ARTFUL, EVER IS.

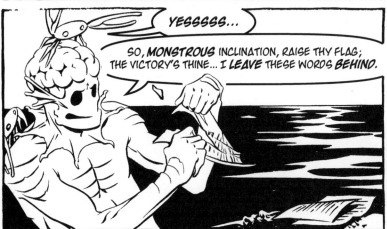

YESSSSS...

SO, *MONSTROUS* INCLINATION, RAISE THY FLAG; THE VICTORY'S THINE... I *LEAVE* THESE WORDS *BEHIND.*

SPLOOSH!

WHERE LIES THE TRACK OF MINDS *DERAILED AND RANK?* WHERE LIES THAT *ROILING* LOCOMOTIVE BLOOD?

WHERE LIES THAT *SIEVE OF LUST,* FROM WHICH I'D *DRINK—*

I THOUGHT YOU WAS *SICK* OF WORDS.

121

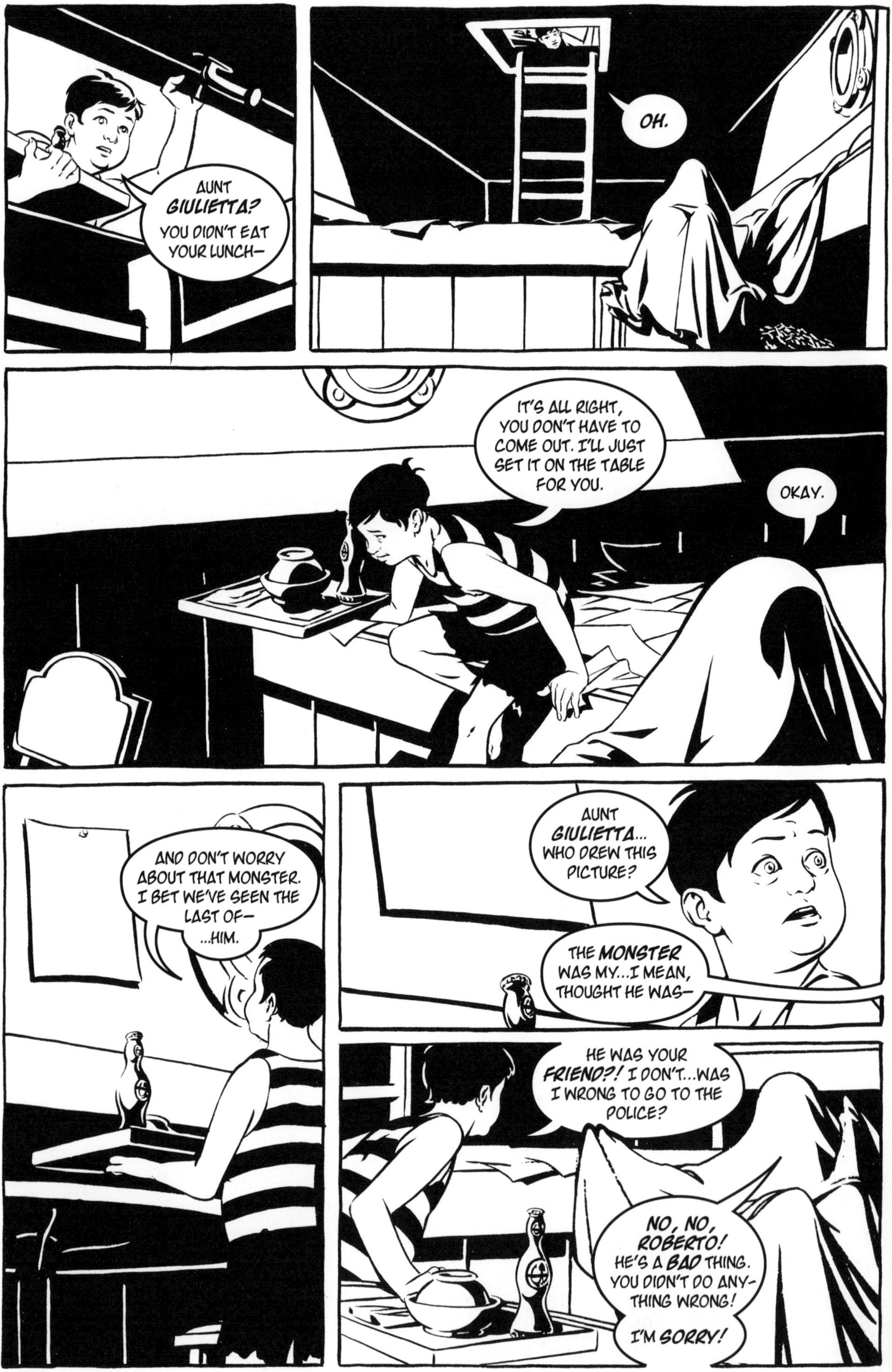
AUNT GIULIETTA? YOU DIDN'T EAT YOUR LUNCH—
OH.
IT'S ALL RIGHT, YOU DON'T HAVE TO COME OUT. I'LL JUST SET IT ON THE TABLE FOR YOU.
OKAY.
AND DON'T WORRY ABOUT THAT MONSTER. I BET WE'VE SEEN THE LAST OF—
...HIM.
AUNT GIULIETTA... WHO DREW THIS PICTURE?
THE MONSTER WAS MY...I MEAN, THOUGHT HE WAS—
HE WAS YOUR FRIEND?! I DON'T...WAS I WRONG TO GO TO THE POLICE?
NO, NO, ROBERTO! HE'S A BAD THING. YOU DIDN'T DO ANYTHING WRONG!
I'M SORRY!

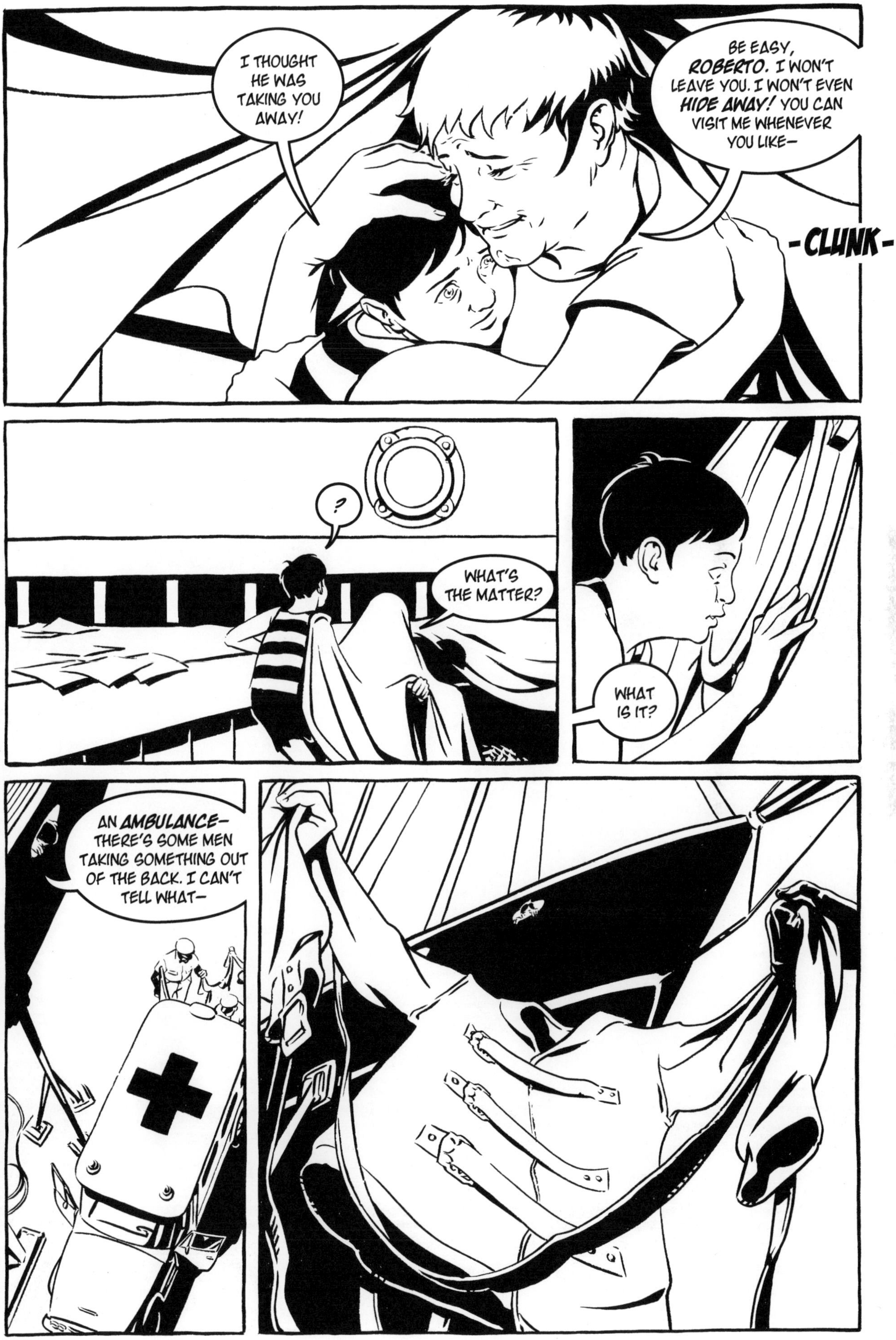
I THOUGHT HE WAS TAKING YOU AWAY!
BE EASY, ROBERTO. I WON'T LEAVE YOU. I WON'T EVEN HIDE AWAY! YOU CAN VISIT ME WHENEVER YOU LIKE—
-CLUNK-
?
WHAT'S THE MATTER?
WHAT IS IT?
AN AMBULANCE— THERE'S SOME MEN TAKING SOMETHING OUT OF THE BACK. I CAN'T TELL WHAT—

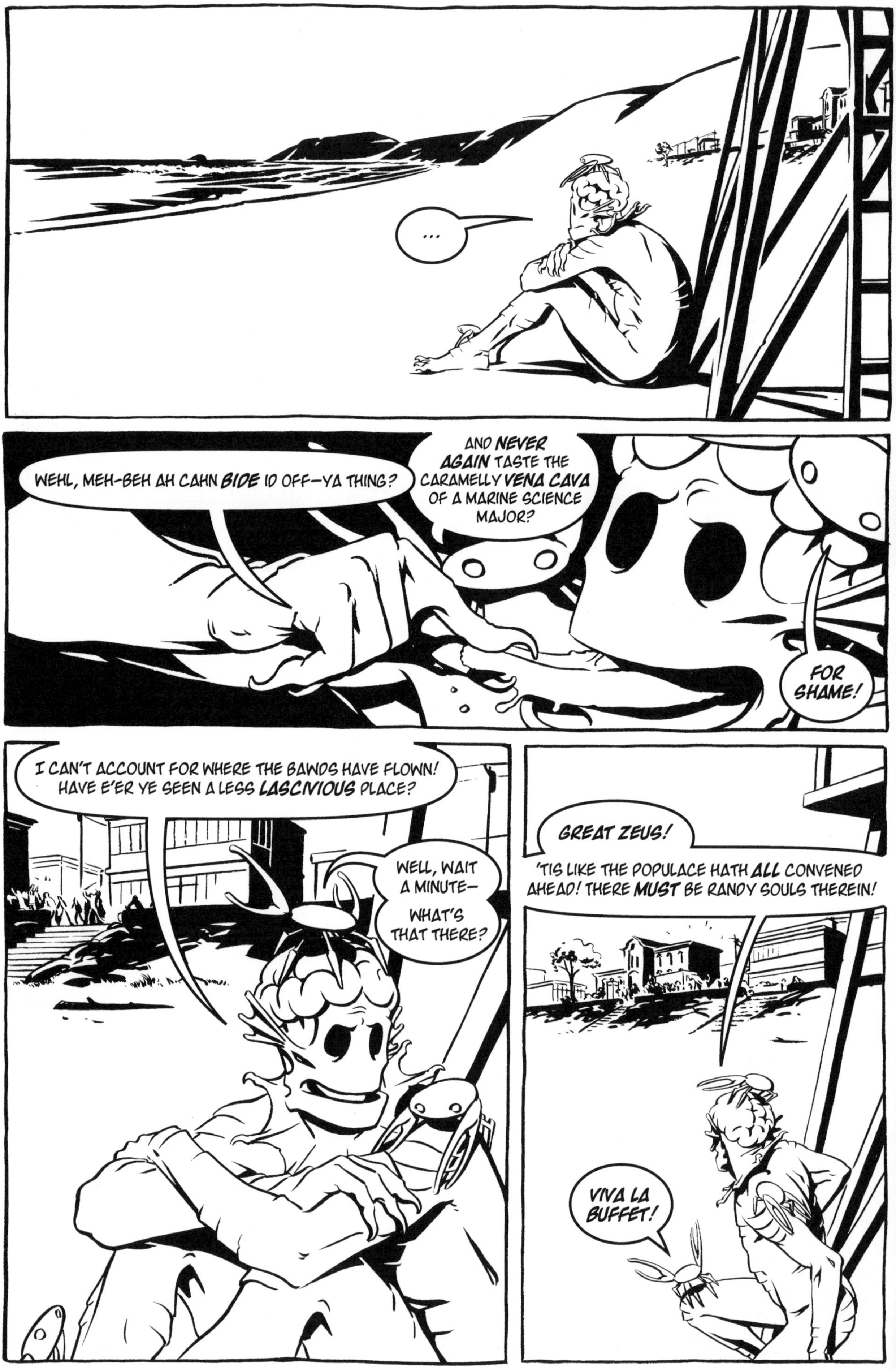
...
WEHL, MEH-BEH AH CAHN BIDE ID OFF—YA THING?
AND NEVER AGAIN TASTE THE CARAMELLY VENA CAVA OF A MARINE SCIENCE MAJOR?
FOR SHAME!
I CAN'T ACCOUNT FOR WHERE THE BAWDS HAVE FLOWN! HAVE E'ER YE SEEN A LESS LASCIVIOUS PLACE?
WELL, WAIT A MINUTE—
WHAT'S THAT THERE?
GREAT ZEUS!
'TIS LIKE THE POPULACE HATH ALL CONVENED AHEAD! THERE MUST BE RANDY SOULS THEREIN!
VIVA LA BUFFET!

GET OUT OF OUR TOWN!

HARLOT!!

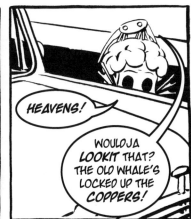

HEAVENS!

WOULDJA LOOKIT THAT? THE OLD WHALE'S LOCKED UP THE COPPERS!

THEY'RE NOT TAKING MY BOY!!

YOU'RE SCUM! YOU'RE SCUM, AND YOUR CHILDREN ARE SCUM!

EYE FOR AN EYE!

YOU CAN ALL ROT! YOUR HEARTS ARE DEAD ALREADY!

COME TAKE A KNIFE IN YOUR DEAD HEARTS! SONO PRONTA, DEMONI!!

COME TAKE IT!!

OOF! DAMN SHAME THIS KILLIN'S NOT PUTTING DINNER ON THE TABLE. FOR AN UGLY CRITTER, THAT GAL PUT OUT SOME KINDA SIGNAL!

BE SILENT, CRAB!...I'VE NOT THE TASTE FOR THIS.

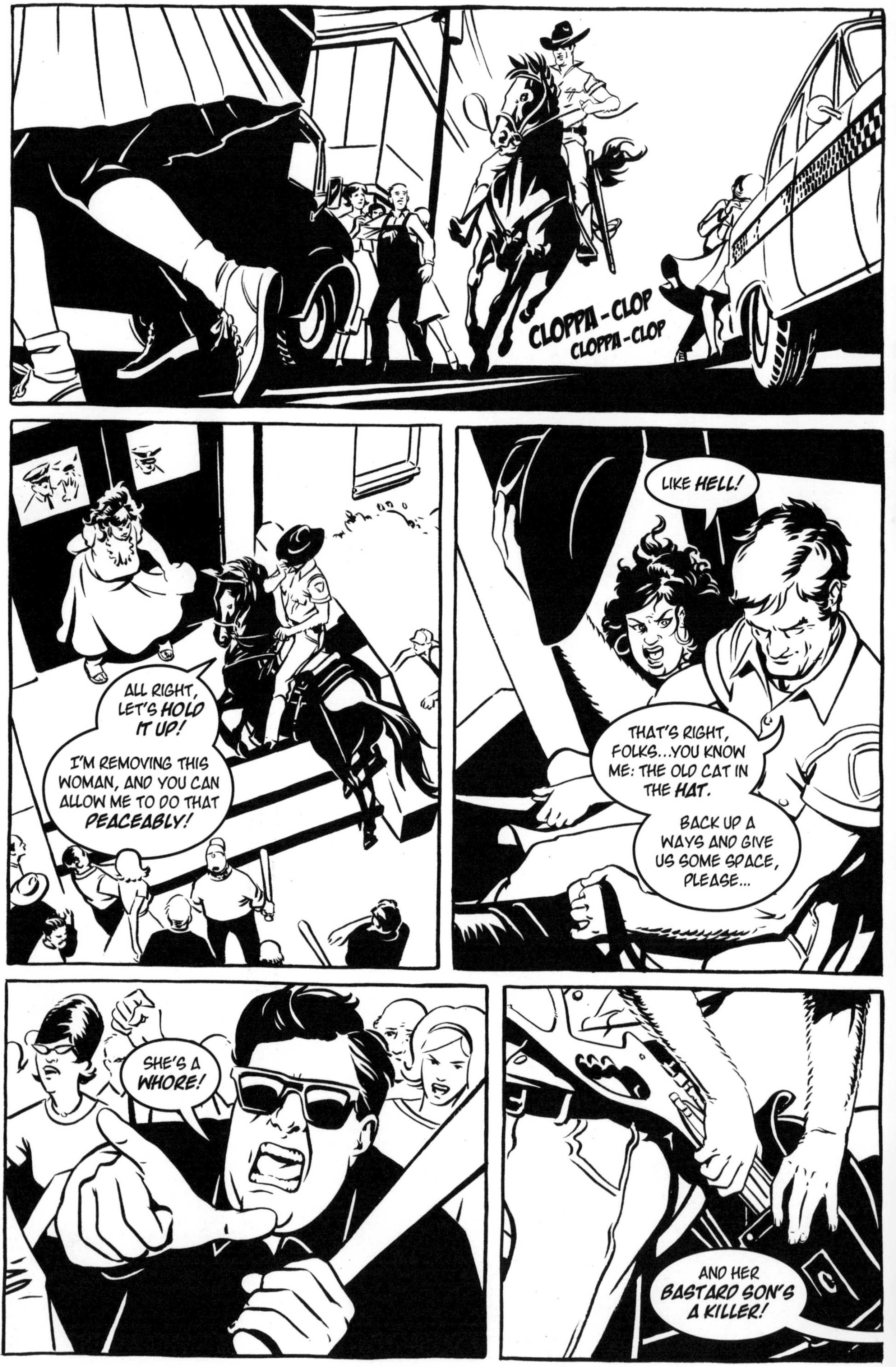
CLOPPA-CLOP
CLOPPA-CLOP
ALL RIGHT, LET'S HOLD IT UP!
I'M REMOVING THIS WOMAN, AND YOU CAN ALLOW ME TO DO THAT PEACEABLY!
LIKE HELL!
THAT'S RIGHT, FOLKS...YOU KNOW ME: THE OLD CAT IN THE HAT.
BACK UP A WAYS AND GIVE US SOME SPACE, PLEASE...
SHE'S A WHORE!
AND HER BASTARD SON'S A KILLER!

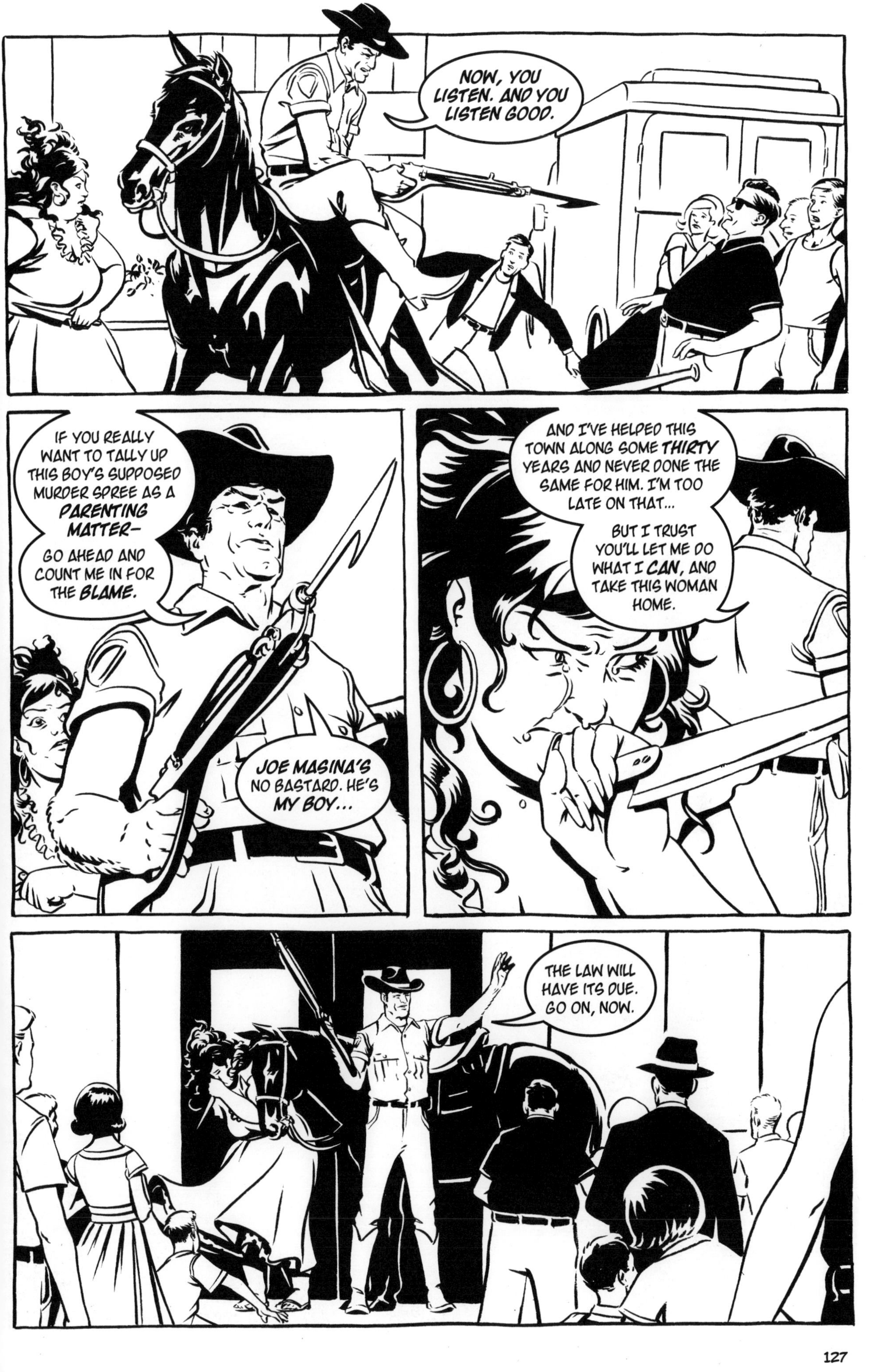
NOW, YOU LISTEN. AND YOU LISTEN GOOD.
IF YOU REALLY WANT TO TALLY UP THIS BOY'S SUPPOSED MURDER SPREE AS A PARENTING MATTER—
GO AHEAD AND COUNT ME IN FOR THE BLAME.
JOE MASINA'S NO BASTARD. HE'S MY BOY...
AND I'VE HELPED THIS TOWN ALONG SOME THIRTY YEARS AND NEVER DONE THE SAME FOR HIM. I'M TOO LATE ON THAT...
BUT I TRUST YOU'LL LET ME DO WHAT I CAN, AND TAKE THIS WOMAN HOME.
THE LAW WILL HAVE ITS DUE. GO ON, NOW.

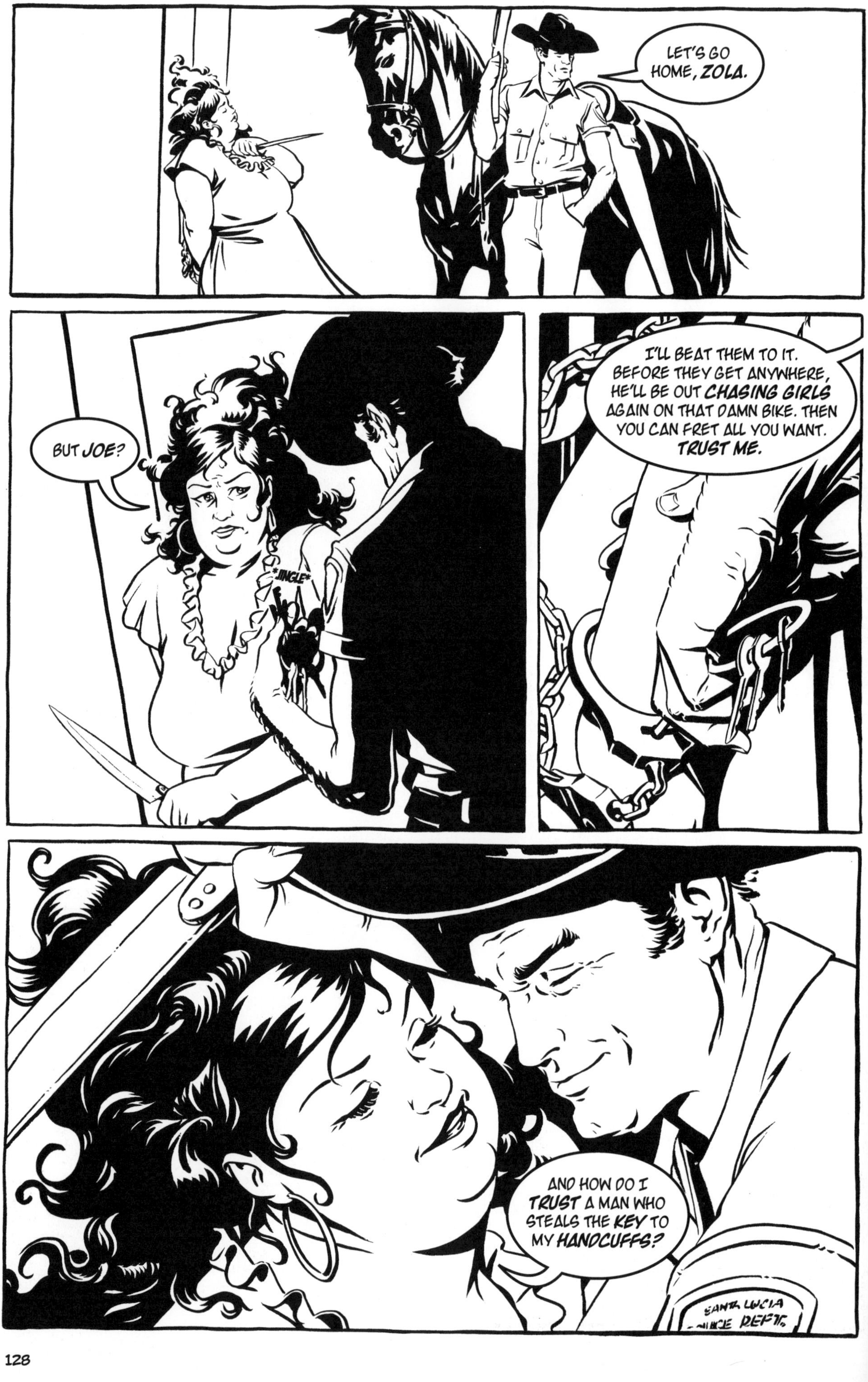
LET'S GO HOME, ZOLA.
BUT JOE?
JINGLE
I'LL BEAT THEM TO IT. BEFORE THEY GET ANYWHERE, HE'LL BE OUT CHASING GIRLS AGAIN ON THAT DAMN BIKE. THEN YOU CAN FRET ALL YOU WANT. TRUST ME.
AND HOW DO I TRUST A MAN WHO STEALS THE KEY TO MY HANDCUFFS?
SANTA LUCIA

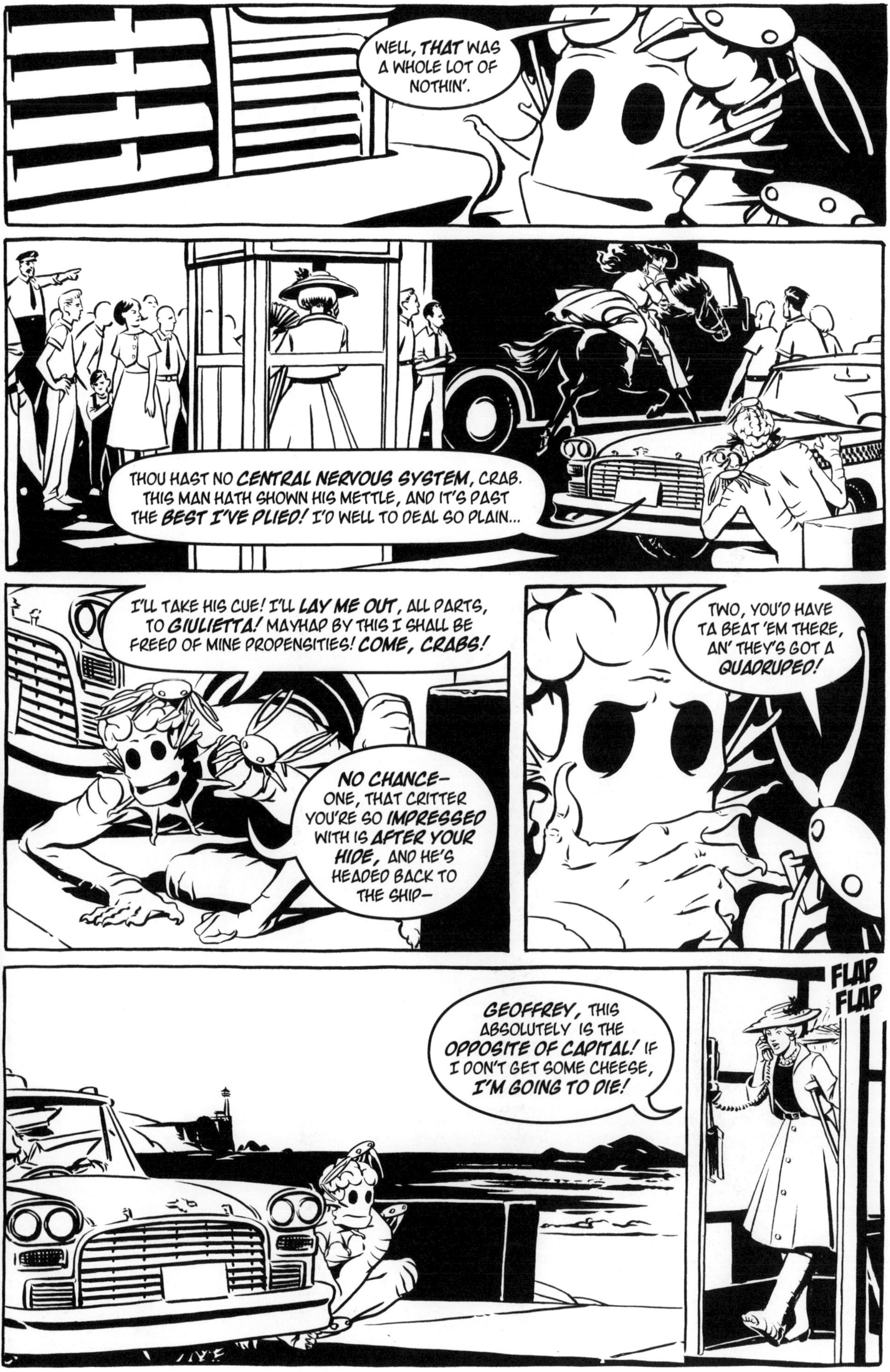
WELL, THAT WAS A WHOLE LOT OF NOTHIN'.
THOU HAST NO CENTRAL NERVOUS SYSTEM, CRAB. THIS MAN HATH SHOWN HIS METTLE, AND IT'S PAST THE BEST I'VE PLIED! I'D WELL TO DEAL SO PLAIN...
I'LL TAKE HIS CUE! I'LL LAY ME OUT, ALL PARTS, TO GIULIETTA! MAYHAP BY THIS I SHALL BE FREED OF MINE PROPENSITIES! COME, CRABS!
NO CHANCE— ONE, THAT CRITTER YOU'RE SO IMPRESSED WITH IS AFTER YOUR HIDE, AND HE'S HEADED BACK TO THE SHIP—
TWO, YOU'D HAVE TA BEAT 'EM THERE, AN' THEY'S GOT A QUADRUPED!
FLAP FLAP
GEOFFREY, THIS ABSOLUTELY IS THE OPPOSITE OF CAPITAL! IF I DON'T GET SOME CHEESE, I'M GOING TO DIE!

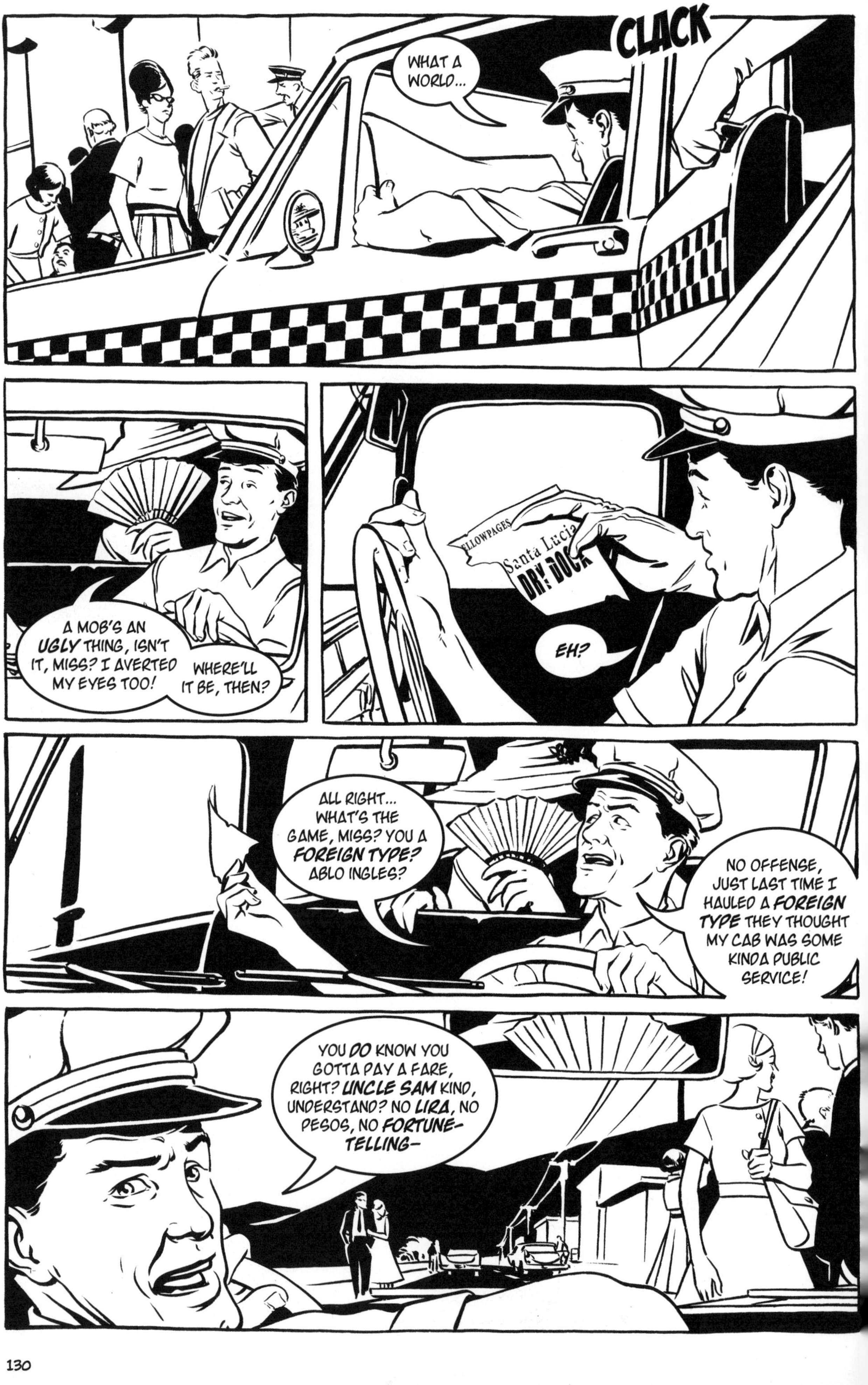
CLACK
WHAT A WORLD...
A MOB'S AN UGLY THING, ISN'T IT, MISS? I AVERTED MY EYES TOO!
WHERE'LL IT BE, THEN?
Santa Lucia
DRY DOCK
EH?
ALL RIGHT... WHAT'S THE GAME, MISS? YOU A FOREIGN TYPE? ABLO INGLES?
NO OFFENSE, JUST LAST TIME I HAULED A FOREIGN TYPE THEY THOUGHT MY CAB WAS SOME KINDA PUBLIC SERVICE!
YOU DO KNOW YOU GOTTA PAY A FARE, RIGHT? UNCLE SAM KIND, UNDERSTAND? NO LIRA, NO PESOS, NO FORTUNE-TELLING–

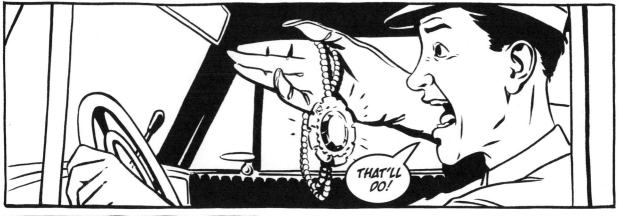

THAT'LL DO!

SKREEEEEEEEEEE

VSHOOOM

WHO SAYS WE CAN'T BEAT QUADRUPEDS?!

GOLLY! THAT'S A LOVELY DRESS, MISS! YOU EVER NEED A LIFT AGAIN, YOU GOT PLENTY OF CREDIT WITH ME!

WHAT A WORLD!

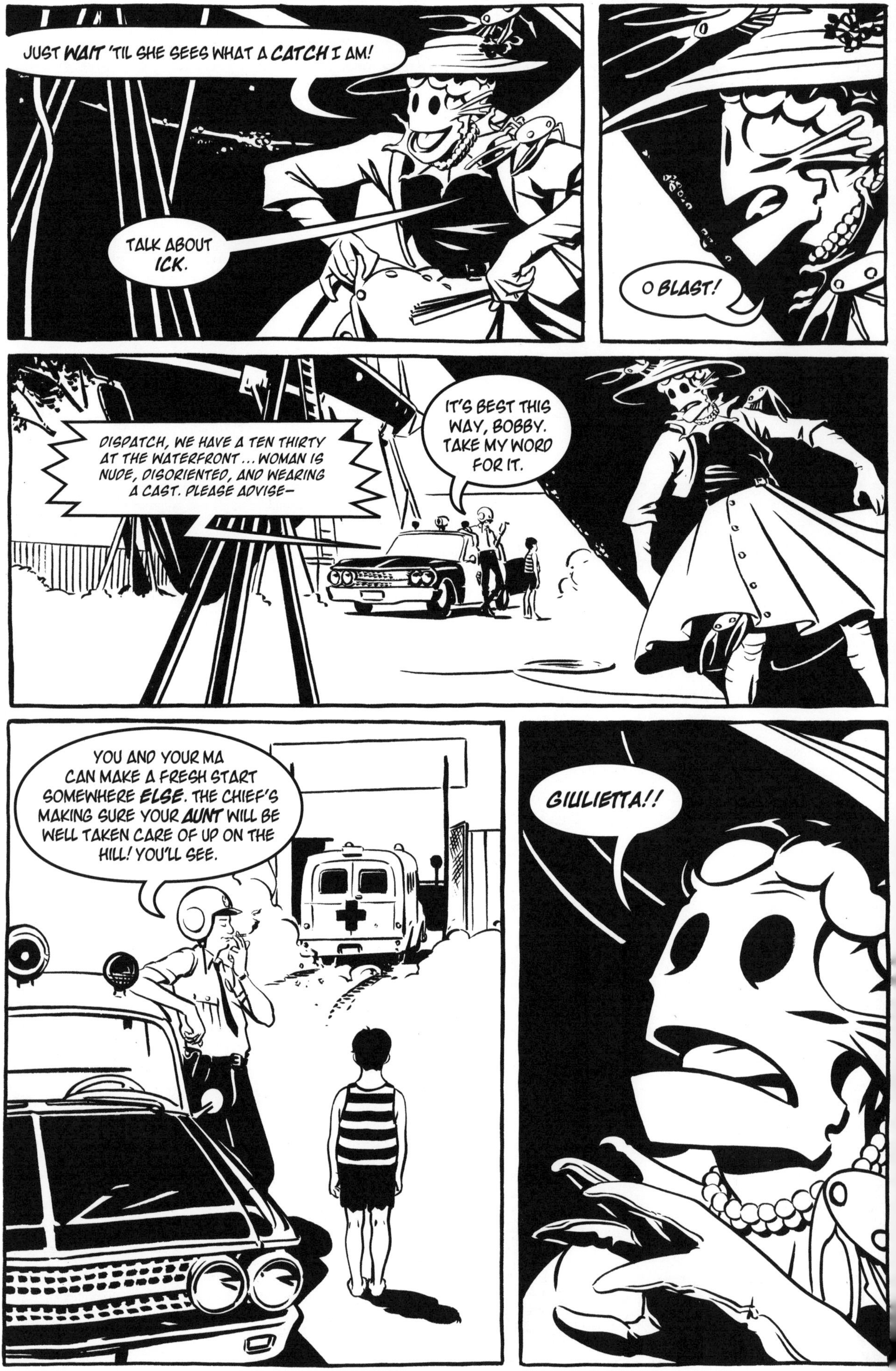
JUST WAIT 'TIL SHE SEES WHAT A CATCH I AM!
TALK ABOUT ICK.
O BLAST!
IT'S BEST THIS WAY, BOBBY. TAKE MY WORD FOR IT.
DISPATCH, WE HAVE A TEN THIRTY AT THE WATERFRONT... WOMAN IS NUDE, DISORIENTED, AND WEARING A CAST. PLEASE ADVISE–
YOU AND YOUR MA CAN MAKE A FRESH START SOMEWHERE ELSE. THE CHIEF'S MAKING SURE YOUR AUNT WILL BE WELL TAKEN CARE OF UP ON THE HILL! YOU'LL SEE.
GIULIETTA!!

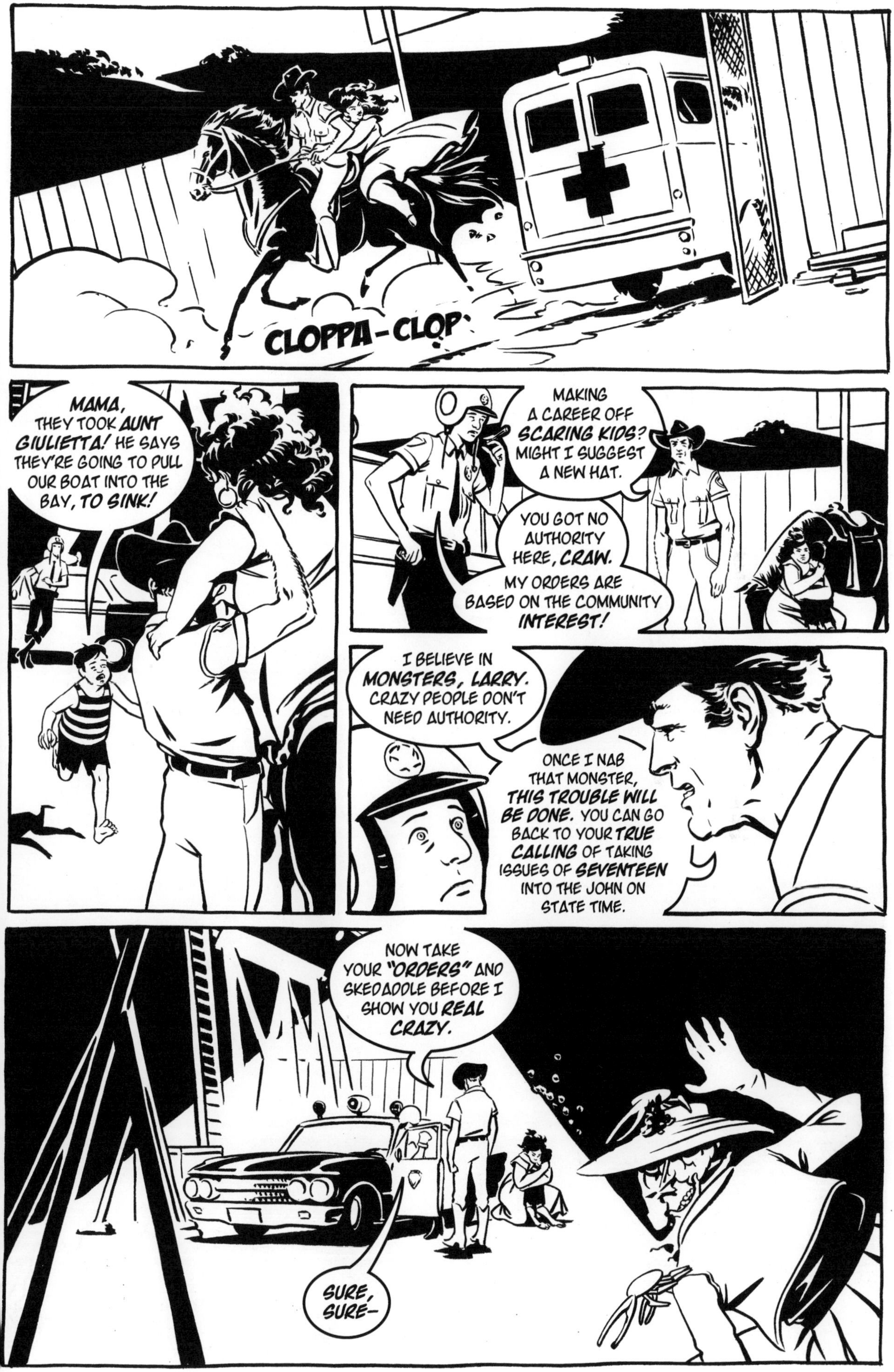
CLOPPA-CLOP
MAMA, THEY TOOK AUNT GIULIETTA! HE SAYS THEY'RE GOING TO PULL OUR BOAT INTO THE BAY, TO SINK!
MAKING A CAREER OFF SCARING KIDS? MIGHT I SUGGEST A NEW HAT.
YOU GOT NO AUTHORITY HERE, CRAW.
MY ORDERS ARE BASED ON THE COMMUNITY INTEREST!
I BELIEVE IN MONSTERS, LARRY. CRAZY PEOPLE DON'T NEED AUTHORITY.
ONCE I NAB THAT MONSTER, THIS TROUBLE WILL BE DONE. YOU CAN GO BACK TO YOUR TRUE CALLING OF TAKING ISSUES OF SEVENTEEN INTO THE JOHN ON STATE TIME.
NOW TAKE YOUR "ORDERS" AND SKEDADDLE BEFORE I SHOW YOU REAL CRAZY.
SURE, SURE-

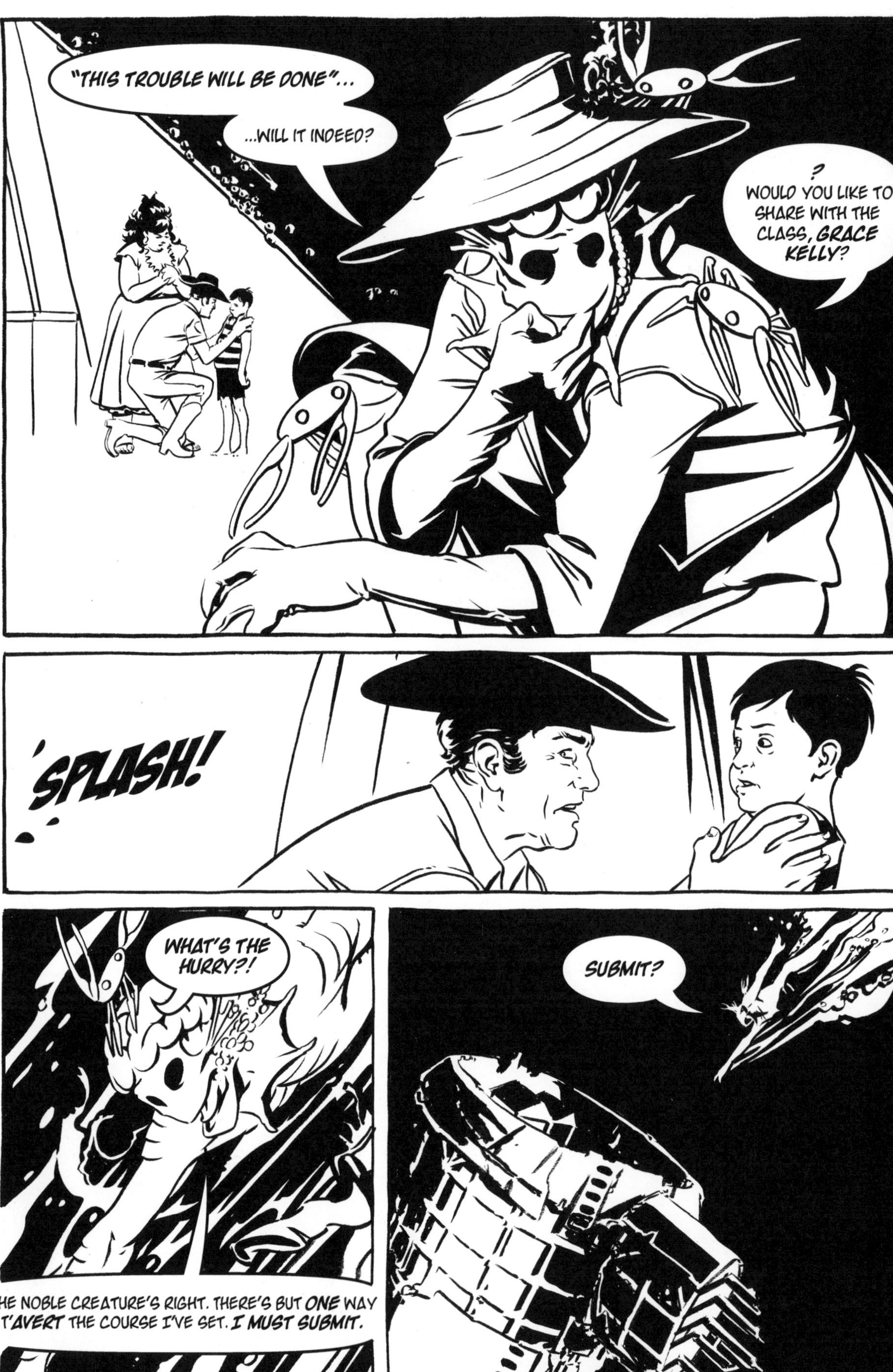

"THIS TROUBLE WILL BE DONE"...
...WILL IT INDEED?
? WOULD YOU LIKE TO SHARE WITH THE CLASS, GRACE KELLY?
SPLASH!
WHAT'S THE HURRY?!
THE NOBLE CREATURE'S RIGHT. THERE'S BUT ONE WAY T'AVERT THE COURSE I'VE SET. I MUST SUBMIT.
SUBMIT?

BUT I'VE ONE CHANCE TO ACT FOR THE IDEAL...

I THOUGHT I'D SAVE MYSELF FROM MONSTERS' WAYS. I'VE **SWUM ENOUGH** TO SEE THAT SHALL NOT **BE**...

HOORAH TO THAT!

TO **PLUMB THE TRENCH**, RETRIEVE MY CHEST OF SPOILS, AND TURN ME IN TO THE AUTHORITIES!

HEH.

HAW. HAW. HAHA!

EH-HAH, HEH...

...HAHA! AHAHAHA HAHA-HA HAHA!

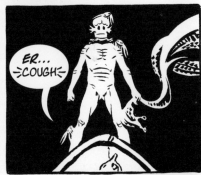
ER... =COUGH=

YOU'RE *SERIOUS?*

...SO IF YOU MAKE IT *BACK* FROM BELOW, YOU'LL TURN YOURSELF IN, AN' BE A *MARTYR* TO A BUNCH OF *FAST FOOD?*

WHY DON'T YA JUST SKIP AIRING THE DIRTY LAUNDRY AND TURN YOURSELF IN NOW, IF ALL YA WANT'S A *DEATH SENTENCE?*

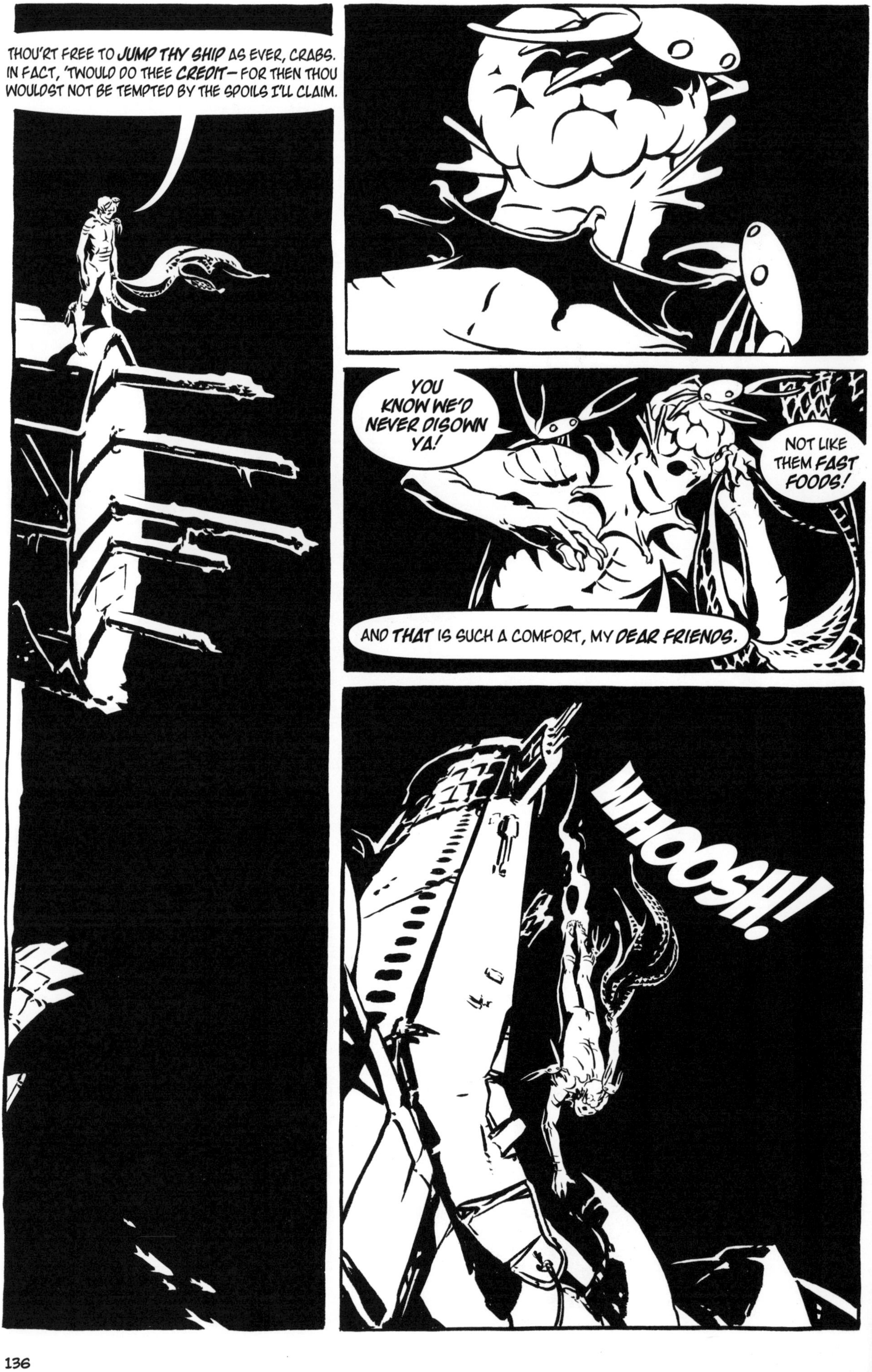
THOU'RT FREE TO JUMP THY SHIP AS EVER, CRABS. IN FACT, 'TWOULD DO THEE CREDIT— FOR THEN THOU WOULDST NOT BE TEMPTED BY THE SPOILS I'LL CLAIM.
YOU KNOW WE'D NEVER DISOWN YA!
NOT LIKE THEM FAST FOODS!
AND THAT IS SUCH A COMFORT, MY DEAR FRIENDS.
WHOOSH!!

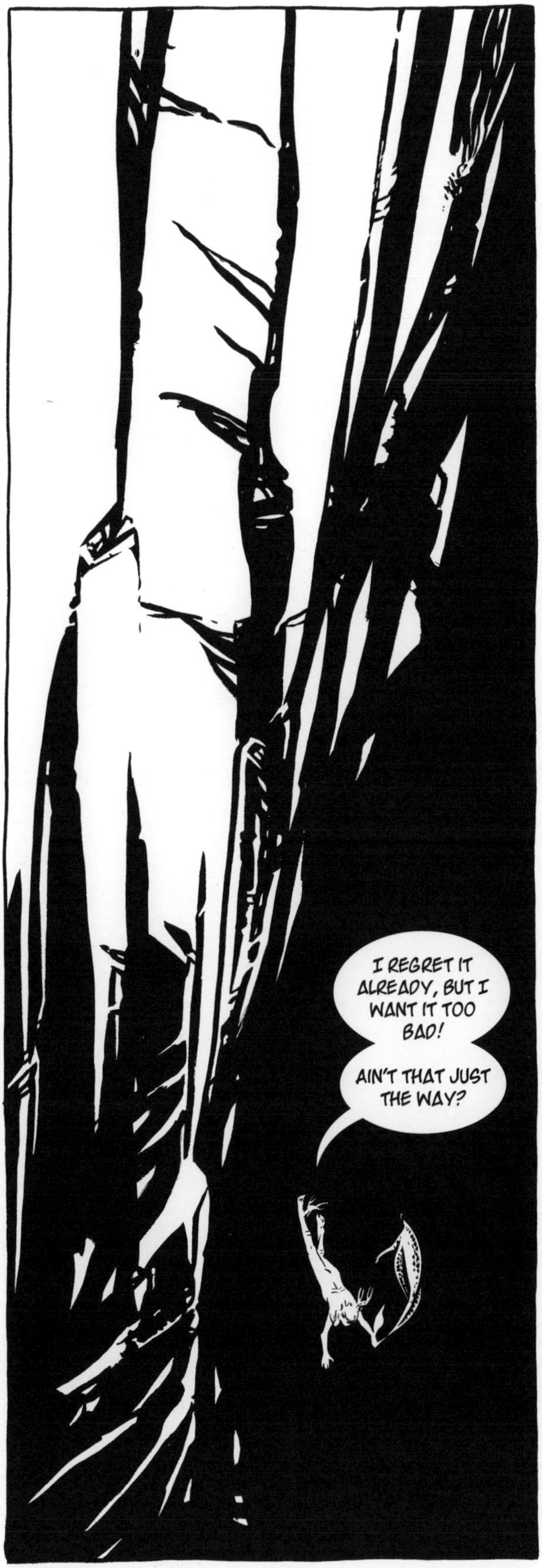
I REGRET IT ALREADY, BUT I WANT IT TOO BAD!
AIN'T THAT JUST THE WAY?

CHAPTER SIX

LOVE HURTS

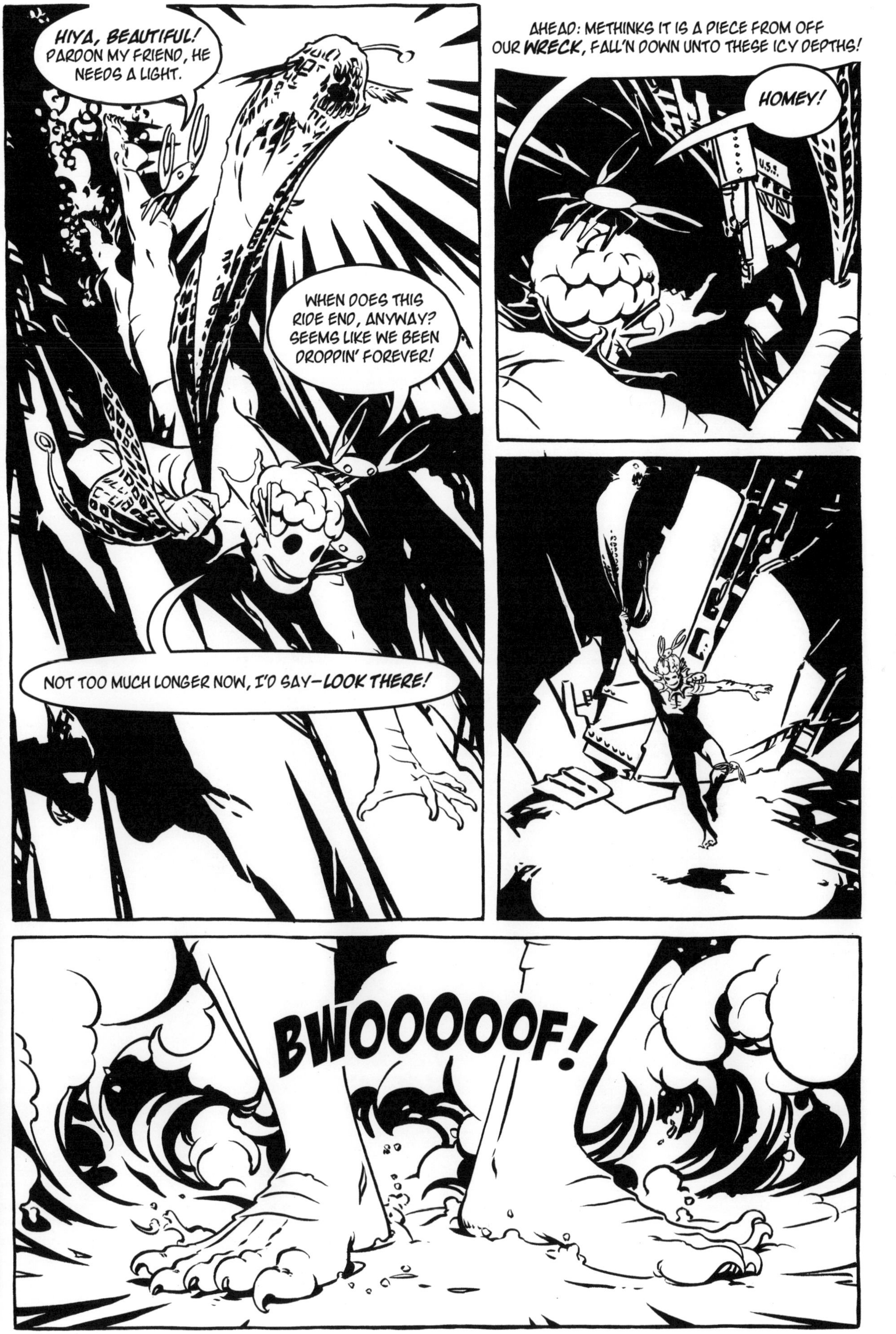
HIYA, BEAUTIFUL! PARDON MY FRIEND, HE NEEDS A LIGHT.
WHEN DOES THIS RIDE END, ANYWAY? SEEMS LIKE WE BEEN DROPPIN' FOREVER!
NOT TOO MUCH LONGER NOW, I'D SAY—LOOK THERE!
AHEAD: METHINKS IT IS A PIECE FROM OFF OUR WRECK, FALL'N DOWN UNTO THESE ICY DEPTHS!
HOMEY!
BWOOOOOF!

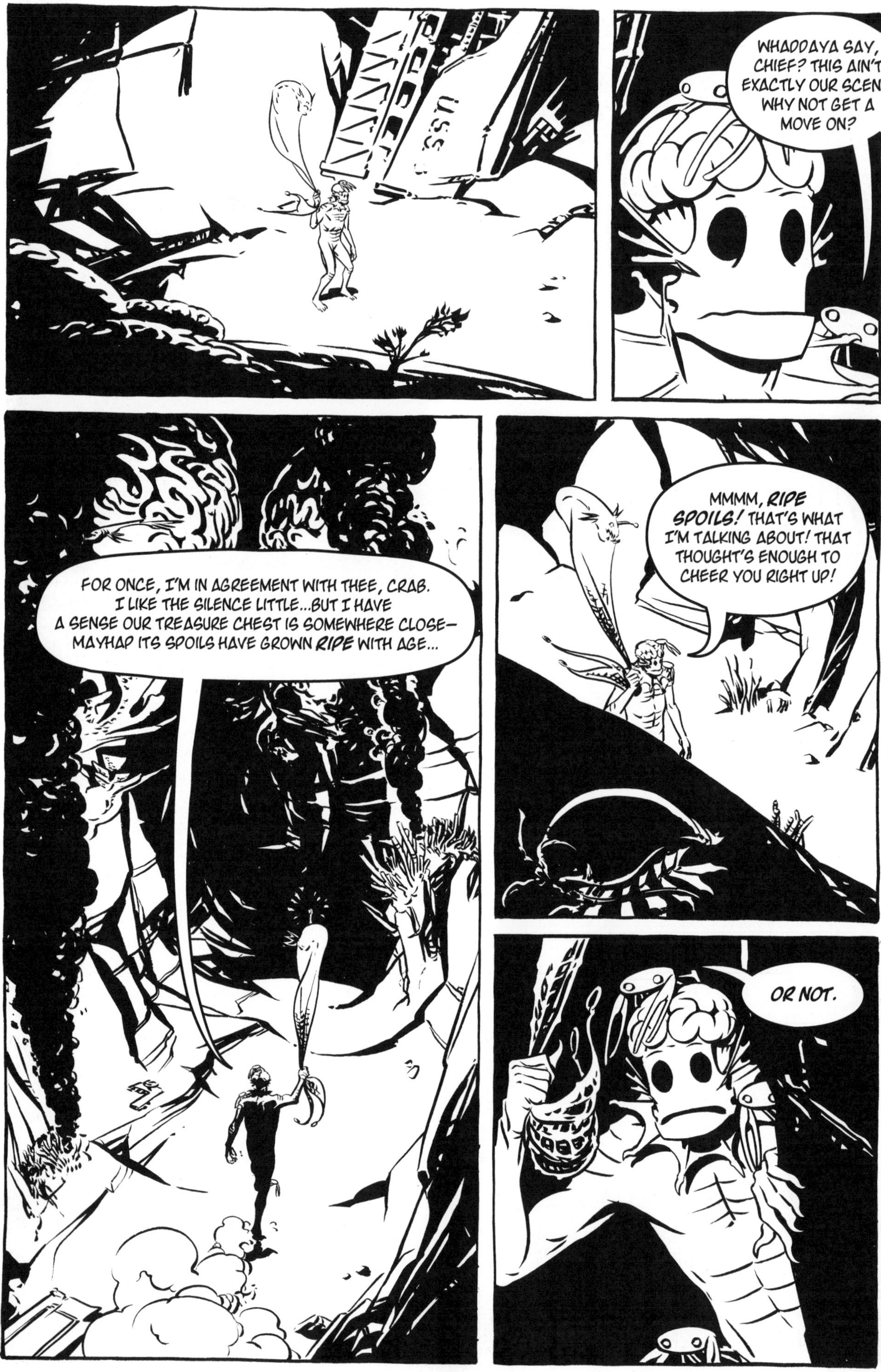
U.S.S.
WHADDAYA SAY, CHIEF? THIS AIN'T EXACTLY OUR SCENE. WHY NOT GET A MOVE ON?
FOR ONCE, I'M IN AGREEMENT WITH THEE, CRAB. I LIKE THE SILENCE LITTLE...BUT I HAVE A SENSE OUR TREASURE CHEST IS SOMEWHERE CLOSE– MAYHAP ITS SPOILS HAVE GROWN RIPE WITH AGE...
MMMM, RIPE SPOILS! THAT'S WHAT I'M TALKING ABOUT! THAT THOUGHT'S ENOUGH TO CHEER YOU RIGHT UP!
OR NOT.

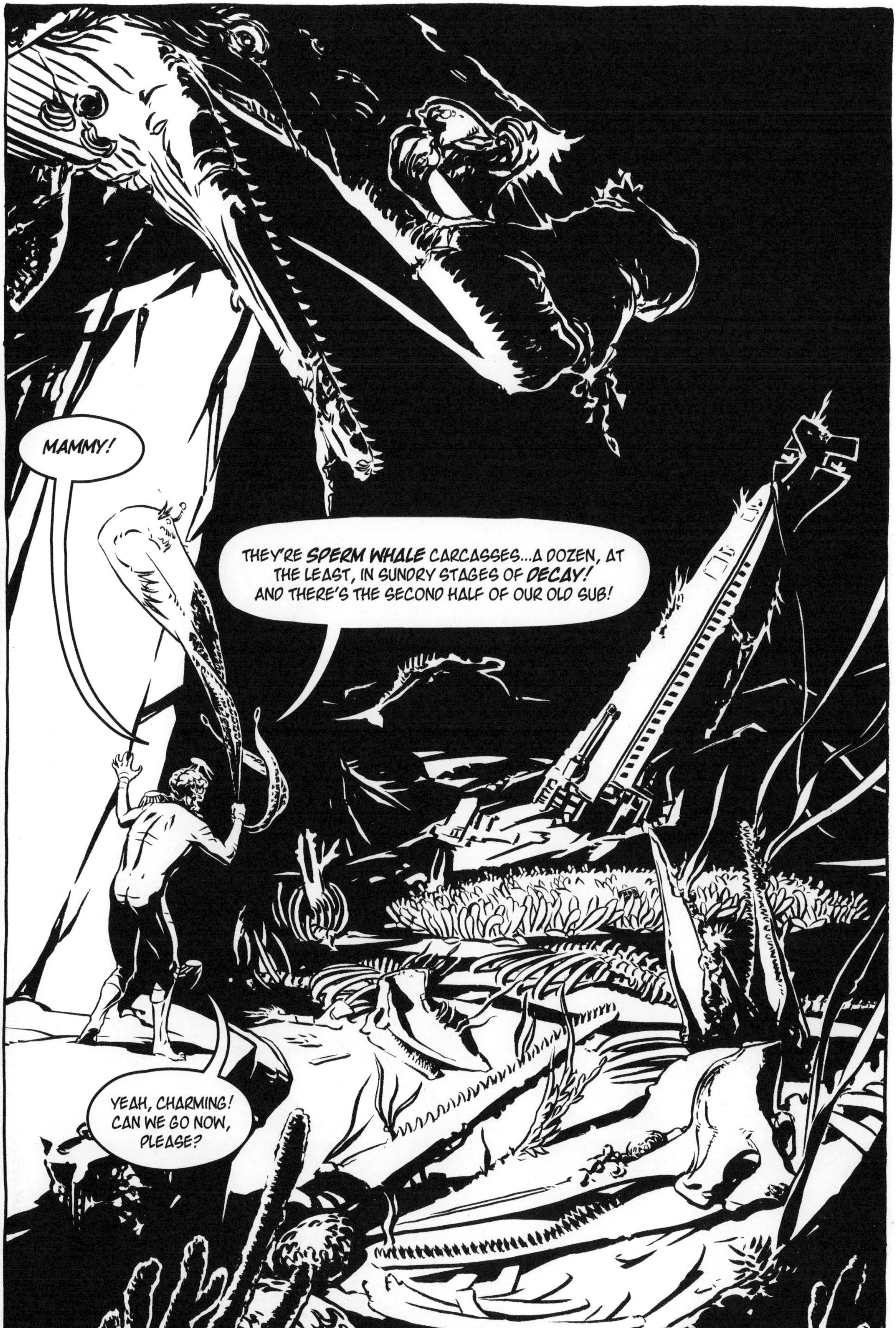
MAMMY!
THEY'RE SPERM WHALE CARCASSES...A DOZEN, AT THE LEAST, IN SUNDRY STAGES OF DECAY! AND THERE'S THE SECOND HALF OF OUR OLD SUB!
YEAH, CHARMING! CAN WE GO NOW, PLEASE?

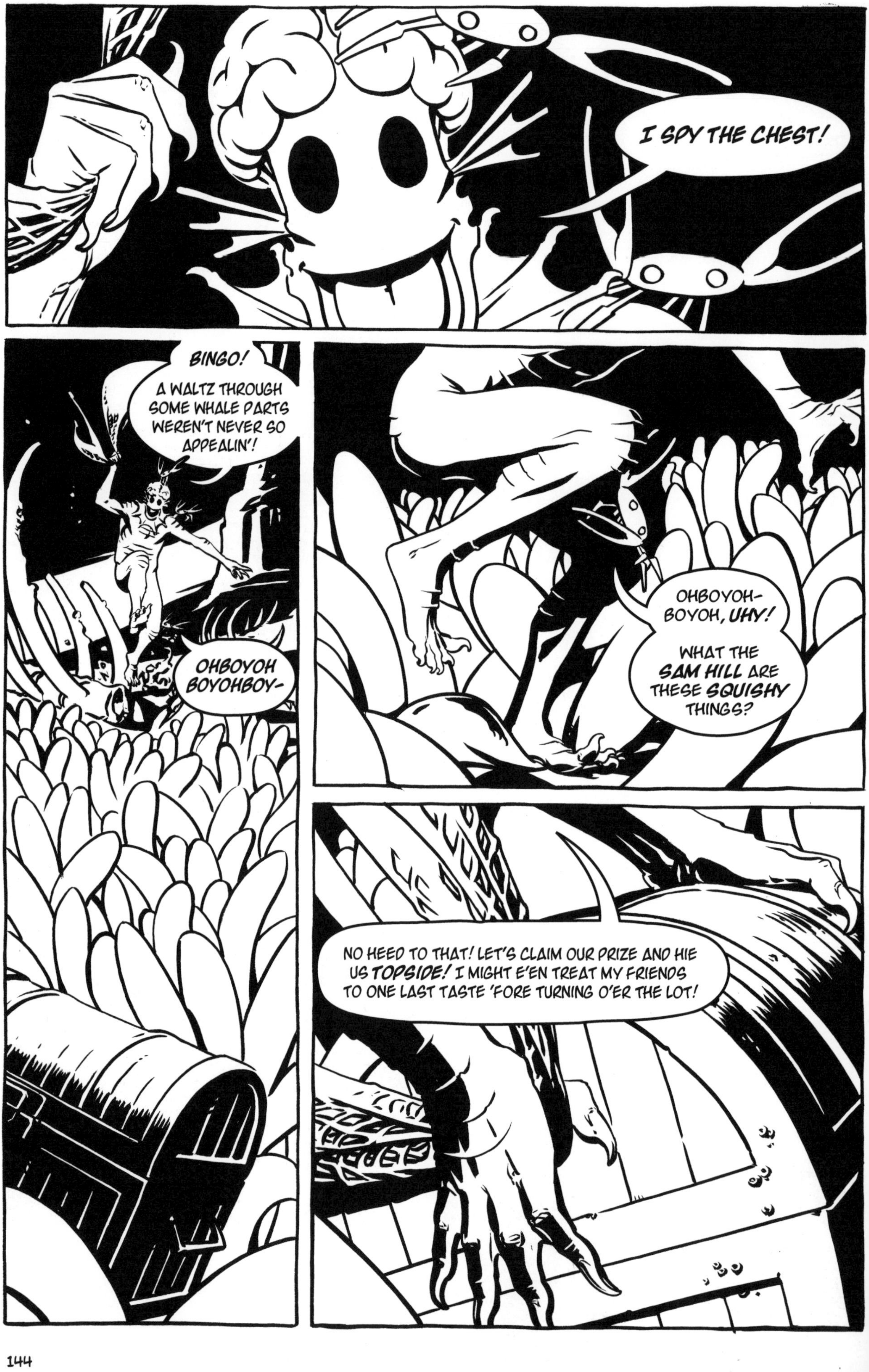
I SPY THE CHEST!
BINGO!
A WALTZ THROUGH SOME WHALE PARTS WEREN'T NEVER SO APPEALIN'!
OHBOYOH BOYOHBOY-
OHBOYOH-BOYOH, UHY!
WHAT THE SAM HILL ARE THESE SQUISHY THINGS?
NO HEED TO THAT! LET'S CLAIM OUR PRIZE AND HIE US TOPSIDE! I MIGHT E'EN TREAT MY FRIENDS TO ONE LAST TASTE 'FORE TURNING O'ER THE LOT!

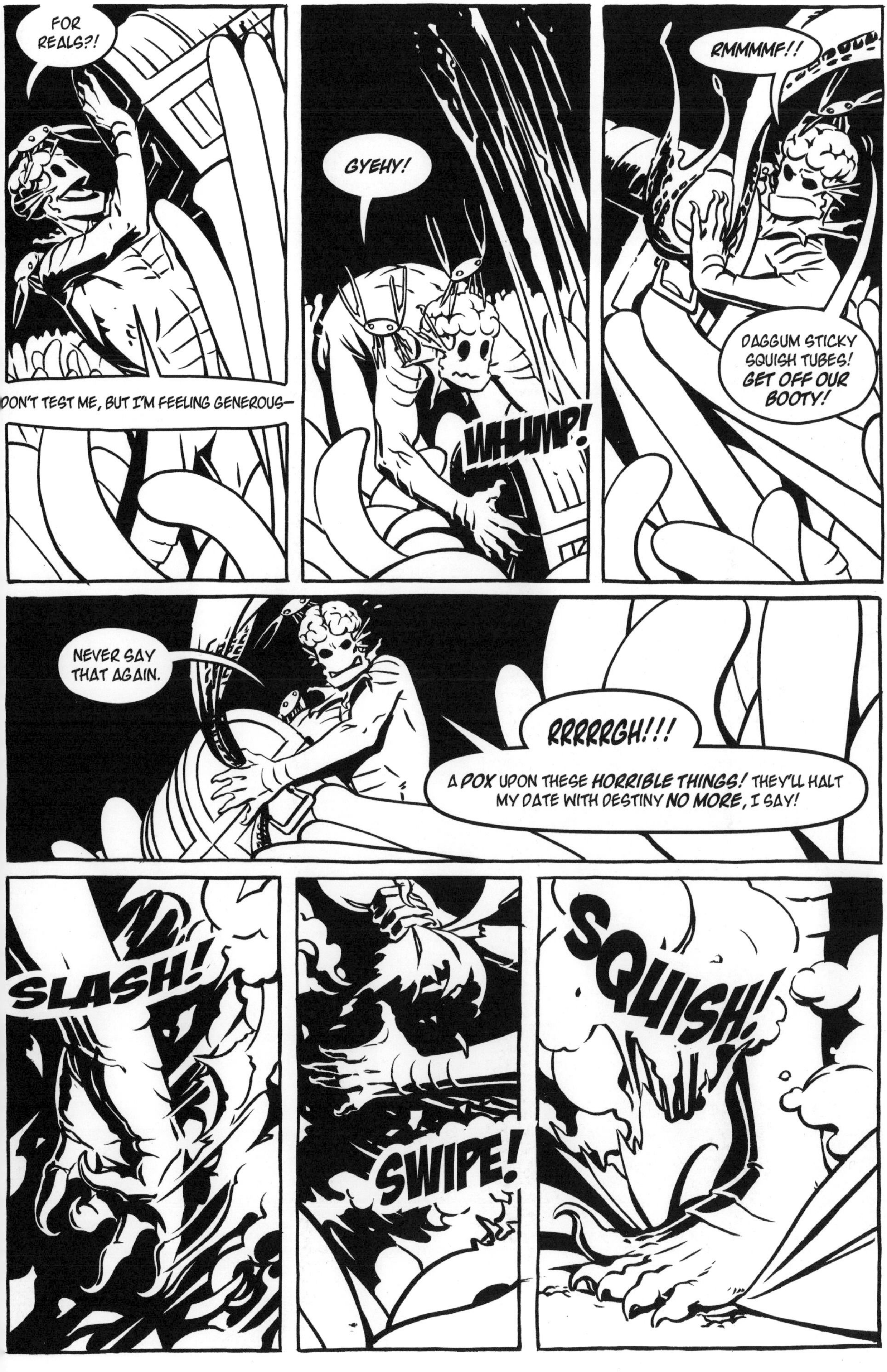
FOR REALS?!
DON'T TEST ME, BUT I'M FEELING GENEROUS—
GYEHY!
WHUMP!
RMMMMF!!
DAGGUM STICKY SQUISH TUBES! GET OFF OUR BOOTY!
NEVER SAY THAT AGAIN.
RRRRRGH!!!
A POX UPON THESE HORRIBLE THINGS! THEY'LL HALT MY DATE WITH DESTINY NO MORE, I SAY!
SLASH!
SWIPE!
SQUISH!

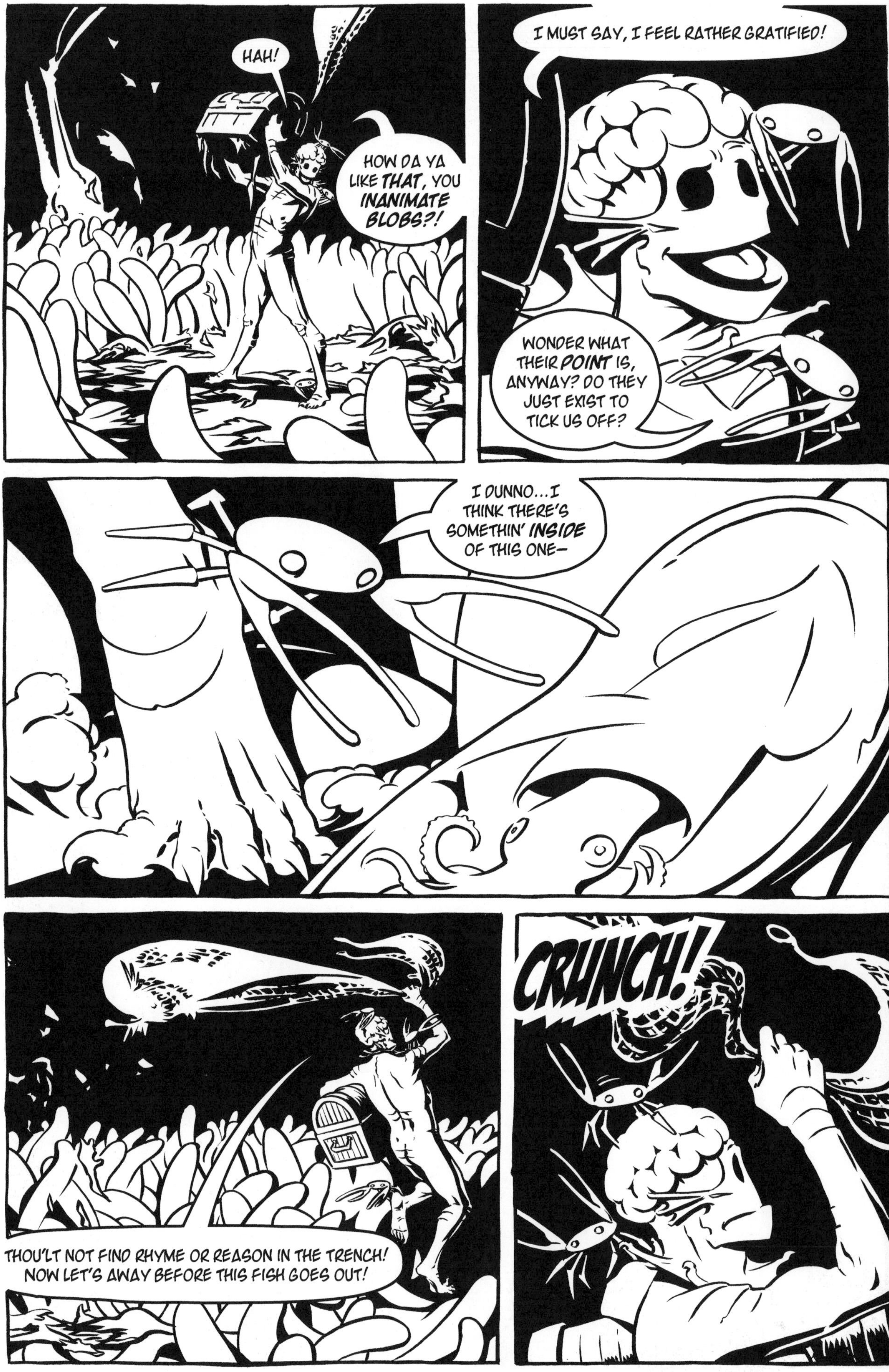
HAH!
HOW DA YA LIKE THAT, YOU INANIMATE BLOBS?!
I MUST SAY, I FEEL RATHER GRATIFIED!
WONDER WHAT THEIR POINT IS, ANYWAY? DO THEY JUST EXIST TO TICK US OFF?
I DUNNO... I THINK THERE'S SOMETHIN' INSIDE OF THIS ONE–
THOU'LT NOT FIND RHYME OR REASON IN THE TRENCH! NOW LET'S AWAY BEFORE THIS FISH GOES OUT!
CRUNCH!

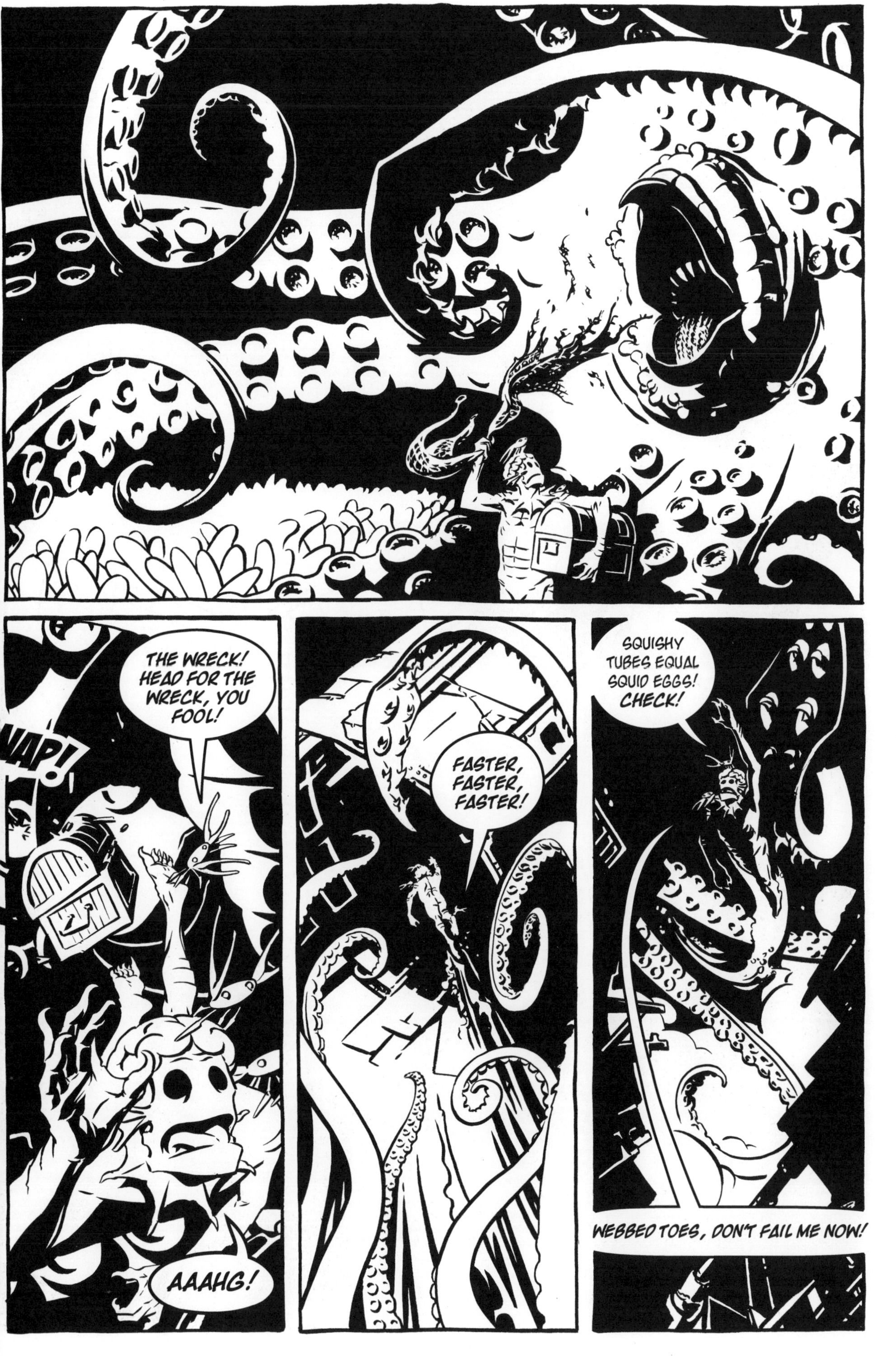
THE WRECK! HEAD FOR THE WRECK, YOU FOOL!
AAAHG!
FASTER, FASTER, FASTER!
SQUISHY TUBES EQUAL SQUID EGGS! CHECK!
WEBBED TOES, DON'T FAIL ME NOW!

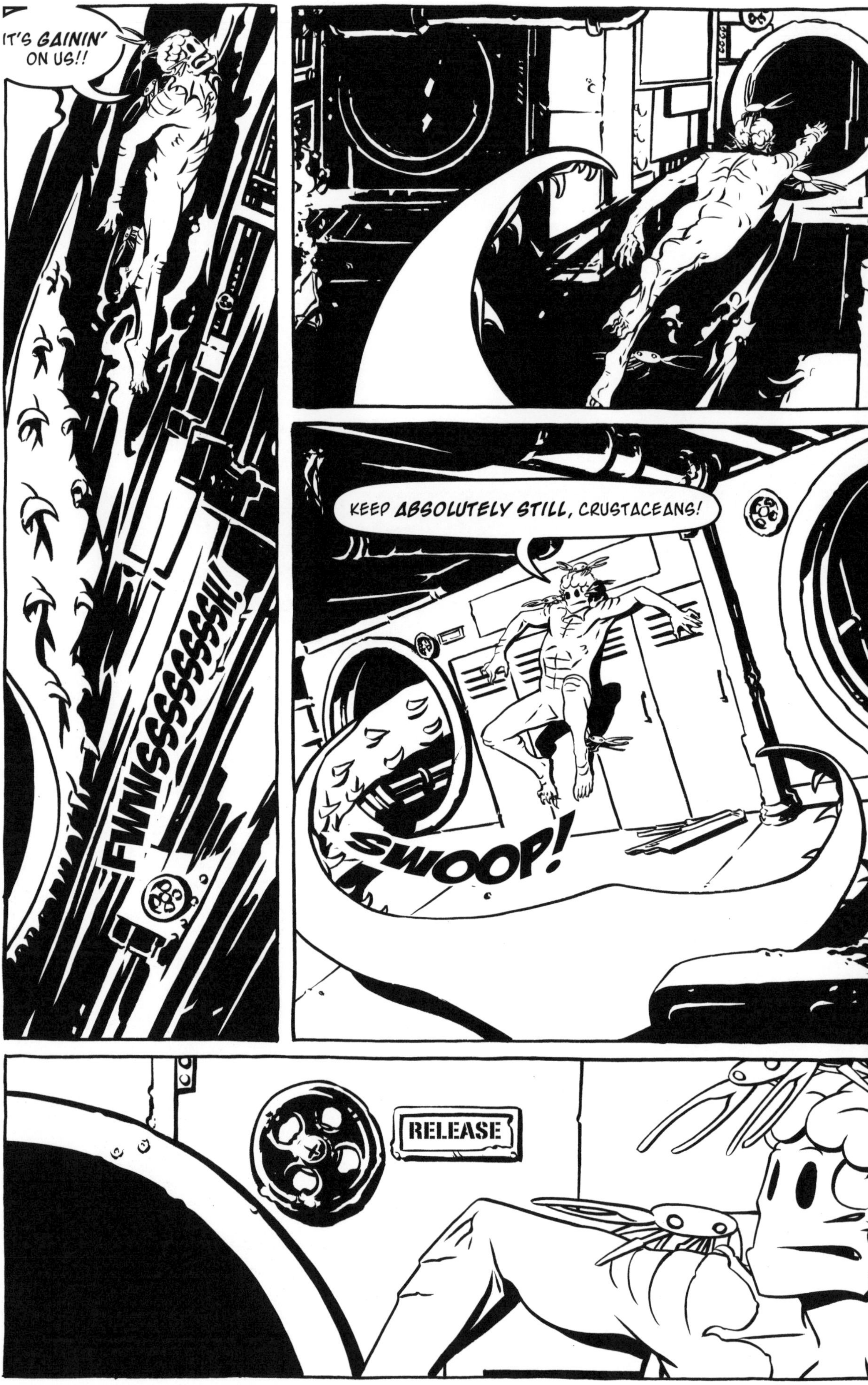
IT'S GAININ' ON US!!
FWWSSSSSSSSH!
KEEP ABSOLUTELY STILL, CRUSTACEANS!
SWOOP!
RELEASE

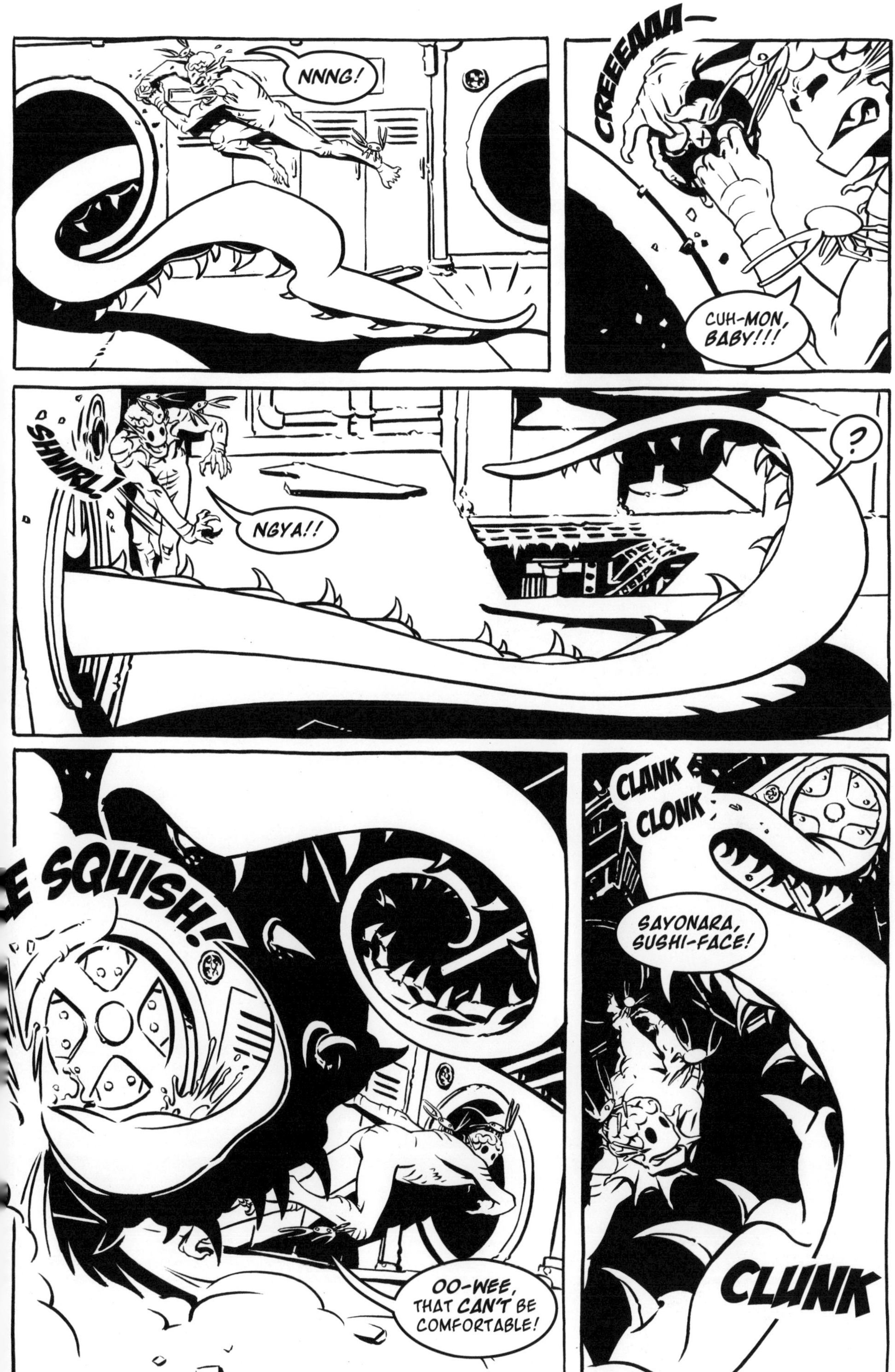
NNNG!
CREEEAAA—
CUH-MON, BABY!!!!
SHWRL!
NGYA!!
?
E SQUISH!
OO-WEE, THAT CAN'T BE COMFORTABLE!
CLANK
CLONK
SAYONARA, SUSHI-FACE!
CLUNK

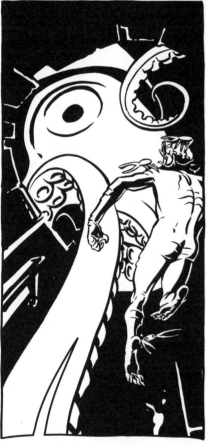

WHO KNOWS HOW LONG OUR TENTACLE RESTRAINT WILL KEEP: IT'S NOW OR NEVER—*HOLD ON TIGHT!*

YEEHAW!!!

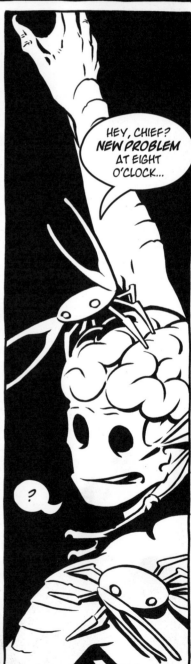

HEY, CHIEF? *NEW PROBLEM* AT EIGHT O'CLOCK...

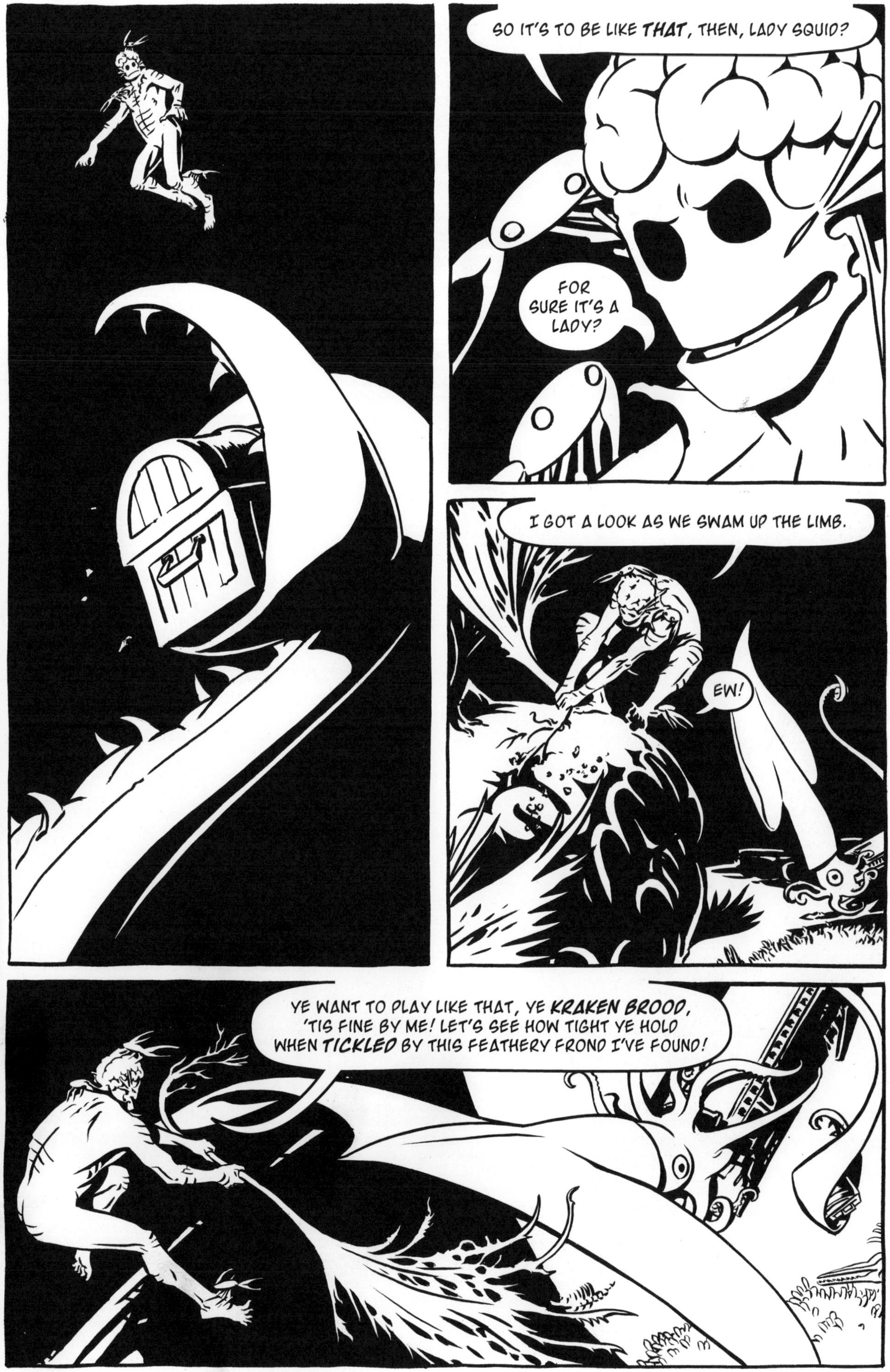
SO IT'S TO BE LIKE THAT, THEN, LADY SQUID?
FOR SURE IT'S A LADY?
I GOT A LOOK AS WE SWAM UP THE LIMB.
EW!
YE WANT TO PLAY LIKE THAT, YE KRAKEN BROOD, 'TIS FINE BY ME! LET'S SEE HOW TIGHT YE HOLD WHEN TICKLED BY THIS FEATHERY FROND I'VE FOUND!

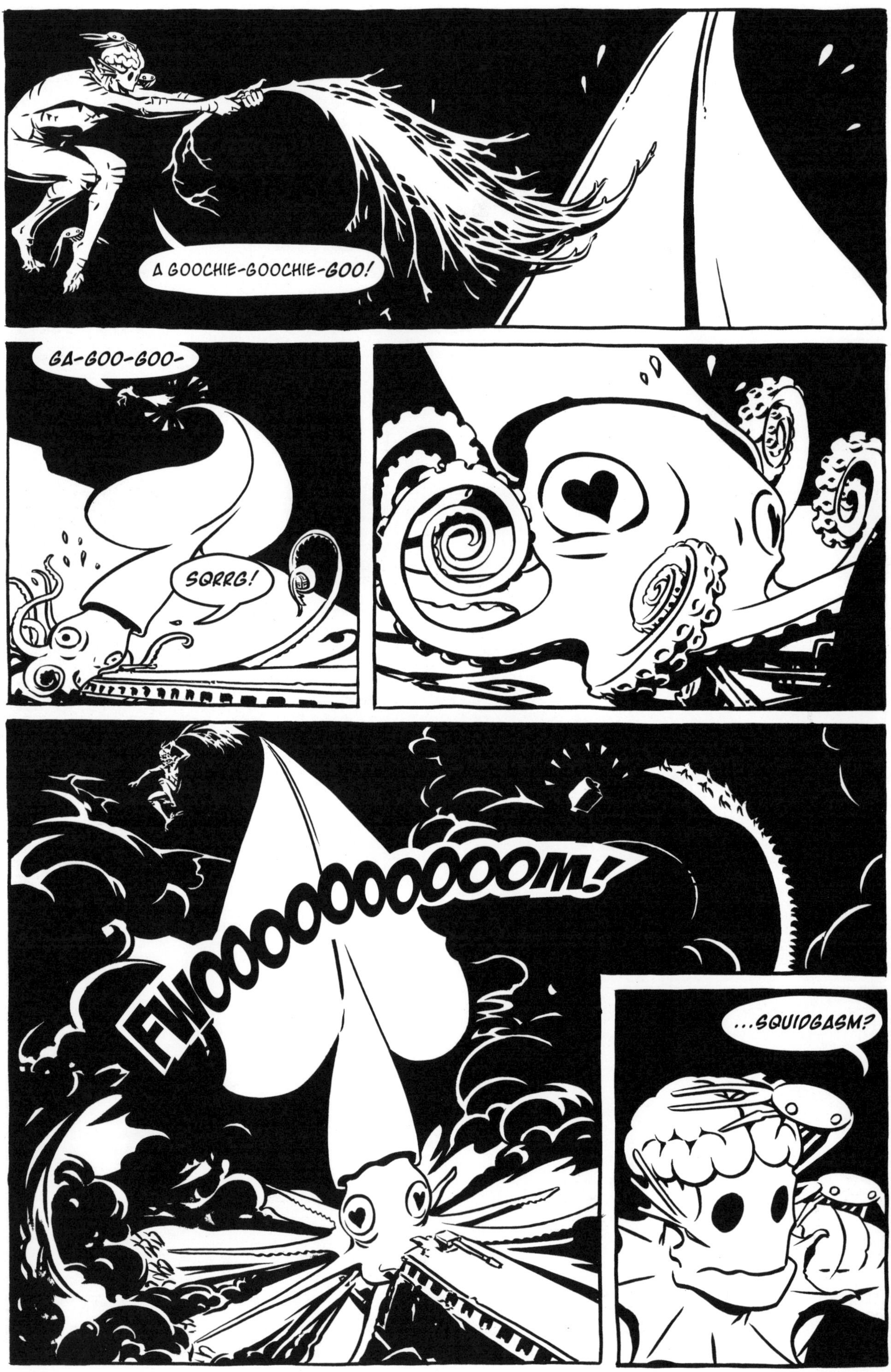
A GOOCHIE-GOOCHIE-GOO!
GA-GOO-GOO-
SQRRG!
FWOOOOOOOOOOOOM!
...SQUIDGASM?

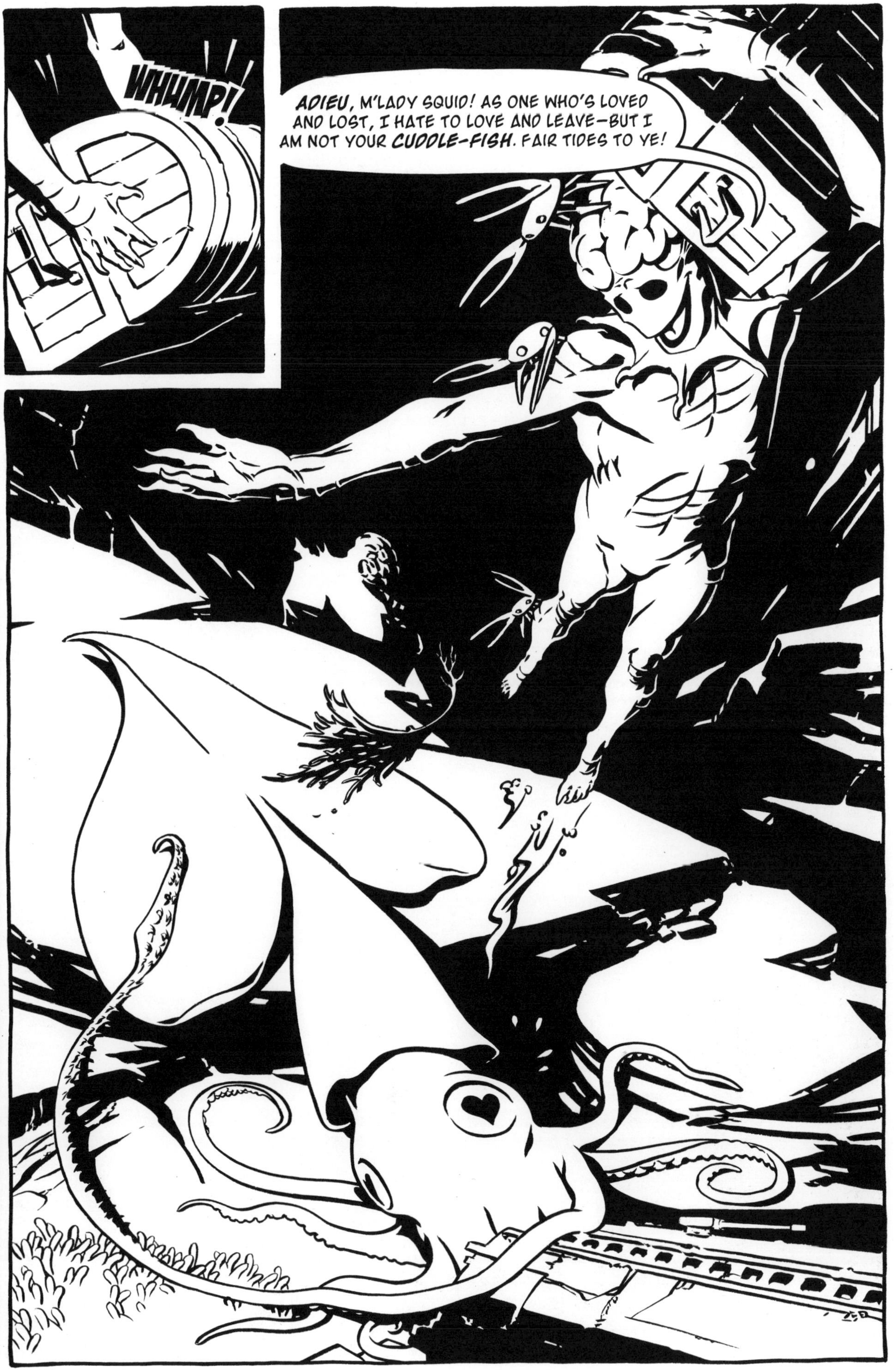
WHUMP!
ADIEU, M'LADY SQUID! AS ONE WHO'S LOVED AND LOST, I HATE TO LOVE AND LEAVE—BUT I AM NOT YOUR CUDDLE-FISH. FAIR TIDES TO YE!

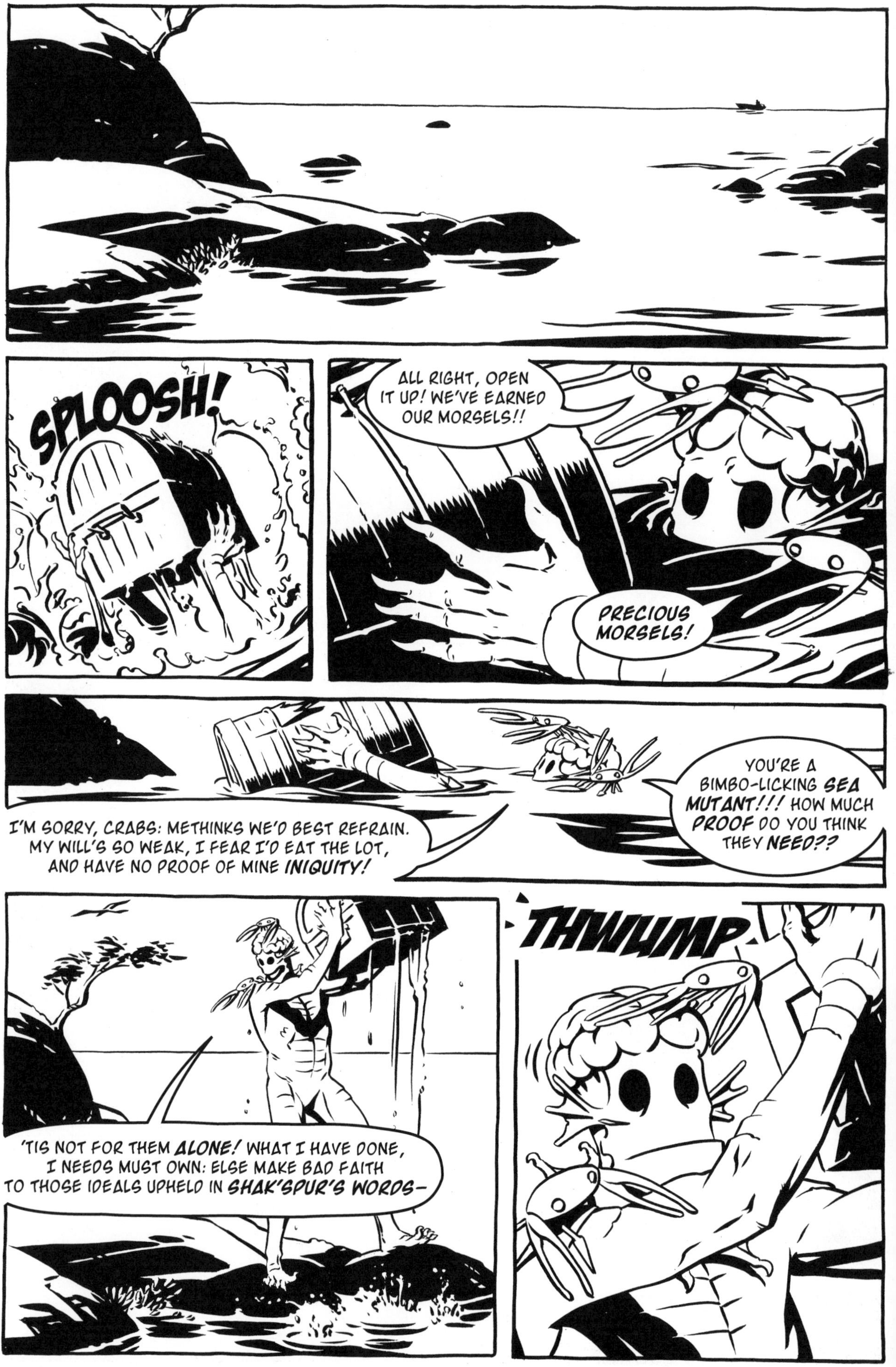
SPLOOSH!
ALL RIGHT, OPEN IT UP! WE'VE EARNED OUR MORSELS!!
PRECIOUS MORSELS!
I'M SORRY, CRABS: METHINKS WE'D BEST REFRAIN. MY WILL'S SO WEAK, I FEAR I'D EAT THE LOT, AND HAVE NO PROOF OF MINE INIQUITY!
YOU'RE A BIMBO-LICKING SEA MUTANT!!! HOW MUCH PROOF DO YOU THINK THEY NEED??
'TIS NOT FOR THEM ALONE! WHAT I HAVE DONE, I NEEDS MUST OWN: ELSE MAKE BAD FAITH TO THOSE IDEALS UPHELD IN SHAK'SPUR'S WORDS—
THWUMP

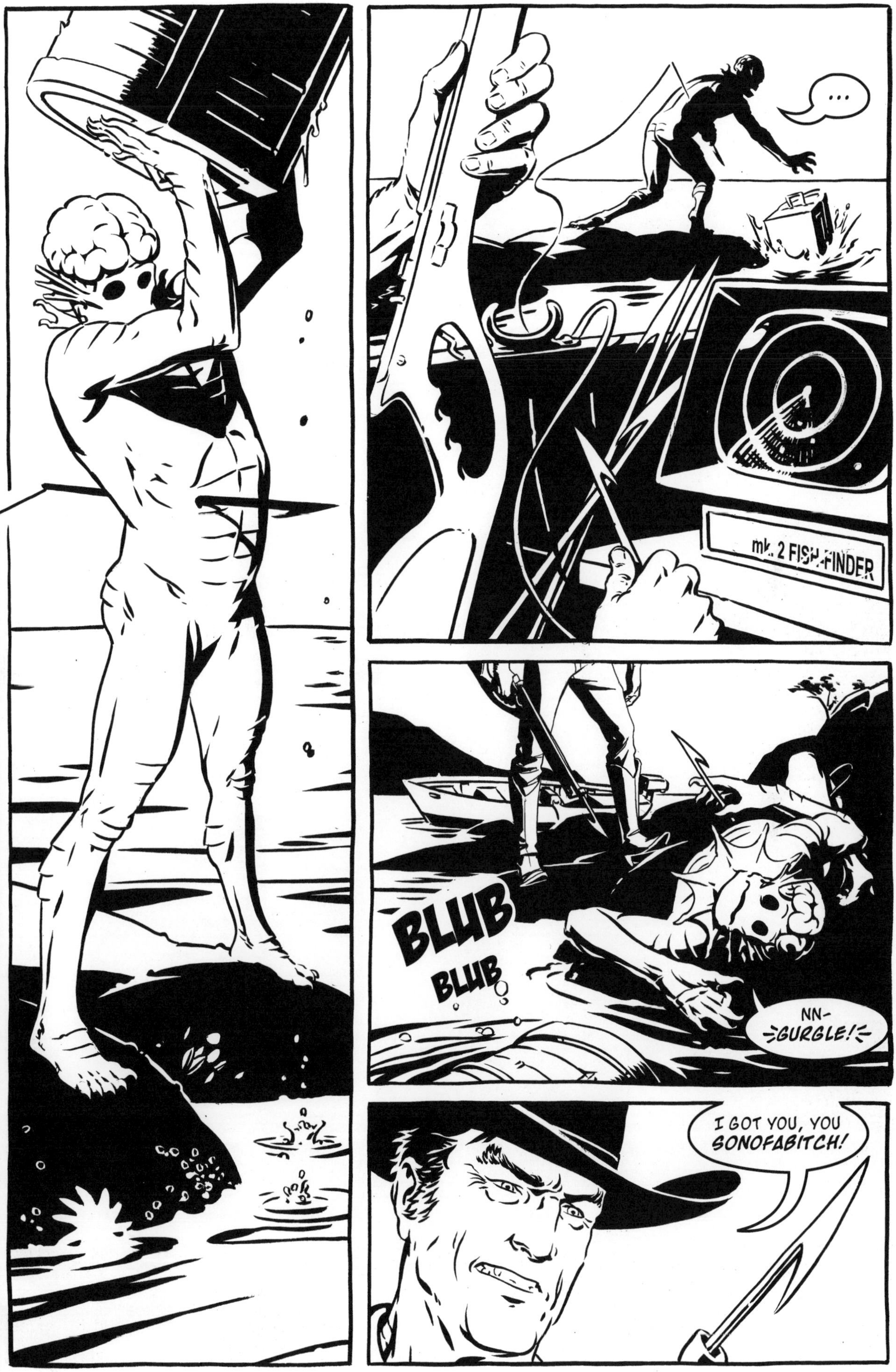
...
mk. 2 FISH-FINDER
BLUB
BLUB
NN-
GURGLE!
I GOT YOU, YOU
SONOFABITCH!

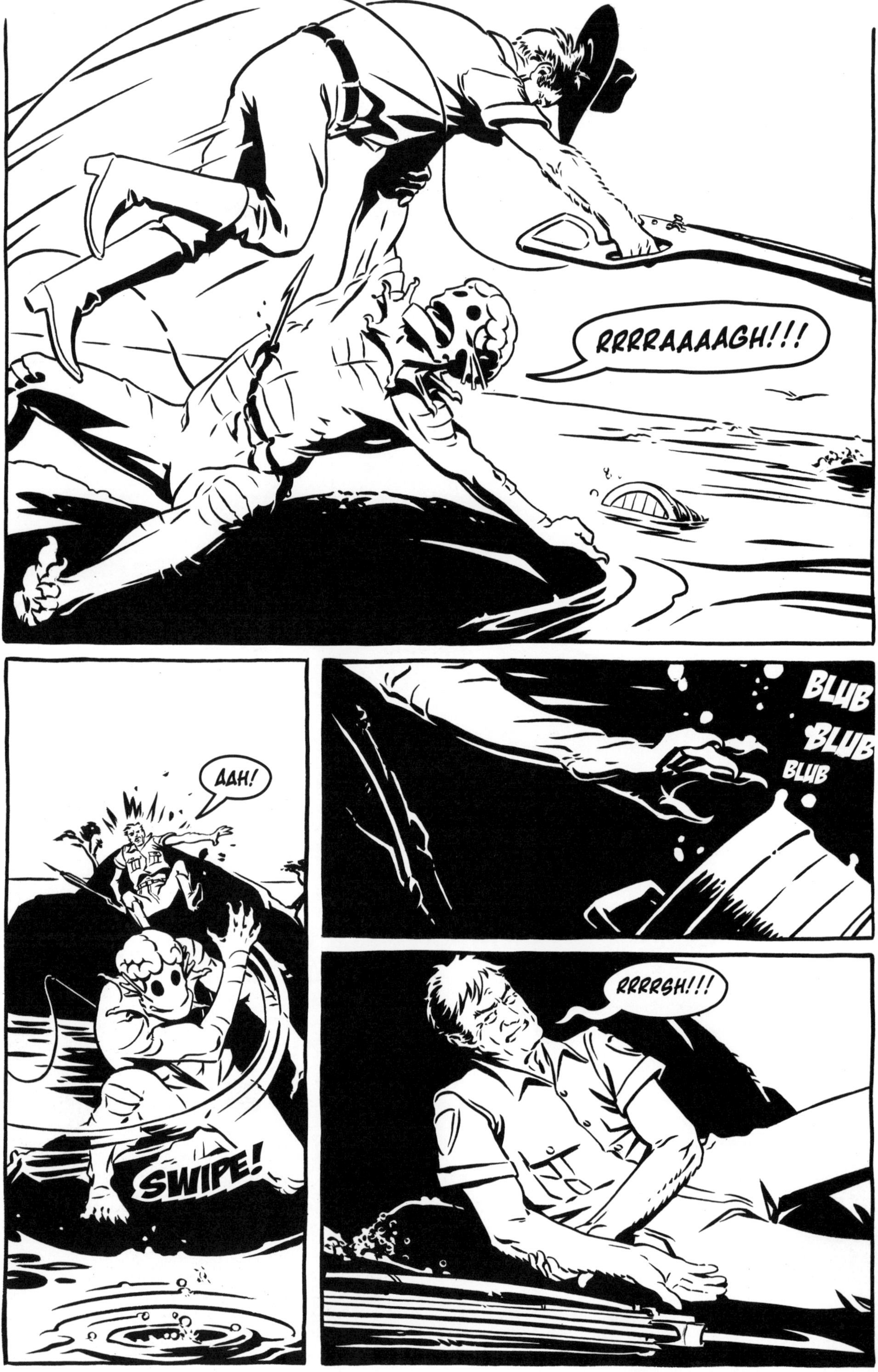
RRRRAAAAGH!!!
AAH!
SWIPE!
BLUB
BLUB
BLUB
RRRRSH!!!

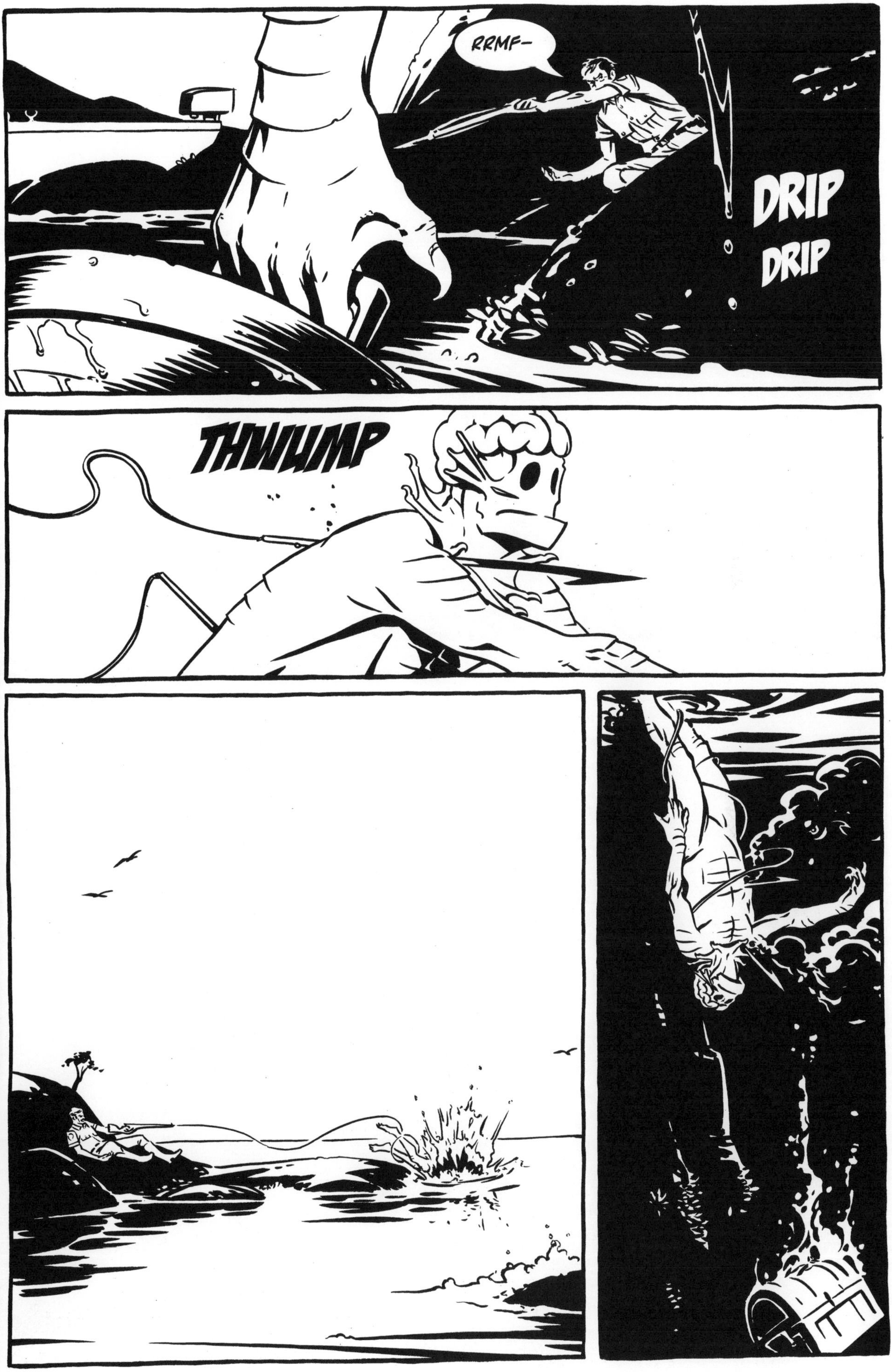
RRMF-
DRIP
DRIP
THWUMP

CHAPTER SEVEN

RUNNING SCARED

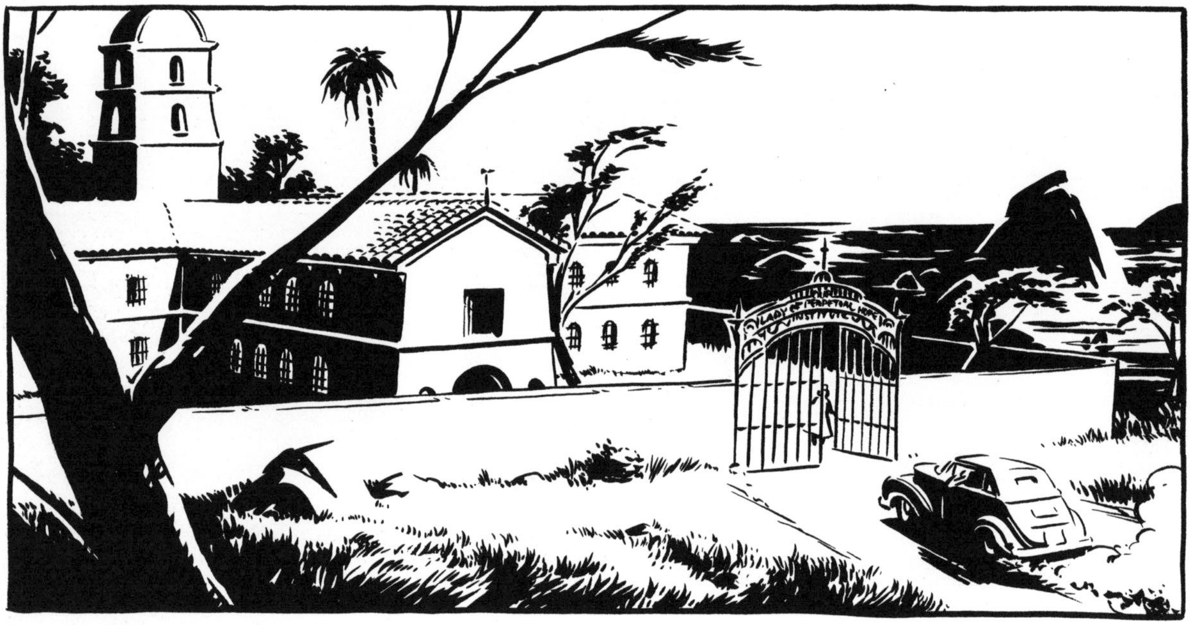
LADY OF PERPETUAL HOPE
INSTITUTE

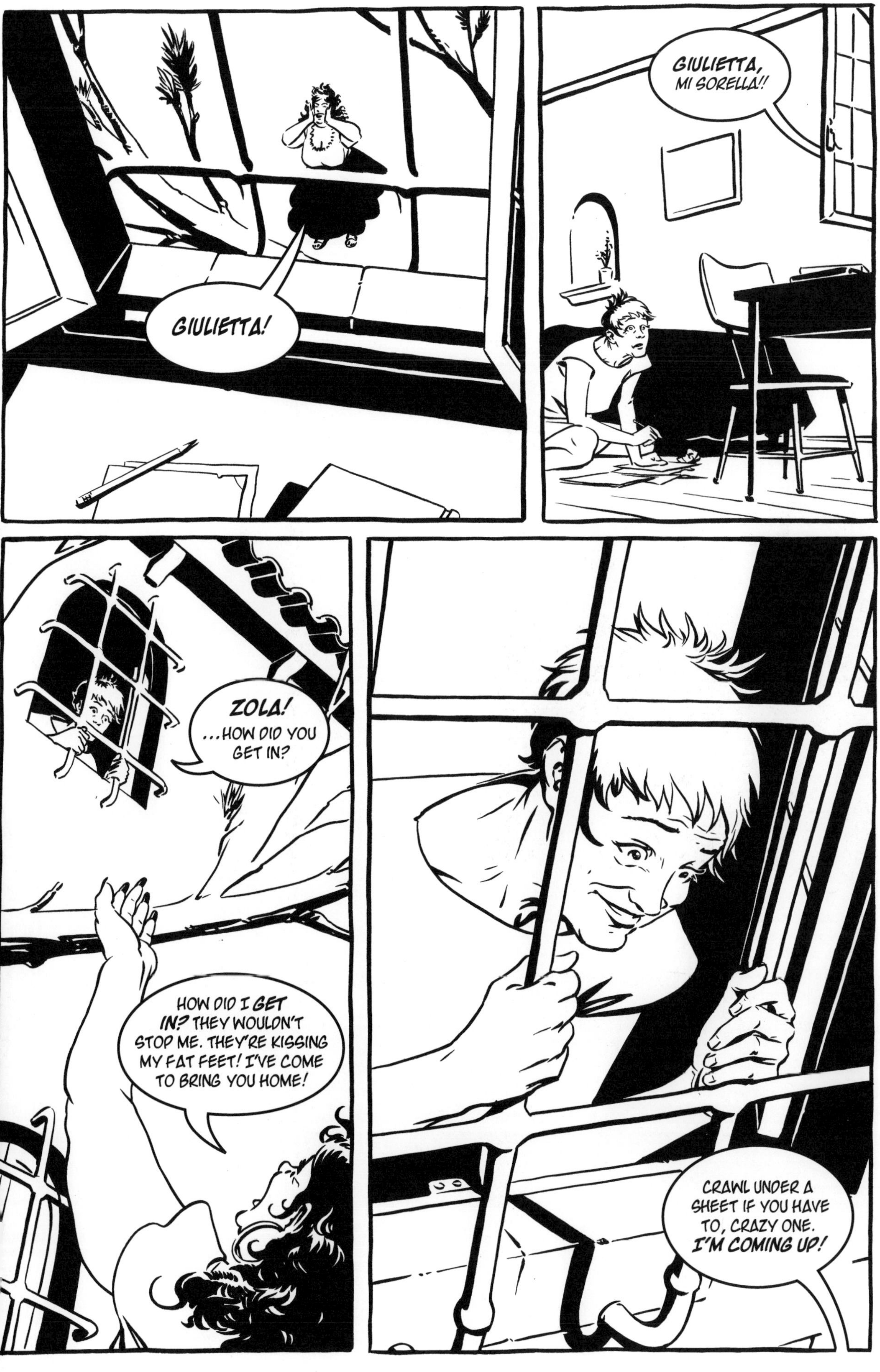
GIULIETTA!
GIULIETTA, MI SORELLA!!
ZOLA! ...HOW DID YOU GET IN?
HOW DID I GET IN? THEY WOULDN'T STOP ME. THEY'RE KISSING MY FAT FEET! I'VE COME TO BRING YOU HOME!
CRAWL UNDER A SHEET IF YOU HAVE TO, CRAZY ONE. I'M COMING UP!

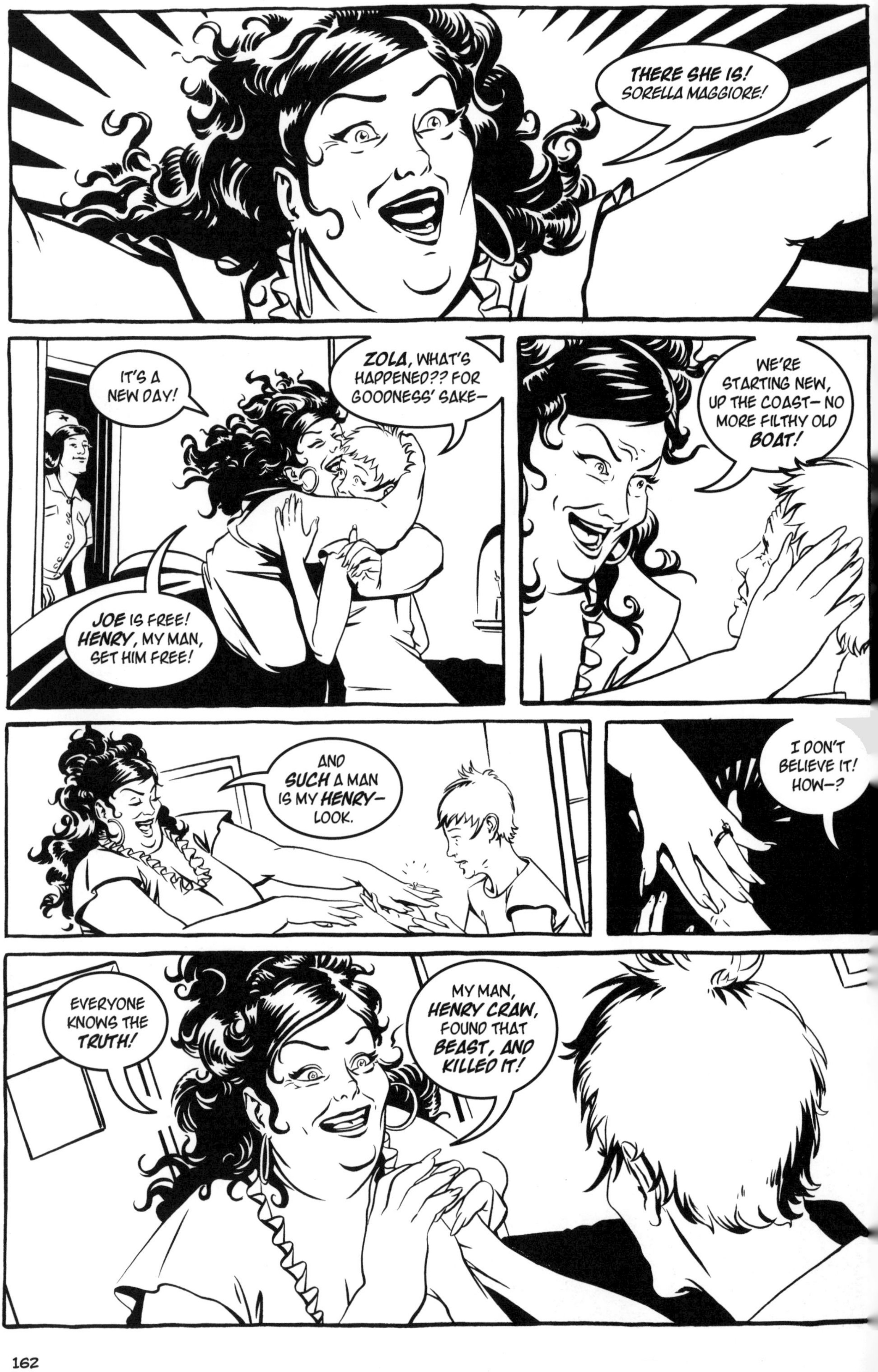
THERE SHE IS! SORELLA MAGGIORE!
IT'S A NEW DAY!
ZOLA, WHAT'S HAPPENED?? FOR GOODNESS' SAKE-
JOE IS FREE! HENRY, MY MAN, SET HIM FREE!
WE'RE STARTING NEW, UP THE COAST- NO MORE FILTHY OLD BOAT!
AND SUCH A MAN IS MY HENRY- LOOK.
I DON'T BELIEVE IT! HOW-?
EVERYONE KNOWS THE TRUTH!
MY MAN, HENRY CRAW, FOUND THAT BEAST, AND KILLED IT!

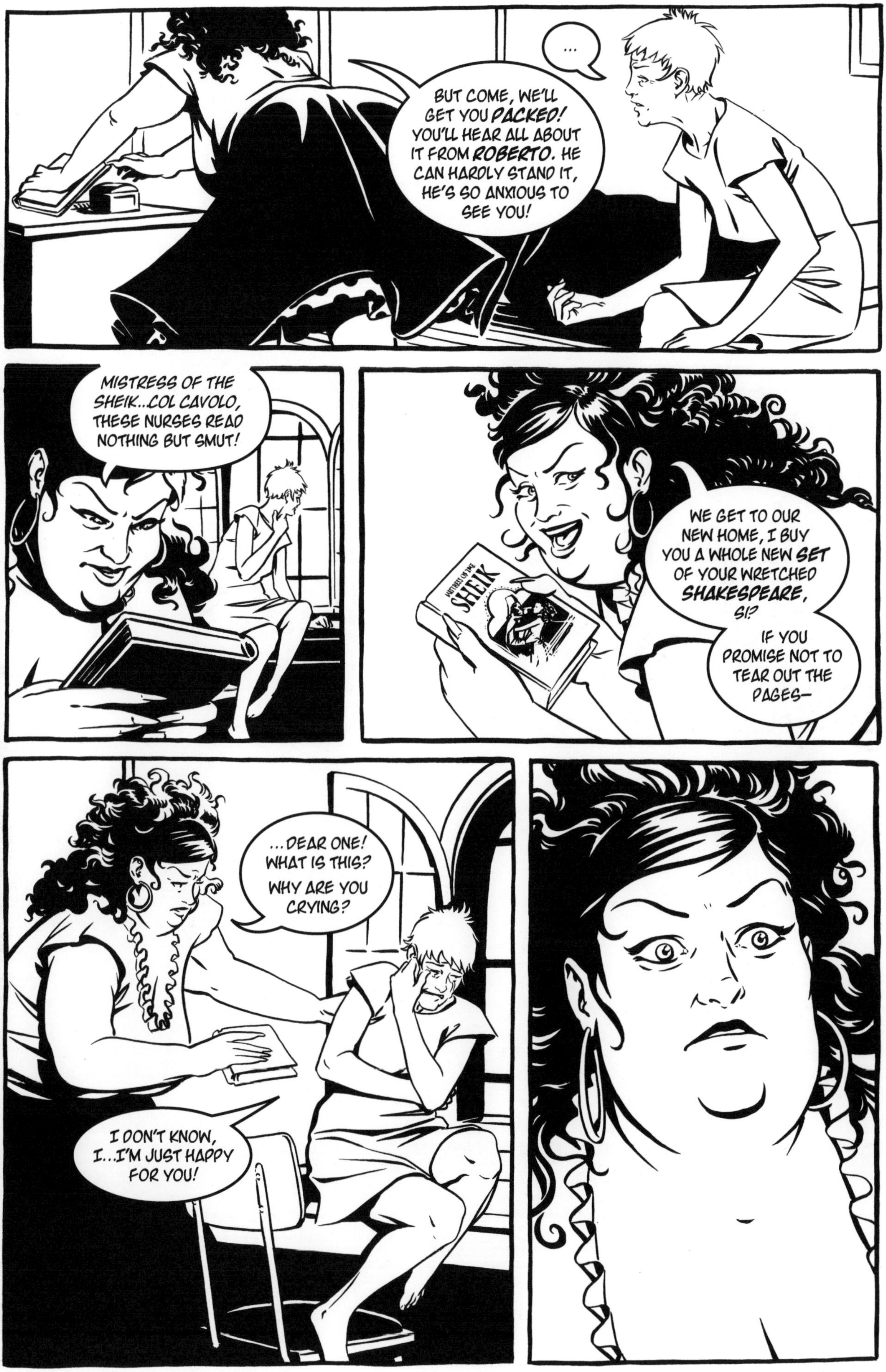
...
BUT COME, WE'LL GET YOU PACKED! YOU'LL HEAR ALL ABOUT IT FROM ROBERTO. HE CAN HARDLY STAND IT, HE'S SO ANXIOUS TO SEE YOU!
MISTRESS OF THE SHEIK...COL CAVOLO, THESE NURSES READ NOTHING BUT SMUT!
MISTRESS OF THE SHEIK
WE GET TO OUR NEW HOME, I BUY YOU A WHOLE NEW SET OF YOUR WRETCHED SHAKESPEARE, SI?
IF YOU PROMISE NOT TO TEAR OUT THE PAGES—
...DEAR ONE! WHAT IS THIS?
WHY ARE YOU CRYING?
I DON'T KNOW, I...I'M JUST HAPPY FOR YOU!

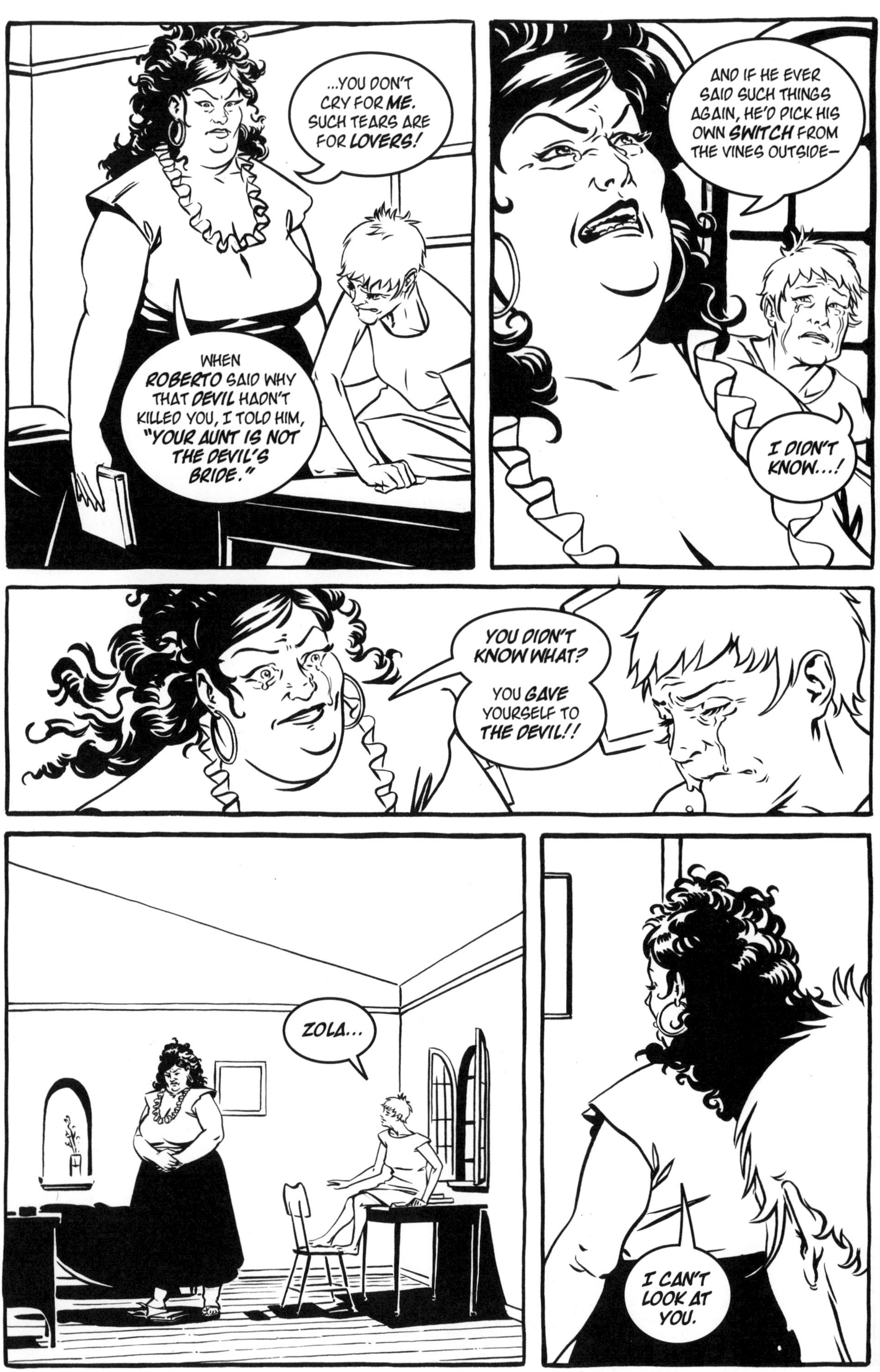
...YOU DON'T CRY FOR ME. SUCH TEARS ARE FOR LOVERS!
WHEN ROBERTO SAID WHY THAT DEVIL HADN'T KILLED YOU, I TOLD HIM, "YOUR AUNT IS NOT THE DEVIL'S BRIDE."
AND IF HE EVER SAID SUCH THINGS AGAIN, HE'D PICK HIS OWN SWITCH FROM THE VINES OUTSIDE—
I DIDN'T KNOW...!
YOU DIDN'T KNOW WHAT?
YOU GAVE YOURSELF TO THE DEVIL!!
ZOLA...
I CAN'T LOOK AT YOU.

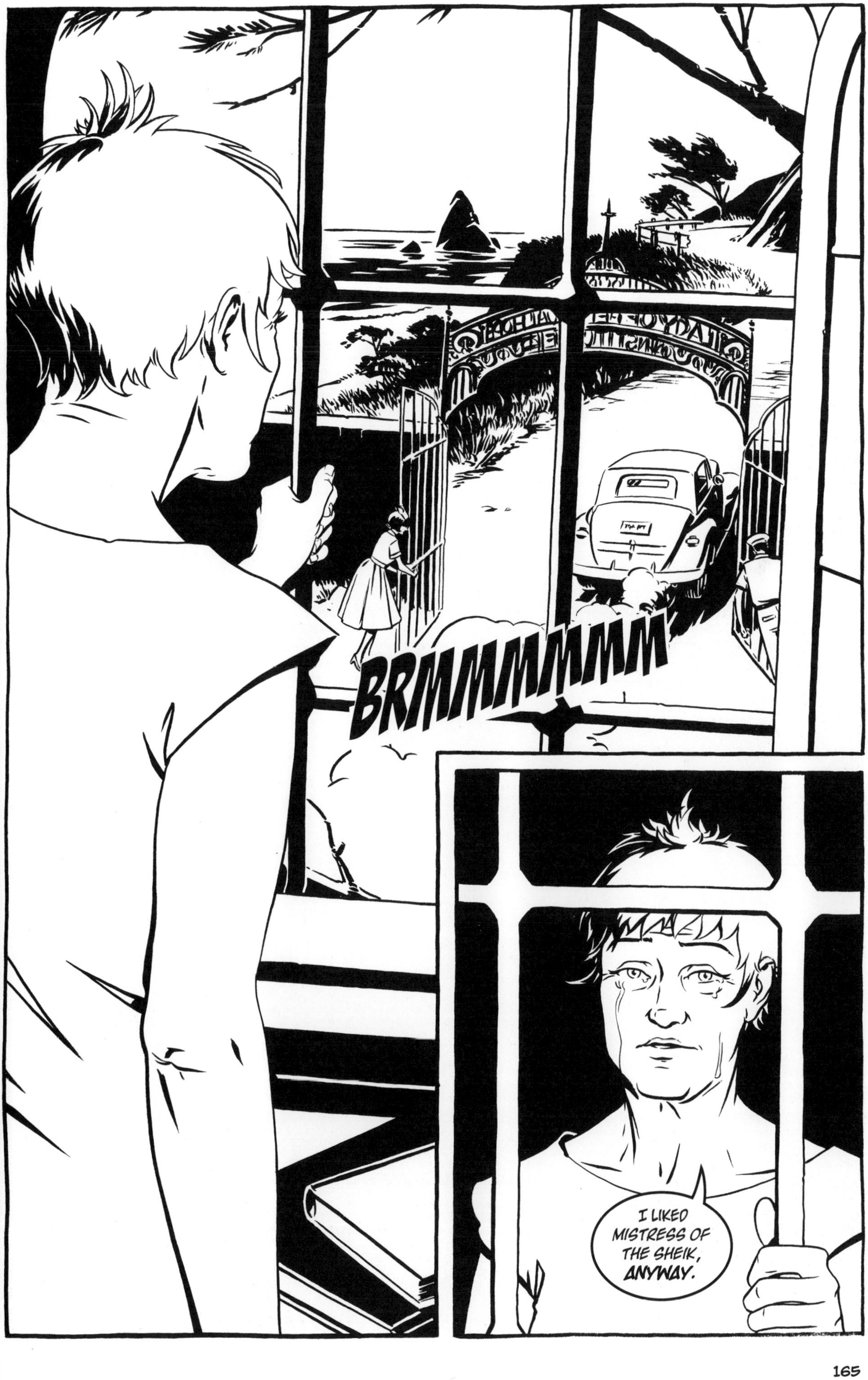
BRMMMMMMM
I LIKED MISTRESS OF THE SHEIK, ANYWAY.

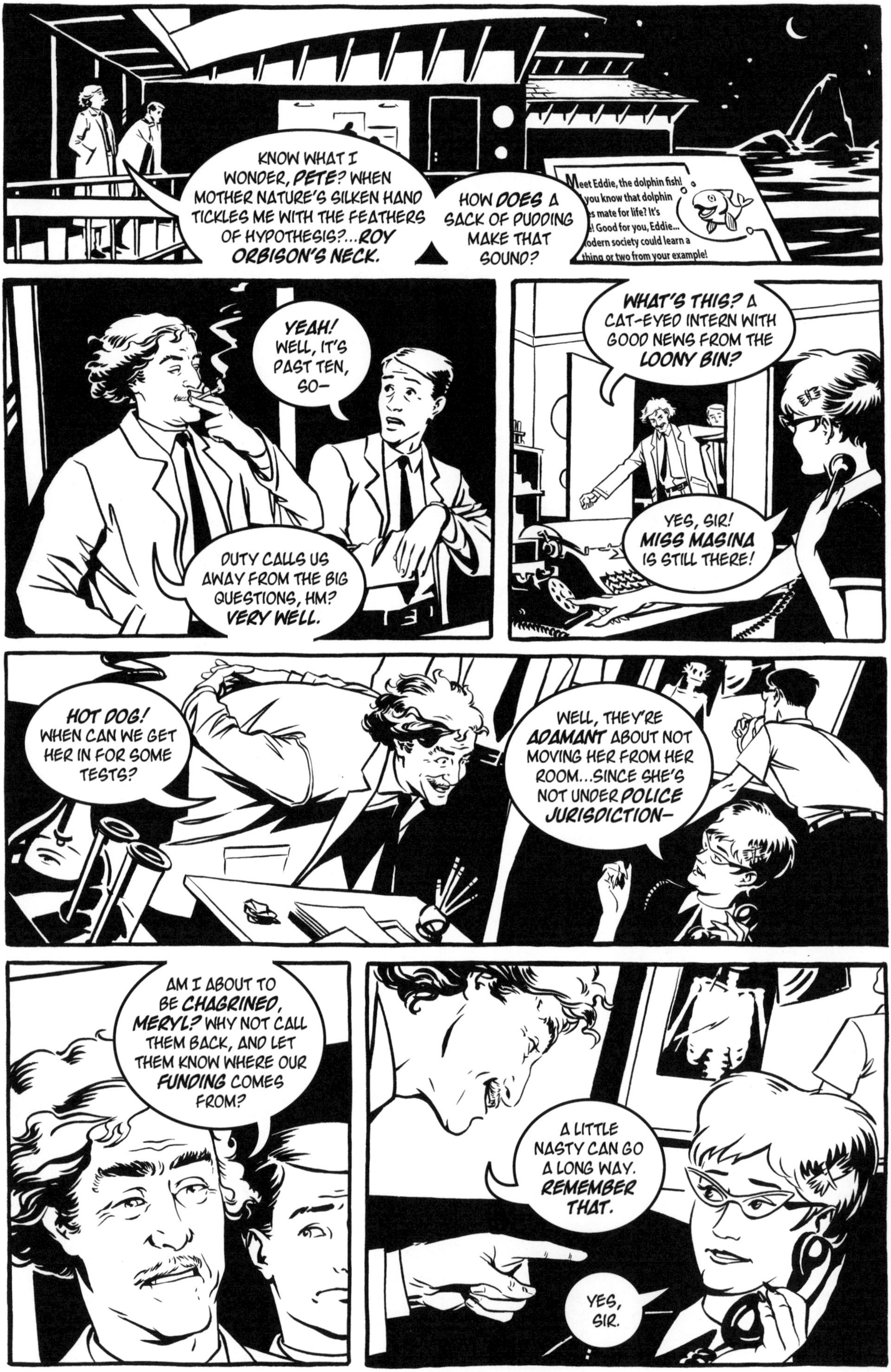
KNOW WHAT I WONDER, PETE? WHEN MOTHER NATURE'S SILKEN HAND TICKLES ME WITH THE FEATHERS OF HYPOTHESIS?...ROY ORBISON'S NECK.
HOW DOES A SACK OF PUDDING MAKE THAT SOUND?
Meet Eddie, the dolphin fish!
you know that dolphin
es mate for life? It's
! Good for you, Eddie...
odern society could learn a
thing or two from your example!
YEAH! WELL, IT'S PAST TEN, SO–
DUTY CALLS US AWAY FROM THE BIG QUESTIONS, HM? VERY WELL.
WHAT'S THIS? A CAT-EYED INTERN WITH GOOD NEWS FROM THE LOONY BIN?
YES, SIR! MISS MASINA IS STILL THERE!
HOT DOG! WHEN CAN WE GET HER IN FOR SOME TESTS?
WELL, THEY'RE ADAMANT ABOUT NOT MOVING HER FROM HER ROOM...SINCE SHE'S NOT UNDER POLICE JURISDICTION–
AM I ABOUT TO BE CHAGRINED, MERYL? WHY NOT CALL THEM BACK, AND LET THEM KNOW WHERE OUR FUNDING COMES FROM?
A LITTLE NASTY CAN GO A LONG WAY. REMEMBER THAT.
YES, SIR.

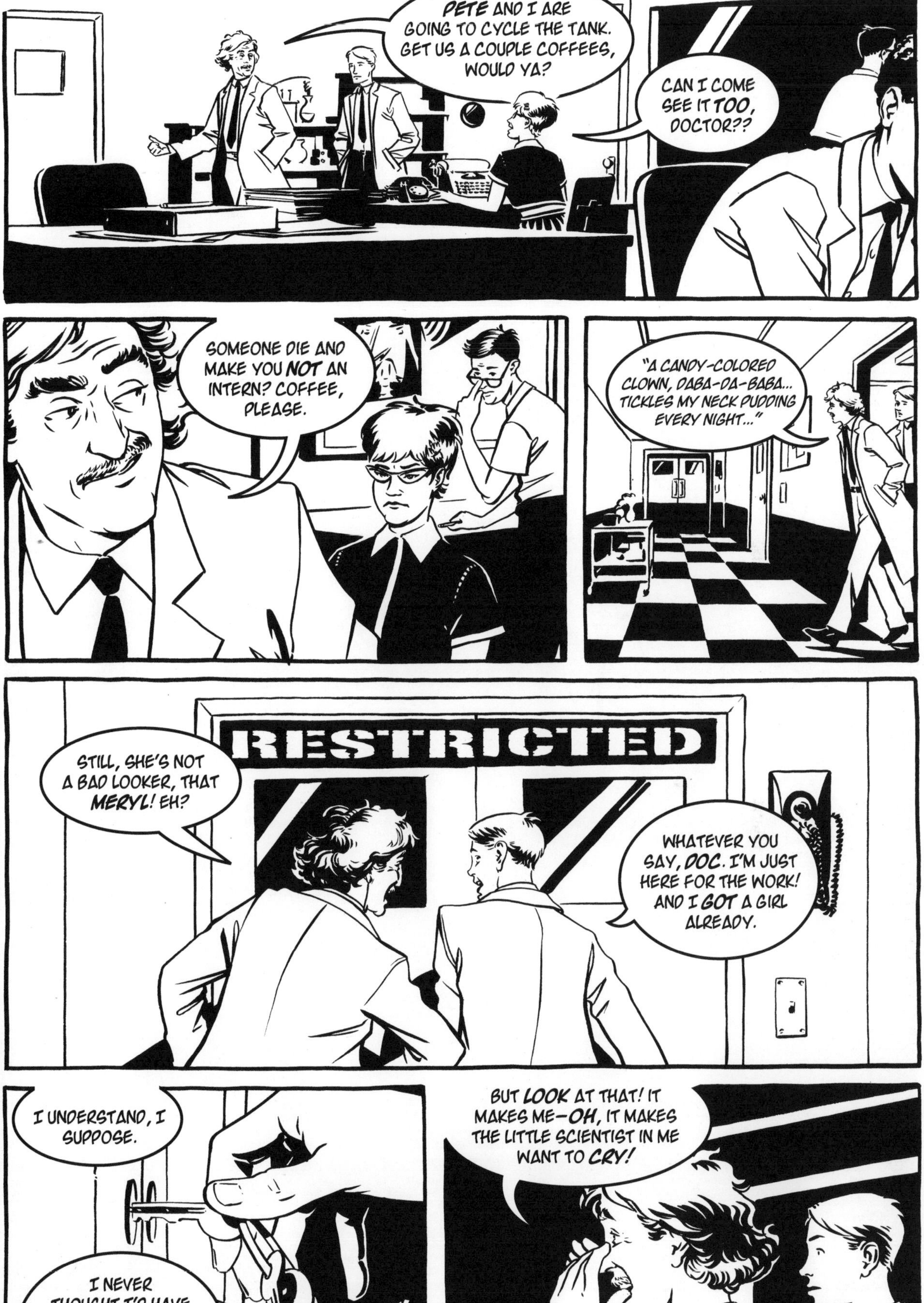
PETE AND I ARE GOING TO CYCLE THE TANK. GET US A COUPLE COFFEES, WOULD YA?
CAN I COME SEE IT TOO, DOCTOR??
SOMEONE DIE AND MAKE YOU NOT AN INTERN? COFFEE, PLEASE.
"A CANDY-COLORED CLOWN, DABA-DA-BABA... TICKLES MY NECK PUDDING EVERY NIGHT..."
RESTRICTED
STILL, SHE'S NOT A BAD LOOKER, THAT MERYL! EH?
WHATEVER YOU SAY, DOC. I'M JUST HERE FOR THE WORK! AND I GOT A GIRL ALREADY.
I UNDERSTAND, I SUPPOSE.
I NEVER THOUGHT I'D HAVE EYES FOR ANYTHING BUT ODONTOCETI AND ARCHITEUTHIS...
CLINK CLINK
BUT LOOK AT THAT! IT MAKES ME—OH, IT MAKES THE LITTLE SCIENTIST IN ME WANT TO CRY!

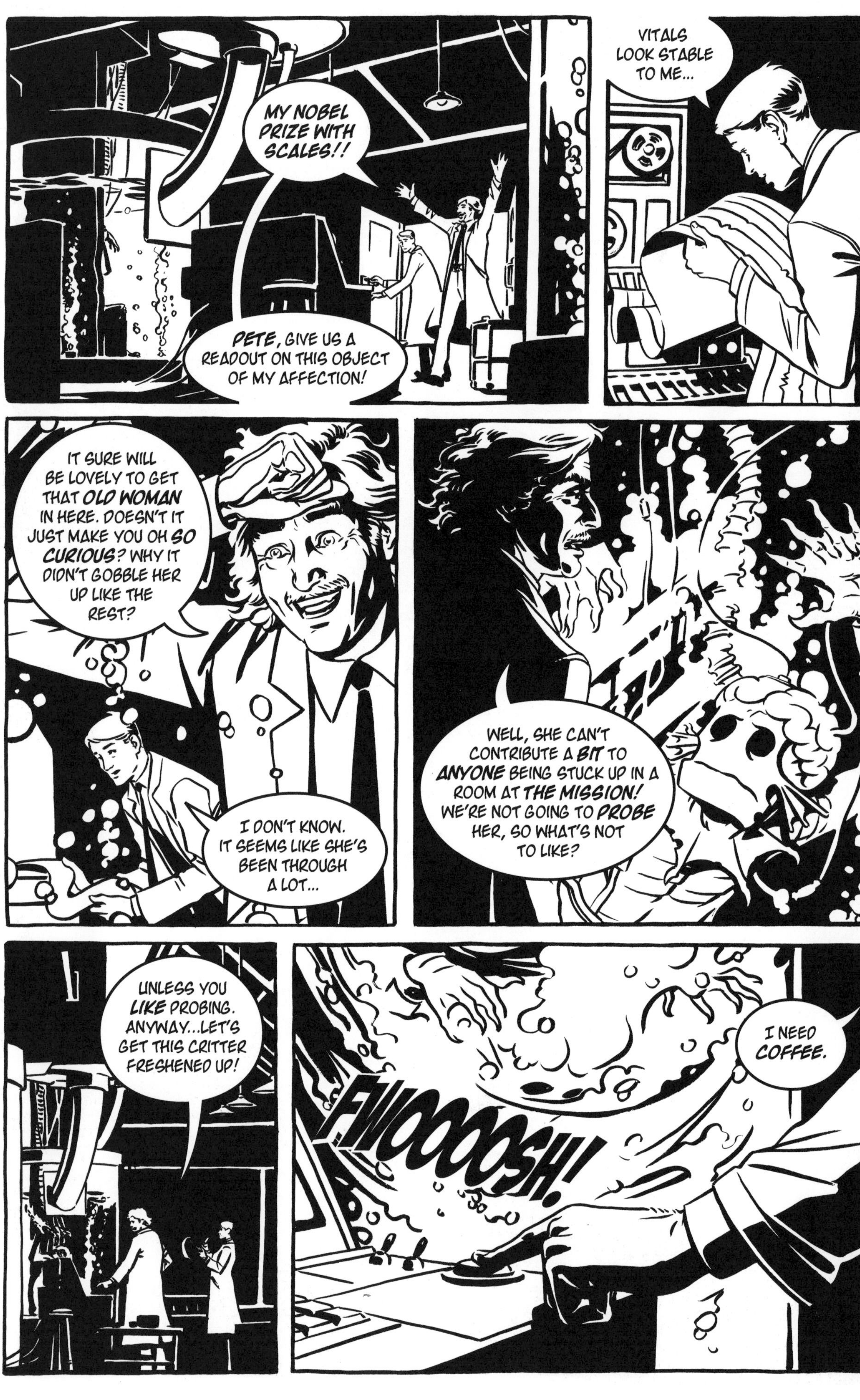
MY NOBEL PRIZE WITH SCALES!!
PETE, GIVE US A READOUT ON THIS OBJECT OF MY AFFECTION!
VITALS LOOK STABLE TO ME...
IT SURE WILL BE LOVELY TO GET THAT OLD WOMAN IN HERE. DOESN'T IT JUST MAKE YOU OH SO CURIOUS? WHY IT DIDN'T GOBBLE HER UP LIKE THE REST?
I DON'T KNOW. IT SEEMS LIKE SHE'S BEEN THROUGH A LOT...
WELL, SHE CAN'T CONTRIBUTE A BIT TO ANYONE BEING STUCK UP IN A ROOM AT THE MISSION! WE'RE NOT GOING TO PROBE HER, SO WHAT'S NOT TO LIKE?
UNLESS YOU LIKE PROBING. ANYWAY...LET'S GET THIS CRITTER FRESHENED UP!
I NEED COFFEE.
FWOOOOOSH!

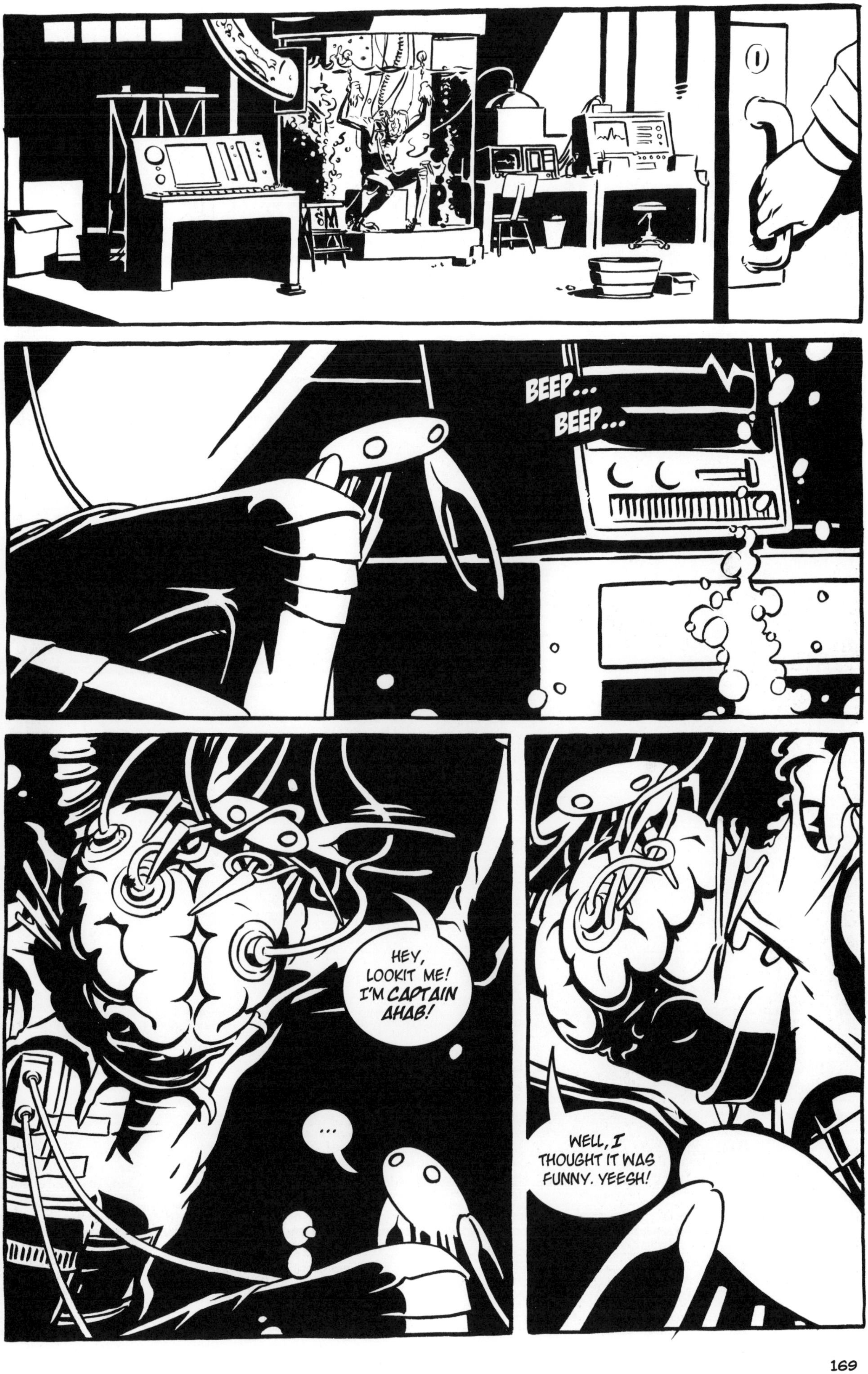
BEEP...
BEEP...
HEY, LOOKIT ME! I'M CAPTAIN AHAB!
...
WELL, I THOUGHT IT WAS FUNNY. YEESH!

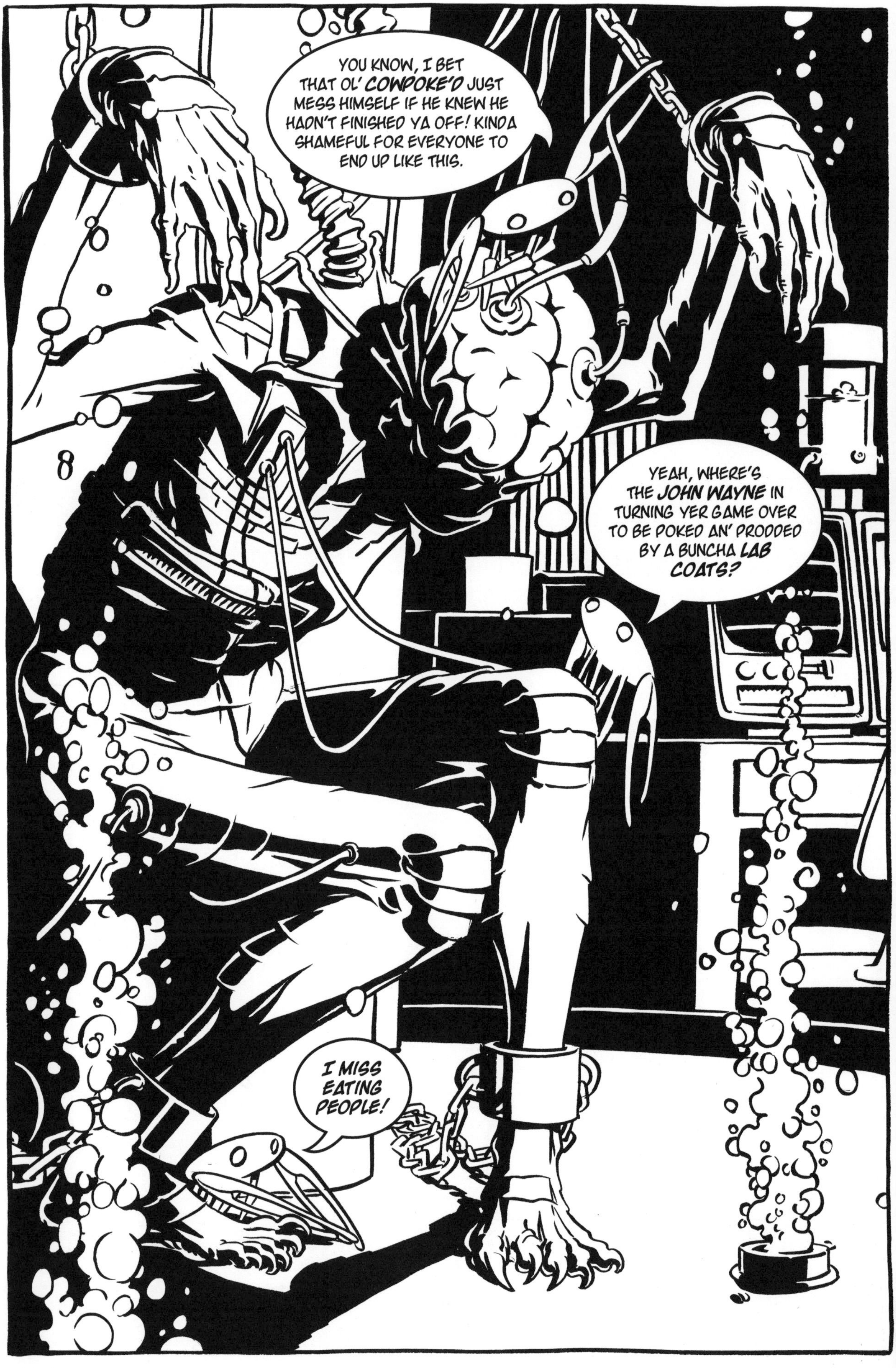
YOU KNOW, I BET THAT OL' **COWPOKE'D** JUST MESS HIMSELF IF HE KNEW HE HADN'T FINISHED YA OFF! KINDA SHAMEFUL FOR EVERYONE TO END UP LIKE THIS.
YEAH, WHERE'S THE **JOHN WAYNE** IN TURNING YER GAME OVER TO BE POKED AN' PRODDED BY A BUNCHA **LAB COATS?**
I MISS EATING PEOPLE!

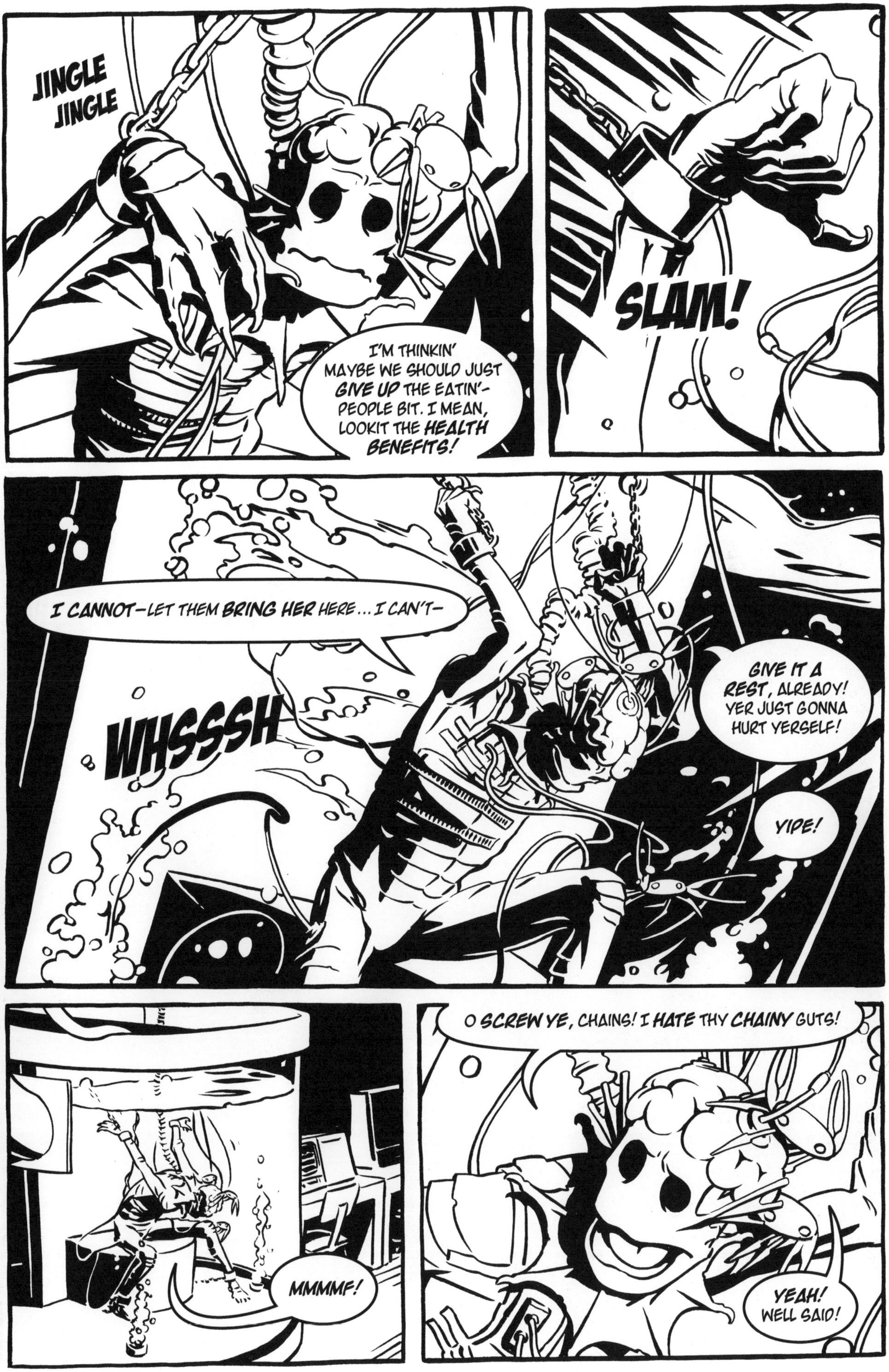
JINGLE JINGLE
I'M THINKIN' MAYBE WE SHOULD JUST GIVE UP THE EATIN'-PEOPLE BIT. I MEAN, LOOKIT THE HEALTH BENEFITS!
SLAM!
I CANNOT—LET THEM BRING HER HERE... I CAN'T—
WHSSSH
GIVE IT A REST, ALREADY! YER JUST GONNA HURT YERSELF!
YIPE!
MMMMF!
O SCREW YE, CHAINS! I HATE THY CHAINY GUTS!
YEAH! WELL SAID!

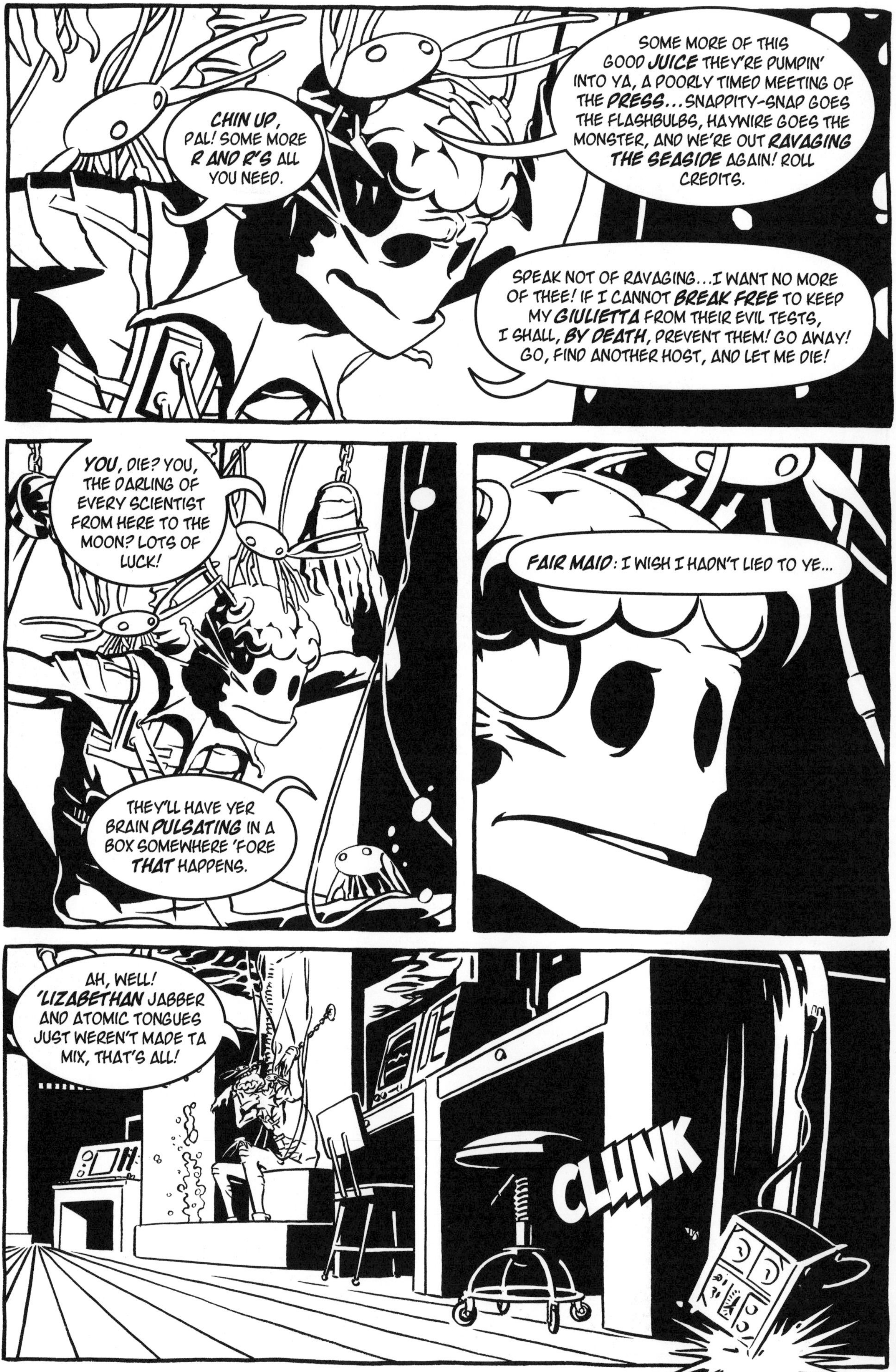
CHIN UP, PAL! SOME MORE R AND R'S ALL YOU NEED.
SOME MORE OF THIS GOOD JUICE THEY'RE PUMPIN' INTO YA, A POORLY TIMED MEETING OF THE PRESS... SNAPPITY-SNAP GOES THE FLASHBULBS, HAYWIRE GOES THE MONSTER, AND WE'RE OUT RAVAGING THE SEASIDE AGAIN! ROLL CREDITS.
SPEAK NOT OF RAVAGING...I WANT NO MORE OF THEE! IF I CANNOT BREAK FREE TO KEEP MY GIULIETTA FROM THEIR EVIL TESTS, I SHALL, BY DEATH, PREVENT THEM! GO AWAY! GO, FIND ANOTHER HOST, AND LET ME DIE!
YOU, DIE? YOU, THE DARLING OF EVERY SCIENTIST FROM HERE TO THE MOON? LOTS OF LUCK!
THEY'LL HAVE YER BRAIN PULSATING IN A BOX SOMEWHERE 'FORE THAT HAPPENS.
FAIR MAID: I WISH I HADN'T LIED TO YE...
AH, WELL! 'LIZABETHAN JABBER AND ATOMIC TONGUES JUST WEREN'T MADE TA MIX, THAT'S ALL!
CLUNK

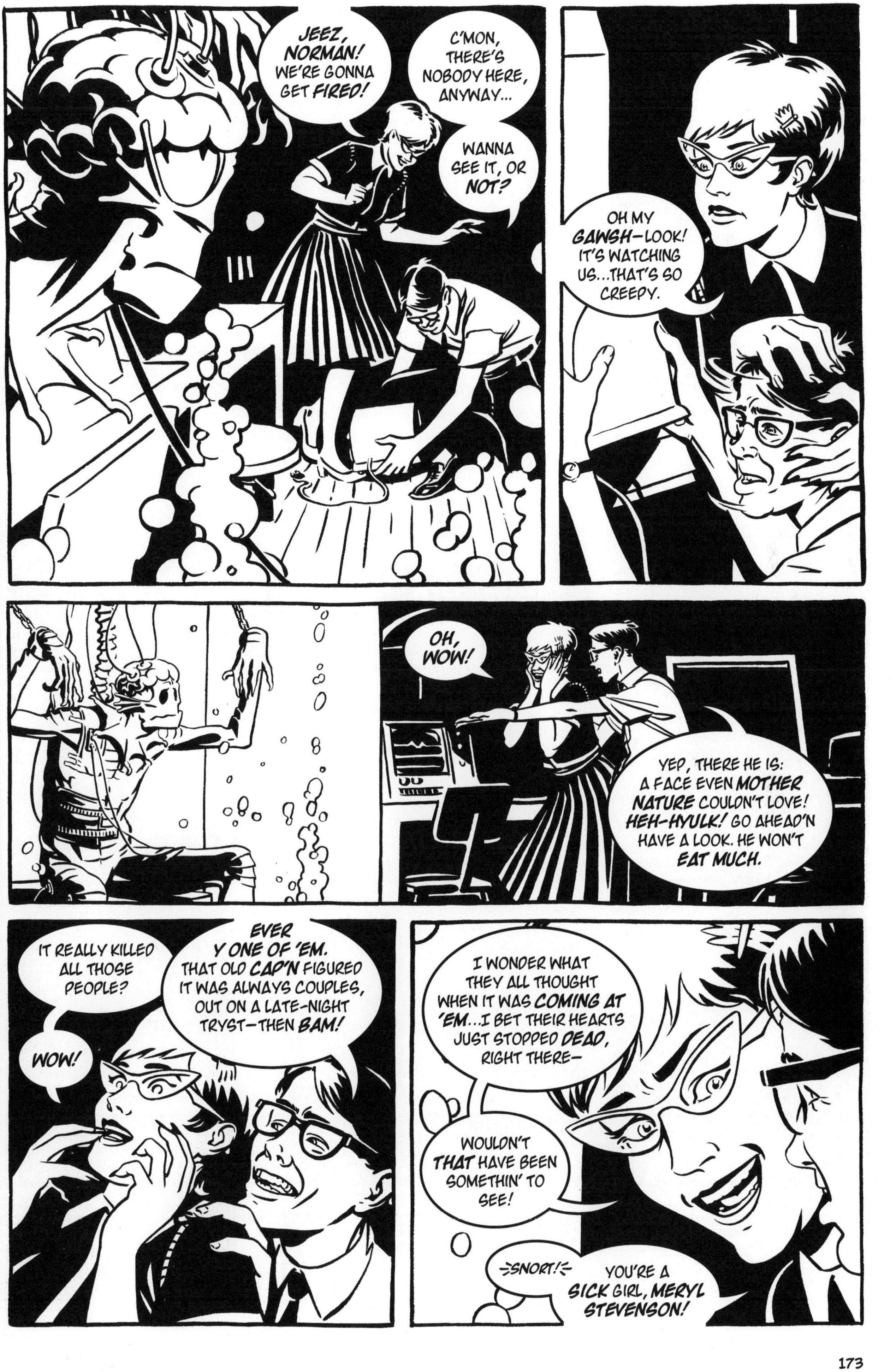
JEEZ, NORMAN! WE'RE GONNA GET FIRED!
C'MON, THERE'S NOBODY HERE, ANYWAY...
WANNA SEE IT, OR NOT?
OH MY GAWSH—LOOK! IT'S WATCHING US...THAT'S SO CREEPY.
OH, WOW!
YEP, THERE HE IS: A FACE EVEN MOTHER NATURE COULDN'T LOVE! HEH-HYULK! GO AHEAD'N HAVE A LOOK. HE WON'T EAT MUCH.
IT REALLY KILLED ALL THOSE PEOPLE?
EVER Y ONE OF 'EM. THAT OLD CAP'N FIGURED IT WAS ALWAYS COUPLES, OUT ON A LATE-NIGHT TRYST—THEN BAM!
WOW!
I WONDER WHAT THEY ALL THOUGHT WHEN IT WAS COMING AT 'EM...I BET THEIR HEARTS JUST STOPPED DEAD, RIGHT THERE—
WOULDN'T THAT HAVE BEEN SOMETHIN' TO SEE!
SNORT!
YOU'RE A SICK GIRL, MERYL STEVENSON!

DO YOU HEAR WHAT I HEAR?

OH, NO...*NOT THIS!*

PLEASE, *ANYTHING* BUT THIS!!!

YEEEHAW! GO, NORMAN, GO, GO!

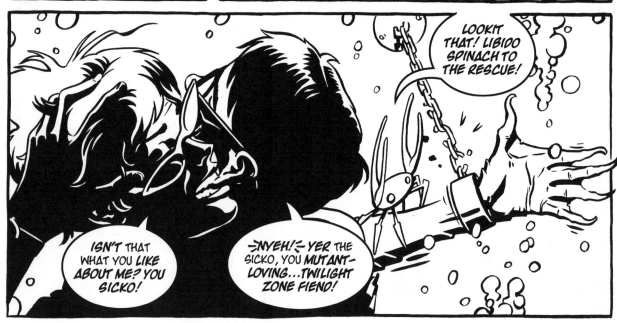

LOOKIT THAT! LIBIDO SPINACH TO THE RESCUE!

ISN'T THAT WHAT YOU *LIKE* ABOUT ME? YOU *SICKO!*

=NYEH!= YER THE SICKO, YOU *MUTANT-LOVING...TWILIGHT ZONE FIEND!*

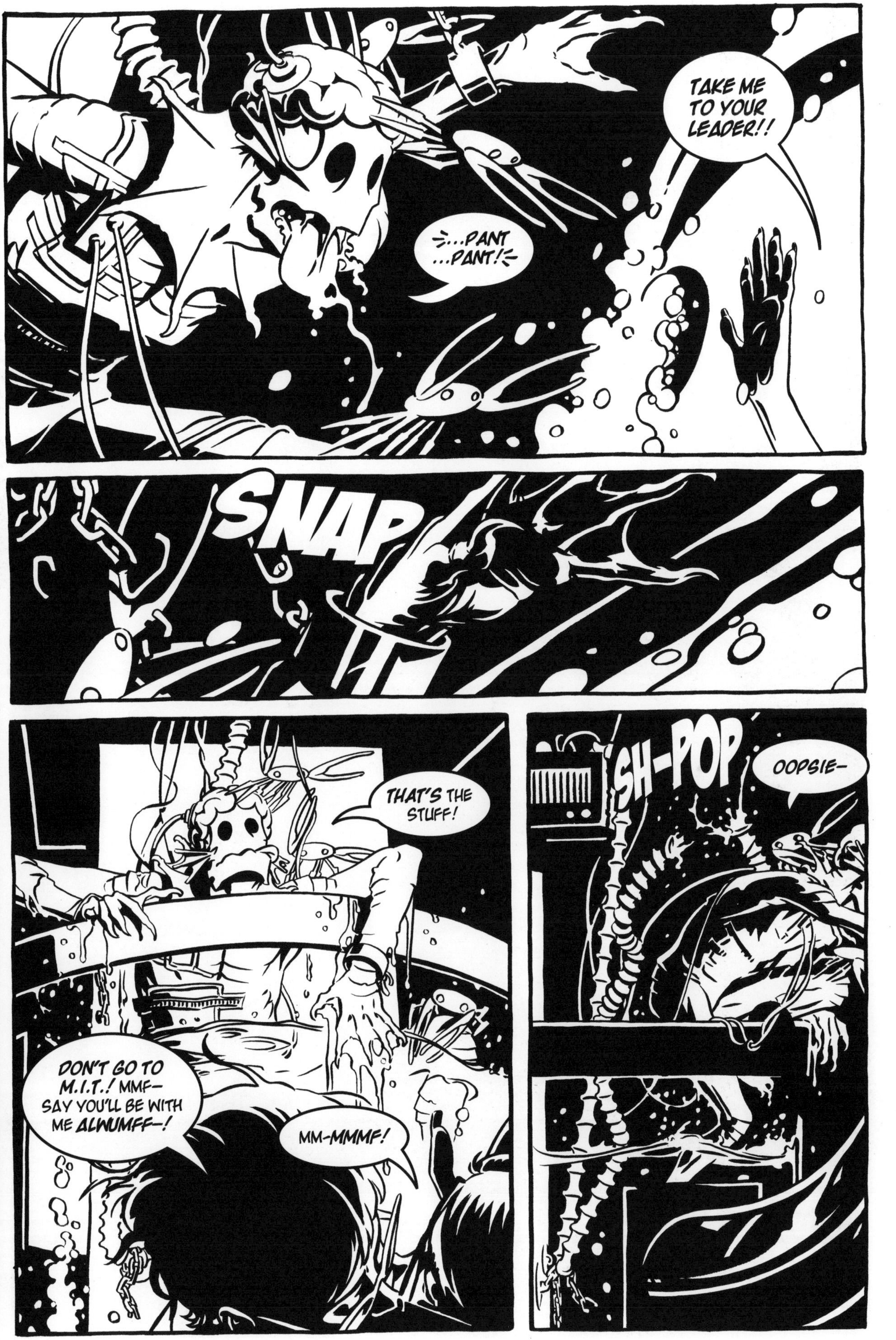

TAKE ME TO YOUR LEADER!!
...PANT ...PANT!
SNAP
THAT'S THE STUFF!
DON'T GO TO M.I.T.! MMF– SAY YOU'LL BE WITH ME ALWUMFF–!
MM-MMMF!
SH-POP
OOPSIE–

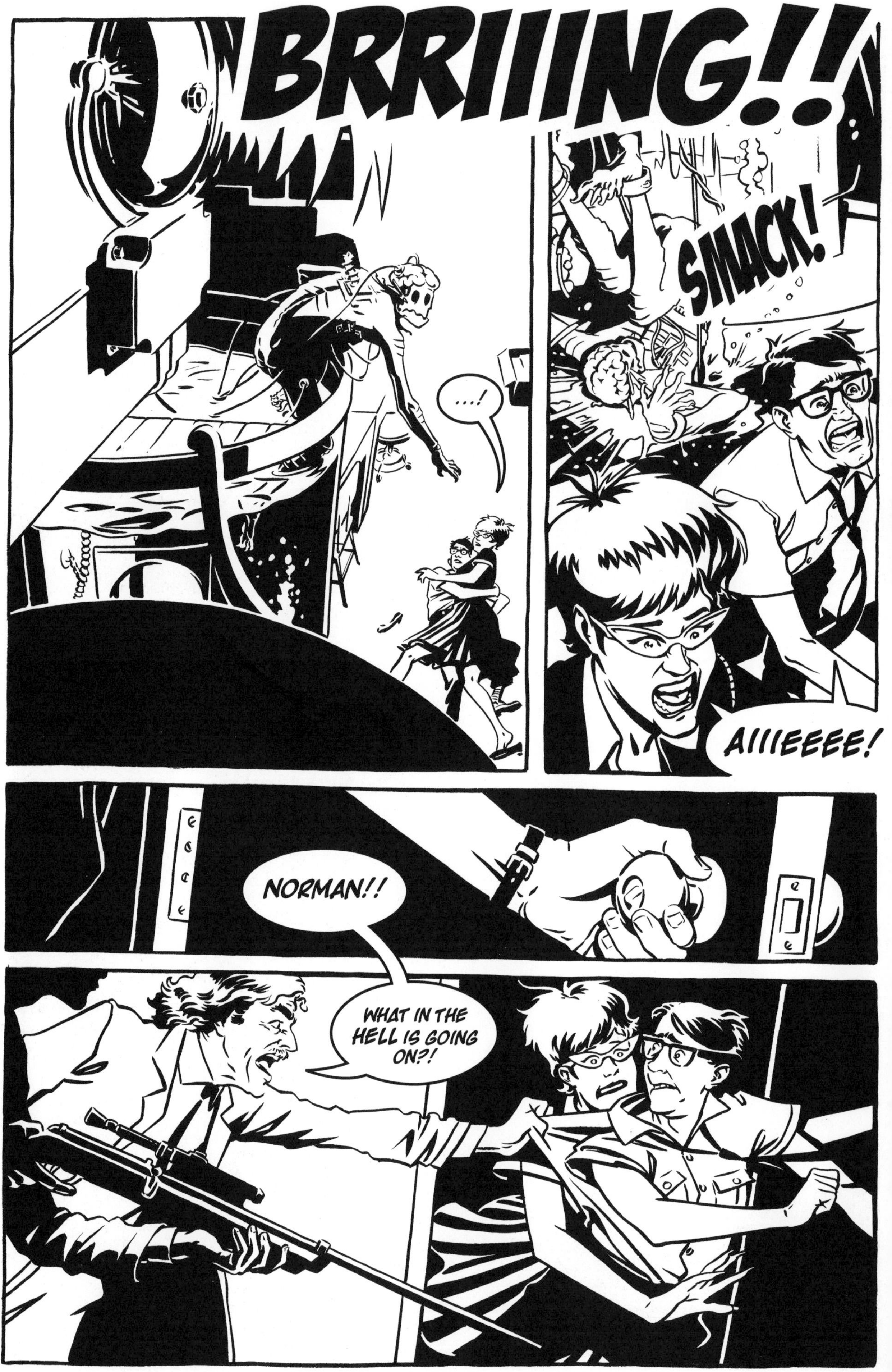
BRRIIING!!
...!
SMACK!
AIIIEEEE!
NORMAN!!
WHAT IN THE HELL IS GOING ON?!

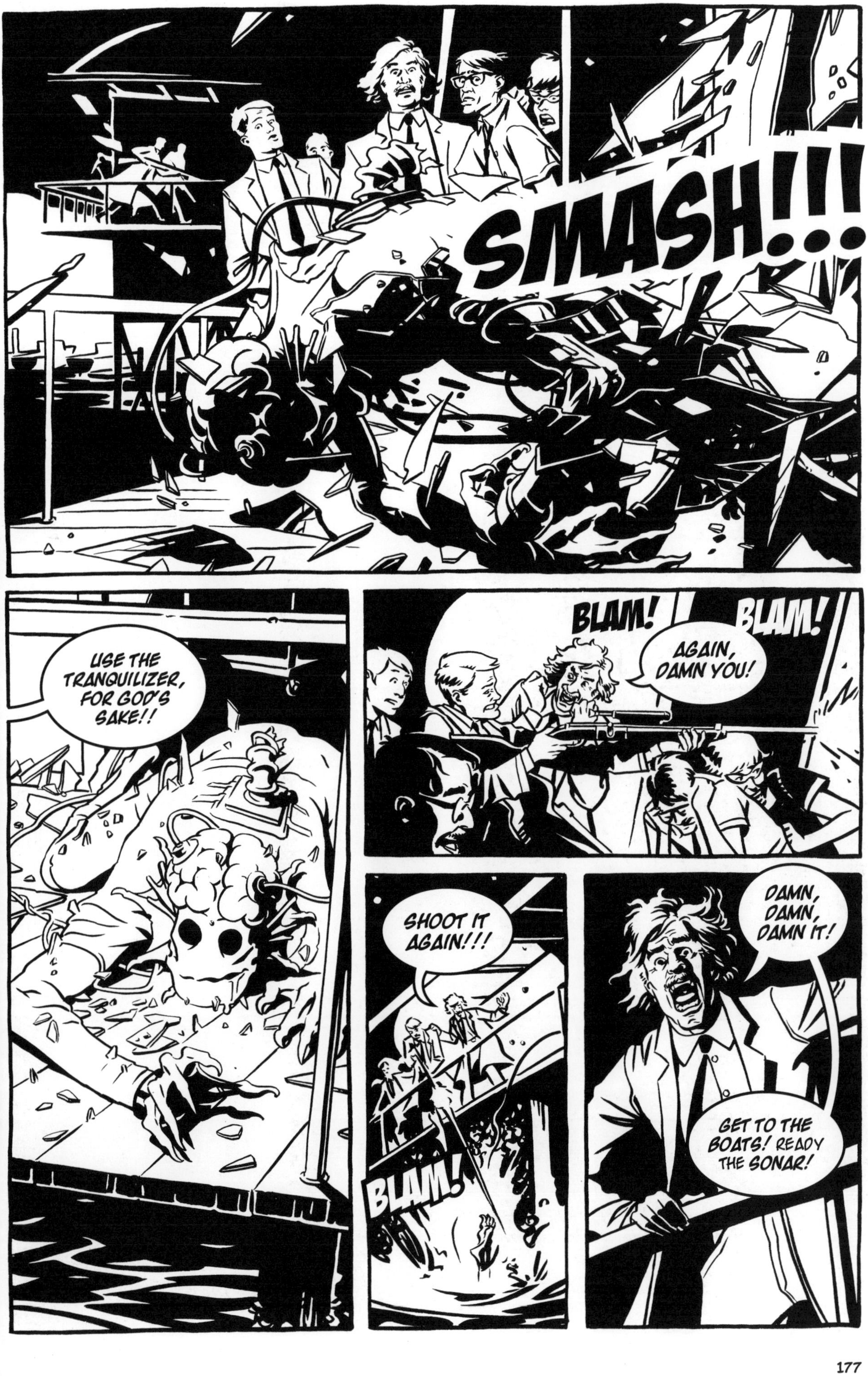
SMASH!!!
USE THE TRANQUILIZER, FOR GOD'S SAKE!!
BLAM!
BLAM!
AGAIN, DAMN YOU!
SHOOT IT AGAIN!!!
BLAM!
DAMN, DAMN, DAMN IT!
GET TO THE BOATS! READY THE SONAR!

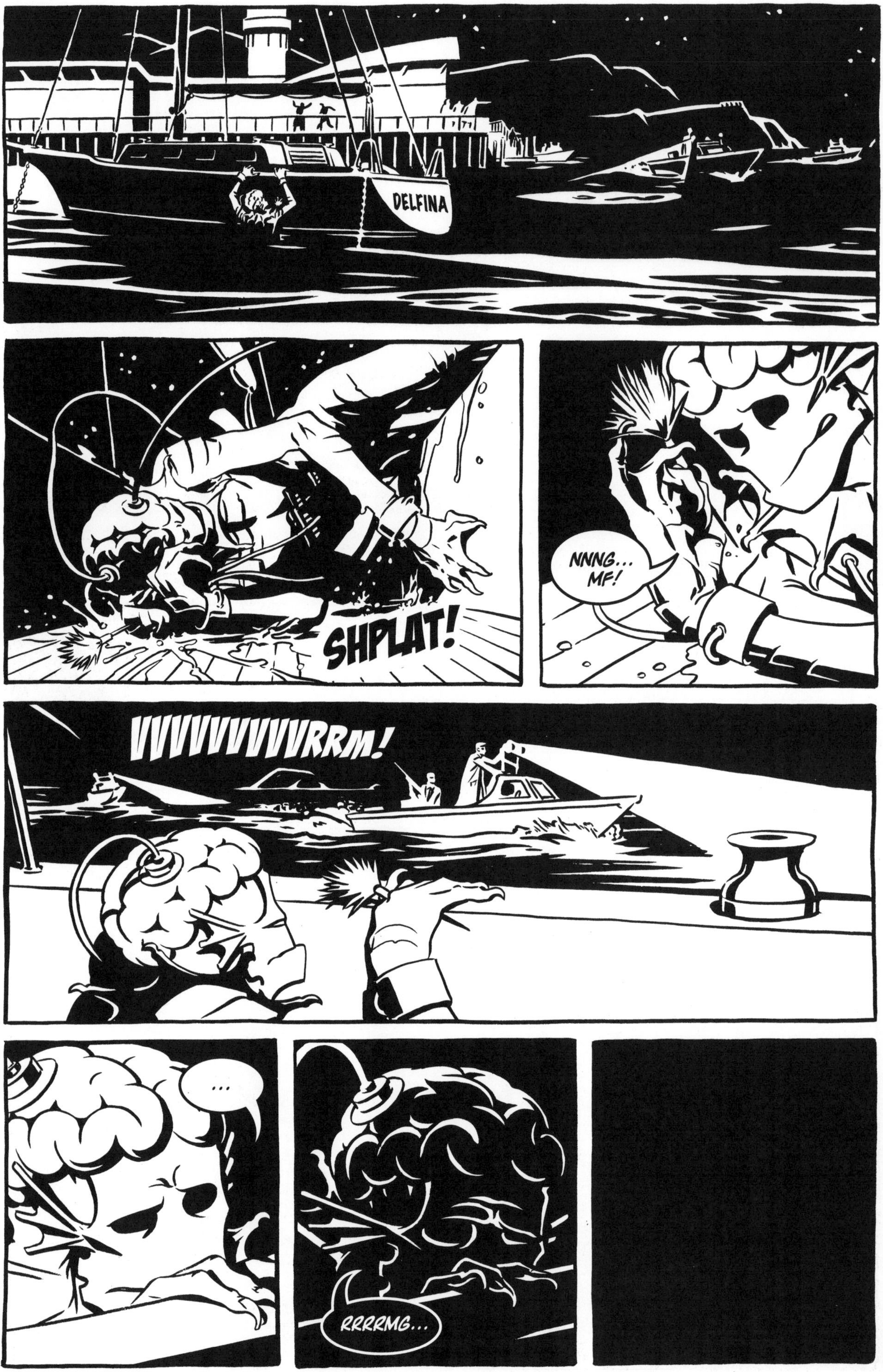
DELFINA
SHPLAT!
NNNG... MF!
VVVVVVVVVRRM!
...
RRRRMG...

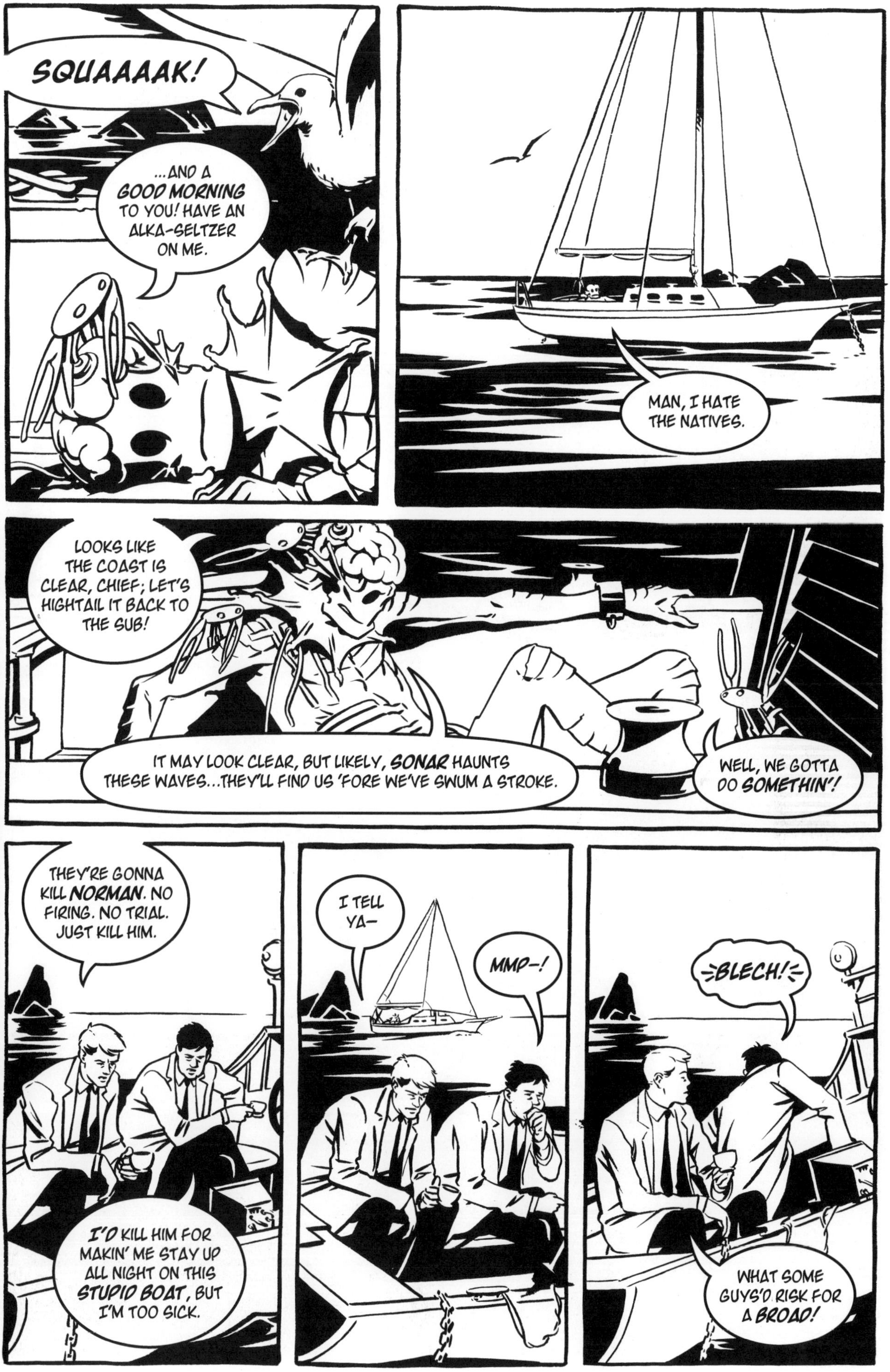

SQUAAAAK!
...AND A GOOD MORNING TO YOU! HAVE AN ALKA-SELTZER ON ME.
MAN, I HATE THE NATIVES.
LOOKS LIKE THE COAST IS CLEAR, CHIEF; LET'S HIGHTAIL IT BACK TO THE SUB!
IT MAY LOOK CLEAR, BUT LIKELY, SONAR HAUNTS THESE WAVES...THEY'LL FIND US 'FORE WE'VE SWUM A STROKE.
WELL, WE GOTTA DO SOMETHIN'!
THEY'RE GONNA KILL NORMAN. NO FIRING. NO TRIAL. JUST KILL HIM.
I'D KILL HIM FOR MAKIN' ME STAY UP ALL NIGHT ON THIS STUPID BOAT, BUT I'M TOO SICK.
I TELL YA-
MMP-!
BLECH!
WHAT SOME GUYS'D RISK FOR A BROAD!

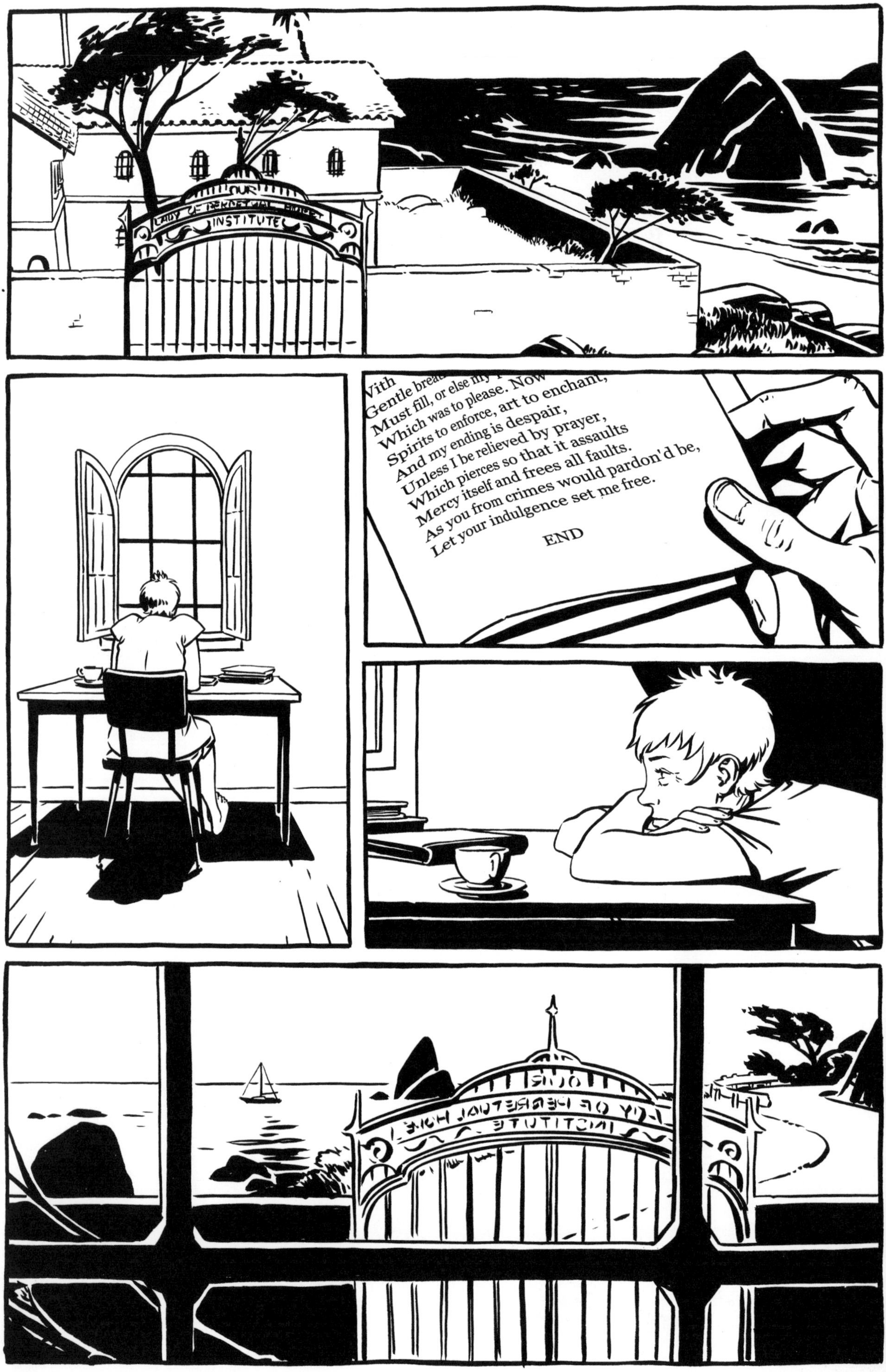
OUR LADY OF PERPETUAL HOPE INSTITUTE
Which was to please. Now
Spirits to enforce, art to enchant,
And my ending is despair,
Unless I be relieved by prayer,
Which pierces so that it assaults
Mercy itself and frees all faults.
As you from crimes would pardon'd be,
Let your indulgence set me free.
END

TO CALL *OUR LADY* BEAUTIFUL IS TRITE. NO WORD CAN SUM HER; I INDEED HAVE TRIED!

HELLO, *FAIR ORGANISM.* FRET YE NOT—YOUR NEPHEW'S SAFE, AND I AM...DISINCLINED TO FURTHER *MISCHIEF!* I COME NOT TO SEEK FORGIVENESS, BUT TO SEE THAT YE BE WELL.

YOU'RE HURT!

A LADY EVER, *GIULIETTA!* CARE NOT FOR ME...I AM A MONSTER, AS YE SAID. BUT HOW FARE *YE*, MY LITTLE CRAZY ONE?

...*ZOLA* TOLD ME THE *CAPTAIN* HAD KILLED YOU!

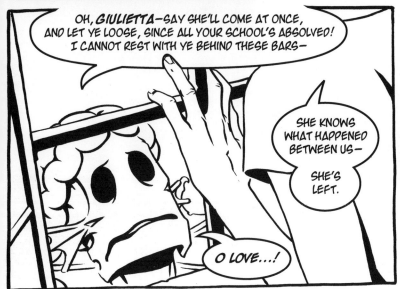

OH, *GIULIETTA*—SAY SHE'LL COME AT ONCE, AND LET YE LOOSE, SINCE ALL YOUR SCHOOL'S ABSOLVED! I CANNOT REST WITH YE BEHIND THESE BARS—

SHE KNOWS WHAT HAPPENED BETWEEN US—

SHE'S LEFT.

O LOVE....!

...I'VE CURSED YE *MORE*—I AM UNDONE!

181

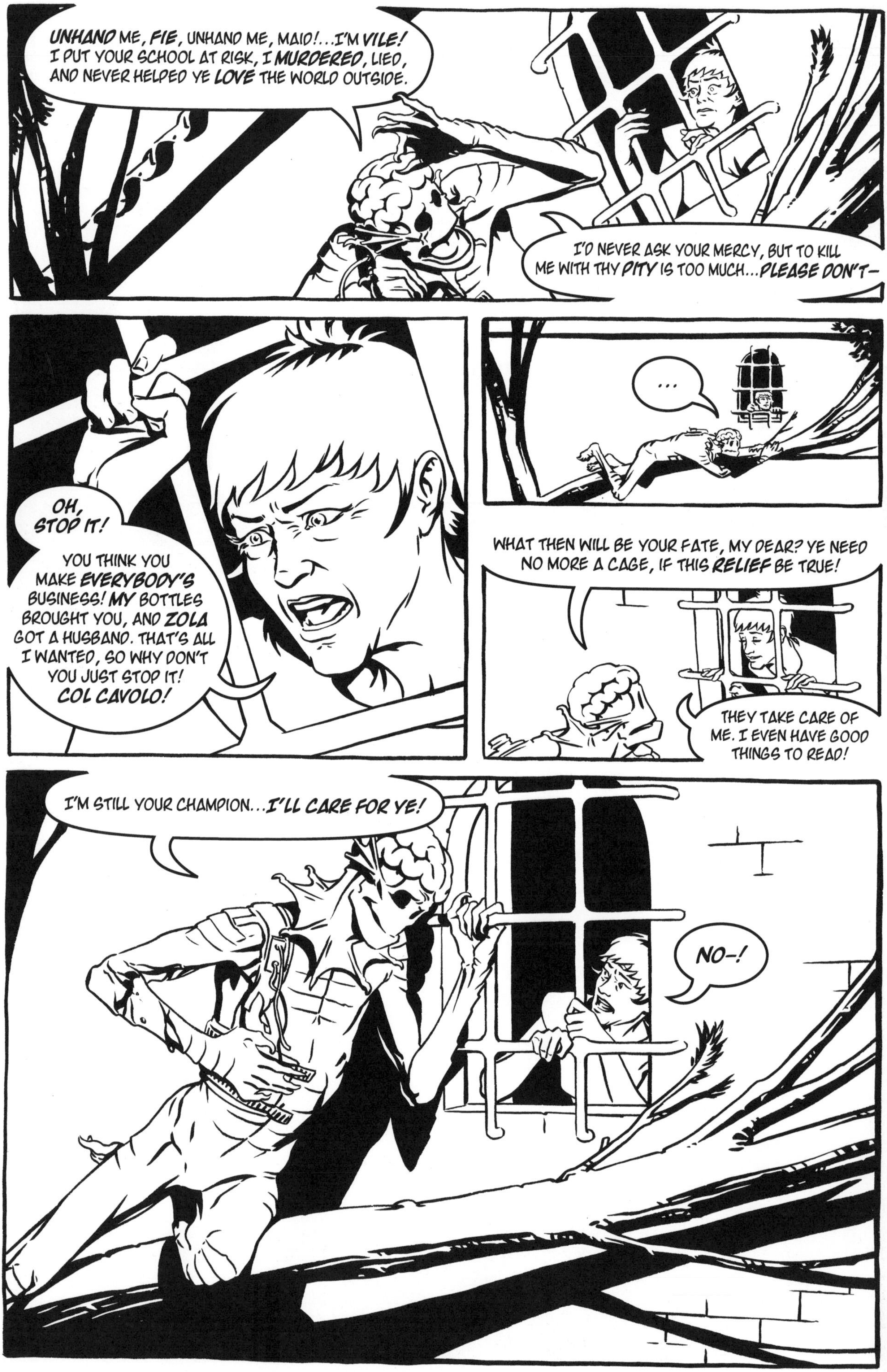
UNHAND ME, FIE, UNHAND ME, MAID!...I'M VILE! I PUT YOUR SCHOOL AT RISK, I MURDERED, LIED, AND NEVER HELPED YE LOVE THE WORLD OUTSIDE.
I'D NEVER ASK YOUR MERCY, BUT TO KILL ME WITH THY PITY IS TOO MUCH...PLEASE DON'T–
OH, STOP IT!
YOU THINK YOU MAKE EVERYBODY'S BUSINESS! MY BOTTLES BROUGHT YOU, AND ZOLA GOT A HUSBAND. THAT'S ALL I WANTED, SO WHY DON'T YOU JUST STOP IT! COL CAVOLO!
...
WHAT THEN WILL BE YOUR FATE, MY DEAR? YE NEED NO MORE A CAGE, IF THIS RELIEF BE TRUE!
THEY TAKE CARE OF ME. I EVEN HAVE GOOD THINGS TO READ!
I'M STILL YOUR CHAMPION...I'LL CARE FOR YE!
NO–!

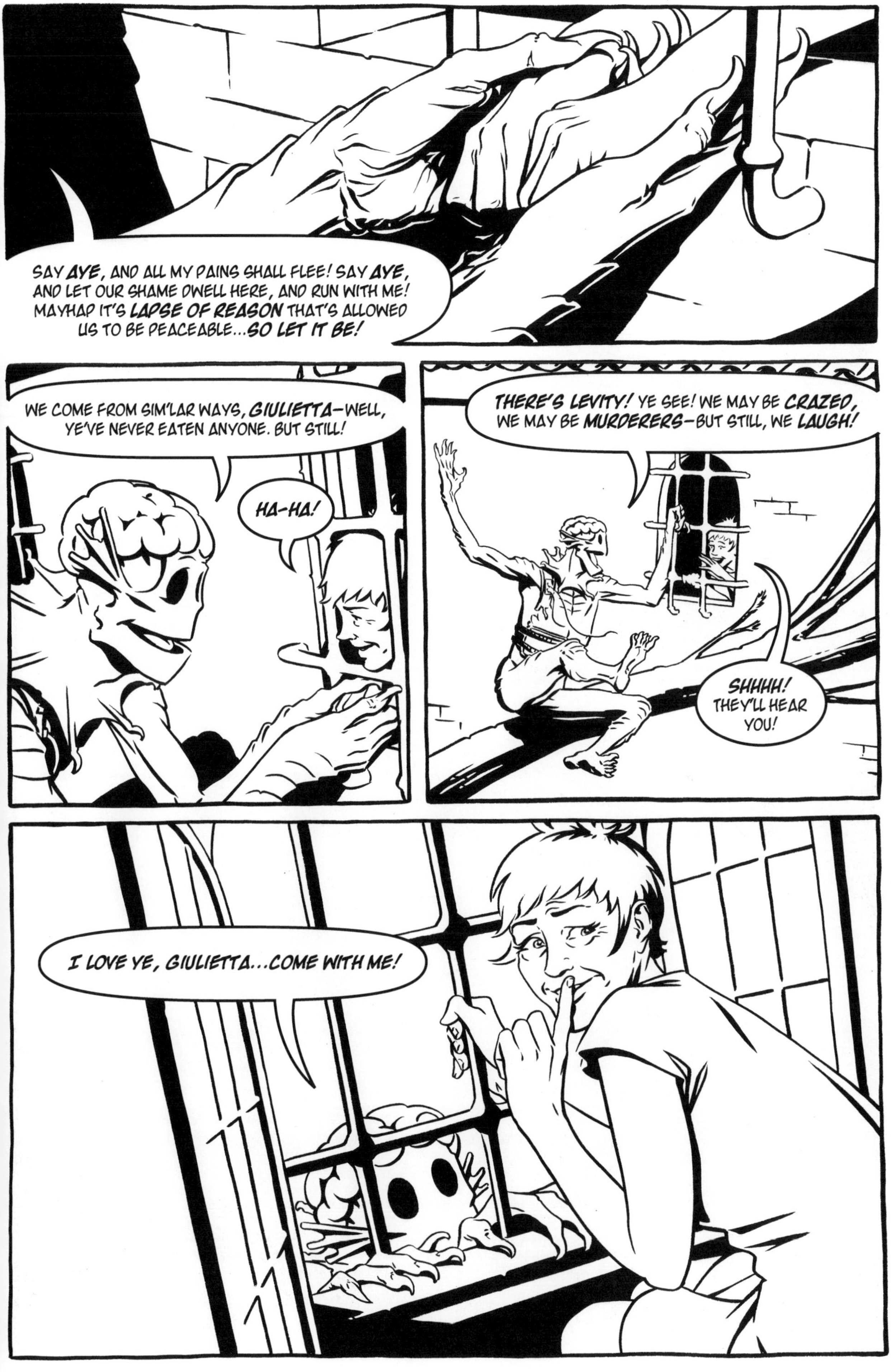
SAY AYE, AND ALL MY PAINS SHALL FLEE! SAY AYE, AND LET OUR SHAME DWELL HERE, AND RUN WITH ME! MAYHAP IT'S LAPSE OF REASON THAT'S ALLOWED US TO BE PEACEABLE...SO LET IT BE!
WE COME FROM SIM'LAR WAYS, GIULIETTA—WELL, YE'VE NEVER EATEN ANYONE. BUT STILL!
HA-HA!
THERE'S LEVITY! YE SEE! WE MAY BE CRAZED, WE MAY BE MURDERERS—BUT STILL, WE LAUGH!
SHHHH! THEY'LL HEAR YOU!
I LOVE YE, GIULIETTA...COME WITH ME!

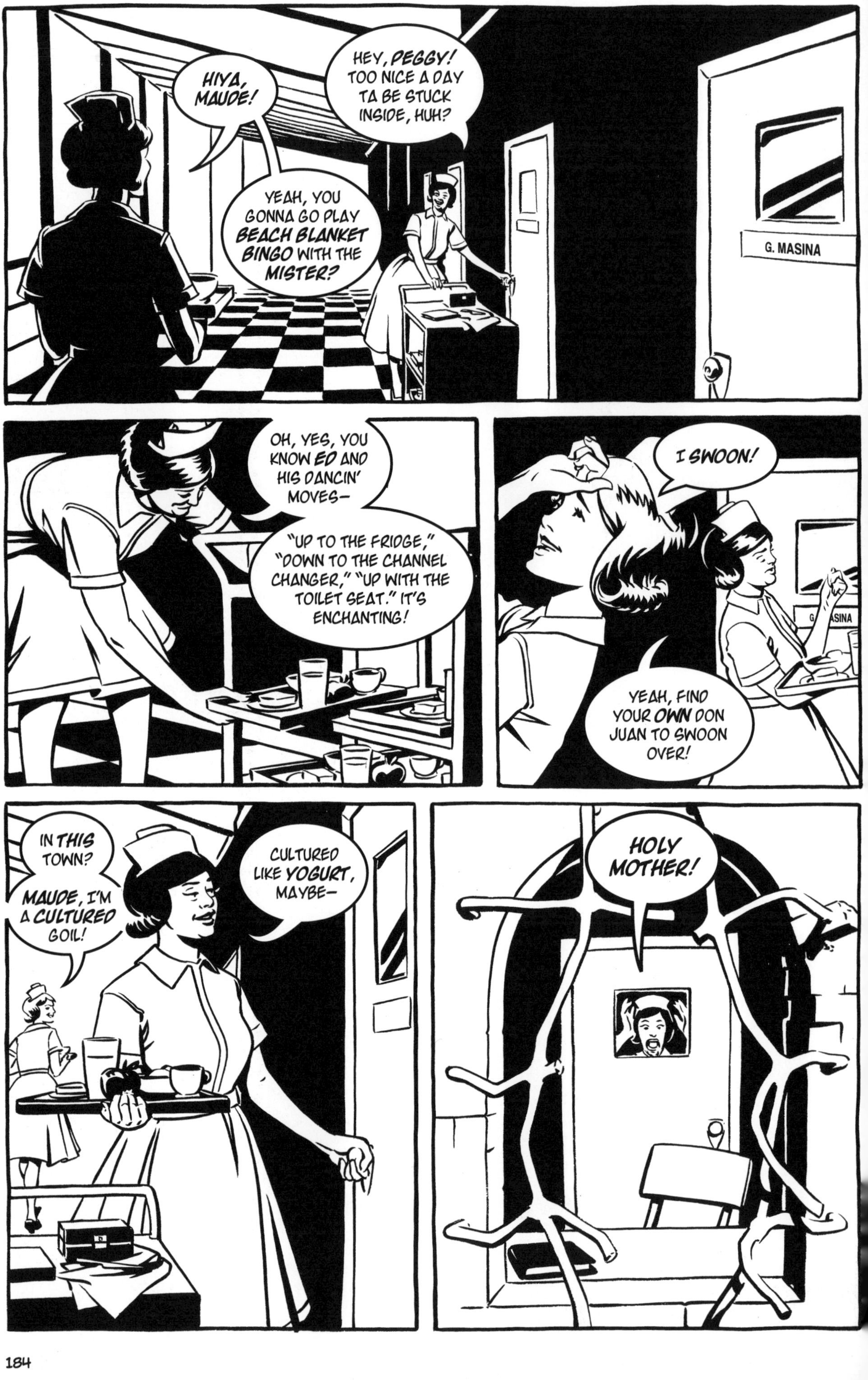
HIYA, MAUDE!
HEY, PEGGY! TOO NICE A DAY TA BE STUCK INSIDE, HUH?
YEAH, YOU GONNA GO PLAY BEACH BLANKET BINGO WITH THE MISTER?
G. MASINA
OH, YES, YOU KNOW ED AND HIS DANCIN' MOVES–
"UP TO THE FRIDGE," "DOWN TO THE CHANNEL CHANGER," "UP WITH THE TOILET SEAT." IT'S ENCHANTING!
I SWOON!
YEAH, FIND YOUR OWN DON JUAN TO SWOON OVER!
IN THIS TOWN?
MAUDE, I'M A CULTURED GOIL!
CULTURED LIKE YOGURT, MAYBE–
HOLY MOTHER!

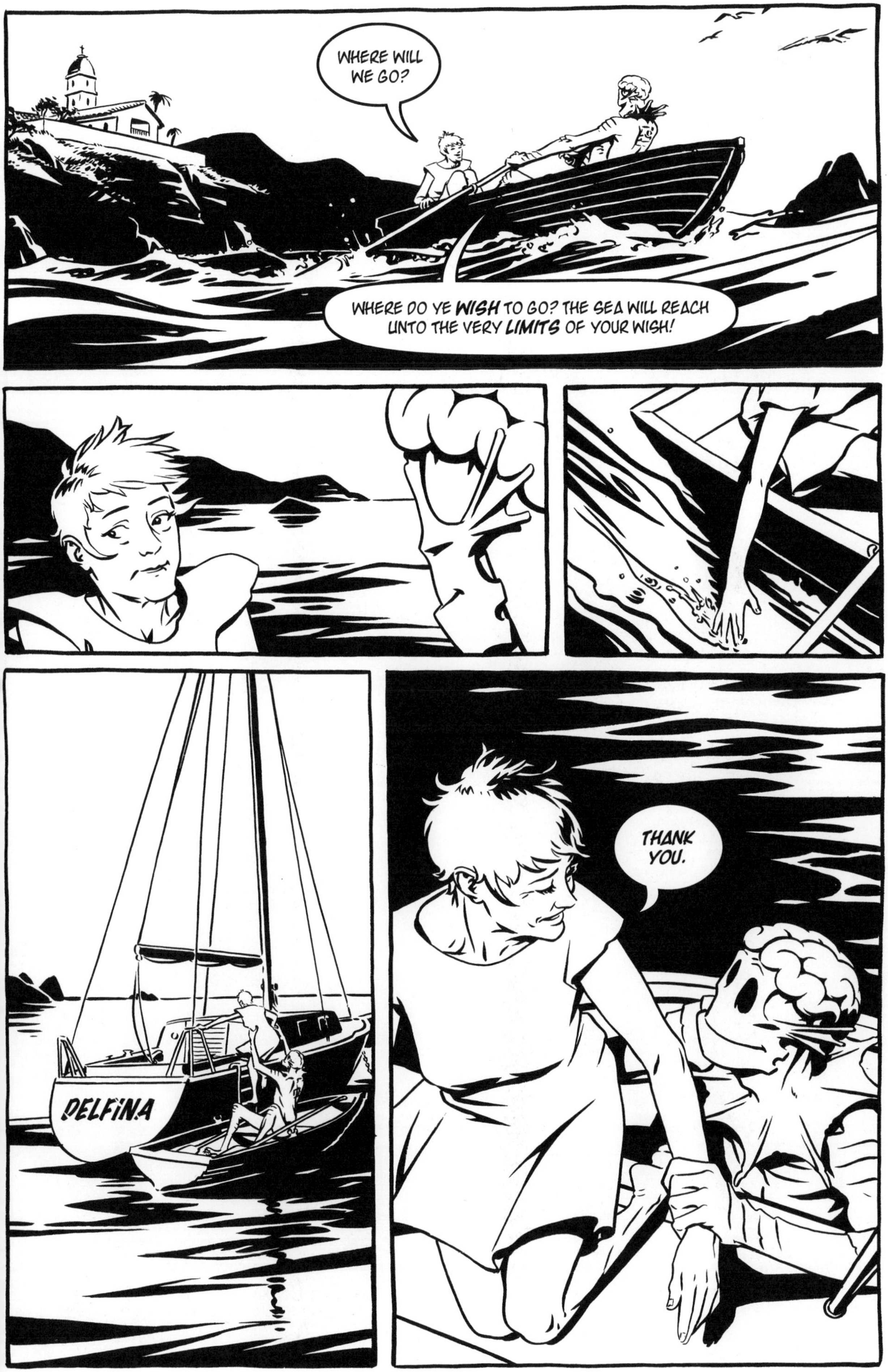
WHERE WILL WE GO?
WHERE DO YE **WISH** TO GO? THE SEA WILL REACH UNTO THE VERY **LIMITS** OF YOUR WISH!
DELFINA
THANK YOU.

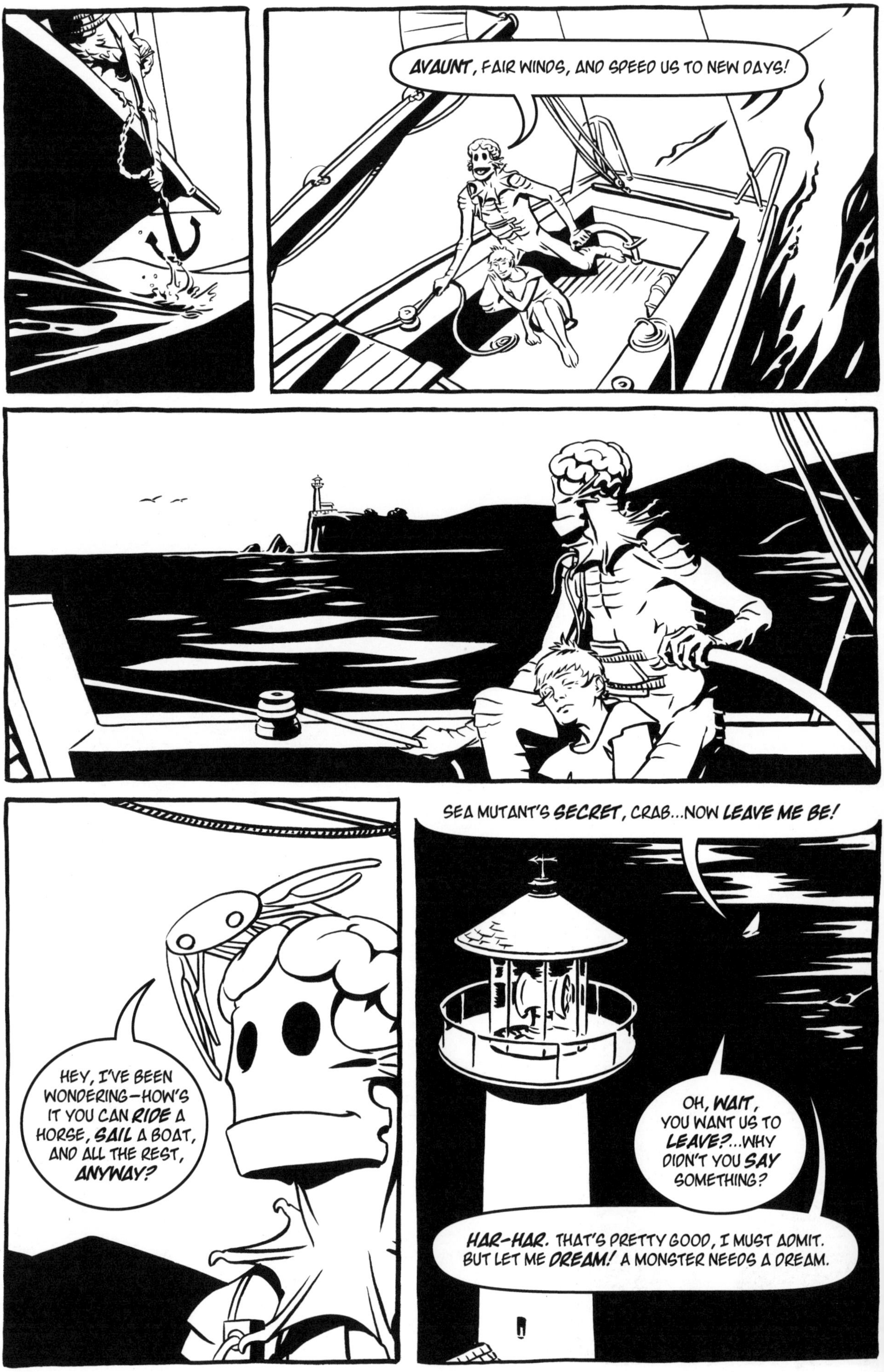
AVAUNT, FAIR WINDS, AND SPEED US TO NEW DAYS!
HEY, I'VE BEEN WONDERING—HOW'S IT YOU CAN RIDE A HORSE, SAIL A BOAT, AND ALL THE REST, ANYWAY?
SEA MUTANT'S SECRET, CRAB...NOW LEAVE ME BE!
OH, WAIT, YOU WANT US TO LEAVE?...WHY DIDN'T YOU SAY SOMETHING?
HAR-HAR. THAT'S PRETTY GOOD, I MUST ADMIT. BUT LET ME DREAM! A MONSTER NEEDS A DREAM.

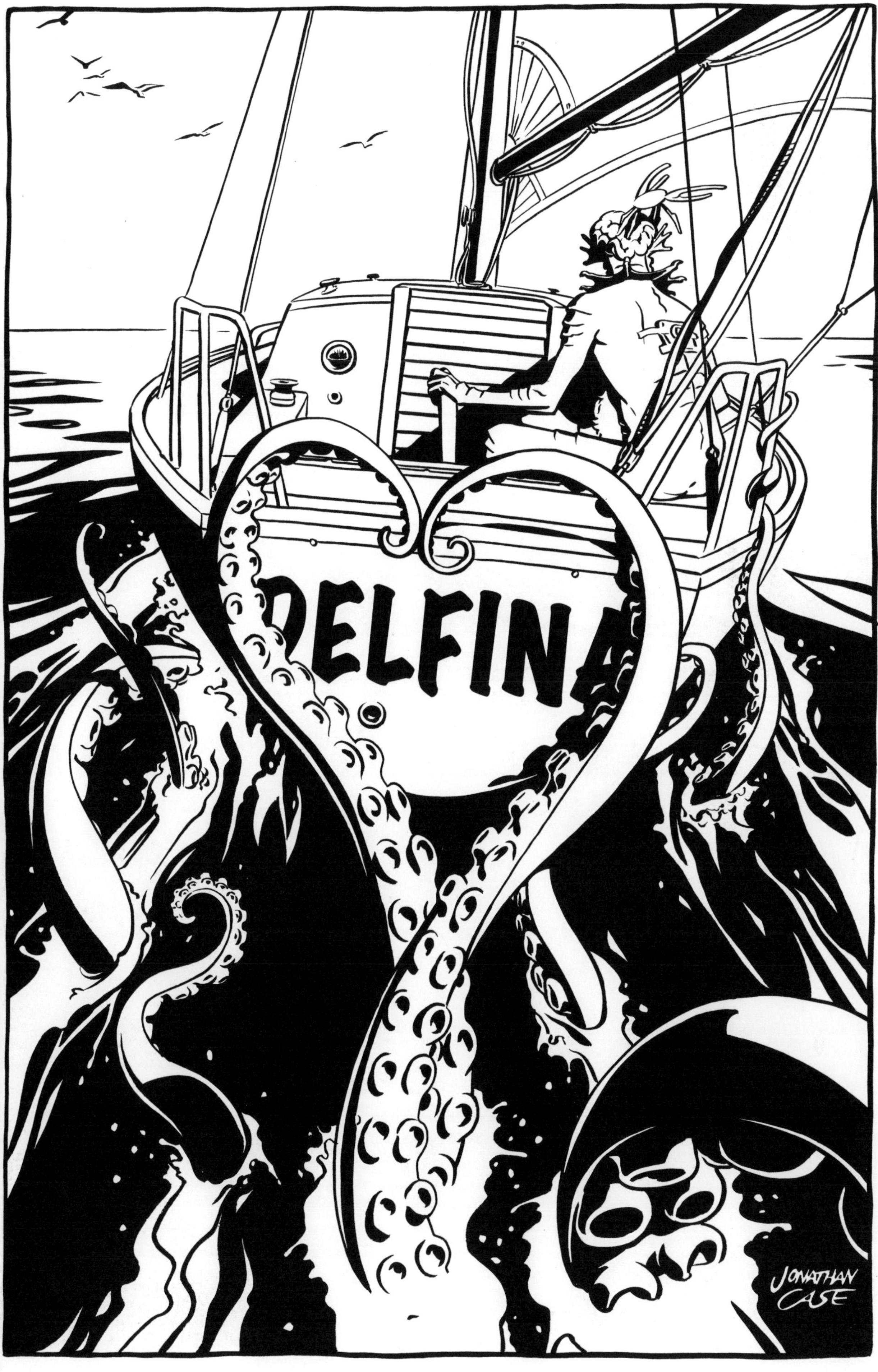
DELFINA
JONATHAN CASE

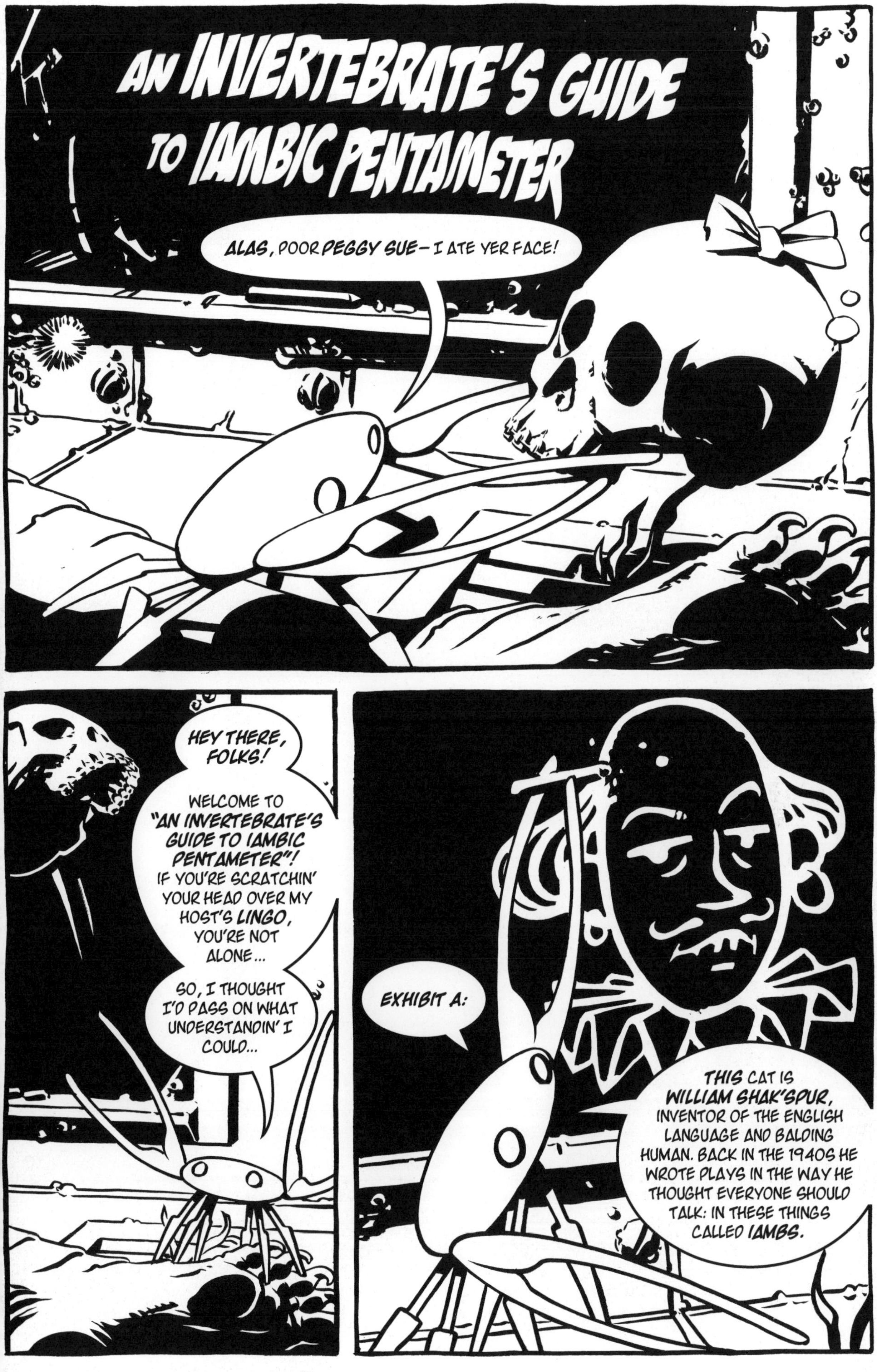
AN INVERTEBRATE'S GUIDE TO IAMBIC PENTAMETER
ALAS, POOR PEGGY SUE– I ATE YER FACE!
HEY THERE, FOLKS!
WELCOME TO "AN INVERTEBRATE'S GUIDE TO IAMBIC PENTAMETER"! IF YOU'RE SCRATCHIN' YOUR HEAD OVER MY HOST'S LINGO, YOU'RE NOT ALONE...
SO, I THOUGHT I'D PASS ON WHAT UNDERSTANDIN' I COULD...
EXHIBIT A:
THIS CAT IS WILLIAM SHAK'SPUR, INVENTOR OF THE ENGLISH LANGUAGE AND BALDING HUMAN. BACK IN THE 1940S HE WROTE PLAYS IN THE WAY HE THOUGHT EVERYONE SHOULD TALK: IN THESE THINGS CALLED IAMBS.

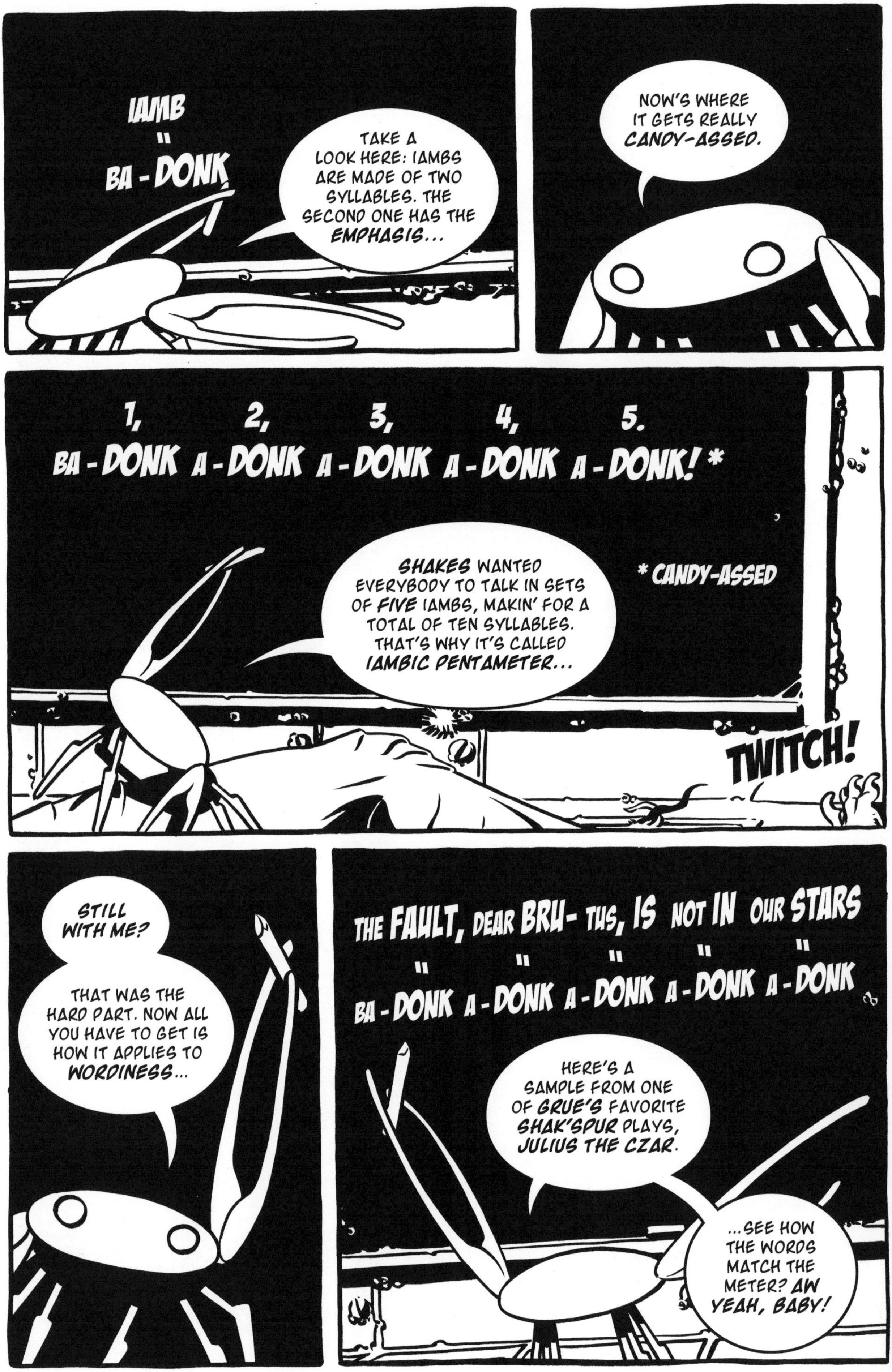
IAMB
"
BA - DONK
TAKE A LOOK HERE: IAMBS ARE MADE OF TWO SYLLABLES. THE SECOND ONE HAS THE EMPHASIS...
NOW'S WHERE IT GETS REALLY CANDY-ASSED.
1, 2, 3, 4, 5.
BA - DONK A - DONK A - DONK A - DONK A - DONK! *
SHAKES WANTED EVERYBODY TO TALK IN SETS OF FIVE IAMBS, MAKIN' FOR A TOTAL OF TEN SYLLABLES. THAT'S WHY IT'S CALLED IAMBIC PENTAMETER...
* CANDY-ASSED
TWITCH!
STILL WITH ME?
THAT WAS THE HARD PART. NOW ALL YOU HAVE TO GET IS HOW IT APPLIES TO WORDINESS...
THE FAULT, DEAR BRU- TUS, IS NOT IN OUR STARS
BA - DONK A - DONK A - DONK A - DONK A - DONK
HERE'S A SAMPLE FROM ONE OF GRUE'S FAVORITE SHAK'SPUR PLAYS, JULIUS THE CZAR.
...SEE HOW THE WORDS MATCH THE METER? AW YEAH, BABY!

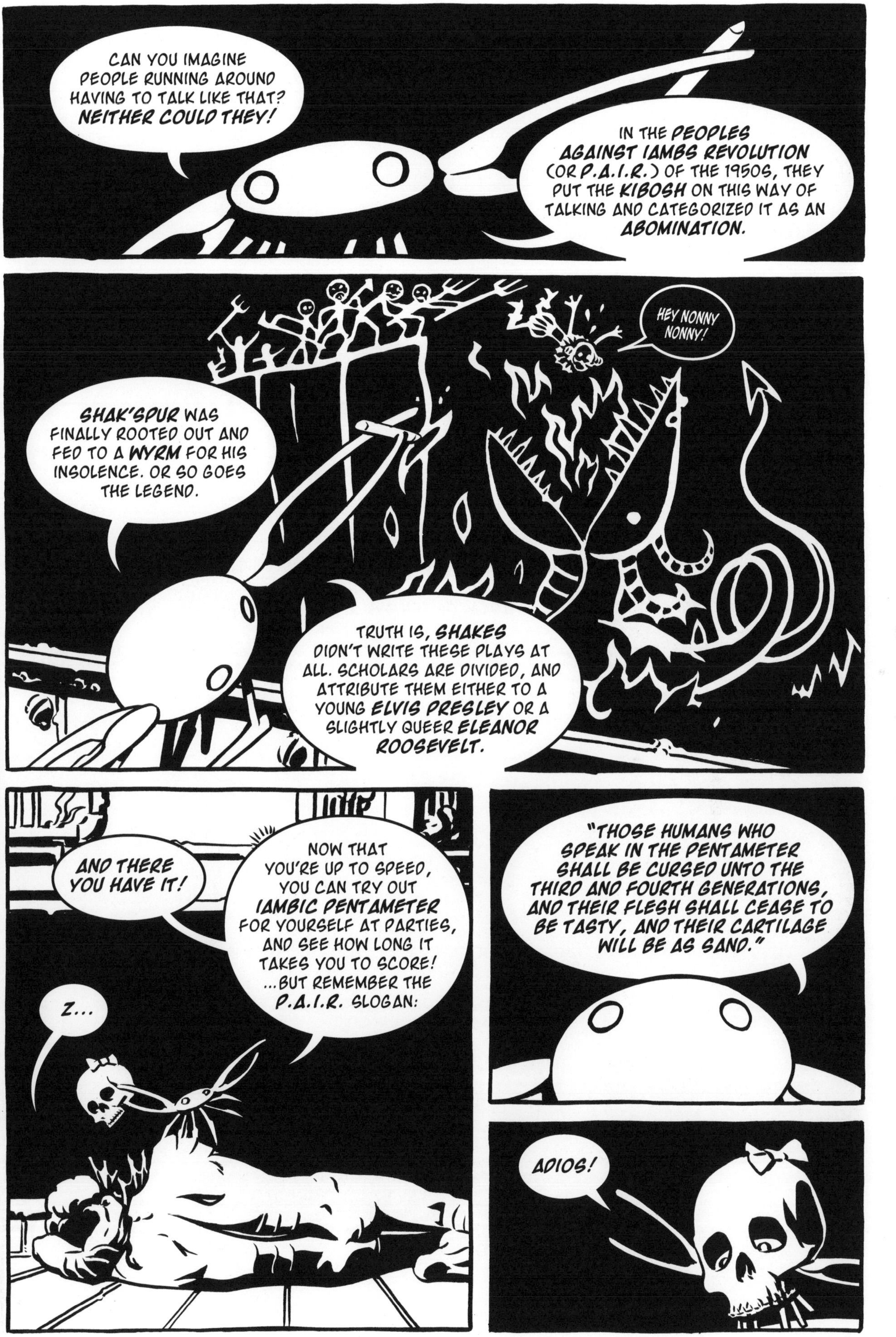
CAN YOU IMAGINE PEOPLE RUNNING AROUND HAVING TO TALK LIKE THAT? NEITHER COULD THEY!
IN THE PEOPLES AGAINST IAMBS REVOLUTION (OR P.A.I.R.) OF THE 1950S, THEY PUT THE KIBOSH ON THIS WAY OF TALKING AND CATEGORIZED IT AS AN ABOMINATION.
HEY NONNY NONNY!
SHAK'SPUR WAS FINALLY ROOTED OUT AND FED TO A WYRM FOR HIS INSOLENCE. OR SO GOES THE LEGEND.
TRUTH IS, SHAKES DIDN'T WRITE THESE PLAYS AT ALL. SCHOLARS ARE DIVIDED, AND ATTRIBUTE THEM EITHER TO A YOUNG ELVIS PRESLEY OR A SLIGHTLY QUEER ELEANOR ROOSEVELT.
AND THERE YOU HAVE IT!
NOW THAT YOU'RE UP TO SPEED, YOU CAN TRY OUT IAMBIC PENTAMETER FOR YOURSELF AT PARTIES, AND SEE HOW LONG IT TAKES YOU TO SCORE! ...BUT REMEMBER THE P.A.I.R. SLOGAN:
Z...
"THOSE HUMANS WHO SPEAK IN THE PENTAMETER SHALL BE CURSED UNTO THE THIRD AND FOURTH GENERATIONS, AND THEIR FLESH SHALL CEASE TO BE TASTY, AND THEIR CARTILAGE WILL BE AS SAND."
ADIOS!

REFERENCE & SKETCHES

THIS WEIRD LITTLE BOOK began life as a piece of outdoor theater during my college years, complete with an ocean-proof monster suit with me inside, tromping onto the beach like a maniac. I chose to end my acting career there, at the top. A bad illness hit me after art school, and all my momentum toward showbiz (even of the make-your-own-monster-suit variety) evaporated. During my recovery I rediscovered my love for drawing, specifically drawing stories. I just sort of tumbled out of my sickbed and into *Dear Creature*. That began my career in comics, or as I like to think of it, acting on paper.

Ahead is a little window into my influences and my creative process (madness) on this book.

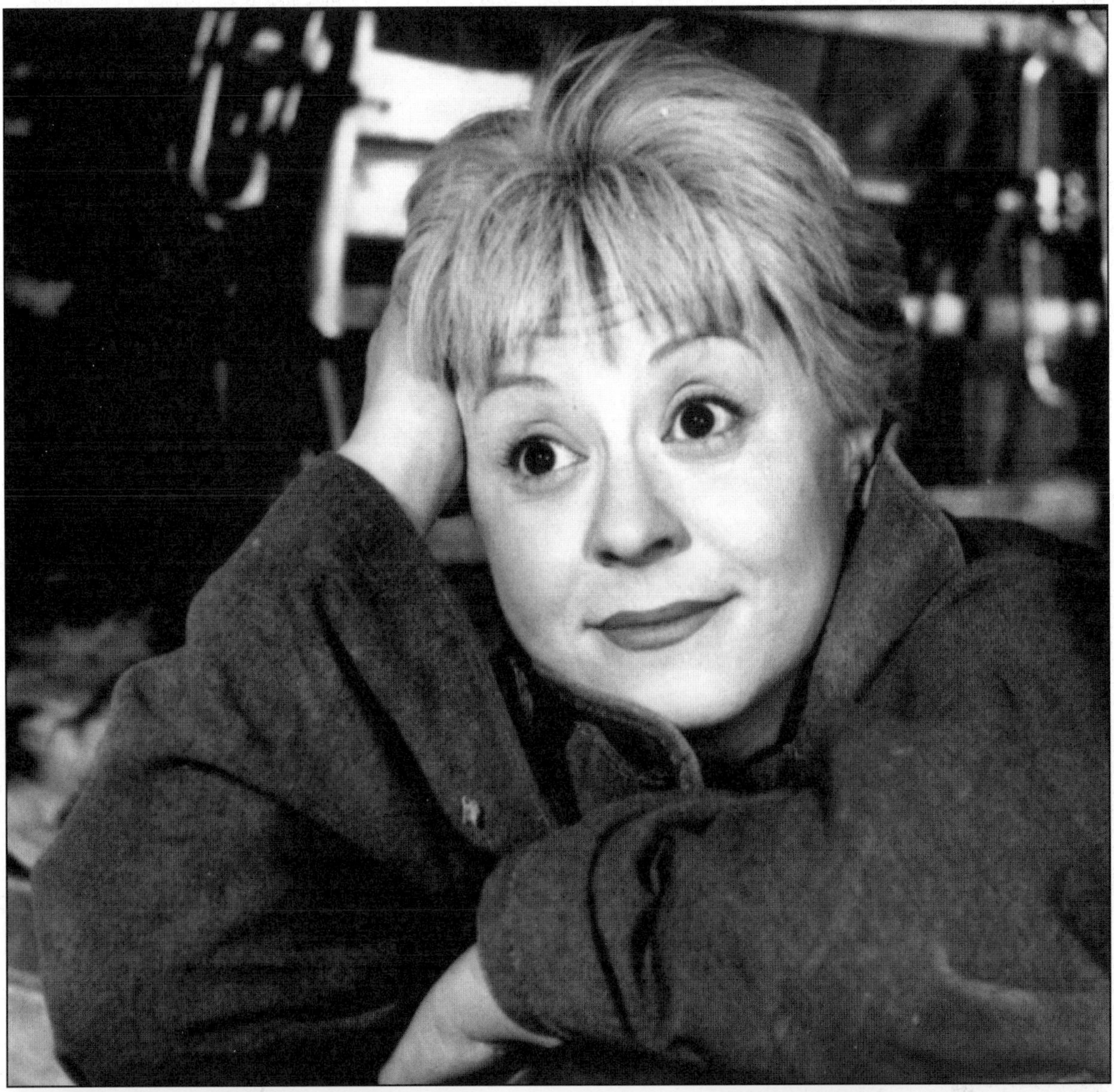

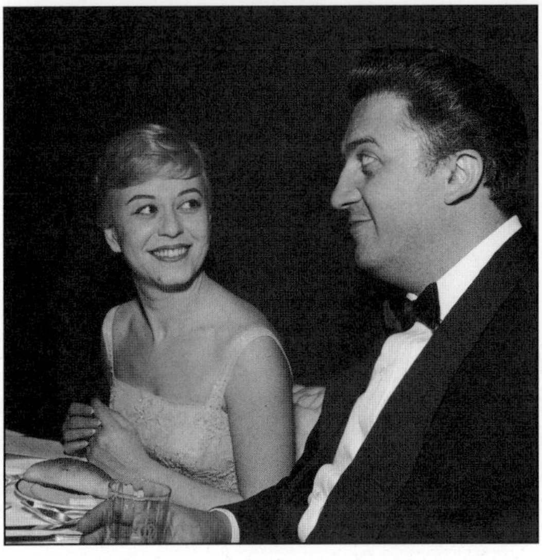

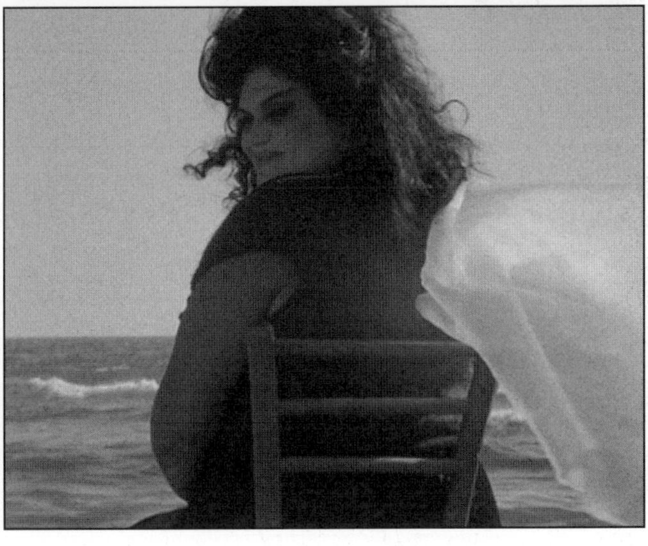

FELLINI'S LADIES: Giulietta Masina, superb actress and wife of Federico Fellini. I stole her outright, name and all. Zola is based on a character from his movie *8½*: Saraghina, the frightening, lascivious woman who lives down on the beach and dances the rumba for curious Catholic-school boys. Turns out the godfather of drive-in B movies, Roger Corman, got a lot of these foreign art-house flicks played in America. I love imagining '60s teenagers going to see a double showing of *This Island Earth* followed by *La Strada*. Today's make-out sessions aren't backed up by anything so well curated.

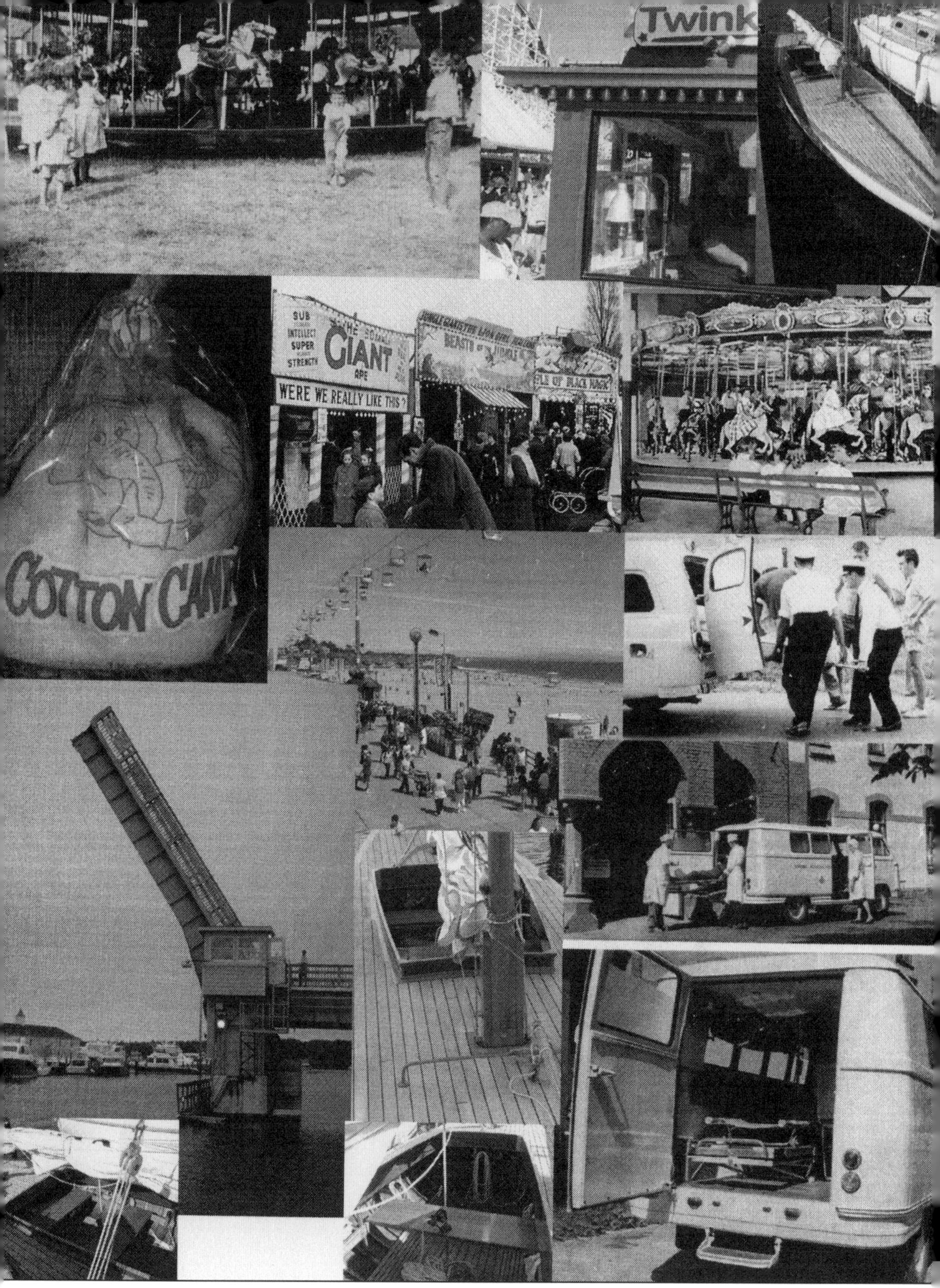
Twink
COTTON CAN
SUB
INTELLECT
SUPER
STRENGTH
GIANT
APE
WERE WE REALLY LIKE THIS ?

I gathered lots and lots of reference material for *Dear Creature*. Among my greatest treasures from the year 1962: a high-school yearbook, a Sears catalog, the digital archive of *Life* magazine . . .

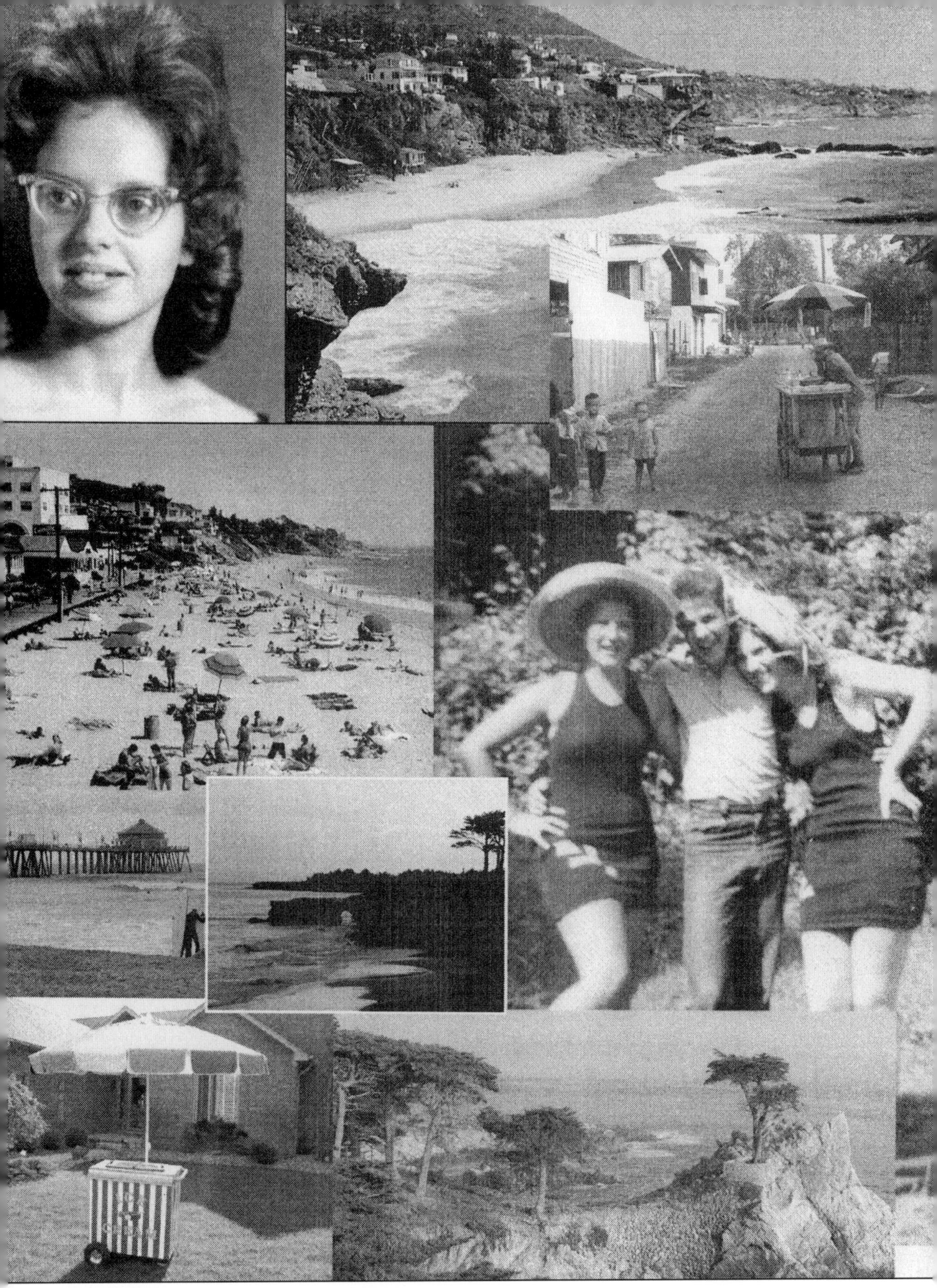

Oh, the towering hair and cat-eye glasses! I probably put in triple the amount of time needed to gather appropriate reference. That was my answer to writer's block, I guess. Too afraid of the blank page? Go find another bouffant.

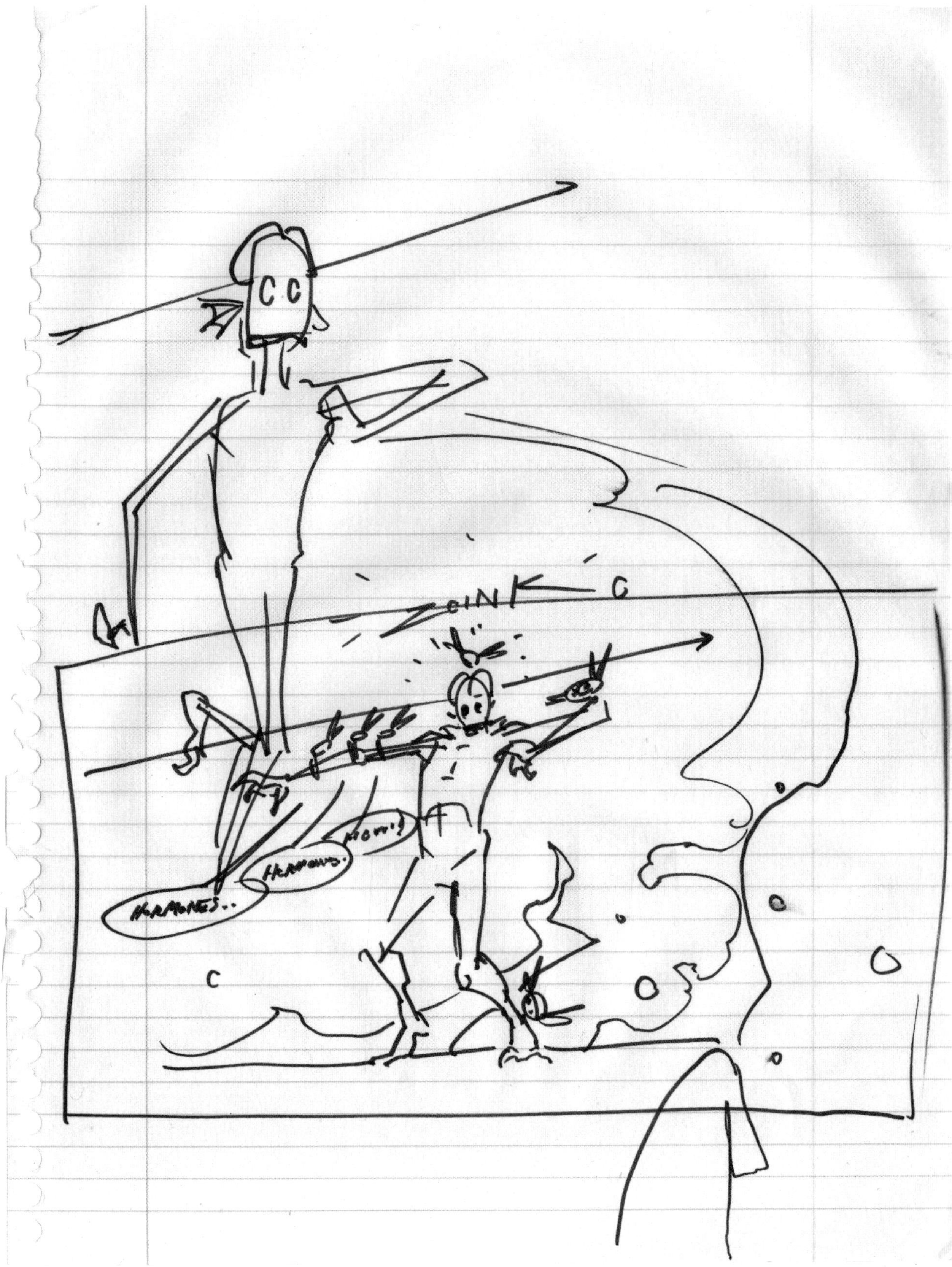
ZOINK
HARMONES..

LAYOUTS: For layouts I mostly used cheap, lined notebook paper. It freed me up to not worry about making pretty drawings, but to just experiment and find the most kinetic gestures I could. I kept pencils loose as well, leaving all the decisions about light sources and shadows for the inks stage. I drew and inked the final art oversized, on 18 x 24–inch paper, in hopes of approximating the brain space of artists from the '50s and '60s. Inks were all done with a Pentel Aquash brush pen—still my favorite!

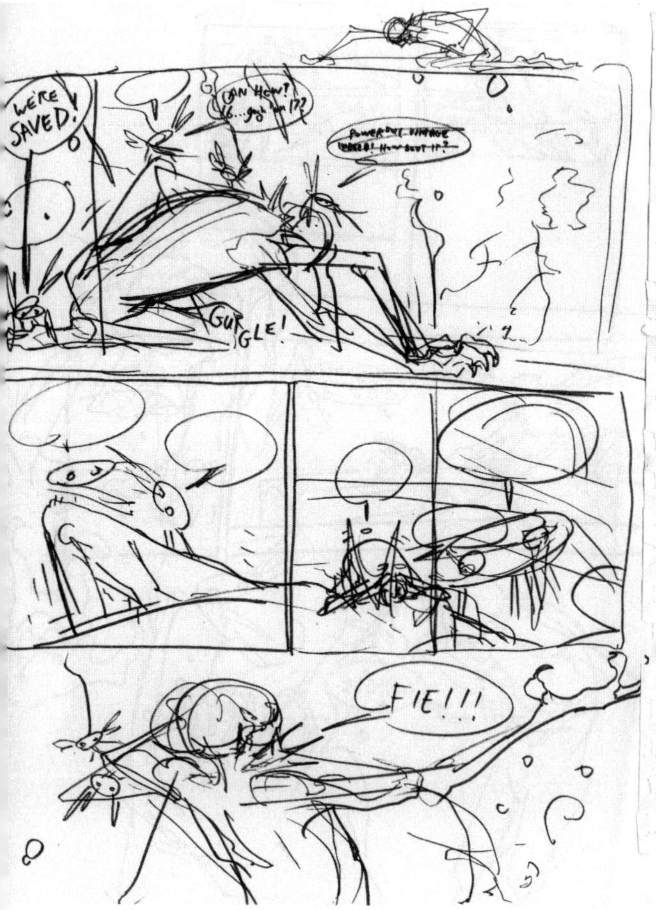
WE'RE SAVED!
GURGLE!
FIE!!!

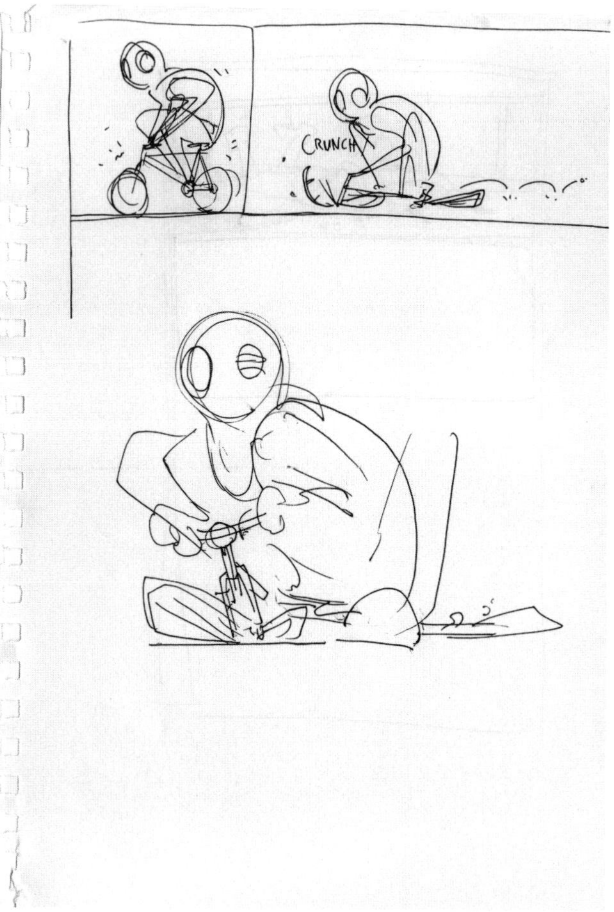
CRUNCH

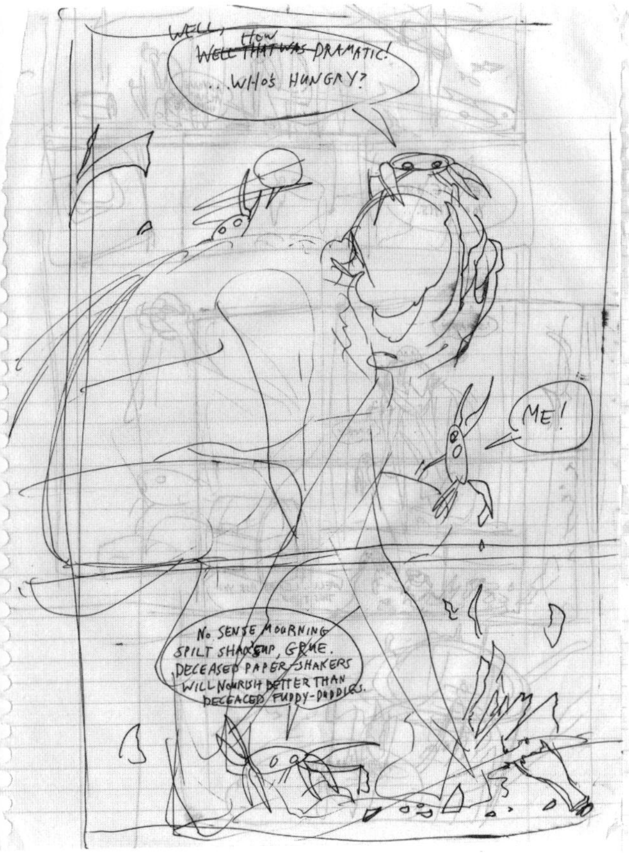
WELL, HOW DRAMATIC!
...WHO'S HUNGRY?
ME!
NO SENSE MOURNING SPILT SHAKESAP, GRUE. DECEASED PAPER SHAKERS WILL NOURISH BETTER THAN DECEASED FUDDY-DUDDIES.

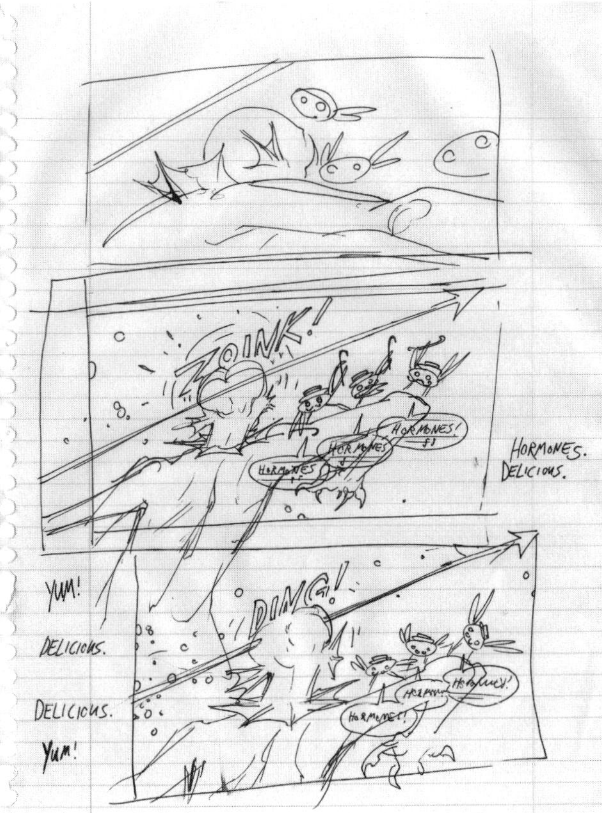
ZOINK!
HORMONES!
HORMONES
HORMONES
HORMONES. DELICIOUS.
YUM!
DELICIOUS.
DELICIOUS.
YUM!
DING!
HORMONES!

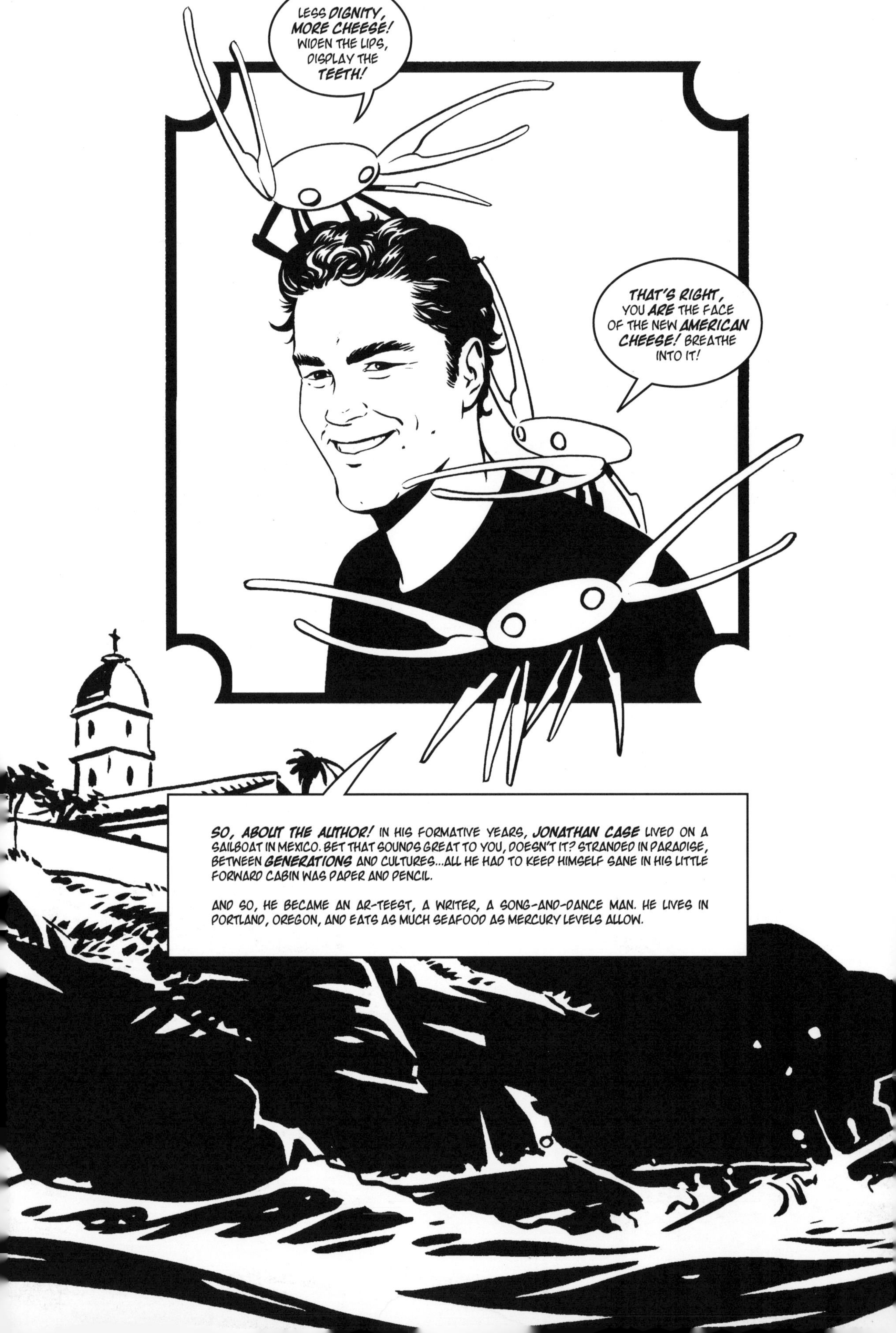
LESS DIGNITY, MORE CHEESE! WIDEN THE LIPS, DISPLAY THE TEETH!
THAT'S RIGHT, YOU ARE THE FACE OF THE NEW AMERICAN CHEESE! BREATHE INTO IT!
SO, ABOUT THE AUTHOR! IN HIS FORMATIVE YEARS, JONATHAN CASE LIVED ON A SAILBOAT IN MEXICO. BET THAT SOUNDS GREAT TO YOU, DOESN'T IT? STRANDED IN PARADISE, BETWEEN GENERATIONS AND CULTURES...ALL HE HAD TO KEEP HIMSELF SANE IN HIS LITTLE FORWARD CABIN WAS PAPER AND PENCIL.
AND SO, HE BECAME AN AR-TEEST, A WRITER, A SONG-AND-DANCE MAN. HE LIVES IN PORTLAND, OREGON, AND EATS AS MUCH SEAFOOD AS MERCURY LEVELS ALLOW.

THANKS

Sarah Case
Alex Kamer
Team Kiki
Mom and Dad
Grandpa
Helioscope
Barbara Williams
and
Dave and Bonnie Zollner,
for giving me the best

---

*For this new hardcover
edition, special thanks to*
Spencer Cushing
Dark Horse Comics
Craig Thompson
Judy Hansen
and
Steven Padnick

MORE FROM JONATHAN CASE

JONATHAN CASE
THE NEW DEAL

THE NEW DEAL

The Waldorf Astoria is the classiest hotel along the Manhattan skyline in 1930s New York City. When a charming woman checks in with a high-society entourage, a bellhop and a maid get caught up in a series of mysterious thefts. The stakes quickly grow perilous, and the pair must rely on each other to discover the truth while navigating delicate class politics.

978-1-61655-731-7 | $16.99

"Terrific. It's got the scariest opening sequence I've read in years, and the novel as a whole makes compelling stay-up-late reading. Great, creepy stuff."
—STEPHEN KING
GREEN RIVER KILLER
A TRUE DETECTIVE STORY
JEFF JENSEN | JONATHAN CASE

GREEN RIVER KILLER: A TRUE DETECTIVE STORY

With Jeff Jensen

"An astounding graphic novel—this is not just a riveting, relentless crime story, but a crackling morality tale pitting the dark glamour of evil against the day-to-day hard work demanded in the upkeep of decency. It's a chilling, unnerving story, with sharp bursts of humor and a strong, true, humane heart. Absolutely fantastic."—Gillian Flynn, *New York Times* best-selling author of *Dark Places* and *Sharp Objects*

978-1-61655-812-3 | $19.99

JOHN ARCUDI
JONATHAN CASE
THE CREEP

THE CREEP

With John Arcudi

A young boy puts a gun in his mouth and pulls the trigger. The police don't care—not about his death or the death of his best friend two months earlier. The dead boy's mom seeks help from an old flame that's employed as a detective. Will the detective's freakish appearance get in the way of uncovering the terrible secrets of these two teenagers?

978-1-61655-061-5 | $19.99

DEAR CREATURE

Deep beneath the waves, Grue discovers love after finding Shakespeare's plays in cola bottles. When his first attempt at companionship in the world above ends . . . poorly, Grue searches for the person who cast the plays into the sea. What he finds is love in the arms of Giulietta. But, with his wicked past catching up to him, Grue must decide if becoming a new man means ignoring the monster he was.

978-1-50670-095-3 | $22.99

AVAILABLE AT YOUR LOCAL COMICS SHOP OR BOOKSTORE. TO FIND A COMICS SHOP IN YOUR AREA, CALL 1-888-266-4226

DARK HORSE BOOKS

For more information or to order direct: On the web: **DarkHorse.com**
E-mail: **mailorder@darkhorse.com**
Phone: **1-800-862-0052** Mon.–Fri. 9 AM to 5 PM Pacific Time.

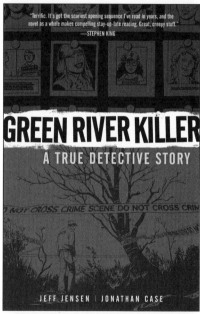

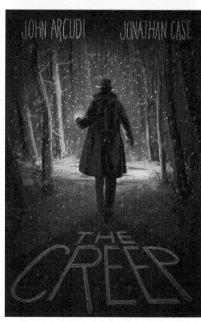